Foundations of the

STEREOSCOPIC CINEMA

A Study in Depth

Lenny Lipton

VNR VAN NOSTRAND REINHOLD COMPANY
NEW YORK CINCINNATI TORONTO LONDON MELBOURNE

Other books by Lenny Lipton

Independent Filmmaking
The Super 8 Book
Lipton on Filmmaking

To be published by Van Nostrand Reinhold:

Futurevisions (with Michael Starks)

Portions of Chapter 1 first appeared, in somewhat different form, in "The Cinema in Depth—From Hollywood to Super 8 3-D," by Lenny Lipton, published in *American Cinematographer,* May, 1978. Permission to reprint is gratefully acknowledged.

Printed in the United States of America
Designed by Loudan Enterprises
Drawings by Christopher Swan unless otherwise credited

Published by Van Nostrand Reinhold Company Inc.
135 West 50th Street
New York, NY 10020

Van Nostrand Reinhold Publishing
1410 Birchmount Road
Scarborough, Ontario M1P 2E7, Canada

Van Nostrand Reinhold Australia Pty. Ltd.
17 Queen Street
Mitcham, Victoria 3132, Australia

Van Nostrand Reinhold Company Limited
Molly Millars Lane
Wokingham, Berkshire, England

16 15 14 13 12 11 10 9 8 7 6 5 4 3 2 1

Library of Congress Cataloging in Publication Data

Lipton, Lenny, 1940–
  Foundations of the stereoscopic cinema.
  Bibliography: p.
  1. Moving-pictures. Three-dimensional.
  I. Title.
  TR854.L56   778.5'341   81-16474
  ISBN 0-442-24724-9   AACR2

This book is dedicated to the memories of
John L. Wasserman, stereoscopic enthusiast, and
Winton C. Hoch, stereoscopic inventor.

"Answers can be given: they are all lies."
Bhagwan Shree Rajneesh, from *The Book of Secrets*

Contents

Preface

It was 1952, and I was twelve years old. I bought a 3-D comic book about a Stone Age hero who used an ax to clobber dinosaurs. I am certain that dinosaurs are supposed to have become extinct several million years before men appeared on earth. Nevertheless, the combination of cave man and tyrannosaurus is a winning one, as any twelve-year-old boy or fifty-year-old movie producer will tell you.

I wore cardboard goggles to see the illustrations in proper 3-D. The goggles had red and blue filters. After looking at the pictures for some time, I noticed that I was seeing the world bluish in one eye and reddish in the other. This occurred when I took off the goggles and looked around the back yards and vacant lots of my youth. Even now, years later, I will blink one eye to see if the world is tinted red and the other to see if it is tinted blue. Sometimes it still happens! Could Mother have been correct? Did those comic books really ruin my eyes?

Soon many other publishers offered anaglyphic comic books, and I bought all I could find. Some were much better than others. The figures in the best ones appeared to be more than cardboard cutouts set against backdrops. Some artists succeeded in giving their drawings a fullness, a roundness. I remember a little girl in one of the drawings. She wore a polka-dotted dress, and the polka-dots followed the contoured folds of her clothes. I remember an aviator falling to his death, hands outstretched right off the page, practically touching my nose. His feet stretched far to the distant sky, a frozen, sculptured doom never achievable in flat comic books.

I became a connoisseur of anaglyphic comic books. I studied them. I even projected their images using an opaque projector that I built. My school friends came to my home to see 3-D comics projected rear-screen on tracing paper, which I buttered for increased brilliance.

I noted that some comic books used green filters instead of blue. Some used blue for the right eye and red for the left and others red for the right and so on. No standardization at all. It concerned me, even at twelve.

I drew my own 3-D comic strips. I invented a character, a giant ape I called Might Mola. He was very much like King Kong. I shopped around for just the right shade of red and blue or green pencils for my drawings. I never found a truly satisfactory blue or green or blue-green. Always too much ghosting, or one image bleeding through to the other eye.

Aug. 28, 1962   M. L. HEILIG   3,050,870

SENSORAMA SIMULATOR

Filed Jan. 10, 1961   8 Sheets–Sheet 3

Fig. 5.

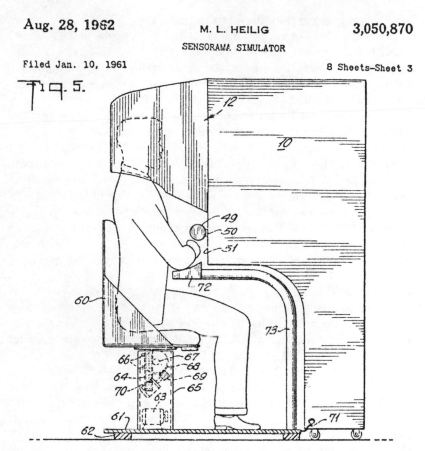

Sensorama simulator, essentially a three-dimensional nickelodeon. The observer sits with head in hood, as shown in this U.S. patent illustration.

My method was to do a master drawing in black pencil and then to overlay a sheet of tracing paper. It was on the tracing paper that I made my red and green drawings, by carefully displacing the tracing paper left or right. The other kids in the neighborhood were playing stickball or running from gangs. I marched to the sound of a different drummer.

Shortly after the first comic books, 3-D movies appeared. I remember my mother taking me to midtown Manhattan to see *Bwana Devil* at a first-run house. I loved it. (I forget what she thought.) Soon 3-D movies were playing at the local movie houses. I remember what I think was the chemical smell of the polarizing glasses as well as that of the blue ink preview pages and rancid buttered popcorn at the Ambassador Theater in Brooklyn.

I don't remember thinking that 3-D movies were better than comic books. They were merely different. The movie glasses were like sunglasses, neutral, not colored. I wondered why. I removed the transparencies from a View-Master card and tried to project them. My method was faulty. I sandwiched the two together and placed them in the gate of a primitive 16mm movie projector. The superimposed images did not appear in 3-D when I wore polarizing glasses. I couldn't figure out why.

By the time I was thirteen, or maybe fourteen, they stopped publishing stereoscopic comic books and making stereoscopic movies. I became interested in puppets, in spaceships, in fourteen-year-old girls.

Time went by, and I went to college. First I studied engineering and then physics. I decided to become a writer and got a job at Time, Inc., and after that I worked as an editor at *Popular Photography*. While there I wrote a story about Morton Heilig's Sensorama simulator. Heilig still is a stereoscopic motion picture fanatic. His dream was to involve the viewer totally in simulated sensual experience. An individual sat with his or her head in a hood, eyes peering into a binocular-type eyepiece, observing stereoscopic motion picture image pairs that covered a great deal of the peripheral visual area. In essence, Sensorama was a stereoscopic nickelodeon, but with added odors, vibrations, winds, and with a pair of built-in speakers providing binocular sound. It was a turn-on!

I left *Popular Photography*, got married, moved to the West Coast, and began a career as an independent filmmaker. To support my habit, I decided to write a book about what I had learned as a fledgling filmmaker. It was called *Independent Filmmaking*. I made many films, I wrote many articles and another book, this one about super 8 techniques.

About six years ago, while rummaging through a San Francisco store that specializes in odds and ends imported from Asia, I suddenly had what I supposed to be a very profound insight into stereoscopic television systems. From the time I was thirteen to the time I was thirty-four, the dream of making stereoscopic films seems to have lain dormant. But this dream of childhood was a deep dream, and it never left me. I got in touch with a former physics classmate who had actually gone through the entire Ph.D. process. He liked my idea. Mel Siegel and I wrote a report to interest investors. He greatly improved my concept, and we came rather close to attracting the kind of money it would have taken to develop such a system. But a miss, as they say, is as good as a mile.

Undaunted, I decided to do what I could and make stereoscopic movies. My proposals to several grant-giving organizations fell on deaf ears, and in March 1976, when two such rejections arrived within a day of each other, I flew into a rage and decided to go ahead anyway. Because of the books and articles I had written about motion picture technology, a channel was opened to me to organizations that distributed motion picture equipment. I was able to borrow the components I needed for my project.

I had to design and build my own stereoscopic system because there was, and in fact still is, no such system available. For small formats there are simple add-on mirror or prism devices, which can be used with existing cameras and projectors, but these have severe limitations. They produce a peculiar vertical field, they are limited to a fixed interaxial distance, and they do not work well with wide-angle lenses. For large formats, the situation is very little better. When I began my work, there were several 35mm motion picture systems available, but they also had a limited range of possible focal lengths and of other creative variables, and they are expensive to lease and operate.

As it turns out, having to build my own dual rig out of two cameras was just the right approach, because with such a system it is possible to vary system and photographic parameters fully. Although my overriding intention was to make stereoscopic movies, I soon became involved in a study of how to build a good system. The best possible approach would be to build a good single-band system, with both left and right images on a single piece of film. But in order to know how to do that properly, dual-band experiments employing two pieces of film, one for the left image, the other for the right, are a necessary first step.

The basic idea of a dual-band approach is to use existing apparatus and systems to the fullest so that as little as possible needs to be developed. This is an economical method, and one that can produce good results. I worked in super 8, because the hardware is small and light, and the software would be correspondingly inexpensive. I decided to use the same approach as many others entering the field. I employed a dual camera, made up of two cameras mounted on a common base for photography and two interlocked projectors for screening footage. These machines needed to be run in precise synchronization, and I was in luck because there was a great deal of interest in super 8 double-system sound. For example, the apparatus used to synchronize a camera and a recorder could be modified with little difficulty to synchronize two cameras.

Like many others who came before me, I had no idea how terribly difficult it is to make such equipment perform properly. The naive position is that since one is simply using two of this and two of that, stereoscopic filmmaking ought to be fairly simple. I had no notion that stereoscopic photography was in many ways substantially different from conventional, or planar, photography.

At the time I began my work, I was giving a class in basic super 8 filmmaking at the Berkeley Film Institute. One of my students, Michael Starks, turned out to be a person of considerable accomplishment as a researcher and writer. Michael's enthusiasm for stereoscopic filmmaking was as great as mine, and he proved it over the next five years by spending countless hours in the library, tracking down every article directly or indirectly related to the subject.

The equipment arrived, and I set to work. In the first few months of our experimental and library research, we learned that the basic information needed for making stereoscopic films had not been published. Whether or not it was known but never written down did not make a difference. What I needed to know was not available. Although there was scattered information about the necessary engineering of a stereoscopic motion picture system, this information had not been codified and was difficult to unearth. Even worse, no straightforward method for doing stereoscopic photography seemed to have been published. Several authors had written their versions of how to vary the photographic parameters involved, but the underlying arguments seemed oblique or incorrect; more important, my attempts to follow these recommendations did not lead to satisfactory results. Other authors seemed to obscure their methods deliberately, perhaps because they did not want competition.

My research efforts were enhanced because there were several theaters in the San Francisco Bay Area engaged in a revival of stereoscopic films. Most of these had been shot in the early 1950s. The theaters screened films such as *Creature from the Black Lagoon, It Came from Outer Space, Kiss Me Kate, The Maze,* and *House of Wax.* With the exception of the last film, they were all screened as they had been originally, using interlocked projectors. Although *House of Wax* was shot with a dual-system, it was projected with a single system, both images having been optically printed side by side onto a single piece of film. I also had an opportunity to view recent efforts: *The Bubble* and *Andy Warhol's Frankenstein.* Although synchronization was not a problem, since these films were shot and projected single-band, there were other terrible problems. The system of photography employed often placed objects too far out into the audience, producing eye fatigue from the muscular effort needed to fuse such images. As bad, the left and right projected image fields usually had eyestraining unequal illumination. With only a single exception (*House of Wax*), all of these films were projected out of synchronization, and it seemed to me that much of the photography was off the mark. To cite one troublesome area, many of the studio rigs produced eyestraining vertical misalignment between left- and right-image pairs when using different lenses, or with changes in focus. I've never yet encountered a double system rig that did not require repeated recalibration in the field, and it seems that the otherwise expert crews took the accuracy of the equipment for granted.

The danger with stereoscopic filmmaking is that if it is improperly done, the result can be discomfort. Yet, when properly executed, stereoscopic films are very beautiful and easy on the eyes.

It took about a year of steady work before I could achieve, on a routine basis, well-photographed and well-projected stereoscopic film. I had to learn how to tune my pair of Nizo 561 cameras and my Eumig projectors to get optimum results. I had to learn how to correlate creative camera controls: focal length, distance from subject to camera, and interaxial distance. After two years, I began to achieve an understanding of the psycho-optical (psychological-optical) nature of the system.

This book is rooted in practicality. A major part of the work involved shooting, cutting, and projection of several stereoscopic films. At the moment, there is a completed stereoscopic work, a half-hour film, *Uncle Bill and the Dredge Dwellers,* which has been screened for audiences in Toronto and Venezuela, at film festivals, and in several cities in the United States. I began work on the film before I knew how to tune my camera projector properly and before my thoughts on transmission systems (the working model used to explain stereoscopic photography) had come together.

I needed to have this experience with actual photography, editing, and projection. I now realize that shooting a documentary-type film in the field, compared to working in a controlled studio situation, is something of a technical tour de force. Working with a tentatively engineered dual rig, with an incomplete notion of how to do the photography, made it even more difficult. Yet the proof is in the pudding, and *Uncle Bill and the Dredge Dwellers* is, I believe, one of the finest stereoscopic films ever made.

In October 1980, my associate, Michael Starks, and I formed Deep & Solid Inc., an organization devoted to the research and development of stereoscopic motion picture and television systems. Together with our partners, General Electronic Services Inc., of Berkeley, California, and in collaboration with video engineer Jim Stewart, we have constructed a successful prototype of a three-dimensional television system which we hope will find acceptance with industrial users.

Several months ago we formed a venture with Stereovision International Inc. to service the film industry with the optics and expertise needed for what we hope will be a flourishing revival of the stereoscopic medium. To date, we have serviced the Oldsmobile Division of General Motors with a promotional film, *The Dimensions of Oldsmobile Quality* (directed by Dave Seago, produced by the Sandy Corp.) and E.O. Corp. with a feature film, *Rottweiler* (directed by Worth Keeter III, produced by Earl Owensby). Both directors forced me to rethink my system of photography, and contributed to my understanding of the medium. The films appear under the *Future Dimensions* mark, using a system that places the stereopairs above and below each other on a single piece of 35mm film. The lenses for our system were designed by Chris Condon of Stereovision.

Readers of my other books may be in for a surprise. This is a more difficult book, and a warning is in order. Although this has certain aspects of a how-to-do-it book, the major portion is, by its nature, a monograph presenting original research. Readers seeking a more simplified approach are referred to *Lipton on Filmmaking* (Simon and Schuster, 1979), which contains a how-to-do-it section devoted to some of the tools used in this study.

The early portions of the book are, by their nature, tutorial and historical. It was necessary to discuss some of the fundamentals, since stereoscopy is an interdisciplinary art, yet lines had to be drawn. For example, trigonometry is used to obtain some results, but obviously this is not a textbook on basic trigonometry. The mathematics is roughly on an advanced high-school, or perhaps freshman college, level. Some readers will thumb through the book and challenge that contention. For them, or for the reader in a hurry, the results of mathematical derivations may be accepted at face value, and I have striven to explain all concepts in simple English.

I admit that I have had a difficult time deciding on the proper tone or level of difficulty of this book. It has been my desire to reach the greatest number of readers; I am hopeful that filmmakers will take up the call so that stereoscopic filmmaking will proliferate. Yet the state of the art is such that large chunks of basic information have not until now existed. I had to invent or discover much of what the reader now has in hand. This book, like my others, contains the information I needed to know in the years before I wrote it.

Having achieved what to my mind is an entirely satisfactory stereoscopic transmission system, I realize that there are a number of stumbling blocks in the path of the beginner, not the least of which is the lack of suitable stereoscopic apparatus. Generally speaking, you cannot go into a store with cash in hand and leave with a stereo camera and projector. The equipment does not exist. Thus a major portion of my concern here is to communicate with the people who will be called upon to design and build stereoscopic motion picture and television equipment. Such advice will also be of great value to the filmmaker striving to create his or her own system. But such an exposition must be more complex than one aimed at the lay reader. It is my hope that this book will appeal not only to filmmakers, technicians, designers, and engineers but also to readers with a more general interest in filmmaking.

When I discuss my system, I am both presenter and popularizer of some rather complex original material. In my desire to present my arguments fully, I may have forsaken simplicity. I feel that the state of the art is such that persuasion and completeness are more important than a streamlined approach. On the other hand, it is also my desire to communicate with those who are not necessarily engineers or scientists. I have omitted some complicated exposition for this reason.

At present, there are very few practitioners of the stereoscopic cinematographic art. Occasional films are produced by only a handful of workers; unfortunately, most of these efforts are a disgrace and in fact retard rather than advance the craft. It is my hope that as a result of this study the situation will change and the stereoscopic cinema will flourish.

Toward that end, I have provided an exhaustive bibliography, which includes selected patents. The inclusion of this material is meant to save the researcher valuable time.

The title of the book, *Foundations of the Stereoscopic Cinema*, needs some explanation. Although I am not without my share of delusions, I am not egotist enough to believe that I and I alone have solved the vexing riddles of stereoscopic cinematography. The title alludes, if the reader will allow, not only to my contribution but to the work of many others as well. Their efforts are reviewed in the historical section and in the portions of the book reviewing transmission systems.

Acknowledgments

I would like to thank, in no particular order, the following persons, who helped with this study and the preparation of the manuscript: Bob Doyle, of Super8 Sound, for his encouragement and outright gift of synchronization equipment for both cameras and projectors; Michael Main, of Super8 Sound, for his help with my projector interlock; Jon Rosenfeld, of Super8 Sound, for documentation enabling the conversion of their crystal control units; Bob White, of Inner Space Systems, for carrying out the crystal control conversion; Joel Adams and William Paul, who patiently listened to my monologues about the future of stereoscopic motion pictures; Michael Sullivan, of Eastman Kodak, who acted as liaison with the library at Kodak Park and arranged the loan of an Ektalite screen; Bob Jones, of Eastman Kodak, who arranged the loan of an Eastman 16mm projector for single-band experiments (optically printed from super 8 originals); John Corso and Jean Binge of W. A. Palmer Films and Michael Hinton of Interformat, for working on optically printing double-band super 8 to single-band 16mm; Christy Stewart, formerly of Hervic Corporation (which formerly distributed Beaulieu cameras), for the loan of a Beaulieu 4008 camera; Ernst Wildi, of Braun North America (formerly distributors of the Nizo cameras), for the loan of a pair of 561 cameras and his personal Bolex stereo projection lens; Stephanie Boris, who typed the bescribbled manuscript; Chloe Lipton, who served as model on many occasions; Chris Condon of Stereovision International, for his technical reading and suggestions; Jeffrey Thielen, of Eumig U.S.A., for the loan of a pair each of Eumig 810 and 824 projectors; Arnold Scheiman of the Canadian Film Board, for his optical printing tests; Maurice Soklov of the Berkeley Film Institute, for the loan of his Bolex stereo camera lens; the friend of Cathy Neiman, whose name escapes me, who graciously lent a Bolex H16M to a virtual stranger (please come and get your camera, or let me bring it to you); Michael Starks, who spent many hours in the library, which I imagine were both tedious and rewarding, ferreting out the many titles which appear in the bibliography and for suggesting many interesting experiments; Bill Hool, for checking the bibliography; Chester Roaman, who edited early drafts of the manuscript, just as he has on my previous three books; Ernest Callenbach, for his encouragement; Daniel Greenhouse, for his technical reading; Christopher Swan, for his illustrations; and Julie Henderson, who helped remind me that I am not out of my mind.

I was fortunate to have this project funded by a grant from the California Arts Council and by three successive grants from the National Endowment for the Arts. In an increasingly mandarin society, where credentials and documentation of qualifications and team effort are the rule rather than the exception, the eccentric loner, the creative nonconforming individual, needs all the help he or she can get.

chapter 1

A Technical History of the Stereocinema

Before Sir Charles Wheatstone discovered the depth sense, stereopsis, inquiry into binocular vision was pursued by only a handful of people. The rest of the world simply went about its business enjoying the benefits of seeing with two eyes, but consciously unaware of the depth sense, stereopsis (literally, solid seeing).

The self-conscious awareness of stereopsis, together with the publication of the discovery of this major perceptual modality, did not take place until 1838. Before Wheatstone, there were perhaps fewer than a dozen writers who were concerned with and made any sort of contribution to the understanding of this, one of the human race's most important survival mechanisms.

The combination of Wheatstone's discovery with photography, which was invented the following year, became a very popular medium, and by the mid-1850s the parlor stereoscope graced many a nineteenth-century living room.

Technical problems, primarily, have retarded the development of stereoscopy, resulting in a culture with a marked planar bias. With the exceptions of theater, sculpture, and of course stereoscopic photography, our visual media are two-dimensional. Certainly depth cues are present, but these are extra-stereoscopic. Photography, rich in depth cues, and cinematography, even richer because of the possibility of motion parallax, nevertheless remain planar, or one-eyed, media.

BEFORE THE STEREOSCOPE

After Wheatstone announced his discovery of stereopsis, another distinguished British physicist, Sir David Brewster, attempted to discredit the discoverer with these words: "It is, therefore, a fact well known to every person of common sagacity that the pictures of bodies seen by both eyes are formed by the union of two dissimilar pictures formed by each. This palpable truth was known and published by ancient mathematicians" (Brewster, 1856, p. 6).

It may have seemed obvious after the fact, but it certainly was not obvious before. Although there are a number of references to the specific issue of vision with two eyes, there is no clear understanding in the prior literature that the two slightly dissimilar left and right images were combined into one image with a new depth sense.

In theorems 23 through 28 of his *Treatise on Optics*, Euclid deals with the geometric problem of observing a sphere with two eyes. He shows that if one looks with both eyes at a sphere whose diameter is less than the interocular distance, more than a hemisphere is visible, and that if one looks at a sphere whose diameter is greater than the interocular, less than a hemisphere is visible. Writers in subsequent centuries repeat and amplify Euclid's remarks, but this hardly serves to substantiate Brewster's claim. Although some philosophers have been interested in the problems of binocular vision, the history of the subject is actually one of repeated exposition of essentially the same facts, without the insight Wheatstone was to provide.

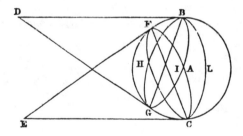

1.1. *Euclid's sphere.* "When the diameter of the sphere is equal to the distance between the eyes we see exactly a hemisphere. In this diagram *E* is the right eye and *D* the left, *CHFI* the section of that part of the sphere *BC* which is seen by the right eye *E*, *BHGA* the section of the part which is seen by the left eye *D*, and *BLC* the half of the great circle which is the section of the sphere as seen by both eyes." (Brewster, 1856)

Galen, the celebrated Greek physician, published his *On the Use of the Parts of the Human Body* in the second century A.D., and it is he who supplied the first common-sense description of left- and right-eye perspective. Today a similar demonstration is often given in terms of holding a finger in front of one's eyes and alternately observing the finger and the background behind it with the left and then the right eye. Galen's description was somewhat different:

> But if any person does not understand these demonstrations [he refers to Euclid] by means of lines, he will finally give his assent to them when he has made the following experiment. Standing near a column and shutting each of the eyes in succession, when the right eye is shut, some of those parts of the column which were previously seen by the right eye on the right side of the column will not now be seen by the left eye, and when the left eye is shut, some of those parts which were formerly seen by the left eye on the left side of the column will not now be seen by the right eye. But when we, at the same time, open both eyes, both these will be seen, for a greater part is concealed when we look with either of the two eyes than when we look with both at the same time.

According to Boring, (*History of Experimental Psychology, A,* 1957, p. 105), it is to Galen that we owe the first physiological insight into the problem, for he attempted to explain the singleness of vision by noting that some of the fibers of the optic nerve cross at the chiasma. Polyak (1957, *The Vertebrate Visual System,* p. 82) does not agree that Galen had such knowledge.

Baptista Porta, a Neapolitan physicist, in his *On Refraction* (published in 1593), quotes both Euclid and Galen and attempts to explain why we see a single image of the world instead of a confused double image. Porta theorized that we actually see with one eye and then the other in rapid succession. The idea is not nearly as foolish as it sounds, since this sort of effect is similar to what occurs in the well-observed phenomenon called retinal rivalry, in which dissimilar images are presented to each eye.

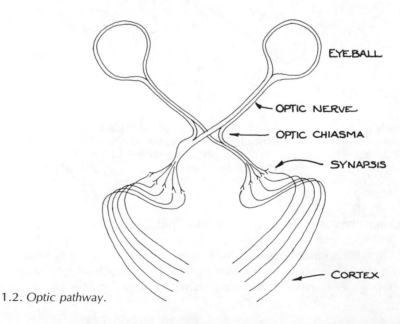

1.2. *Optic pathway.*

With the coming of the Italian Renaissance, painters suddenly became concerned with depicting depth. Prior to the fifteenth century, painting in Europe was primarily used as a means to express religious motifs for church decorations, but with the Renaissance and the rise of the merchant princes, painters had new clients to satisfy. The psychologist Kaufman (1974, *Sight and Mind*, p. 215) suggests that "one factor in the development of three-dimensional space in painting was a need for more adequate and lifelike representation of those who paid for the paintings . . . painters had to create lifelike images of their patrons."

Leonardo da Vinci, one especially well-known figure in the Italian Renaissance, wrote in 1584 in *Trattata della Pictura, Sculptura* (Wheatstone, 1838. On some remarkable, and hitherto unobserved, phenomenon of Binnocular vision, p. 372), "A painting, though conducted with the greatest art, and finished to the last perfection, both with regard to its contours, its lights, its shadows, and its colors, can never show a relief equal to that of the natural objects unless these be viewed at a distance and with a single eye." He follows this with an example of looking at a sphere, similar to that of Euclid's.

Leonardo codified the monocular depth cues, among them the rules of rectilinear perspective, which had been discovered, or invented if you like, by Renaissance painters. It is instructive to quote Kaufman (p. 218) on this:

> Nearly all of the so-called cues to depth were discovered by artists. The only contribution of psychologists was to formalize the notion that there are distinctive sources of information about depth; and, as we shall see, they did not do this very well. It is only in recent years, particularly in the important work of James Gibson (1950), that any real progress has been made in developing what the Renaissance gave us with regard to pictorial cues.

Johannes Kepler was wall-eyed and myopic and suffered from monocular polyopia (double vision). Kaufman speculates that Kepler's double vision might have caused him to wonder whether other people also saw double. When he realized that this was not the case, he offered as explanation his projection theory, in 1611. Kepler imagined that mental rays travel outward from the eyes, in straight lines. Objects would then be perceived as single if the object point is at the intersection of the two mental rays.

A historian of psychology, Boring (1957), points out that this concept is similar to that advanced to explain why a pencil, for example, feels like a single object even when held between, and therefore perceived by, two fingers. Kaufman holds that Kepler's construct is actually isomorphic with the modern projection theory of stereopsis. That is, it is structurally identical and produces the same explanations of phenomena despite the fact that modern scientists no longer believe in mental rays of light originating from the eyes, a concept, by the way, that did not begin with Kepler but originated with the ancient Greek philosophers, the Pythagoreans.

Both Porta and Kepler attempted to explain how two-eyed vision becomes single. Galen, as has been mentioned, may have been first to recognize that the answer may be physiological, if he truly identified the optic chiasma with respect to this function. The fibers of each retina cross over at the chiasma, a phenomenon known as decussation. Actually, only some of the fibers from each eye cross over (partial decussation). To quote Boring: "That fact suggests that the projections of the two retinas on the brain by the nerve fibres are superimposed, and that singleness of vision results when the brain pattern coincides point-for-point with the other." Newton in the eighteenth century and Muller, the nineteenth-century psychologist, followed this view.

It was the Jesuit Francis Aguillon, or Aguilonius as he is usually known, who in 1613 in his *Optics* proposed the concept that the horopter, or the locus of points lying before the eyes, will be seen as single. (Aguilonius proposed a horopter that was a straight line parallel to a line drawn between the two eyes.) In other words, retinal images of these objects will have zero

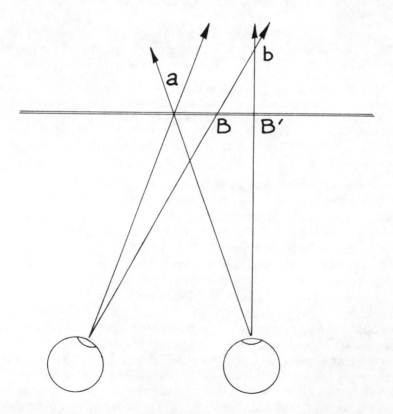

1.3. *Kepler's projection theory.* Mental rays cross at point *a*, leading to perception of a single image. Object at point *b* will then be seen to be double. The straight line containing points *B* and *B'* is the horopter of Aguilonius.

disparity. The geometric concept of the horopter made manifest that objects lying on it will appear single, while objects not on the horopter will appear double. This concept has been refined by later workers, and their work has proved influential in stereoscopic transmission theory.

We have seen that various people sought to understand the nature of binocular vision and that it took two thousand years to properly formulate the problem. Euclid explained, from a purely geometric point of view, that we can see slightly more of an object, especially a close object, with two eyes than with one. Galen gave a physiological explanation for the singleness of vision. Porta and Kepler offered psychological theories in an attempt to explain this singleness of vision, and Aguilonius was the first to realize that singleness of vision exists not only for the one point in space on which the eyes converge, but also on a locus of points, or a horopter. As we shall see, these men set the stage for Wheatstone's great discovery of stereopsis, that unique depth sense that arises from the binocular nature of our vision.

THE STEREOSCOPE

Following Aguilonius, writers attempted to understand why doubleness of vision is not ordinarily seen as such. Doubleness of vision was handled as if it were a problem, but it was Wheatstone who, using his invention of the stereoscope in 1833, turned the problem into the solution. In his *Contributions to the Physiology of Vision—Part the First: On some remarkable, and hitherto unobserved, Phenomena of Binocular Vision* (1838), he explained that doubleness of vision, caused by retinal disparity, actually produced the depth sensation stereopsis. By using line drawings with ambiguous monocular depth cues in his stereoscope, he demonstrated that stereopsis, the sense of depth created by two eyes, existed independently of monocular cues and that in some fashion the eye-brain was able to synthesize a solid view of the world out of disparate images. Some of the drawings that Wheatstone made are reproduced here, and we can only speculate at the pleasure and delight it must have given him to see two planar perspective representations take on the aspect of a truly solid body.

Before this, writers simply did not take into account that the minute differences between the left and right retinal images produced this depth sensation.

> Yet they [Wheatstone wrote (p. 371)] seem to have escaped the attention of every philosopher and artist who has treated the subject of vision and perspective. I can ascribe this inattention only to this circumstance, that the results being contrary to a principle that was generally maintained by optical writers, viz., that objects can be seen single only when their images fall on corresponding points of the two retinae. If the consideration ever arose in their minds, it was hastily discarded, under the conviction that if the pictures presented to the two eyes are under certain circumstances dissimilar, the differences must be so small that they need not be taken into account.

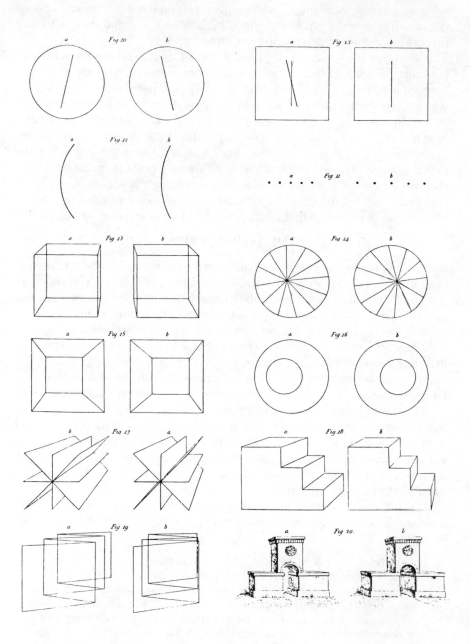

1.4. *Wheatstone's original stereopair drawings.* (Wheatstone, 1838)

Indeed, we have very much the same situation today with stereoscopic filmmaking, in which the virtually identical left and right frames of motion picture film together produce such a dramatic sensation of depth.

In 1833, Wheatstone invented the mirror stereoscope, which is made up of an arrangement of mirrors, as shown here in the original published drawing. The device is still employed for observing three-dimensional X-rays too large to be used in the more common form of the stereoscope developed by Brewster in 1844. In the Wheatstone mirror stereoscope, the pairs of images are separated and the greater distance from the eyes to the surfaces of the images eliminates the need for the lenses to help the eyes focus.

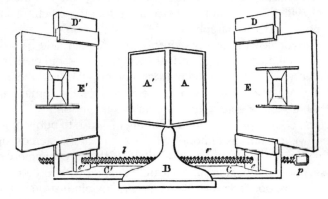

1.5. *Wheatstone's mirror stereoscope.* The head is brought up to mirrors A' and A, and pictures E' and E are viewed stereoscopically. (Wheatstone, 1838)

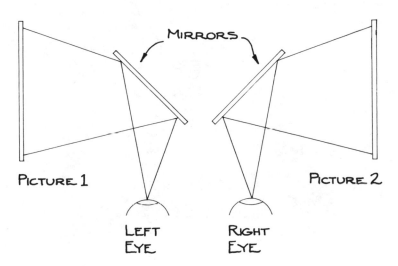

1.6. *Diagrammatic view of mirror stereoscope.* This device is still employed for viewing large stereopairs, such as X-rays. Note that the images must be reversed left to right, or a mirror image view will result.

Brewster's enclosed stereoscope uses lenses to help the eyes accommodate the shorter distance between them and the stereopair. The optics of Brewster's stereoscope are interesting. He used a lens cut in half along a diameter for the left and right lenses. This ensured that left and right optics would match, and it added a prismatic effect that helped the viewer fuse stereograms that were often mounted so that conjugate points were further apart than the interocular.

Brewster's stereoscope, far more compact and easy to use than Wheatstone's mirror stereoscope, with both images mounted on a single card, survives in one variation or another in virtually all modern devices such as the ubiquitous View-Master, which is virtually the spitting image of the creator's original device with the exception that circular rather than rectangular cards are used to mount the stereographs.

Brewster advocated the use of stereopairs mounted side by side on a single card, of miniature formats, and of transparencies rather than paper prints. The latter two suggestions did not become popular until the introduction of the View-Master in 1940, and of the Stereo Realist camera and film format in 1949, about a century after Brewster's invention.

Wheatstone could not be accused of being in a rush to publish; it was in 1852, fourteen years after his announced discovery of the stereoscope and stereopsis, that the *Philosophical Transactions* of the Royal Society of London ran the second and final part of his article dealing with further improvements of the stereoscope, adapting it to a more flexible instrument for psychological research, to photographic stereoscopy, and the invention of the pseudoscope. As peculiar as it may seem, the stereoscope was invented before photography.

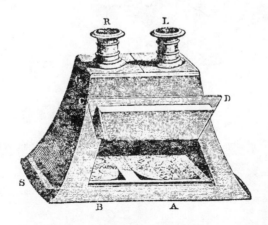

1.7. *Brewster's lenticular stereoscope.* The hinged flap *D* is left open when viewing prints. The design is also readily adaptable for viewing transparencies. (Brewster, 1856)

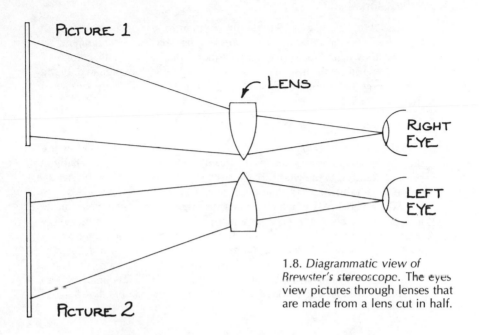

PICTURE 1

LENS

RIGHT EYE

LEFT EYE

PICTURE 2

1.8. *Diagrammatic view of Brewster's stereoscope.* The eyes view pictures through lenses that are made from a lens cut in half.

1.9. *Gruber's lenticular stereoscope.* Stereographs in the form of a circular card are introduced through a slot. Note similarity of the View-Master viewer and Brewster's design. (From U.S. Patent No. 2,511,334)

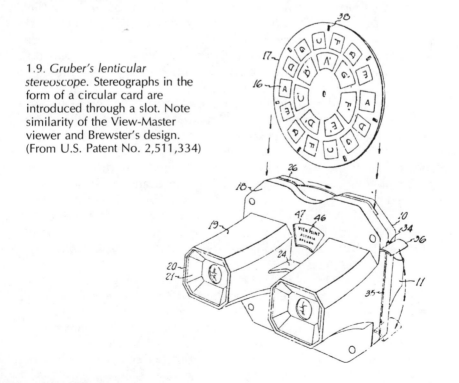

Wheatstone had this to say:

It was the beginning of 1839, about six months after the appearance of my memoir in the *Philosophical Transactions,* that the photographic art became known, and soon after, at my request, Mr. Talbot, the inventor, and Mr. Collen [one of the first cultivators of the art] obligingly prepared for me stereoscopic Talbotypes of full-size statues, buildings, and even portraits of living persons.

In the previous paragraph, he wrote,

At the date of the publication of my experiments on binocular vision, the brilliant photographic discoveries of Talbot, Niepce, and Daguerre, had not been announced to the world. To illustrate the phenomenon of the stereo-scope, I could therefore, at that time, only employ drawings made by the hands of an artist. Mere outline figures, or even shaded perspective draw-ings of simple objects, do not present much difficulty; but it is evidently impossible for the most accurate and accomplished artist to delineate, by the sole aid of his eye, the two projections necessary to form the stereo-scopic relief of objects as they exist in nature with their delicate differences of outline, light, and shade. What the hand of the artist was unable to ac-complish, the chemical action of light, directed by the camera, has enabled us to effect.

The first stereoscopic photographs were taken with a single camera that was moved through a distance of about 2½ in. for the second exposure. Brewster can be credited with conceiving the idea of the twin-lens stereo camera in 1849. For years Brewster attempted to persuade British instrument makers to produce devices based on his designs. He finally succeeded in France, where he made an agreement with the firm of Jules Duboscq, a Parisian optician, in 1850 (Gernsheim, 1956).

But Brewster had his difficulties in France as well, when his representa-tive, the Abbé Moigno, attempted to obtain endorsements for the stereo-scope from member of the Section de Physique of the Académie des Sci-ences. He had incredibly bad luck with the men he visited. Arago, Savat, Becquerel, and Poillet were all stereoblind and had, respectively, diplopia, some sort of serious defect in one eye, only one eye, and strabismus. A fifth, Boit, failed to observe a stereo effect, although no reason is given for his inability. Finally, Moigno took the stereoscope to another member of the Académie, Regnault, who fortunately had normal vision. (Linssen, 1972, and Cornwell-Clyne, 1954; the original source is Clerc's *Photography: The-ory and Practice.*)

Kaufman (1974) estimates that 8% of the population cannot see depth through the stereoscope. There are individuals who are stereoblind and those who have various degrees of deficient stereoscopic perception.

If we assume that some one out of twelve members of the population, or about 8%, have sufficiently anomalous stereoscopic perception to make it impossible for them to see a stereo view properly through a stereoscope,

then the chances of meeting five consecutive members of the French Académie so afflicted were $(1/12)^5$, or about 4 in 1 million.

The greatest single stroke on behalf of the stereoscope came at the London Exhibition in 1851 when Queen Victoria was evidently amused by various stereo views. Brewster lost no time in making the queen a gift of an
instrument, and the press made much of this. In the next five years, half a
million stereoscopes were sold, and many Victorian homes were graced
with the device and cabinets stocked with views. The stereoscope became
widespread on this side of the Atlantic, most often in a form designed by the
physician and author Oliver Wendell Holmes, Sr., in 1859. (His son was the
well-known jurist.)

In their day, the stereoscope and stereo views were the equivalent of
television and photojournalism. From the middle of the nineteenth century
and for a decade, followed by a gradual decline, the stereoscope introduced
people to events of the day with the regular issue of up-to-date stereo views
by a number of firms active in the field. In addition to timely subjects, people
enjoyed scenic views, illustrated literature, erotica, and views of popular
personalities. Views were often hand colored.

The stereoscope reached its peak of popularity shortly after Brewster's
successful efforts to exploit it, but by the latter part of the century people
began to lose interest in the medium. After the novelty wore off, they may
have become disenchanted with the system, since it called for observing the
stereopair through the stereoscope, and only one person at a time could look
at a view.

We must remember that there was increasing interest in ordinary photography; and planar paper prints, which are easier to view and may be seen
by a number of people at the same time, probably seemed almost as good as
the stereograph. Layer (1974) speculates that photomechanical reproduction
introduced in books and magazines at that time was a contributing factor to
the decline of stereoscopy.

Although factors external to the actual technology of stereoscopy itself
might possibly account for the decline, my interest is in technical factors. As
it turns out, system defects are very similar to those that have led to the
modern decline of motion picture stereoscopy, since the psycho-optical circumstances for viewing stereopairs in a stereoscope are similar to the psycho-optical factors of viewing motion pictures by the polarized-light method
of image selection. In other words, the principles of binocular symmetries
(page 213) apply to both. Viewing stereopairs and stereo movies are optically similar.

The same sort of abuses that existed in the cinemas of the 1950s also
existed in the parlours of the nineteenth century; in this belief I am support-
ed by Linssen (1952) in his chapter on "Stereoscopists and Abuses," and by
the August 1899 *Photo-Miniature* (a magazine of photographic information,
as it claimed to be), which related the actual errors themselves. The major
nineteenth-century difficulties seem to have been that the paper prints were

improperly mounted, that views were poorly photographed, and that many firms offered badly constructed stereoscopes.

THE EARLY DAYS OF MOTION PICTURES

After Wheatstone's publication of the discovery of stereopsis and his invention of the stereoscope, and following the improvement and popularization of the form by Brewster, a number of scientists began to study with great zeal the psychology of perception and the physiology of the eye, vis-à-vis stereopsis. Two such scientists were Helmholtz and Czermak. Helmholtz, in his *Optik*, first described moving-image stereo views in general and then Czermak's invention in particular: "Revolving stroboscopic disks may also be inserted in the panorama stereoscope instead of the pictures, and then the moving figures can be seen in their bodily forms." The names of these machines are interesting: the stereophantascope, the bioscope, the stereophoroscope, and the stereotrope.

The earliest of these devices may well be Czermak's stereophoroscope, of 1855. This is Helmholtz's description of it (1910, p. 357):

> He selected the ordinary lens stereoscope in which both pictures are mounted side-by-side on the same cardboard. These cardboards were attached to the plane faces of a polygonal wooden prism, which could be revolved around a horizontal axis. Surrounding the prism, and at a distance of several inches from the pictures, there was a cardboard cylinder with slits made in it at such intervals as to allow the pictures to be seen at the proper instants. Beyond this cylinder there was the optical arrangement in Brewster's stereoscope to enable the observer to look through it and view the images through the slits as they passed by.

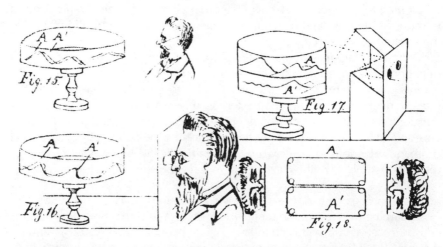

1.10. *Hymmen's panoramic stereo views.* British Patent No. 24,804 of 1897 shows, among other novelties, this spinning drum and stereoscope for viewing three-dimensional images.

Terry Ramsaye (1964) tells us that Coleman Sellers's Kinematoscope of 1861, almost thirty years before the invention of motion pictures, used a paddle-wheel arrangement of stereopairs made up of still photographs. These individual still poses were synthesized into motion when viewed in "flip-book" form, and also three-dimensionally through a stereoscope.

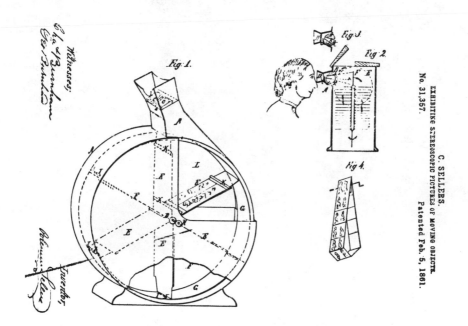

1.11. *Sellers's moving-image stereoscope.* In one version (left), we see flip-type cards mounted on a drum, to be viewed through a stereoscope hood. It anticipates later monocular viewing devices for motion pictures. Sellers used drawings on cards. In another version (right), stereo views are arranged on a belt, with pivoting hinges.

It is Friese-Greene, the British photographic pioneer, who usually gets the credit for the first camera that could rightfully be called a stereoscopic motion picture instrument. It was built in 1889, hard upon the heels of Edison's invention of the motion picture camera, which unlike the systems mentioned above used real-time photography of motion instead of drawings or stills assembled into a movie. Sources often vary by a year or so on dates, perhaps because it is difficult to know when an invention was actually publicly presented and because a delay of up to several years in the granting of patents is common.

No sooner does any development become public than someone is bound to combine it with existing systems to create a new and patentable variation. Given the stereoscope and photography, photographic stereoscopy must follow. Add the airplane, and aerial stereophotogrammetry will be

1.12. *Friese-Greene's stereoscopic camera film.* (1889, reprinted in George Sadoul, *Histoire Générale du Cinema*, 1948)

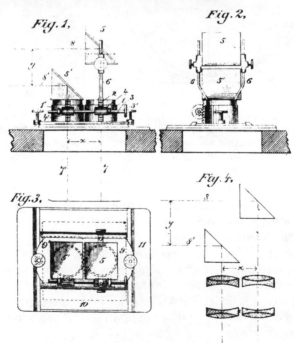

1.13. *Dickson's stereoscopic movie camera.* Figure 4 shows a diagrammatic view of how the optical system functioned. Lenses saw at right angles to their axes with prisms separated by distance y. Although this British patent was applied for in 1893, it was not granted until 1899.

developed. So, given the invention of motion pictures, stereoscopic motion pictures are similarly inevitable. Who did it first is not nearly as important as who did it well enough to make the medium useful. Usually this is the result of the work of many people, over a period of years, involving a synergetic interdisciplinary combination.

The Friese-Greene invention, no matter how lovely the mahogany woodwork of the camera (Smith, 1977), used a peculiar and unworkable film format, and the only means for viewing at that time must have been through a stereoscope. But those working in an individual field, one supposes, ought to have knowledge of other workers' efforts, and although Friese-Greene's invention was never used on a commercial basis, it probably influenced subsequent inventions. Friese-Greene's was the first camera to combine both left and right images of a stereopair onto a single band of motion picture film.

At about this time Edison and his erstwhile assistant Dickson filed patent applications for stereoscopic motion picture cameras. Edison discussed such a camera in his abandoned patent application No. 403,535 (Ramsaye, 1964) in 1891, and Dickson applied for a stereocamera in British Patent No. 6,794 in 1893.

THE ANAGLYPH AND ECLIPSE SYSTEMS

But these interesting developments were suitable only for viewing in conjunction with a stereoscope, which is entirely in keeping with Edison's concept of the cinema as "peep show."

We should also consider related inventions in the area of the projection of slides. Two-lens dissolving-type magic lantern projectors were confusingly known at this time as stereopticons. The term denotes devices for planar projection purposes. Both the eclipsing shutter method and the anaglyph method for viewing stereo slides were shown in 1858. In the eclipse technique shutters are placed in front of both left and right projection lenses and shutters are used in the spectacles worn by the audience. When the left shutter is opened at the projector, the left is opened at the viewing device, and so on. In this way the observer sees only the image meant for the appropriate eye.

The anaglyph, proposed by D'Almeida (in one form at least) in 1858, used complementary-colored filters over the left and right lenses to superimpose both images on a screen. Viewing devices with red and green lenses separated the images and selected the appropriate view for each eye. According to Helmholtz, D'Almeida was preceded in 1853 by Rollmann, who first demonstrated the principle using red and blue lines on a black background and red and blue glass goggles to view the effect.

Du Hauron, the pioneer inventor of color photographic systems in 1891, first proposed a method for combining left and right images on a single print. Although meant for still paper prints, the idea has obvious applications for motion picture work, since a combined print eliminates the need to project with two lenses or, in some cases, two machines.

Both the eclipse and the anaglyph methods were commercially employed in the early 1920s. Inventor Laurens Hammond's eclipse system, using individual viewers mounted to theater seats, was introduced by Teleview in 1922 and received fairly good reviews in the press (*New York Times,* December 28, 1922). Projector and analyzer motors were run off the same alternating current, keeping their shutters in synchronization.

Whatever its merits, the eclipse system has the crippling defect of not being able to present left and right images to the corresponding eyes essentially simultaneously. It is important that this be the case for any stereoscopic motion picture system, for if it is not, peculiar visual effects result from the introduction of spurious temporal parallax. This blurred or rippling or gelatinous effect is seriously disturbing for rapidly moving objects, but it presents difficulty even with the blinking of an eye or the movement of lips. The eclipse system will work for slide presentations; but once movement is introduced, the impossibility of simultaneous left and right images probably rules out the system.

Although the Fairall anaglyph system, presented by Multicolor, Ltd., in 1923, did not suffer from this defect, anaglyphs do create eyestrain for many people. Since color coding is the basis of image selection, color photography is ruled out, while Hammond's approach allowed full-color cinematography. Nevertheless, the eclipse system has not been used for commercially exhibited motion pictures since that time, whereas anaglyphic presentations

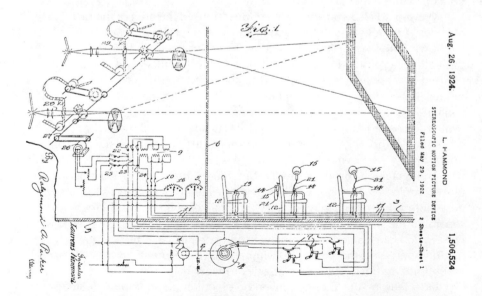

1.14. *Hammond's eclipse system.* Projectors (upper left) have occluding shutter blades that run in synchronization with similar devices mounted on each seat.

are unfortunately with us to this day. Whatever their defects, anaglyphs can be projected without any modification to equipment, and it is not necessary for everyone in the house to have a motorized viewing device.

A similar anaglyph system was used for the Plastigram films which were produced by J. F. Leventhal and were theatrically distributed with success between 1921 and 1924.

In 1936 and 1937, commercially successful anaglyphic motion picture shorts were distributed by MGM. These were shot for them by Leventhal and John Norling under the series title Audioscopiks. MGM also presented in 1941 a comedy called *Third-Dimension Murder,* shot with the studio's camera. Early two-color processes lent themselves to the making of anaglyphic prints. In the case of the Fairall process, one side of duplitized stock was printed with red and the other with blue images. Today any black-and-white stereoscopic film can be converted to an anaglyph by successive passes through a printer onto color stock, with left and right images illuminated through appropriate color filters. The economy and simplicity of the system, so easily compatible with existing laboratory and projection practices, remains attractive, but the results rarely warrant the effort.

POLARIZED-LIGHT IMAGE SELECTION

A number of interesting ways of producing polarized light have been suggested and used, including birefringent crystals called Iceland spar or nicol prisms, and a device called "piles-of-plates," which uses a sandwich of glass plates. Compared with sheet polarizers, these methods are inconvenient and costly and have optical limitations. Sheet polarizers may also be used for a wide cone of illumination, whereas nicol prisms have a restricted angle of view. Sheet polarizers are lightweight and fairly rugged, can be cut to shape, are essentially neutral in color, and are very inexpensive compared with alternatives.

Sheet polarizers were first discovered in Britain in 1852 by William Bird Herapath (Linssen, 1952). One of his students produced crystals "formed by accident in a bottle containing a large quantity of the mixed disulphates of quinine and cinchonine." Herapathite sheet polarizers were commercially available for much of the nineteenth century but were reportedly of very poor quality and in very small sizes. In 1928, Edwin H. Land, of what is now the Polaroid Corporation, took out his first patents based on improvements of Herapath's work. At this time, or shortly thereafter, Bernauer, a researcher with Zeiss, in Germany, and Marks, in the United States, invented similar filters.

Anderton, in his American patent of 1891 (No. 542,321), first suggested the use of polarized light for image selection for stereoscopic projection. Although he did not rule it out, he did not specify Herapathite. He does mention the nicol prism and the piles-of-plates devices. By implication, this does not speak well for the quality of Herapathite.

It was not until 1935, when Land showed stereoscopic films to the Society of Motion Picture Engineers in Washington, D.C., that a successful public demonstration of sheet polarizers in this context was given, according to Ryan (Quigley, 1953). Ryan also tells us that "their [Land and his associate, Wheelwright] first laboratory being a rural dairy building with few technical

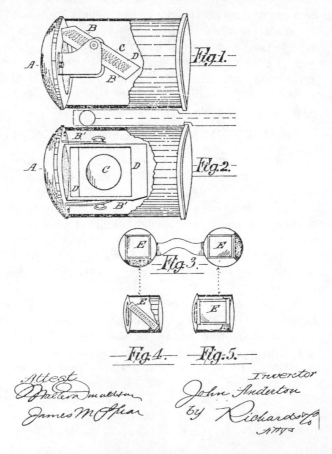

(No Model.)   2 Sheets—Sheet 1.

J. ANDERTON.
METHOD BY WHICH PICTURES PROJECTED UPON SCREENS BY MAGIC
LANTERNS ARE SEEN IN RELIEF.

No. 542,321.   Patented July 9, 1895.

1.15. *Anderton's polarized light system.* Shown here in the U.S. patent drawings of 1895, it provides the basis for modern three-dimensional projection. The significant improvement came forty years later with the perfection of the sheet polarizer. Figures 1 and 2 show projector polarizers, at right angles to each other, made up of a "thin bundle of glass plates." A similar arrangement used for viewing glasses is shown in Figure 3. Anderton also specified a nondepolarizing screen.

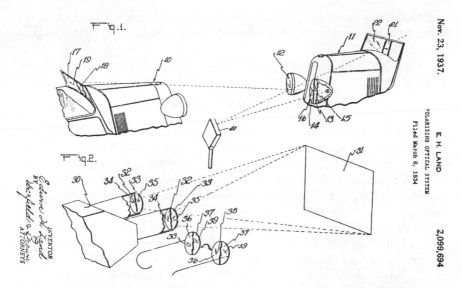

1.16. *Applications for sheet polarizers.* Land patented a method for dimming on-coming polarized automobile headlights, when viewed through a polarized windshield (top). Also shown (bottom) is the modern method for viewing stereoscopic movies using sheet polarizers for image selection.

Feb. 25, 1947.   **E. H. LAND**   **2,416,528**

COMBINED TICKET STRIP AND VIEWING VISOR

Filed March 13, 1942

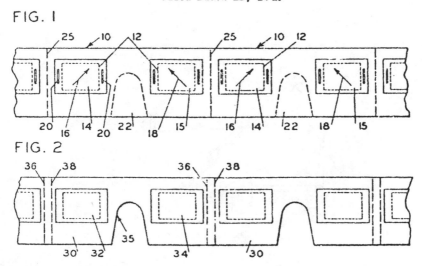

FIG. 1

FIG. 2

1.17. *Combined ticket and viewer.* Land is a prolific inventor, and this logical but somehow goofy patent of 1947 describes a technique for simplifying ticket sales and selection device distribution. The viewers have no temples.

facilities, these films [early Kodacolor] were developed, by an intricate reversal process, by Wheelwright while locked in the icebox, the only darkroom available!"

Polarized light, as a method for image selection, will be discussed more fully on page 80.

NORLING AND SPOTTISWOODE

In 1939, a stereoscopic film using the polarized-light method of image selection was commissioned by the Chrysler Corporation for the New York World's Fair. The film, produced by John A. Norling and using stop-motion animation, showed the building of a car. He used a dual camera-projector system, and the presentation more or less established the system that would be employed commercially for many years to come. Double camera rigs like Norling's avoided the great research and development costs that would have been incurred in the creation of a single-band system, and they achieved production and distribution economies by sticking to existing hardware and production systems. Essentially, everything was simply doubled up.

In 1951, the Telekinema, a special 400-person theater constructed for the Festival of Britain, used this double-band approach. It was specially designed for stereoscopic projection, and several films were commissioned for it and played to well-attended houses in 1951. Under the directorship of

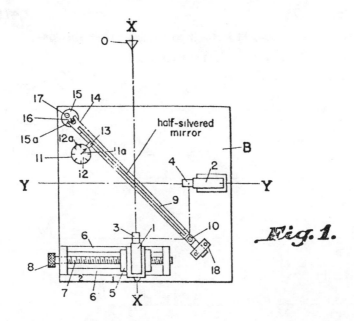

1.18. *The Ramsdell camera.* An interesting design that can allow for very low values of interaxial separation. The semisilvered mirror will result in a light loss of about a stop.

Raymond Spottiswoode, the Telekinema helped to popularize the stereo-scopic medium, specifically that employing polarized light for image selec-tion. Two animated films (*Around Is Around* and *Now Is the Time*) were made by Norman McLaren of the Canadian Film Board, and live-action sub-jects were also presented on the program, one of which (*London Tribute*) was shot in black and white at the London Zoo with a camera designed by Leslie Dudley (British Patent No. 17.086150), based on the Ramsdell still camera. The lack of availability of integral tripack color stock, like modern Eastman Color, prevented the production from being shot in color, since the bulky Technicolor machines were not used by Dudley. However, the Tech-nicolor Company modified a pair of their cameras so that color film was shot of the River Thames (*Royal River*). The film was photographed mostly in long shots, from a floating platform. The size of the machines prevented the interaxial distance from being less than 9.5 inches, but comparatively few of those responding to an audience questionnaire noticed any distortion (Spot-tiswoode, 1953).

BEFORE THE BOOM

Land and others had attempted to interest people in the theatrical film industry in the polarization method of image selection for some time, but without any direct success. It took a combination of factors from within and without the film industry in the early 1950s to finally convince the moguls that stereoscopic filmmaking was a good way to get people back into the neighborhood theaters.

Between 1946 and 1952, weekly attendance in American theatrical cinemas had dropped by nearly half, from 82.4 million to 46 million. There were rumors in 1952 that the studios were headed for major corporate shake-ups, and that labor cutbacks were in the offing. The inquiry, or witch hunt, of the House Committee on Un-American Activities into Communist infiltration into Hollywood had put a dent into some of the finest creative talent in the industry, but it was the growing popularity of television that was blamed for declining audiences. Things looked grim for Hollywood, and something was needed to save the day. Obviously that something was spec-tacle, as the Roman emperors had learned twenty centuries before.

To an outsider the introduction of Ansco Color and subsequently East-man Color materials would hardly seem to be of earth-shaking importance to the Hollywood film industry. Yet these color films directly paved the way for Cinemascope, Cinerama, and the dual-camera projector system of stere-oscopic films. Any studio camera could now become a color camera when loaded with one of these new integral tripack films. Before the early 1950s, a producer who wanted first-rate color had to use one of the monstrously large Technicolor machines, actually three cameras built into one unit. Now mul-tiple combinations of studio cameras for the panoramic Cinerama or the stereoscopic Natural Vision became more manageable. It is doubtful that these systems would have been tried with the old Technicolor rig.

On September 30, 1952, *This Is Cinerama* opened at New York's Broadway Theatre and played to record attendance. Essentially a triptych process similar to that used by Gance in his 1927 Polyvision effort, *Napoleon,* Cinerama used a triple array of cameras and projectors in an attempt to boggle the mind with the sweep of its screen. It relied on travelogue spectacle rather than dramatic elements.

On November 27, 1952, the first American feature film to be made in color and 3-D, in the Natural Vision process, *Bwana Devil,* was shown in Los Angeles. In one week at this single theater, *Bwana Devil* grossed $100,000. The scramble was on. The studios, shown the way from indepen-

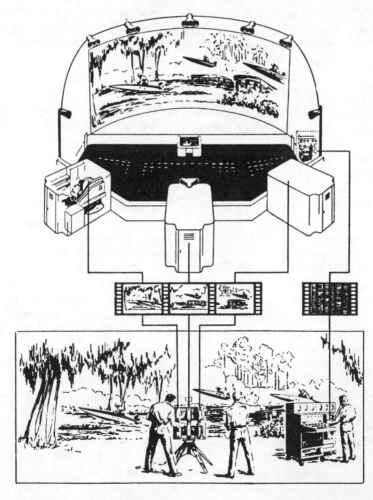

1.19. *This is Cinerama.* Three cameras and three projectors, plus sound equipment, were synchronized for presentations on large, curved screens.

1.20. *Natural vision camera.* On the set filming *House of Wax.* (Gunzberg, "The Story of Natural Vision," *American Cinematographer,* Volume 34:534–5, 1953. Reprinted by permission.)

dent producers, wanted a piece of the action. Since *Bwana Devil* was promoted as the first stereoscopic feature film, it's important to note the priority of the German effort, *You Can Almost Touch It* (*Zum Greifen Nah*), which was shot in the Zeiss single-band process invented by Boehner and premiered at the Berlin Ufa Palast Theater on May 27, 1937.

The Gunzburg brothers, Milton and Julian—a script writer and an eye surgeon—with the help of cinematographer Friend Baker, put together a rig made up of two Mitchell cameras after the fashion of Dudley's device prepared for the Festival of Britain. After unsuccessfully approaching the majors, the Gunzburgs finally persuaded independent producer Arch Obler, of "Lights Out" radio fame, to use their stereoscopic process for his film *Bwana Devil*. The rest, as they say, is history. The box office success of *Bwana Devil* had to be explained in terms of 3-D, and only 3-D, since the film had little merit.

Industry decision makers thought history was repeating itself, and they did not want to be unprepared, as they been had at the end of the silent era. The instantaneous stereo craze created a technological revolution, and once again the studios were virtually asleep. According to Gavin (*American Cine-*

matographer, March 1953), only one studio, Paramount, had a 3-D rig on hand, made years before.

In such a year, the studios made about three hundred films. In 1953 about forty-five films were released in 3-D, with another twenty in 1954 (Limbacher, 1968). Clearly a conversion to stereo was in progress in 1953, or at least the studios were flirting with the possibility. One of the reasons usually offered to explain the rapid decline of the stereo film—the boom lasted no more than nine months—is that the films were of low quality, and exploitation films at that. Hollywood has always made exploitation films, exploiting stars, fads, or gimmicks, and it was to be expected that three-dimensional films would be handled in the worst possible taste. Many distasteful objects were hurled out of the screen at the audience.

Even a bleary-eyed examination of the films shows a number of "A" 3-D pictures, including *Kiss Me Kate, Dial M for Murder, Hondo,* and *Miss Sadie Thompson.* (Fortunately for the author, there are theaters in the San Francisco Bay Area that frequently play stereoscopic films.) These would probably pass muster, although they were projected flat for most bookings because of the public's antipathy to 3-D by the time they were released. But good work was also done in "B" films such as *Creature from the Black Lagoon* and *House of Wax.* Stereo films were not any worse than the flat product, and they were made up of the same mixture of good and bad that Hollywood has always turned out.

The decline and fall of the stereo film can be attributed to problems in the shooting rigs themselves, a lack of stereoscopic photographic experience on the part of otherwise expert technical crews and cinematographers, inadequate quality control in the laboratories, a system of projection not matched to the abilities of normal human projectionists, and penny-pinching exhibitor practices. It all added up to headaches, eyestrain, and the demise of 3-D movies in under a year. Although Hollywood remains open to a good stereoscopic process, the memory still smarts, despite the many millions the stereoscopic films made.

Let us start with the shooting rigs themselves. A number of basically similar schemes were developed, usually involving two studio cameras mounted on a single lathelike base. Some rigs, such as the Gunzburgs' set-up, used cameras facing each other shooting into mirrors. Another, the Fox unit, used two cameras set at right angles, one camera shooting the subject's image reflected by a semisilvered mirror, with the other shooting through a mirror. The Universal stereo camera used two machines mounted side by side, but one upside down, to obtain the necessary short interaxial distances.

RKO had an agreement to use the services of John A. Norling and a stereoscopic camera of his design, which appears to have been the most sophisticated and advanced machine of its time. In fact, the Norling camera (patent No. 2,753,774) remains a very interesting stereoscopic camera for feature film production and appears to be the precursor of the Soviet Stereo

1.21. *Posters from the boom.* (Gunzberg, "The Story of Natural Vision," *American Cinematographer,* Volume 34:554–6, 1953. Reprinted by permission.)

70 camera. Essentially a 70mm camera itself, the Norling machine used two 35mm rolls of stock, immediately adjacent to each other, exposed through two side by side apertures. Lenses of various focal lengths featured continuously variable interaxial separation using a periscope-type device that maintained image orientation through a range of rotation. Unlike all other stereo cameras of the time, jury-rigged from existing machines, the Norling device was engineered from the ground up and appeared to be less bulky or awkward to operate. At present, the Norling camera is owned by Stereovision International.

In passing, let us note that a similar camera was used by Frederic Eugene Ives from 1900 to 1905, with lenses set at a fixed interaxial distance of 1.75 in. Twin 200-ft magazines were mounted within the camera body, according to Norling (Quigley, 1953).

Nine features were shot with the Natural Vision rig (Gunzburg, 1953), including all of Warner Brothers' efforts. The minimum interaxial distance for this unit was 3½ in. (about 90 mm). My tests have convinced me that this separation for many focal lengths and subject-to-camera distances produces

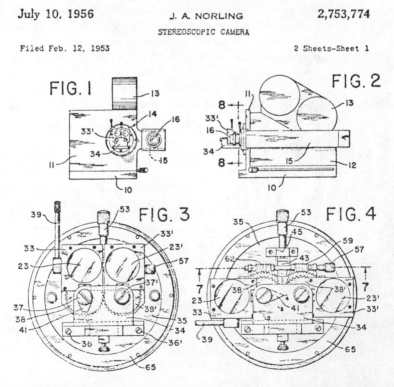

July 10, 1956   J. A. NORLING   2,753,774

STEREOSCOPIC CAMERA

Filed Feb. 12, 1953   2 Sheets—Sheet 1

1.22. *The Norling Camera.* First page of the drawings of the 1956 patent. Figures 1 and 2 show front and side views of the camera, and Figures 3 and 4 show how lenses (23 and 23') can be adjusted for interaxial separation.

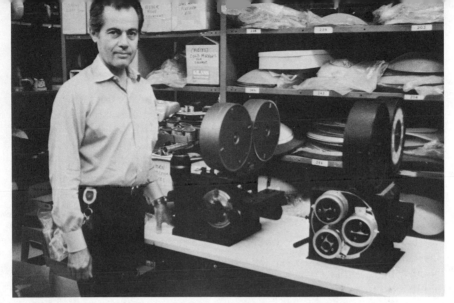

1.23. *Chris Condon, optical designer*. Condon shown here with two camera systems he did not design, the Norling (left) and the Dunning (right). His company, Future Dimensions, offers these machines to the film industry. They are of very similar design.

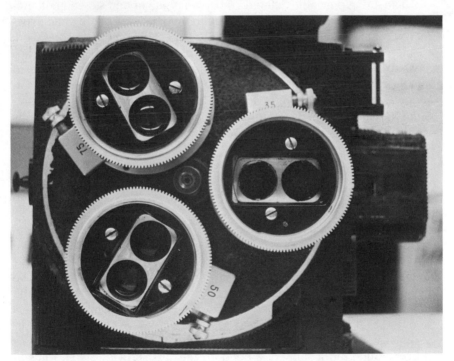

1.24. *Front of the Dunning camera*. Lens turret with three focal lengths mounted in place with fixed 1.5-in. interaxial. As with the Norling camera, left and right images are exposed on adjacent rolls of 35mm film. Originally designed as a color camera, it makes more sense as a 3-D machine. Many of the early color motion picture devices are similar to 3-D designs.

eyestrain in many viewers because of the resulting large values for screen parallaxes. Many situations call for photography that is better accomplished at interaxials equal to or less than the nominal 2½ in. (about 65 mm) accepted as the human interocular. However, a case can be made for using a fixed 3.5-in. interaxial setting for studio photography. Usually focal lengths greater than the diagonal of the format are employed, with correspondingly greater distances from camera to subject. Given these longer focal lengths and longer subject-to-camera distances, the somewhat expanded interaxial setting can provide natural-appearing photography with adequate depth range (see page 190 for an explanation of depth range).

Films that I had an opportunity to view (photographed with a number of rigs) often showed recentration of optics for closeups or for certain focal lengths; that is, there was a shift in the position of the optical axes of the taking lenses resulting in spurious screen parallaxes, the most serious being the addition of vertical parallaxes. If one image point is shifted upwards with respect to the other by even very small values (more than 0.2°), the attempt at fusion results in an upward sheering of one eye with respect to the other. For most people this muscular effort causes eyestrain.

There are appreciable differences between planar and stereo photography, and cinematographers in Hollywood in the 1950s had little or no experience with stereoscopic work. It is unfair to expect anyone to do good work in a medium without some practice, yet this is exactly what the studios expected of their cameramen. Several shooting systems were devised to guide the cinematographer. One was published by Spottiswoode and Spottiswoode, another by Hill in the form of a calculator offered by the Motion Picture Research Council, and another in the form of charts and graphs by Levonian. My work with all three has convinced me that the cinematographer would have been better off without such help.

The laboratory's part in all this is crucial. Timing and processing for the left and right prints must be precisely the same, or one dark and one light print can result. Even small differences between left and right image illumination strain the eye.

A number of serious errors can take place in the projection booth. Focal lengths of both projection lenses have to be matched to within the required 0.5%. This was not always done. If both arcs do not receive the same amperage, the images will have unmatched illumination. The projectionist must be on guard for shifted framelines to correct for vertical parallax. Although the projectors were electrically interlocked to keep them in sync, the shutters also must be substantially in phase (opening and closing together), a condition not automatically guaranteed with the equipment employed. The Polaroid Corporation did a study of a hundred theaters showing stereo films in 1953 (Jones and Schurcliff, 1954) and found that twenty-five of them had images enough out of synchronization to be disturbing.

Five to 10% of the population cannot see stereo, and up to another 10% have anomalous stereo perception. These figures may seem discouraging, but the fact that there are tone-deaf people has not diminished activity on the part of musicians. The real problem here is that projectionists with anomalous stereo vision might set their equipment to match the needs of their eyes while producing strain in just about everyone else in the theater.

Next we come to the exhibitor, who sometimes sought to save money and wound up helping to kill stereo. Sprayed screens usually cannot do the job that aluminum-surfaced ones can do. Screens painted with pigment usually have much higher ghosting, or spurious images, or left and right image cross-talk, than screens coated with aluminum. Nor are they as bright, and they tend to have hot spots. Distributors sought further to save pennies on stereoglasses of inferior quality. Nothing could be more foolish than to have

Jan. 13, 1959   A. W. TONDREAU   2,868,065
STEREOSCOPIC CAMERA SYSTEM

Filed May 11, 1953   5 Sheets-Sheet 1

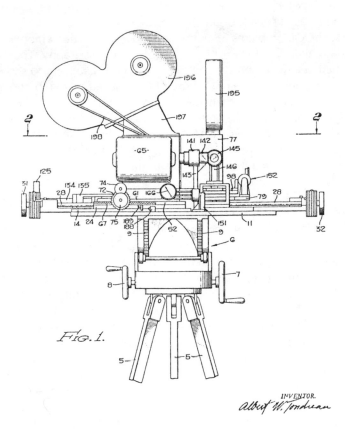

1.25. *The Tondreau camera for Warner Brothers.* Cameras at right angles, one seeing into a mirror.

patrons looking at the show through second-rate optics, but this was done. The glasses are often singled out as the greatest drawback to public acceptance of stereo films. But I believe they became the scapegoat of the medium, taking the blame for the difficulties I have enumerated, although it is perfectly obvious that they are an encumbrance, especially for people who already wear glasses.

Given all of these difficulties, which quite literally add up to a big headache, it is not hard to understand why the studios, distributors, exhibitors, and, most important, the public preferred the major alternative to 3-D: "scope," or in its initial personification, Twentieth Century-Fox's CinemaScope—perhaps the first word in the English language with a middle letter capitalized. The first CinemaScope film, *The Robe,* opened on September 16, 1953, at the Roxy Theater in New York.

Despite the claims in the advertisements I knew even as a thirteen-year-old that CinemaScope was not 3-D without glasses. But there was a special thrill in watching the curtain open to twice normal width and listening to the blare of the Fox fanfare while the logo showed carbon arcs scanning the Hollywood skies in search of a new gimmick.

The technical problems of anamorphic or wide-screen cinematography are trivial compared to those of stereoscopic cinematography. That is not to say that there are not technical challenges. But it is far easier to show a film through an anamorphic lens or to crop off the top and bottom of the frame to obtain a wide-aspect ratio than it is to produce and present stereoscopic films. While public complaints may have centered on the stereoglasses, people in the industry must have had a clearer view of the difficulties, and they took the course of least resistance, opting for a wider aspect ratio.

After 1954, comparatively few films had been shot stereoscopically, and the saving grace of those that had been, from the distributor's point of view, was that, by showing one band of the two-band process, a planar version of the film could be shown.

The double-band system could have been made to work in road-show presentations (that is, in first-run houses in major cities where extraordinary care is taken with the projected image). Cinerama required three projectionists one at each machine, a soundman to run the interlocked multichannel magnetic playback unit, and a specialist in the house itself who corrected for deficiencies in synchronization among portions of the triptych and sound.

The projection of double-band stereoscopic films is no less difficult to achieve successfully, as I have learned from conversations with two projectionists who were operators in San Francisco theaters in the 1950s and from the literature, which includes instruction books sent with the prints.

Quite obviously there was a great incentive to play stereoscopic films in neighborhood as well as road-show houses. CinemaScope, the poor man's Cinerama, as it was dubbed, had the great virtue of being adaptable to any theater. Cinerama could only be shown in a special house with special care. Probably the great difficulty with the double-band system is that it was attempted in neighborhood theaters, when it should have been saved for theaters that had been specially equipped and staffed.

In an effort to do away with the problems of double-band stereo, Nord and also Dudley in 1953 showed single-band systems, following the vertical similar sense rotation scheme shown in the illustration. Although Columbia adopted the Nord system and encouraged its use, it did not succeed.

In the early 1950s, several single-band systems were also offered for the amateur enthusiast. Bolex and Elgeet manufactured similar dual-lens optics, and Nord produced a prismatic converter lens meant to be mounted before the taking and projection lenses. The Bolex unit, to be used with their 16mm camera, was a remarkably good performer, although it suffered from an awkward vertical format. Today these camera and projector optics are sought by collectors and enthusiasts.

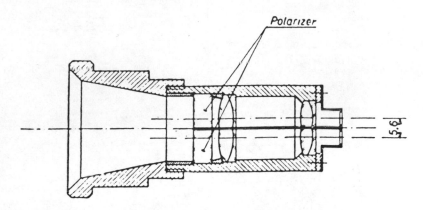

1.26. *Paillard projector lens design.* Two lenses mounted in one barrel. (Paillard, 1953)

There is also a tradition of amateurs and others concocting their own dual camera and projector stereo systems, just as I did. Accounts of these workers, who experimented with small format cinematography, can be found in the 1953 volume of *American Cinematographer.*

Bernier in 1966 produced a single-band system (Space Vision, U.S. Patent No. 3,531,191), splitting a full 35mm frame into halves with a horizontal separation. This results in what is known as two Techniscope frames, with the usual scope-aspect ratio. Others, such as Condon, Marks, Findlay, and Symmes, have shown similar systems. The Bernier system has the distinction of having been the first used to shoot feature films, such as *The Bubble* (1966) and *Andy Warhol's Frankenstein* (1974). In 1981 Condon's optics were used for two features, *Rottweiler* (under the Future Dimensions mark) and *Parasite* (under the Stereovision mark).

It is difficult to analyze which portion of a system has gone wrong when viewing the end product, but it is evident that only the synchronization

Sept. 29, 1970   R. V. BERNIER   3,531,191
                    THREE DIMENSIONAL CINEMATOGRAPHY
Filed Oct. 21, 1966   12 Sheets-Sheet 10

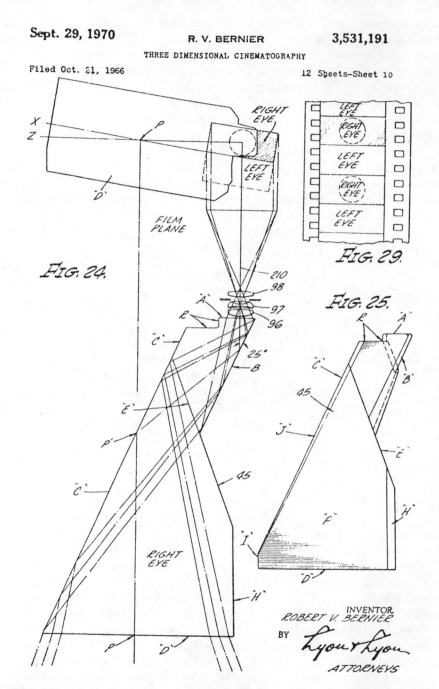

1.27. *The Bernier Spacevision three-dimensional lens.* A horrendously complicated optical design, it produces first-rate over-and-under images when properly used.

problem has been successfully solved with Bernier's over-and-under or stacked-format approach. Photography and projection have been abominable, and the situation is aggravated because only one focal length (32mm) and one interaxial setting (65mm) are available. Despite the fact that the Bernier optics are rarely put to good use, I believe they are of high quality.

One of the most financially successful stereoscopic films in recent years was shot for about $100,000. *The Stewardesses,* a silly, softcore pornographic film, was released in 1969 and grossed $26,000,000. The format design positioned two frames side by side on a single band of 35mm. I suffered severe eyestrain after a few minutes of trying to view the film, although some other patrons seemed to have a better time of it—or maybe they were just more determined to look at the screen.

The middle and late 1970s experienced scattered stereoscopic motion picture activity. Only a handful of newly produced stereoscopic films have actually made their way into theaters. Some of these have been the inevitable sexploitation, horror, and ultra-violent films, in technically inferior single-band systems. I have attended revivals of dual-band 1950s films in Berkeley and San Francisco. Audience reaction was enthusiastic.

THE SOVIET STEREOCINEMA

Many major contributions to stereoscopy have come from the West, as has been reflected in this account. However, since 1940 the Soviets have embarked on a steady program of developing a stereoscopic cinema, and, with the exception of the war years, have made at least one stereo film (shorts and features) every year.

The history of the Soviet stereocinema is closely tied to developments in the field of autostereoscopy (see page 69). In recent years, I am told by two visitors to the Soviet Union, the autostereoscopic system has been completely replaced by the polarized-light method of image selection. Apparently audiences prefer to wear stereoglasses and see a decently sharp and bright image rather than a blurry and dim image autostereoscopically. The glasses employed are very high-grade instruments, using glass filters, manufactured by Zeiss Jena in East Germany. Patrons return the glasses and they are used for subsequent screenings.

At present the Soviets employ their Stereo 70 system, which uses a 70mm camera and projector. The system was developed by NIKFI, the Motion Picture and Photography Scientific Research Institute, and is certainly the most complete stereoscopic filmmaking system.

Essentially, two 35mm frames are photographed side by side on a single 70mm band of film, and twin optics are used for projection. Full details of the system are given in a paper by Ousjannikova and Slabova (1975), which I will discuss in Chapter 5. A similar camera and projection system was developed in 1972 by Stereovision of Burbank, California, and is compatible with the Soviet effort.

What the Russians have done is a straightforward job of design, producing a system that ought to give a good, bright image of very high quality. In addition, the usual six-channel stereophonic sound available with 70mm is incorporated. Screenings are wisely confined to relatively small theaters, and the aspect ratio employed is 1.33:1.

A 70mm system was also developed in Europe by Jacobsen (U.S. Patent Nos. 3, 425, 775 and 3, 433, 561) that photographs anamorphically squeezed images side by side on 65mm camera stock for wide-aspect ratio projection. Several films were produced in the early 1970s, such as *Lieb im 3-D,* and *Frankenstein's Bloody Terror.*

THE UNITED ARTISTS SYSTEM

In November 1978 and January 1979, I witnessed early tests of a system developed by United Artists Theater Circuit, using interlocked 70mm cameras and projectors. The images were projected on a screen nearly fifty feet wide at the United Artists Theater in Pasadena, California. If properly used, this system promises to produce very high-quality three-dimensional motion picture images. The 70mm cameras, similar to the Fox rig of 1954, face at right angles to each other, shooting into a semisilvered mirror. Lenses with a wide range of focal lengths and variable interaxial settings from zero to 4 inches have been provided.

This system is meant only for road-show presentations, or first-run, specially equipped and staffed houses. A return to double-system under such circumstances, reminiscent of the effort it took to present early three-projector Cinerama, could be made to work. It is important to point out that such a system cannot be considered for neighborhood houses, where a solution employing single-band projection must be found. (However, film shot with the system can be optically printed into a single band of film.)

WED enterprises, a subsidiary of Walt Disney Productions, is producing a short 3-D film for the Kodak Pavilion at the EPOCT Center at Disney World in Florida. The system, designed and built by Disney, uses interlocked 65mm cameras and 70mm projectors, just like the UATC system. The film will be projected on a 54-by-22 foot screen.

The hopes for a stereoscopic filmmaking revival depend upon the success of two single-system films, using the over-and-under format. The summer of 1981 saw the Filmways release of a western shot in Spain, titled *Comin' at Ya.* Production values were low, the acting was terrible, the dialogue moronic, the stereoscopic process, Optrix, was an optical catastrophe, and the filmmakers attempted to place every shot behind the heads of the audience. The stereoscopic system suffers from left and right images of unequal sharpness, severe vertical parallax, and strange watermark-like spots hovering in one or the other image field.

The film has apparently been doing good business, and for that reason many major studios and producers are considering employing the three-dimensional medium. The situation brings to mind *Bwana Devil.*

Hollywood insiders are awaiting the release of the first quality stereoscopic feature shot in the United States in twenty-five years, *Rottweiler* from the E.O. Corporation. My company, Future Dimensions, supplied the three-dimensional system, and I worked on the film in the summer of 1981 as stereographer. I am certainly not unbiased, but this is one of the best shot stereoscopic films ever produced. Its performance in the market place will be keenly observed.

THE INDEPENDENT STEREOCINEMA

At just about the same time that the commercial stereo boom was taking place, there was also activity on the part of independent film artists. Dwinell Grant preceded the boom of the early 1950s, having received a Guggenheim grant in 1945 to pursue his *Composition #4*. The animated image pairs were printed, or shot, side by side on a single band of film to be projected with a prismatic attachment. Although shot in color, the original camera film has decomposed, and a print in black and white is now available from the Anthology Film Archives in New York.

On January 11, 1977, the Pacific Film Archive at the University of California in Berkeley presented a program that included Grant's film and the work of other animators who had pursued the stereoscopic medium. The program was put together by William Moritz, a poet and filmmaker who has been working in binocular forms exploiting retinal rivalry.

Grant's severely abstract film was followed by Norman McLaren's previously mentioned *Now Is the Time* and *Around Is Around* (both 1950). Prints had been supplied by Harold Layer of San Francisco State College, who managed to secure copies from the National Film Board. Projection was extremely good, using interlocked 16mm machines. The stereo effects were fun, but the graphics seemed terribly dated.

It is impossible to comment in detail on any of the other films on the program, since difficulties in projection made them unviewable. Oskar Fischinger's *Stereo Film* (1952) was obviously meant to be projected in a parallel-lens-axes system, unlike McLaren's, which is a crossed-lens-axes film, as are practically all modern efforts. However, no adjustment was made in projection for this different standard, so that Fischinger's stereopairs became unfusable. The short film was prepared as part of an application for funding that was not forthcoming.

Harry Smith's *Film #6* (1952) was meant to be viewed anaglyphically, but red and green glasses were not presented to the audience, so I can only guess at the possible effects.

Hy Hirsh's *Come Closer* (1952) was also improperly projected, so no comments are possible. (The projectionists did the best they could. I believe there were no instructions with the films.)

Moritz's experiments in retinal rivalry, in *Allee* and *Hot Flashes* (1970), were also shown at the Pacific Film Archive and I found that these invited fusion because the left and right fields were so similar. In my binocular "rivalry" work I have presented totally dissimilar left and right films, linked only thematically, not visually, so that attempts at fusion, which in such a case will probably cause eyestrain, is avoided.

Other independents have worked in the stereoscopic medium, and because of projection difficulties these films are rarely seen. Ken Jacobs has performed stereo shows using shadow forms of rear-projected anaglyphs and has also exploited the Pulfrich phenomenon by equipping audience members with neutral-density monocles.

Standish Lawder has shown me his elaborate 35mm dual-band system using optical positioning equipment and digital-control circuitry, but at the time of writing I have seen no footage shot with this promising system.

It has been one of my major intentions in writing this book to make the fundamental principles of the medium available to the filmmaking community in general, and especially to the independent film artist. The opportunities for exploration of the binocular cinema are literally limitless, since so little work has been done. The specific kind of double-band system I worked with in the course of this study could be assembled rapidly at relatively low cost by a skilled filmmaker. It is my hope that film artists will take up the call and go to work making curious and beautiful films in this, the binocular cinema.

chapter 2

Stereopsis and Stereoscopy

I will discuss many of the basic facts about stereopsis and stereoscopy here in an effort to give the reader some foundation in the physics, psychology, and physiology of binocular vision and in the depth sense, stereopsis. I will also make an attempt to relate stereopsis to stereoscopy, or the art of photographing binocularly three-dimensional images. Stereoscopic systems will be classified, and some of the basic facts about transmitting such information will be given. Discussion of the work of Gibson should provide a pathway between stereopsis and stereoscopy, so that the reader will gain some further insight into the difference between perception of the visual world and perception of a transmitted stereoscopic image. Finally, I will discuss polarized light and its applications to stereoscopy. The primary display technique assumed in this book is the polarized-light method of image selection.

DEPTH CUES

All filmmaking is three-dimensional in the sense that motion pictures provide many cues to depth that also help us perceive the visual world. Certainly planar films depict a three-dimensional world, and observers rarely feel that anything is missing. Space, as it is depicted, seems full, and the images appear to be real and lifelike. The actors quite clearly are not part of the background, but separate from it; they are rounded, not flat, and they look like the human beings we see every day.

These planar films lack only one depth cue, since all the other psychological depth cues can be perceived on a flat screen. Stereopsis, sometimes called binocular stereopsis to emphasize the fact that two eyes are needed, cannot be conveyed in the conventional cinema.

The following is a cursory exposition of the cues to depth as usually given in textbooks, most of which were first enumerated by Renaissance painters. The reader interested in learning more is advised to consult a basic book on perceptual psychology, such as that by Kaufman (1974), *Sight and Mind*.

Retinal Image Size. Larger retinal images tell us that the object is closer, because objects closer to the eye are seen as larger.

Perspective, or Linear Perspective. This cue is based on the notion that objects, often man-made, diminish in size as they recede from the observer. For example, parallel railroad tracks seem to converge at the horizon.

Interposition, or Overlapping. One object in front of another prevents us from seeing the one beind. A teacher in front of a blackboard cuts off part of the view of the blackboard and must, therefore, be closer to the student than the blackboard.

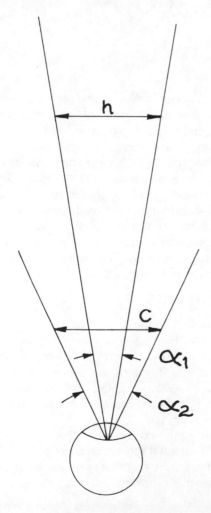

2.1. *Retinal image size.* Lines c and h are the same length, but c subtends angle α_2, greater than α_1, thus appearing closer than h.

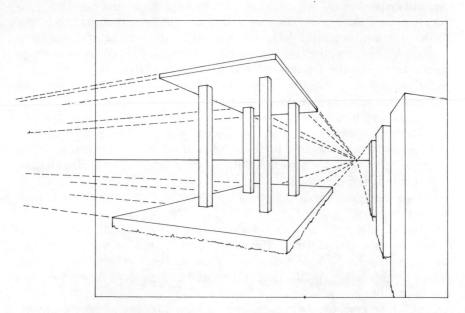

2.2. *Perspective.* Dashed lines extend to "vanishing points" on horizon.

2.3. *Interposition.* The top rectangle appears to be closer than the bottom one.

Aerial Perspective. At this moment I am looking out across San Francisco Bay to Mount Tamalpais. It is a very hazy day, and the mountain is barely visible in the glare of the haze illuminated by the setting sun. The haze intervening between me and the mountain makes it look far away. Atmospheric haze provides the depth cue of aerial perspective.

Light and Shade. Cast shadows provide an effective depth cue, as does light coming from one or more directions modeling an object.

These depth cues can provide information about the volume of space filled by objects or how far apart one object is from another. Some cues also help us perceive the solidity of an object or understand its roundness. The extent of space between objects and the way individual objects fill space are different but related entities.

One such cue discussed at great length by J. J. Gibson (1950) is termed textural gradient.

Textural Gradient. A tweed jacket seen up close has a coarse texture that is invisible from a great distance. The leaves of a tree are clearly discernible up close, but from a distance the texture of the leaves becomes less detailed. Silver photography is particularly well suited to the recording of finely detailed texture.

All these cues can be picked up in still photography, whereas the following cue can be seen only in motion pictures.

Motion Parallax. This cue is a post-Renaissance discovery, probably discussed first by Helmholtz. A most dramatic example of motion parallax is the rapid movement of nearby foliage as one rides in a car, while the sky and

2.4. *Aerial perspective.* The haze contributes to making the background look far away.

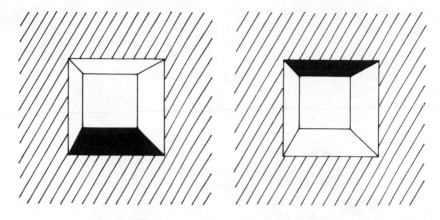

2.5. *Light and shade*. Because of the direction of the cast shadow, the left shape seems to pop out, and the right shape pops in.

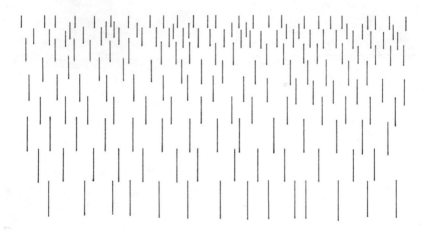

2.6. *Textural gradient*. A field of needles driven into a plane. The density of spacing decreases in the foreground.

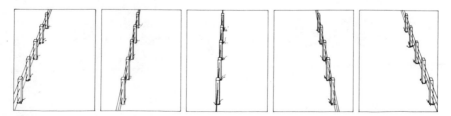

2.7. *Motion parallax*. Movie frames of a fence as the camera moves by.

the distant hills seem to remain relatively fixed in position. This cue is closely related to the cue of stereopsis, which is the major concern of this study.

The depth cues that have been enumerated above are usually classified as psychological cues. They have been studied by psychologists as separate entities, and certain rules can be specified for each. The following depth cues, usually categorized as physiological cues, are more readily explicable in terms of anatomical function.

Accommodation. Just as the camera lens focuses by moving closer to or farther away from the film the lens of the eye focuses images on the retina by actually changing shape as it is pulled by muscles. The muscular effort involved in focusing could provide a feedback or proprioceptive mechanism for gauging depth.

Convergence. The lens of each eye projects a separate image of objects on each retina. In order for these to be seen as a single image by the brain, the central portion of each retina must "see" the same object point. You can see

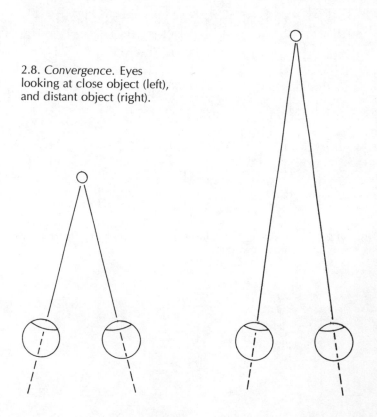

2.8. *Convergence*. Eyes looking at close object (left), and distant object (right).

the tip of your finger as one finger, but if you look behind it you change the point of convergence and your finger will look blurry or doubled. The muscles responsible for this vergence, the inward or outward rotation of the eyes, may provide distance information such as a camera range finder does. **Disparity.** When the eyes converge on an object in space, it is seen as a single image, and all other objects, in front of or behind the point of convergence, can be seen to be double images.

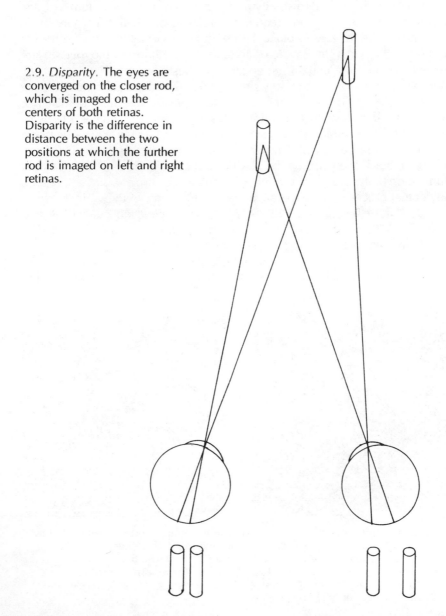

2.9. *Disparity.* The eyes are converged on the closer rod, which is imaged on the centers of both retinas. Disparity is the difference in distance between the two positions at which the further rod is imaged on left and right retinas.

Objects behind the point of convergence are said to have uncrossed disparity, and those in front of the locus of convergence have crossed disparity. Different groupings of cells in the brain are activated by crossed or uncrossed disparity of the retina.

The drawing shows that retinal images of objects that are not being converged on will have some measurable distance from the central portion of the retina where convergence occurs. The difference between these two distances is a measure of disparity and can be given either in terms of distance on the retina or, more frequently, in terms of angular measure.

The eye-brain seeks to place the image points of interest on the central portion of the retina, the fovea, or actually on a portion of the fovea. Here the eye's acuity or ability to see detail is greatest.

Stereopsis. Stereopsis is the only depth sense that depends on our having two eyes. Stereoscopists use the term *interocular* to describe the distance between the eyes, usually 65mm for males and 63mm for females. Physiologists call this the *pupillary distance,* or *P.D.* The distance between camera and projector lenses is called the *interaxial.* Although it is a separate depth sense, stereopsis depends on the other depth cues in order to form a visual impression of the world. This ought to come as no surprise, since the entire perceptual process is a cooperative effort on the part of the various cues.

Both the convergence and disparity cues depend on our having two eyes, but neither can be described as being a sense. Both aid in the formation of the stereoscopic image created by the mind.

It can be demonstrated through the use of Julesz figures, for example, that a stereogram totally lacking any extrastereoscopic cues can have depth

2.10. *Julesz figure.* My only attempt to reproduce an image stereoscopically in this book, which I feel says something about the "state of the art" of printing. Some people have the knack and can "free vision," or fuse the two together into a three-dimensional effigy. (Julesz, *Foundations of Cyclopean Perception.* Chicago: University of Chicago Press, 1971. Copyright 1971 by Bell Telephone Laboratories, Inc. Reprinted by permission.)

when viewed through a stereoscope. In the figure shown here, which has been reprinted time and again in the literature, the viewer with functioning stereopsis will see a rectangle emerge from the background field.

There are many rival psychological theories that attempt to explain stereopsis. For now, let us discuss stereopsis in terms that will be helpful to the filmmaker or photographer. Although it is an independent depth sense, stereopsis works in conjunction with monocular depth cues, especially perspective, and is dependent on memory.

Although many texts and articles for the stereographer attempt to explain this mechanism in terms of convergence, it has been repeatedly established for a century and a half, since the work of H. W. Dove, that convergence has little to do with gauging distance and simply functions to fuse left and right image pairs to prevent doubling of the image. Perceptual psychologists have not as yet established a totally convincing theory to account for all the known observations of stereopsis. Physiologists, studying brain function on an individual cellular level, may come closest to unravelling the functional mechanism through their observations that groups, or pools, of cells discriminate between crossed and uncrossed disparity and that these disparity pools may well be the key to the functioning of stereopsis.

The mind transforms two essentially planar retinal images into a single view of the world with stereoscopic or three-dimensional depth. In whatever way this happens, slight horizontal shifts of left and right image elements on the retinas are turned into the useful and pleasurable sensation, stereopsis.

THE VISUAL PATHWAY

The visual pathway begins with the eye.

The eye, like a small camera 1 in. in diameter, has a focal length of about 25 mm, a maximum f stop of about 2.8, and a minimum stop of about f/22. The commonplace analogy between the eye and a camera is remarkably accurate (Wald, 1954). The retina, the light-sensitive surface or film of the eye, when called upon to see in dim illumination, increases its speed through a chemical process very much like using faster film or pushing film for increased sensitivity.

The cornea and the lens of the eye bend light rays to form what is called a real image, upside down and backwards, on the retina. Focusing is accomplished by muscles that pull on the lens, changing its shape. When one looks at some object, the six muscles attached to each eye aim it at that object so that the image falls on the fovea. The foveal portion of the retina is packed with specialized nerve cells called cones, and this region of the eye provides us with maximum visual acuity.

The density of cones (there are a total of about 120 million of them) falls off as we move away from the fovea, where the rods (there are 7 million of them) are responsible for vision in dim light, essentially seen as monochromatic.

The eye, like a camera lens, uses an iris diaphragm for controlling the level of illumination that reaches the retina. In bright light the lens is "stopped down," and in dim light it "opens up."

The optic nerves carry the visual signal initially processed by the retinas further into the brain, although the eye-retina is quite clearly an extension of the brain itself (see Fig 1.2). A funny thing happens on the way to the brain, where most of the left and right fibers of the optic nerve cross over at the optic chiasma. Some of the fibers of the right eye go to the right hemisphere and some to the left hemisphere. A corresponding partial crossover, or partial decussation, also takes place for the left eye.

About 70 percent of the fibers originating at an eye cross over at the chiasma. The bundle of fibers from each eye can be thought of as made up of two bundles, temporal and nasal, from corresponding halves of the retina. The temporal fibers go to the hemisphere of the brain on the same side of the head as the eye from which they originated, and the nasal fibers go to the opposite cerebral hemisphere.

What happens from this point on becomes increasingly complex as information is fed back from one portion of the visual pathway to another. The interested reader is advised to consult Kaufman (1974), Julesz (1971), or Polyak (1957).

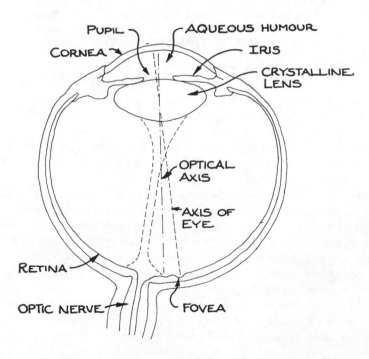

2.11. *Cross section of an eye.* A diagrammatic view of an eye.

THE STEREOPHOTOGRAPHIC FIELD

J. J. Gibson, in his classic book, *The Perception of the Visual World* (1950), makes this distinction between the visual world and the visual field: The visual world is the world of daily experience, of ordinary life, the room one may be in, the streets one drives through, the parks one walks through. It is a visual world not subject to introspection. It is taken for granted.

On the other hand, we perceive the visual field only when we become consciously aware of seeing. Gibson suggests that the difference can be illustrated by looking around the room you are in as you usually would. There are all the things you expect to be there, a chair, a book lying on top of a table, and so on. Now try fixating your eyes on some particular point in the room, but at the same time remaining aware of the entire area of vision. As you continue this exercise, what you see takes on the appearance of a picture, and this conscious effort has turned the visual world into the visual field. There are some very interesting differences between the two, and these have a direct bearing on stereoscopic filmmaking.

The visual field, unlike the visual world, is bounded. This may seem a peculiar notion at first, but the visual world exists in a totality of extent in space, or throughout a full 360° sphere. You are not able to see more than a fraction of that sphere at one time, but you are nonetheless aware of the world extending beyond in all directions. If you continue to fixate one eye (close or cover one eye) on a particular point in the room, still paying attention to the boundaries of vision, you will soon see that the extent of vision is limited by your nose at one edge of the field and gradually diminishes at the opposite side. The drawing shown here, by the physicist Ernest Mach, illustrates the extent of the visual field of a single eye. Both eyes together cover a field of about 180° horizontally and about 150° vertically. It may come as a surprise to many that the nose actually extends into the visual field to a significant extent. It has been there all our lives, but most of us never really notice it.

One of the most interesting things about the visual field, which you can demonstrate for yourself if you continue to fixate on a point, is that it is sharpest at its center. As you move your attention away from the center of the field without moving your point of fixation, you will notice that the edges of the field become progressively less clear and distinct. Try fixating on a single word on this page. Only that word, or the few adjacent ones, are sharp. All the other words on the page become less distinct away from the center of the field.

The visual world, on the other hand, gives the impression of being totally sharp over its entire extent. Undoubtedly some sort of visual memory is at work here; the various movements of the eye from point to point in the field produce images that are somehow stored and summed up to construct a sharp visual world.

The eye sees very poorly while in motion. Only when at rest does it see clearly. And, as the eyes move, the visual world remains fixed. This is quite unlike the results one obtains when panning a camera, in which the world does seem to move when you look at the footage. That is probably why pans are so difficult to execute gracefully. The result of a pan is quite unlike anything we are used to seeing when looking at the visual world.

If you push on the corner of one eye with a finger, while fixating on a point (closing or covering the other eye will help with this experiment), you will notice that the world actually moves. The commonly accepted theory to explain this is that there is an internal frame of reference of visual direction. When the eye initiates movement, the frame of reference moves in the opposite direction with equal magnitude, so the visual world remains at rest. A push on the eyeball disassociates the movement of the eye from this mechanism.

Gibson points out that when we tip our head vertically, or look through our legs at the world upside down, if we pay attention to the visual field, the orientation of the image is defined with respect to the boundaries of the field, as would be the case when looking at a painting or photograph. The visual world, on the other hand, has distinct upward and downward directions that are gravity-defined, undoubtedly, by the mechanism of the inner ear.

2.12. *The visual field.* Ernst March in the 1880s was probably the first person to introspect and come up with a drawing like this. Artist Christopher Swan has drawn this version.

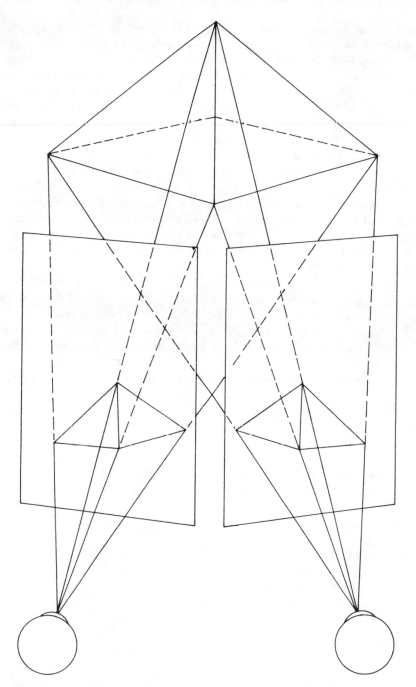

2.13. *Two perspective points of view.* The eyes, like a double-lensed stereoscopic camera, see objects from two perspective viewpoints. Shown here are the geometric projections onto two plane surfaces of a three-dimensional object. (After Gibson, 1950).

In addition, linear perspective is a quality of the visual field, and probably a learned one that operates only when we introspect. Gibson asserts also that when objects are observed in an introspective or pictorial sense, especially with one eye closed, they appear flat, like shapes without depth.

The visual field, observable only through conscious effort, is more readily available to the person who is trained in its perception. Filmmakers and photographers train themselves to see the visual field. It is their life's work. Only the visual field, not the visual world, can be photographed.

The naive photographer for example, has not been trained to understand the compositional necessities of the visual field. His or her attempts to create effigies, no matter how worthy and ambitious in intent, may fail. It may be impossible to translate such ideas photographically because of the perceptual limitations of the creator. The snapshot shooter attempts to translate the visual world directly into a good photograph. The accomplished photographer learns to interpret the visual world photographically by concentrating on the visual field.

The role of memory in our perception of the photographic world is important. When observing the photographic field, our recollections of qualities of objects, such as their shape, color, and texture, may all contribute to a heightening of the sense of presence of their effigies. Similarly, poorly photographed objects may not withstand such comparison with the genuine article.

Artists and photographers are trained in the methodology of making the visual field and the photographic field correspond in terms of planar, or two-dimensional, representations. In other words, because of technological limitations, our photographic field is a mono-optical one that interfaces with a monocular visual field.

Audiences experience the projection of images, which are essentially recordings of the visual field (not the visual world) translated into the photographic field. But carried along by the dynamic of the work, they are transported into the *photographic world*. Thus, good filmic construction creates a new entity, based on the moving photographic field, transforming it into a reality that is more nearly like the visual world. This new entity, the photographic world, is made up not only of the photographic field but also of the additional elements of plot, characterizations, or whatever human interest and other related qualities are inherent in the film.

Throughout this book I am attempting to show how the binocular visual field may be translated into the stereophotographic field.

EVOLUTION AND THE NEED FOR STEREOPSIS

Binocular stereopsis is a relatively rare facility among animal species; it is possessed only by primates and a few other animals, such as owls, despite the fact that all species that have eyes have pairs of eyes. The fact is that the vast majority have eyes on opposite sides of the head. It is interesting to speculate why the human race possesses stereopsis and how it developed.

For stereopsis to be possible, both eyes must be able to converge on an object so that the image can be fused into a single three-dimensional view. Eyes placed on opposite sides of the head simply cannot accomplish this. They do have a distinct advantage over eyes that can converge: excellent coverage of the visual field, a nearly panoramic view of the world. (The advantage of such a view is obvious. For example, a grazing animal can constantly be on the lookout for predators without having to move its head.) Binocular vision, on the other hand, restricts the field of view to the direction faced.

There is a peculiar analogy between the wide-screen and stereo cinema and animals with panoramic vision and primates with stereoscopic vision. It is as if the Great Producer decided that panoramic vision was more important than stereoscopic vision and, as a result, made most species to see that way.

Of the few species possessing stereoscopic vision, the human race has made the most of it. Although almost entirely taken for granted (it was not even recognized as a separate depth sense until the last century), stereoscopic vision has materially aided human intelligence and technology in fields as diverse as primitive agriculture, where we have been able to accomplish weeding, for example, and in modern technology, for example, in the assembly of cameras. These tasks, and a myriad of eye-hand coordinated efforts that have directly led to human exploitation of the material universe, would be practically unimaginable without binocular stereopsis. As the renowned physiologist Polyak (1957) put it, "The development of stereoscopic vision appears to have been one of the essential factors in the evolution of the human intellect."

It has been suggested that our arboreal ancestors found stereopsis particularly helpful for estimating distances when jumping from tree limb to tree limb. Obviously, being able to land on the limb is an important survival characteristic. If you have the opportunity, cover one eye in a wooded region where there is a confusion of limbs and shrubs. The confusion will be multiplied a hundredfold. When other depth cues lead to confusion, stereopsis often helps to separate elements of the visual world.

Man is a hunter, and a predatory animal seeking prey has a distinct advantage if it has a well-developed stereoscopic visual system. Not only can this help him gauge the distance to animals, but it also helps him see through tricks of camouflage to reveal the existence of an otherwise unsuspected creature. Since the predator may become the prey, stereopsis also helped with the early detection of a hunter in a difficult visual environment, such as brambles and forested areas. In dim light I have observed stereopsis provides an additional perceptual advantage; the ability, at least to some extent, to separate foreground from background.

CLASSIFICATION OF STEREOSCOPIC SYSTEMS

There have been a number of approaches to the problem of creating stereoscopic effigies, but I shall confine my discussion to systems actually employed for the transmission of moving images and concentrate on those that are more or less commercially successful.

In this book, specifically, I have in mind the production of stereopairs, which are projected through sheet polarizers onto a polarization-conserving screen. The twin images are sorted out for the spectator through viewers with sheet polarizers similar to those at the projectors. This system has been in commercial use for almost fifty years, but image selection based on polarized light was suggested before the turn of the century.

A similar scheme employs complementary-colored filters of images to produce an anaglyph. The left image may be printed green and the right red (but there is no standardization) on color print stock. The original photography is usually done with black-and-white film. The combined red and green image is viewed with a selection device (glasses) made up of one red and one green filter. The red filter occludes the red image and transmits the green, and vice versa. Julesz (1977) has dubbed these devices anaglyphoscopes, and by a similar stroke of linguistic hokum we could call sheet polarizer glasses polarizoscopes.

Image selection by polarization and by complementary-colored filters have a great deal in common. Black-and-white stereopairs may be displayed either way. In fact, all of the arguments in this book about stereoscopic transmission may be applied to either system.

STEREOGRAM CINEMATOGRAPHY

Most three-dimensional motion picture systems use a stereogram, or left and right image pairs, to recreate the depth sensation of binocular vision, stereopsis. Whereas some photographic systems have used two existing monocular cameras in dual rigs, others have employed stereoscopic cameras or lenses designed to place both images on a single piece of film. Both methods of image selection, the anaglyph and polarized light, may be applied to black-and-white photography taken with either type of camera. Only the latter method is suitable for color photography (although there are some advocates of the color anaglyph, which depends on binocular color mixing).

Projection of specially coded left and right pairs in superimposition, with an appropriate image selection device worn by the viewer, has been the most successful method devised. But other approaches have been used for the display of stereograms.

In one approach the images are projected side by side so that they resemble image pairs mounted for viewing in a stereoscope. One way to view such images would be to use prismatic glasses to align each image with the appropriate eye. Since such a method relies on exact placement of the observer's head, it obviously presents grave difficulties.

Some people have actually advocated "free vision" for viewing such side-by-side projected image pairs, requiring the observer to exercise muscular effort to fuse these normally unfusable images. It is difficult to imagine a system like this ever becoming successful, since it requires such a departure from normal viewing of objects and demands so much skill on the part of observers.

Another technique for individual selection of stereograms, the eclipse method, was employed commercially in the 1920s for theatrical films. It uses motorized shutters in spectacle frames rotating in synchronization with the projector shutters. The major failing of this scheme is that both photography and projection of left and right fields of the stereogram must take place simultaneously. This method alternately occludes each half of the stereogram, so it is difficult to provide the necessary simultaneous presentation of image sensation.

It can be shown that photography must use shutters that are in phase to within a few degrees out of the 360° intermittent cycle. Slow object or camera movement is less demanding than rapid movement, but a camera must have shutters in phase to better than 5° to cover most subjects. The tolerances for rapid movement are probably stricter.

For projection it can be readily demonstrated that shutter phase requirements for the standard 24-fps rate must be better than 100°. Thus the standards for projection are more relaxed than those for photography. Nevertheless, eclipse systems for projection employ shutters that must be out of phase by 180°. This will result in a peculiar rippling effect for objects in motion or for camera movement. Because the effect is one never observed in the visual world, it is difficult to describe. Viewing for even a short time will be unpleasant for most people.

Inventors have also turned their attention to eclipse television systems. Prior art was forced to use cumbersome mechanical shutter devices, but the development of electro-optical shutters like PLZT ceramics and liquid crystal material has reawakened interest in the scheme, which uses the obvious idea of presenting left and right images on alternate odd and even fields.

AUTOSTEREOSCOPY

The panoramagram is another class of stereoscopic photograph, but with image selection taking place at the screen or photograph, without a selection device worn by each observer. The general term "autostereoscopy" is usually applied to such techniques. The panoramagram for still photography often uses a camera with a vertically striped shutter, or raster, moving at the film plane in synchronization with the camera movement. Such cameras usually move in arcs measured in feet and require several seconds to make an exposure. For this reason the method is totally unsuited to the requirements of cinematography.

For many years these displays have had some commercial success and have been marketed in the form of record album covers, postcards, and magazine and advertising illustrations. In Europe, especially France, there are even portrait photographers offering panoramagram technology to the individual sitter. In the United States and Japan, commercial interests have developed techniques for mass reproduction of panoramagrams. These photographs are overcoated with a corduroy type of transparent layer of lenses, usually called lenticules. Behind each lenticule lies an image stripe that contains a succession of partial views of the subject, from the extreme left camera position to the extreme right.

A variation of the parallax panoramagram, to give this class of device its full name, is the parallax stereogram, which is made up of two (or more) views rather than continuously varying views. Each half of a stereogram may be cut up into strips and each alternate left and right pair of strips laid behind one tubular lenticule of the viewing screen. In fact, no physical cutting of the stereopair need be undertaken, since optical methods may be used to interdigitize or multiplex the stereogram. The Nimslo camera, designed for amateur still photographers uses this system to interdigitize four separate views creating an autostereoscopic snapshot.

The major deficiency of the parallax stereogram is that it can be viewed only from a limited number of positions and the relationship between the viewer and the display must be strictly fixed. The parallax panoramagram, compared with the parallax stereogram, has the advantage that one can see the image from a wider range of head angles before encountering rather confusing pseudoscopic zones, or areas with reversed stereo effect.

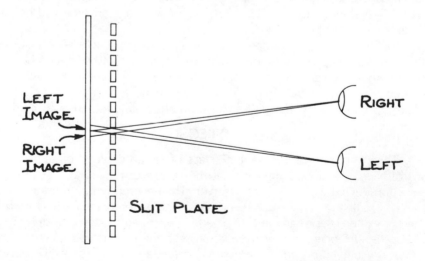

2.14. *Parallax stereogram*. The slits select the appropriate view for the appropriate eye.

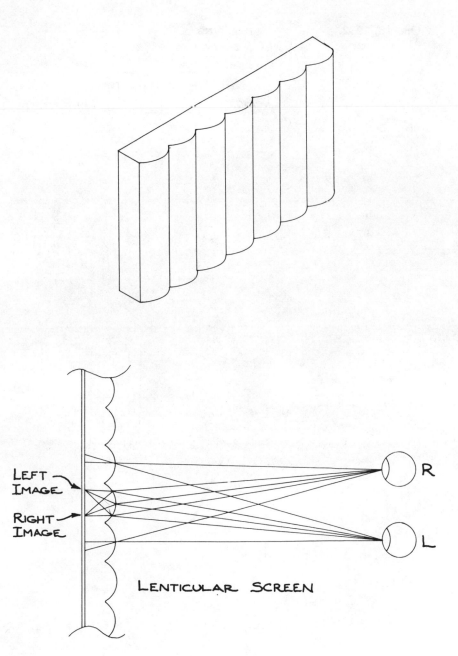

2.15. *Lenticular screen and panoramagram image.* Refraction of lenticules selects the appropriate image for the appropriate eye.

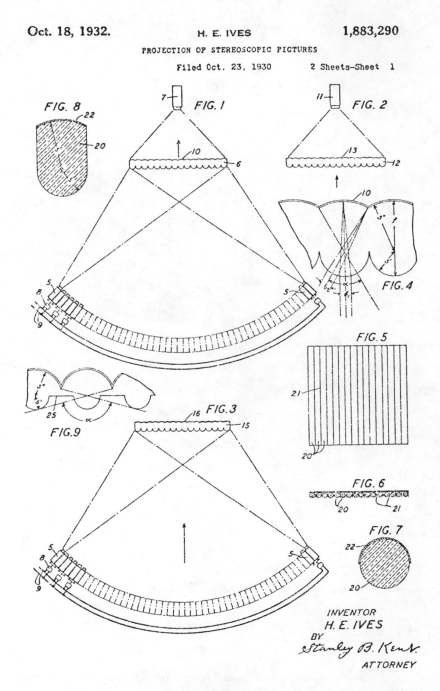

Oct. 18, 1932.   H. E. IVES   1,883,290

PROJECTION OF STEREOSCOPIC PICTURES

Filed Oct. 23, 1930   2 Sheets—Sheet 1

INVENTOR
H. E. IVES
BY
Stanley B. Kent.
ATTORNEY

2.16. *Ives's lenticular projection scheme.* Many cameras are used to produce the many perspective views needed for the true panoramagram.

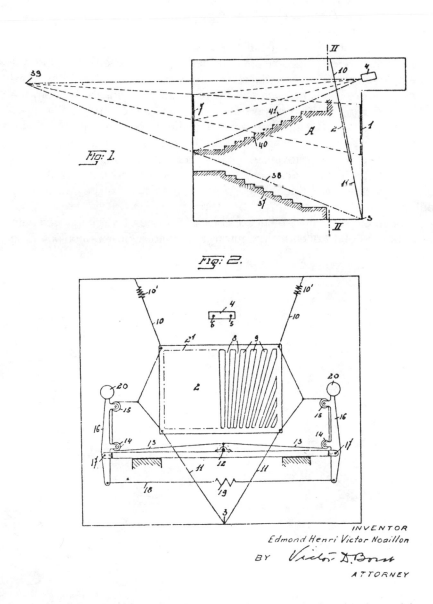

Aug. 12, 1930.   E. H. V. NOAILLON   1,772,782

ART OF MAKING CINEMATOGRAPHIC PROJECTIONS

Filed Dec. 18, 1928   3 Sheets—Sheet 1

Fig. 1.

Fig. 2.

INVENTOR
Edmond Henri Victor Noaillon

BY

ATTORNEY

2.17. *Noaillon autostereoscopic display*. A vibrating grid, placed in front of the screen, oscillates left to right in this arrangement.

Developing the work of Noaillon, a Belgian, and the Frenchman Savoye, the Soviets since the 1940s have been displaying projected stereopairs autostereoscopically. In such parallax stereogram systems, image selection takes place at the screen, thereby eliminating the need for individual selection devices. At first Soviet screens, engineered by Ivanov and improved by others, were raster barriers, made up of piano wire strung vertically in front of the screen. Next lenticular systems were employed, but these efforts were discontinued in 1976.

One might suppose that parallax stereograms would be satisfactory for theatrical display, since people are confined to seats. Nevertheless, the system employed by the Soviets placed severe restrictions on the observer, allowing little or no head movement. Even the slightest shift away from the preferred viewing position renders the image a rather confusing blur.

In an effort to offset the disadvantages of the stereogram, the Soviets and others have experimented with using additional views so that four, eight, or more points of view approximate the continuously varying information afforded by the true panoramagram. Such systems have not yet been perfected, and whether or not autostereoscopic technology can be successfully applied to the cinema remains to be seen.

Nonetheless, there are other possible approaches. I was impressed with the work of Robert Collender, a California inventor whose prototype of the

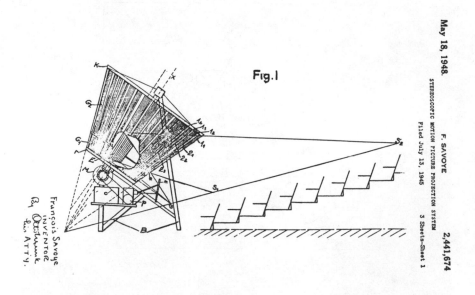

2.18. *Autostereoscopic projection of Savoye.* A spinning frustrum of a right circular cone ruled with stipes contains the projection screen. The projector projects through the spinning cone onto the screen. Reports are that it worked well, if the viewer did not move his or her head too much.

Stereoptiplexer device projected delightful three-dimensional movies auto-stereoscopically on a small screen made of metal with a brushed surface. His invention turns motion parallax into spatial parallax information. All photography must be done when either the camera or the subject is in motion.

The reader seeking more information about autostereoscopy would do well to read articles and patents by Bonnet, Collender, Dudley, Gabor, Ivanov, Ives, Kanolt, Montebello, Noaillon, Okoshi, Savoye, and Valyus, all listed in the Bibliography.

2.19. *Robert Collender with prototype stereoptriplexer.*

VOLUMETRIC AND OTHER TECHNIQUES

Spottiswoode (1953) places all the systems just described into a category he calls plano-stereoscopic. Left and right image pairs are synthesized by the mind into stereoscopic effigies, which are not in fact optical images, since they cannot be reflected or refracted. Another technique, stereo-stereoscopic, may have been originally proposed by the French motion picture pioneers, the Lumières. Such images actually have depth, just like the depth of the visual world, and can be optically transmitted. The film image would actually resemble a bas-relief. No technology exists for the direct creation of stereo-stereograms. These images, a subclass of the technique known as volumetric displays, might be projected on gaseous screens or on a series of layers of screen surface.

The Lumières suggested using a series of rear-illuminated transparencies, one mounted in front of the other. The transparencies would be filmed with a large-format camera whose lens and setting provided little depth of field. The exposures would be on the thin side, and the lens would be selectively focused for each exposure. For a portrait, for example, one would focus first for the tip of the nose, then farther back, perhaps on the eyes, and so forth, until perhaps a half dozen or more photos were taken and mounted one on top of the other, with some space between.

When I was fifteen years old, I stumbled onto the method and applied it to the photography of flowers using 35mm transparencies stacked on top of one another. The technique would be very difficult or impossible to apply to

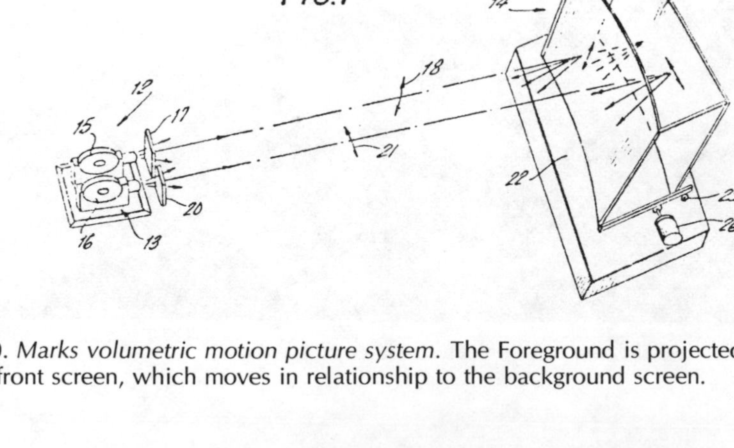

April 26, 1966   A. M. MARKS ET AL   3,248,165

MOVING SCREEN PROJECTION SYSTEM

Filed Feb. 24, 1964   4 Sheets–Sheet 1

FIG. 1

2.20. *Marks volumetric motion picture system.* The Foreground is projected onto the front screen, which moves in relationship to the background screen.

the moving image, but this has not stopped inventors from trying to perfect such a system. For example, Alvin and Morimer Marks have come up with several intricate schemes, one of which uses separately projected foregrounds and background.

Volumetric systems are limited in their depth effect by the thickness of the display itself. This and other drawbacks make it hard for me to believe that the system could be applied to motion pictures.

Lately, inventors have tried to use other techniques to create volumetric images. One scheme employs moving, or rotating cathode ray screens, and another uses polyester film mounted in a contraption that is very much like a loudspeaker. Movies are projected onto the plastic sheet, which is driven like a speaker cone in synchronization with the images. These inventions have been suggested for three-dimensional data display, but they present serious limitations in terms of more general applications, since the images are translucent. The rear of the object can be seen through the front of it.

Holography has attracted a great deal of attention in the last decade, and in the popular mind the term has come to mean any high technology that can provide stereoscopic images without special eyeglasses. The most successful commercial application has been the multiplex white-light moving holograms invented by Lloyd Cross. Combining aspects of holography and the panoramagram, the system presents a ghostly, false-colored image within the confines of a cylindrical loop of film. These efforts can be classified as motion pictures because the effigy appears to move when the cylinder is rotated. Strictly speaking these are not really holograms, but rather a panoramagram technique using a holographic display.

A great deal of effort on the corporate research level has gone into perfecting holographic motion pictures, so it is instructive to note that Mr. Cross's efforts were made beyond the corporate yoke and may well be the only commercially successful example of a holographic three-dimensional imaging technique. Although several researchers, the Soviets included, in particular Komar (1977), have reported partial success in creating holographic motion pictures, the problems are formidable and probably insoluble. Some limited success has been achieved using laser light for photographing and illuminating relatively small areas, but any successful system of photography needs to employ the sun and other available light sources.

STEREOSCOPIC DEPRIVATION

Some individuals actually experience a sense of panic or psychological stress when first observing stereoscopic films. In interviews and discussions after screenings of my three-dimensional films, some people indicated that they were puzzled by the experience, even claiming they had never seen a stereoscopic image before, in spite of the fact that their daily world is perceived stereoscopically. One possible explanation for this is that to a large extent we learn about our environment through the media. Our present media, because of technological restrictions, are almost invariably planar, from films to photographs to book and magazine illustrations and so forth. Sculpture and theater are examples of two media that evoke the stereoscopic depth cue. Layer has written an interesting article (1971) about our having become culturally deconditioned to stereopsis.

In addition, it is well known that people under stressful or unfriendly situations react unfavorably to change. Many individuals, presented unexpectedly with a new experience, may perceive it as unpleasant, whereas the same person in a better mood, or more comfortable, might find that the same stimulus produces pleasurable sensations.

Culturally conditioned persons, used to planar motion pictures, may be disturbed by the stereoscopic film because of the unaccustomed tactility of the stimulus. The additional sensual involvement of the medium has erotic implications, and some people may respond unfavorably because of sexual inhibitions.

Children, on the other hand, have little trouble viewing stereoscopic films for the first time, and they frequently enjoy sitting so close to the screen that adults, so positioned, would experience eyestrain. Children are not yet fully conditioned to cultural biases, and just as important, their eye muscles are more supple.

There are difficulties apart from technological considerations with respect to the stereoscopic film. Among them are unfavorable individual responses because of cultural and perhaps unconscious bias against media employing stereopsis. However, for most people this can be rapidly overcome after even relatively short exposure to well-produced and well-presented three-dimensional films.

ANAMALOUS STEREOSCOPIC PERCEPTION

Stereoscopic perception is highly idiosyncratic. There is evidence, according to Lundberg (1947) that our perception of physical space changes at various times in our lives or even throughout the day. There may be some connection between this phenomenon and the fact that a relatively large part of humanity has varying degrees of anomalous stereoscopic perception.

Perhaps 5 to 8% of the population has defective stereopsis. Sherman (1953) supplies the former figure, Kaufman (1974) the latter. Julesz's impression is that some 2% of the people at his lectures, in which he presents his special stereograms (often called Julesz figures), are stereo-blind.

My observations concur with Julesz; about 2% of the people looking at my stereo movies are indeed stereo-blind. Another 2 or 3% experience fatigue or discomfort from watching even the best stereo-projections. Another small segment of the audience experiences fatigue to a lesser degree. I am not talking about the pathology of the eye, but rather about people's perception of stereoscopic films, even though the areas are closely related and hard to isolate experimentally.

It appears, then, that no matter how perfect a three-dimensional motion picture system, a significant number of audience members will not see the film stereoscopically or will experience various degrees of fatigue.

Sherman (1953) tells us that 2% of the population suffers from hyperphoria, a condition in which one of the eyes deviates upward relative to the other. The optical axes of such eyes cannot cross on a point in space, so coordinated convergence leading to fusion is impossible. He also believes that hyperphoric projectionists have misaligned stereoscopic projectors to suit their own visual needs. Although this may have satisfied the small minority of similarly afflicted members of the audience, most patrons of such a theater suffered in attempting to fuse images with vertical disparity.

There are other visual defects that produce either a total lack of stereopsis or varying gradations of stereoscopic ability. Strabismus (cross- or wall-eyes) is a fairly common defect. And obviously, people who are blind in one eye cannot see stereoscopically. The overall situation probably breaks down to something like this: Perhaps 2 to 5% of the population lacks the sense of stereopsis; another 10 or 15% have varying degrees of the sense, from those with very little stereopsis to those having only a mild loss of the sense. Twelve to 20% is a significantly large segment of the population, and this may be a factor in the stereocinema's inability to gain popular acceptance.

There is comfort in the fact that, despite the appreciable number of people who have anomalous color perception, color motion pictures are commonplace. The incidence of color-blindness is on a par with stereo-blindness. The interested reader is referred to Linksz (1964) for details on classifications of color defects.

There are also a number of individuals who cannot tolerate less than perfect projection. Another way to put this is that some people are troubled with certain symmetrical imbalances (see Chapter 6) between left and right eye. Sherman states that 2% of the population will have difficulty fusing images in which one of a stereo pair is 12% dimmer than the other. This condition might seem to be easily avoidable, but in fact, in the theatrical cinema, this has not been the case, especially for double-band projection using interlocked machines.

In various single-band projection schemes I have seen, the binocular symmetry of illumination should be held to tighter tolerances, but all is far from perfect. While Sherman is concerned with total illumination, unevenness of illumination is just as important; unless optics are properly aligned, this cannot be guaranteed.

In my studio, I employ a dual-projection system with two low-voltage dichroic reflector lamps. The lamps are matched (sometimes with the help of color correction filters), and remain matched after many hours of life—indeed, until they burn out. The ongoing change to xenon arcs (from carbon arcs) in the theatrical cinema could have a similarly favorable effect for double-band projection.

Some other projection factors, such as unequal size of the projected images because of the lenses' mismatched focal lengths may influence the ability of audience members to fuse the image or, just as important, to fuse the image comfortably for prolonged periods.

My research leads me to conclude that strain induced from any source either is felt to be an unspecific kind of irritation or (often) is felt in specific parts of the body other than the eyes. For example, strain or discomfort induced by uneven illumination may produce the same bodily sensation as strain produced by unequal image size resulting in misaligned homologous points. Some will interpret these effects as blurriness, others as nausea, and still others as headaches.

Such strain is cumulative and in time can turn mild sensations of discomfort into serious disturbances. There are rich opportunities to annoy people with stereoscopic projection. But if it is properly done, the stereoscopic cinema can be free from strain for the great majority of people. Images of incomparable beauty can be presented in this medium—so perfectly beautiful, in fact, that the planar cinema might begin to lose much of its appeal.

POLARIZED LIGHT

Image selection by polarization is commonly employed for stereoscopic projection; sheet polarizers are mounted at the projector lenses, and viewers incorporating sheet polarizers are worn by audience members. With proper orientation, the right eye will see only its intended image, as will the left. The left image is occluded by the right viewer filter, which transmits only the right image; the opposite effect occurs with the viewer's left filter.

One of the models that physicists use to describe light is that of an electromagnetic wave. Light has two components, an electric and a magnetic vector. As light travels through space, or a medium like glass, the electric and magnetic vectors exhibit an up-and-down wave motion. A simple equation relates wavelength, frequency, and the speed of light:

$$\lambda = C/f$$

Here λ, or wavelength, is given in centimeters; f, or frequency, is given in cycles per second; C, the speed of light through a vacuum, is 2.99×10^{10} cm/sec.

If we were able to see the electric vector of light as it emerged from a source like an electric lamp, a candle, or the sun, we would see that the planes in which the electric vectors travel are randomly oriented, or unpolarized. The amplitude, or height, of the wave in the drawing varies with time as the wave moves in the X direction. The electric component of light in the drawing is moving in the Z-X plane. The usual light sources encountered will produce a multitude of light waves traveling along the X axis but with their electric vectors oriented randomly at various angles to the Z axis.

Light produced by a source or reflected by most objects usually behaves this way. When it does, it is said to be unpolarized. If the light were produced by a source or some optical means, or reflected from certain surfaces

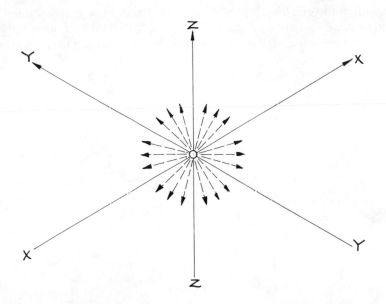

2.21. *Natural, unpolarized light.*

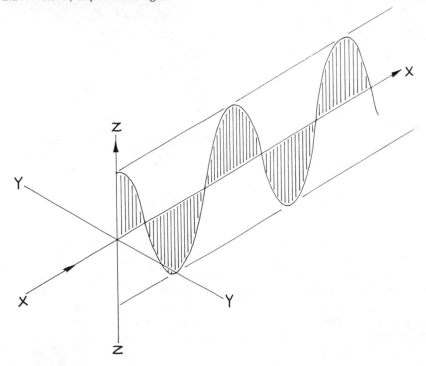

2.22. *Polarized light.* Shown in a single wave vibration in the X-Z plane.

so that all of the electric vectors of the light waves were parallel, the result would be what we call plane polarized light. It is that form of polarized light that is most often used for image selection in stereoscopic projection.

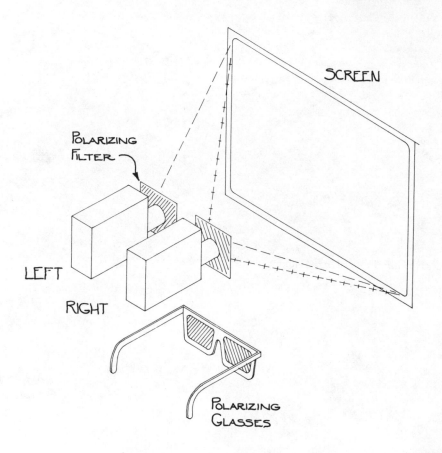

2.23. *Basic system of image selection using polarized light.*

If such a polarizing filter is held over the right projector lens, the light for the right image will be polarized in a plane (perpendicular to the filter surface) that can be controlled by rotating the filter in its plane. Once the projected light is reflected by a suitable surface (a movie screen), one that does not depolarize light, it can pass through the right spectacle filter because its axis of polarization matches that of the projection filter. However, the left filter of the viewer has its axis oriented at right angles to the right lens filter axis and will allow little or no light to pass through it.

Electromagnetic radiation, like light, is thought to be made up of two parts, a magnetic vector and an electric vector. The axis of polarization corresponds to the orientation of the electric vector of light. A polarizing filter acts to absorb the components of light at right angles to its axis. The filter does not create polarized light; it merely absorbs at least half the available light and transmits approximately the other half (usually somewhat less).

Unpolarized light can be represented by light waves with electric vectors oriented at right angles to each other, with half the energy of the wave in each right angle component. The sheet polarizer therefore absorbs the energy of light with its vector represented at right angles to the filter's axis. For this reason, sheet polarizers must always lose at least half the light they transmit. In actual practice, the sheet polarizers employed transmit only about 40 to 30% of the total light.

When one considers that polarizing filters must be used both at the projectors and for the viewers, it is not surprising to learn that more than two-thirds of available projection light is lost in 3-D transmission.

PHYSICAL PROPERTIES OF SHEET POLARIZERS

The transmittance of a sheet polarizer is called k and varies between a maximum value k_1 and a minimum value k_2. In the case in which we are most interested, polarized light produced at the projector and then transmitted by the spectacle filters, k varies according to the rule

$$k = (k_1 - k_2) \cos^2\Theta + k_2$$

If, at the lens of our projectors, we introduce a single sheet polarizer, the transmittance of nonpolarized light through the polarizer is

$$K = \frac{k_1 + k_2}{2}$$

For the transmittance of the left image, or light through the sheet polarizer of the left lens and through the left spectacle filter, which is the case of identical sheet polarizers with parallel axes, the transmittance for the projector's source of nonpolarized light is

$$H_0 = \frac{k_1{}^2 + k_2{}^2}{2}$$

Similarly for the case of right-image transmittance through the left filter, or for the lens axes crossed with identical sheet polarizers:

$$H_{90} = k_1 k_2$$

As for the chemistry or actual physical structure of sheet polarizers, the following is from the Polaroid Corporation's 1970 booklet, *Polarized Light:*

> In the early '40s, Polaroid developed the type 'H' and 'K' linear dichroic polarizers which are in current use. These linear polarizers are not microcrystalline (as were former products), but are oriented linear polymeric materials. The 'H' polarizer, which is most popular, is made by absorbing iodine in a sheet of thin polyvinyl alcohol that has been stretched to arrange the molecules in long parallel chains. The light-absorbing molecules are often referred to as dichromophores. (p. 4)

The parentheses are mine. The K-type polarizers, which were used in theater projection ports because of their ability to withstand heat better than the H-type, are no longer manufactured.

Two transmission graphs for Polaroid HN32 and HN38 sheets are reproduced here. Another type, HN35, is also available, and these three are of most interest to the stereoscopist. The number in each case refers to the maximum transmission. For example, a single HN32 sheet introduced into a beam of unpolarized light transmits 32% of the light, provided that the illumination is a standard source known as C.I.E. illuminant C. However, the transmission figure quoted provides a good approximation for the projection lamps used in most situations. The maximum transmission is represented by the upper curve, *A*, and, as you can see, varies with the wavelength of light.

The second curve, labeled *B*, gives the percent transmission for light passing through two parallel axes polarizers. This is an indication of the overall efficiency of the polarizers in stereoscopic projection. In the region of green light, 500 to 550mμ, the total transmission for two HN32 sheets with parallel axes, say two left filters, is about 28%. Therefore, 72% of the projection light is lost to polarizer absorption in this case. For HN38s the

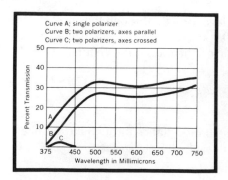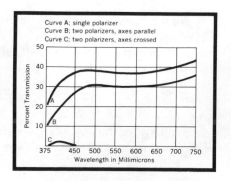

2.24 *Transmittance curves for sheet polarizers.* HN32 material (left) and HN38 (right). Note that transmittance varies with the color of light. HN38 or material of similar specifications is usually employed in stereoscopic applications. (Courtesy of Polaroid Corporation)

situation is hardly an improvement, for the transmission in this case is about 30%. The use of a high-gain metal surface screen can, in some cases, make up for this light loss, and the polarization of the incident light is preserved by such a metallic surface.

The curve labeled C is often called the leakage. It gives the percent transmission for polarizers with orthogonally crossed axes, say the left projection lens filter in conjunction with the right spectacle filter. The leakage, or extinction transmission, of HN32 sheets is 0.005%.

A lower-extinction transmission can be obtained only by accepting a lower total luminous transmission. The HN32, HN35, or HN38 sheets that are available have low enough leakage to satisfy the most demanding applications for stereoscopy. The problem is not so much the leakage when the filters' axes are properly orthogonally oriented, but rather the fact that alignment of the filters depends on the posture, or head tipping, of audience members. The basic relationship governing this, where θ is the angle between linear polarizer axes, has already been given as

$$k = (k_1 - k_2) \cos^2 \Theta + k_2$$

As θ changes at the 90° position, k changes very rapidly, and even small rotations of the head lead to a greatly increased leakage or crosstalk (sometimes called ghosting) of the left image through right filter, and vice versa.

This can be demonstrated to the reader's satisfaction by holding two sheet polarizers, one behind the other, a few inches in front of a light source, such as a 40- or 60-w tungsten lamp. The extinction transmittance is generally visible as a dark blue or violet color, as is indicated in the extinction curves labeled C. Transmission increases very rapidly with small changes of angle away from the maximum extinction position where the polarizers' axes are orthogonal.

The situation is hardly improved by using filters with lower extinction-transmittance. In most cases this cannot be sanctioned, since a low leakage is accompanied by a lower total transmission.

PRACTICAL CONSIDERATIONS

Several factors play an important part in the actual choice of sheet polarizers in any given installation, although one will not go very far wrong by installing HN38s, HN35s, or HN32s in just about any situation for both projection and spectacle filters. It is most usual to purchase stereoglasses already made up. Usually manufacturers choose sheet polarizers that are equivalent to HN38 sheets. But it is possible for zealous workers to assemble their own stereoglasses. I have used plastic frames to install various types of sheet polarizers.

I have found that the HN35 polarizers are particularly convenient because they are manufactured with their axes at angles of 45° to the edges of the sheets. This makes it easy to cut out filters, especially if you're making your own viewers (glasses, goggles, spectacles, selection devices, polarizo-scopes, or whatever you call them).

Given stereoglasses manufactured with HN38s, it is possible to experi-ment by substituting various projection filters, say from HN22s for very bright projectors or very small screens to HN38s for larger screens or less bright projectors. The HN42 sheets also available have too much leakage. A large number of combinations are possible. When evaluating performance, it is advisable to use ordinary footage, not test charts. Image contrast plays a great part in determining the visibility of the spurious images arising from left-image crosstalk through the right filter and vice versa. This spurious im-age may be the result of filter leakage and possible depolarization of light by the screen. But there are other factors; for example, images with high con-trast photographed so that they have large parallax values when projected are very likely to ghost. Another factor is that the more ambient light in the projection room, the lower the ghosting.

The standard orientation for sheet polarizers for stereoscopic projection is for the axes to be at right angles but to form an inverted V, $+45°$ for the right projector and viewer filter and $-45°$ for the left filters. This choice makes it possible to fold cardboard temples in either direction while main-taining the proper orientation of axes. If the axes were at right angles but aligned with the horizontal and the vertical, there would be the danger of seeing the left image through the right eye and vice versa when these com-monly used viewers are improperly folded. This results in a pseudoscopic image with stereopsis in conflict with all other depth cues, which is unpleas-ant in most instances. (If you turn the glasses upside down, you will see this effect.)

Sheet polarizers ought to be aligned to each other and the projectors to an accuracy of better than 1 degree. I can see no good reason for accepting lower standards for the viewers' axis-to-axis tolerances. Using well-chosen, good-quality, accurately oriented sheet polarizers and a good screen, with good photography, will produce images with very low ghosting, far lower than was or is seen in usual theatrical circumstances. However, a system of image selection that depends on audience posture cannot be considered perfect, and this, not the actual wearing of the glasses, is the system's great-est defect. People like to relax at the movies, and they have every right to get into any position they find comfortable without having restrictions imposed by the system of image selection. Nevertheless, if the standards I have indi-cated are maintained, moderate head tipping of a few degrees is possible for linear polarizers. The degree of tipping is impossible to specify with a single number, since it will vary principally with the contrast of the shot and the placement of the objects with respect to the plane of convergence.

In an effort to reduce the positional constraint imposed by linear polar-izers, I tried some experiments with circular polarizers. The drawing shows that a circular polarizer is made up of a linear polarizer and a special quar-ter-wave plate of stressed material. In plane polarization, all the electric vectors of light are oriented in parallel planes. In circular polarization, the electric vectors rotate in the same direction. As shown in the drawing, polarized right circular light becomes left-handed on reflection from the screen surface. Thus, if right and left circular polarizers (the right one turned around) were used for image selection, head tipping is allowed, since the selection process depends not on relative orientation of axes but on left or right rotation of the electric vector and its relationship to the handedness of the sheet polarizers.

Land patented this suggestion in 1931, but as far as I know it was never employed commercially. I found it very hard to make it work in my studio because of low transmittance and poor extinction. I am pessimistic about circular polarizers in this context, since their advantage is marginal and the filters are expensive and not efficient.

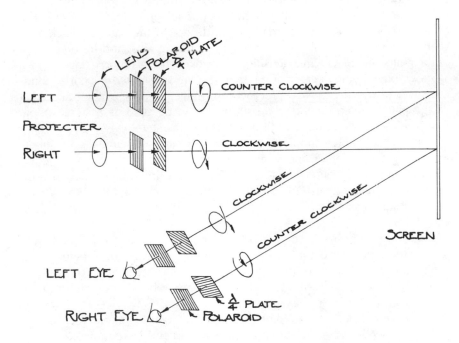

2.25. *Circular polarization for image selection.*

My experiments with anaglyphic projection convinced me that more head tipping could be tolerated in a system in which filter orientation was not a consideration. It was for this reason that I experimented with circular polarization. However, misalignment of homologous points also plays a part in limiting head rotation.

I should mention that modern polarizers are available in acrylic plastic or cellulose acetate sheets of various thicknesses and as glass laminates. I think sheets 0.01 in. thick will be found suitable for both viewers and projection filters. (Some people prefer thinner filters for glasses.) Products from Polaroid and Marks Polarized had very good properties. They are sharp, neutral in color, without optical distortion, and showed no signs of fading or alteration of properties even with prolonged use. (Arc projection places greater demands on these materials.) I taped a pair of Marks glasses to the inside of my studio window to an eastern exposure with several hours of sunlight a day; at the end of three months they showed no visible fading. With care a soft cloth or tissues can be used to clean these materials.

THE VECTOGRAPH

In 1938, Joseph Mahler, a Czechoslovakian inventor who had supplied sheet polarizers in Europe, approached Land with the concept of the Vectograph (Cornwell-Clyne, 1954), which was publicly introduced in 1940. The density of the photographic image is made up, in the case of black-and-white materials, of a collection of metallic silver grains, and in the case of color materials, of varying densities of dyes in three colored layers. In a Vectograph, varying degrees of polarization are substituted for corresponding silver or dye densities. A Vectograph image, made up of left and right image pairs printed on the same support, can be seen as a stereoscopic image when viewed through the usual polarizing stereoglasses.

The Vectograph is similar to the anaglyph, since both images are superimposed on each other and may be projected with a standard projector without any modification. Because the coding of information depends on polarization rather than color, one would assume that full-color Vectographs might also be possible, and these, as still photographs, have been shown.

At the end of the Second World War, the Polaroid Corporation was renting the Cinecolor plant to experiment with motion picture Vectographs. Cinecolor was a two-color process using green and red dyes. According to Ryan (Quigley, 1953), several reels of black-and-white Vectograph motion pictures were printed in this Los Angeles facility.

The Vectograph is an imbibition process, similar to the old Technicolor printing process or the Eastman dye transfer process. To manufacture color Vectograph prints would have taken a facility capable of printing color matrices (actually two pairs of cyan, magenta, and yellow matrices). No such facility existed, although I suppose it might have been possible to prepare prints with two passes through the imbibition Technicolor process.

The Vectograph promised to be the most elegant system for the production of stereoscopic prints using the polarized-light method of image selection. Ordinary projectors could have been employed without straining the skill of the projectionist. Projected, these prints would have had a very high light output compared to the usual method of mounting sheet polarizers in front of the left and right lenses. However, technical or economic factors

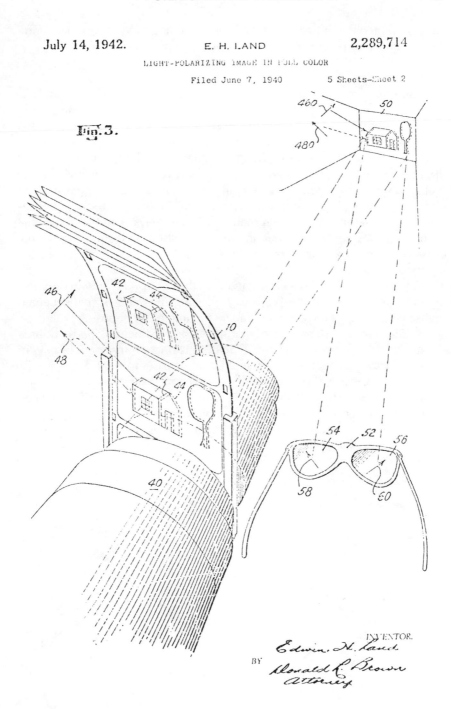

July 14, 1942.   E. H. LAND   2,289,714
LIGHT-POLARIZING IMAGE IN FULL COLOR
Filed June 7, 1940   5 Sheets—Sheet 2

Fig.3.

INVENTOR.
Edwin H. Land
BY   Donald L. Brown
Attorney

2.26.*Vectograph projection of 3-D images.* The most dramatic patent illustration I have encountered.

have prevented the utilization of the process, although Vectograph technology continues to be employed for still photography.

GHOSTING

Ghosting, or spurious images or crosstalk, is a function of the inclination of the viewer's head. If we draw an imaginary line through the eyes of the viewer and compare that with the horizontal, assuming well-adjusted projector and spectacle polarizers, tipping of only 1 or 2° is permissible for some high-contrast shots. For the great majority of shots, however, head tipping of several degrees is possible, and for low-contrast shots where the major portion of the subject is essentially at the plane of convergence, up to perhaps 10° of tipping is permissible. It may well be that viewers will unconsciously and automatically align their heads with respect to the image that produces the least ghosting, but any motion picture projection system that depends on posture may prove to be fatiguing for some members of the audience.

If the viewer's head is well aligned with the horizontal, or with the sheet polarizers employed at the projector, ghosting may still occur in certain high-contrast shots. However, this can be minimized by choosing projection sheet polarizers and stereoglasses that have good extinction and by using a screen that does not depolarize incident projection illumination. The axes of polarization of the sheet polarizers in the stereoglasses must also be within 1 or 2° of the axes of polarization in the projection polarizers.

Despite the fact that high ghosting may be present in a poorly designed display, the stereoscopic effect may remain undiminished even with relatively high crosstalk between left and right images. However, a well-designed stereoscopic projection system ought to have virtually no ghosting.

chapter 3

The Stereoscopic Field

We will now discuss some of the fundamental psycho-optical concepts of photographic stereoscopic motion picture systems. The term *psycho-optical* signifies an optical system whose final link is the human eye-brain. It was Ronchi (1957), I believe, who first clearly understood that many physical explanations are incomplete without inclusion of the eye as part of the optical system. Certainly this is the case for the stereophotographic motion picture process. It ought to be pointed out that many, perhaps most, of the concepts presented here and elsewhere in this book are also valid for still photographic stereoscopy, and for television.

FRAME AND OBJECT MAGNIFICATION

There is a distinction between frame magnification M and object magnification m. *Frame magnification* is defined as the ratio of the screen height (or width) of the projected image to the frame height (or width):

$$M = \frac{H_s}{H_f} = \frac{W_s}{W_f}$$

Object magnification is defined as the ratio of the height (or width) of the object to the height (or width) of the image of the object:

$$m = \frac{H_o}{H_i} = \frac{W_o}{W_i}$$

Motion pictures are generally projected on screens whose M values vary from about 150 to 500. Super 8 projected on a screen 1m wide has a magnification of about 180; 35mm on a screen about 4m wide also has a frame magnification of about 180.

The image of a man 1.5m tall projected full height (head and toes touching the top and bottom screen edges) on a meter-wide screen (0.75m high) will have an object magnification of ½, but the same image projected the same way on a screen 4m wide will have an object magnification of 2.

Because super 8 is usually projected on screens that are about one-tenth to one-quarter the width of 35mm screens, object magnifications will be proportionately lower, despite the fact that frame magnifications can be more or less equal.

SCREEN PARALLAX

The drawings here illustrate four classes of screen parallax. Screen parallax is the distance between corresponding left- and right-image points measured at the screen. In the literature, in addition to "corresponding," one will also find the terms "conjugate" and "homologous" used. In Figure 3.1, left- and right-image points coincide and screen parallax is zero. Left and right eyes converge on the plane of the screen for which they are focused. Image points with zero parallax will have a stereoscopic cue placing them in the plane of the screen. For the polarized-light method of image selection, head tipping will produce a minimum of ghosting for image points at or near zero screen parallax. Since image points for both fields coincide, the ghost image coincides with the image point. Images at or near the zero parallax condition will have little or no strain caused by the breakdown of the habitual accommodation/convergence response (see page 100).

Figure 3.2 shows the case of positive (uncrossed) screen parallax with a value equal to the average interocular. Homologous, or corresponding, left and right points with this value may be thought of as being at stereoscopic infinity, since the optical axes of the eyes will be parallel when viewing them, a condition that also exists in the visual world when looking at very distant objects. Image points with positive screen parallaxes will appear to be behind the plane of the screen, in screen space.

Figure 3.3 shows image points with negative, or crossed, screen parallax equal to the value of the interocular. Negative screen parallax occurs when the lines of sight from the eyes to the image points cross. Such points will appear to be in front of the plane of the screen in theater space. By geometrical analysis they will appear halfway between the observer and the screen.

In the fourth and final case, Figure 3.4, we have a situation similar to that given in Figure 3.2 with positive screen parallaxes, but the value for screen parallax is greater than the average interocular distance. When this occurs, the lines of sight from the eyes to the image points will no longer be parallel, as was the case for Figure 3.2, and the eyes must now diverge, or angle outward, in order to fuse such image points. If the eyes are called upon to fuse stereoscopic images with large angular values of divergence, then fatigue and discomfort will result.

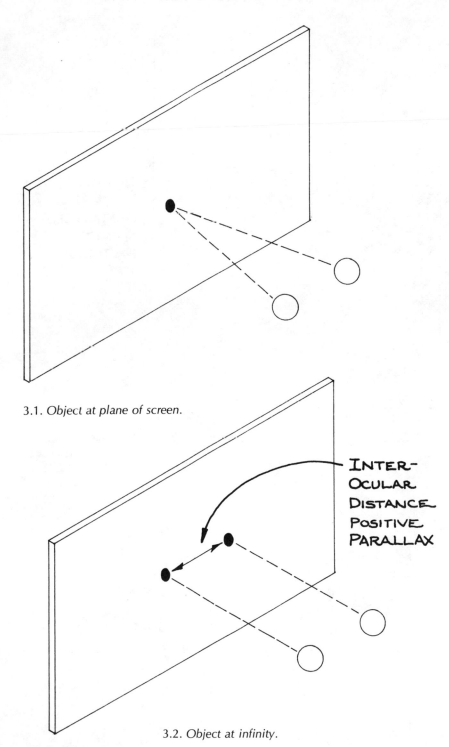

3.1. *Object at plane of screen.*

Inter-
Ocular
Distance
Positive
Parallax

3.2. *Object at infinity.*

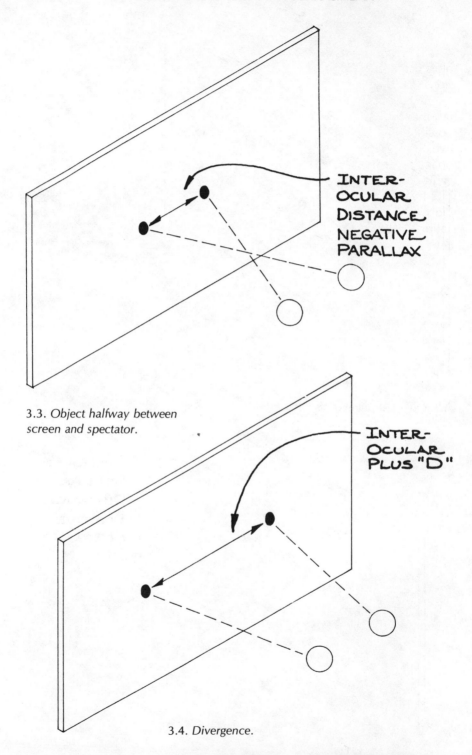

INTER-
OCULAR
DISTANCE
NEGATIVE
PARALLAX

3.3. Object halfway between
screen and spectator.

INTER-
OCULAR
PLUS "D"

3.4. Divergence.

CROSSED-LENS-AXES PHOTOGRAPHY

The crossed-lens-axes, or CLA, system will be discussed more completely, but it is important to understand it now so that the following discussions will be clear.

The geometrical or optical conditions of projection determine the method of stereoscopic cinematography. The CLA mode is only one of several possibilities, but for reasons that will be discussed later it is the best alternative. For a dual-band approach, the projection lenses are set so that their optical axes cross at the surface of the screen. A target film may be used to achieve this end.

If we were using a single-band system (left and right images on the same piece of film) in the CLA mode, we would employ similar test target film and calibration procedures. In any event, in the CLA mode of projection, we want to have two prints struck from the same master looking like a single print projected by one projector.

From this it follows that objects at the point of intersection of the left and right camera lens axes will appear to be in the plane of the screen.

Camera lens convergence may be achieved by using the Target, or Smee's, Method (Brewster, 1856). Cross hairs at the center of each finder are made to coincide with the object to be placed in the plane of convergence. The objects upon which the lens axes cross or actually converge in space will appear, upon projection, to be in the plane of the screen. For the CLA mode, the term "stereo window" is synonymous with the plane of the screen for projection, which corresponds to the plane of convergence for photography.

This technique provides the stereoscopic cinematographer with a volumetric compositional device that can place objects where he or she chooses with respect to the plane of the screen. Objects in front of the plane of convergence will stick out of the screen and appear to be in *theater space,* and those behind the plane of convergence will appear within the screen, or in what I call *screen space.*

There is a parallel here between what occurs on the retinas and what occurs on the stereo screen. The term *retinal disparity* describes the retinal distance between corresponding image points, and *screen parallax* the distance between corresponding left and right screen points. In stereography, these corresponding points are called homologous points.

By convention, uncrossed parallax, which corresponds to objects in screen space behind the plane of convergence or plane of the screen, are assigned positive values, and those with crossed parallax (in front of the plane of convergence and the screen) are assigned negative values of parallax. And just as we speak of crossed and uncrossed disparity, it is possible to speak of crossed and uncrossed parallax, which could refer to film parallax but more often concerns the measurable distance between homologous points at the screen.

In some ways the CLA mode corresponds to the functioning of the eyes, but it is best not to press the analogy too far, since there are important differences. However, it is instructive to note that when the eyes converge on an object in space, this corresponds nicely with the convergence of the stereocamera lenses on an object in space. In the case of the eyes, fusion takes place and the object has zero disparity and is seen singly. For stereocinematography, the object will have zero parallax, and can be seen clearly without the aid of stereoglasses. Other objects with negative or positive values for screen parallax will be seen blurred or doubled without the use of the stereoglasses. In the same sort of way, objects with disparity are perceived as double or blurred.

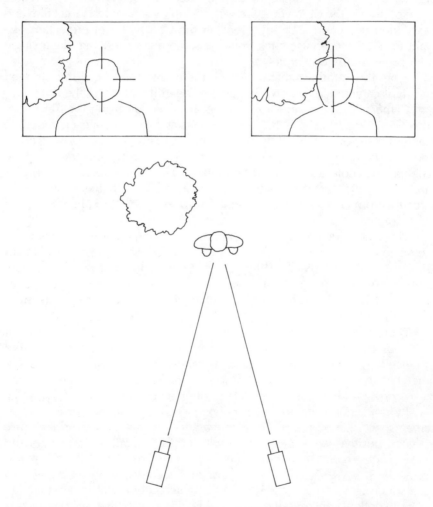

3.5. *Target method for setting convergence.* Left and right finder cross hairs are aligned on subject that is to appear in plane of convergence.

Before leaving the subject, it should be noted that convergence can be achieved either by the lateral shifting of the lens axes or by rotating the cameras. These methods are sometimes called *toe-in* instead of convergence, and the two terms will be used interchangeably in this book.

When a double-band system is used, either one or both of the cameras may be rotated in order to get convergence. When a single band of film records both left and right images, the lateral shifting of the lens or lenses may be the best method for setting toe-in, since the left and right halves of the camera are not separated and cannot be moved. In such a situation, small lateral shifts of the lens axes accomplish the same effect as convergence. Lenses are usually aligned so that their optical axes intersect the center of the frame. If the axes are shifted either to the left or to the right, usually by only a fraction of a millimeter, film parallax can be altered at will. This small shift in the lens(es) will leave t_c, the interaxial, substantially unaltered, but the effect on film parallax can be considerable. Lenses used for this purpose must cover a slightly greater area than the usual designs, to avoid vignetting the corners of the frame when shifts are made.

For either technique, the Target Method may be used for accurately setting lateral lens shifts or camera rotation.

CONVERGENCE ANGLE

PHOTOGRAPHY

If we say that the left and right lenses of a stereocamera are at L and R and that these lenses are converged on point Z in space, we can measure the angle of convergence with either θ, β, or α, as shown in Figures 3.6 and 3.7. Psychology texts usually specify the angle identified as α as the angle of convergence. In Figure 3.6, I have assumed that we have an isosceles triangle, so that the line ZM bisects angle α, in which case left and right exterior angles θ are equal, as are left and right interior angles β.

For stereoscopic photography, we will call angle(s) θ the angle(s) of convergence. Convergence can be asymmetrical; for example, the angles corresponding to θ shown here, let us say θ_l and θ_r, need not be equal. Your eyes can converge on objects in space asymmetrically, and so can camera lenses, as we will see.

For the camera lens, we are assuming that LZ and RZ are the optical axes and that points L and R are rear nodal points. The angle of convergence may be specified trigonometrically (for the symmetrical case) by

$$\tan \Theta = \frac{t_c}{2D}$$

where t_c is the interaxial distance and D is the distance from camera to subject Z. For everything but extreme closeups, we can take the distances LZ or RZ to be equal to D or ZM.

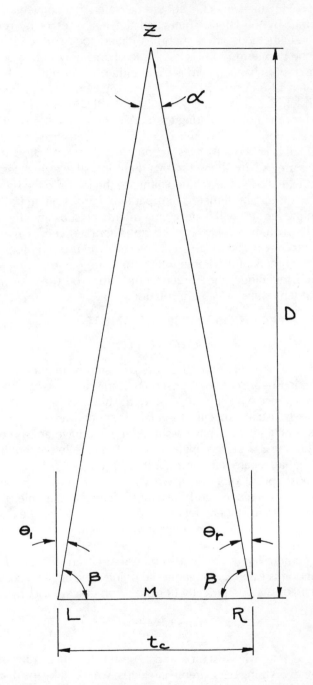

3.6. *Convergence angle.* Stereoscopists define θ_l and θ_r as convergence angles.

PROJECTION

Convergence angle of the eyes and screen parallax are equivalent quantities and may be expressed by the relationship

$$\tan \Theta_e = \frac{t_e \doteq P}{V}$$

Figure 3.7 shows the asymmetrical case where rR, the line of sight between the right eye R and the right image point r, is at right angles to the base line LR. The angle θ_e is the total angle of convergence, V is the distance from the screen, P is screen parallax or the distance between image points l and r, and t_e is the interocular distance.

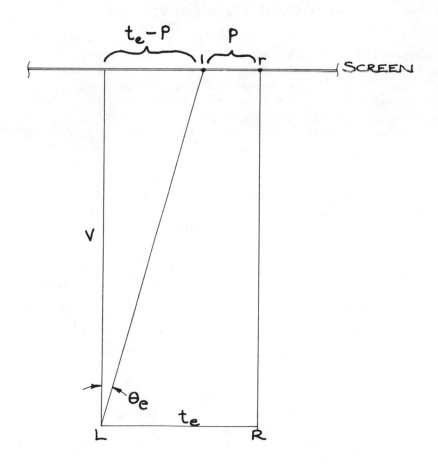

3.7. Convergence angles of eyes and screen parallax.

Since the angle θ_e is very small, the relationship could have been given in radians. Similar results can be derived for various symmetrical and asymmetrical cases for both negative and positive parallaxes, and for the divergent case. By our definition, the example shown is for positive parallax.

When observing stereoscopic films, the eyes must do work to which they are unaccustomed: They must converge. That is to say, when observing planar films, the eyes converge for the surface of the screen and remain converged at one, more or less, constant distance. For stereoscopic films, as the eyes scan the shot, they need to reconverge from point to point. This muscular effort is interpreted by some people to be an unpleasant sensation, which may be heightened by the breakdown of the habitual accommodation/convergence muscular response.

ACCOMMODATION/CONVERGENCE

The muscles that focus (accommodate) the eyes are controlled by neurological systems separate from those that converge the eyes. But we become used to the habitual, seemingly coordinated response of these two sets of muscles. Any departure from the usual effort of accommodation and effort of convergence (the accommodation/convergence ratio as it is called) may become a source of discomfort.

When the eyes converge for a given distance, there is a zone of single, clear binocular vision. Once we move out of the zone, or exceed the limits of the A/C relationship, one of two things will happen. Either fusion breaks down (in which case there is double vision) and accommodation remains, or fusion is maintained and accommodation is lost (the image is out of focus). Relative convergence is the ability to change convergence relative to the distance for which the eyes are accommodated. Valyus (1966, p. 373) notes that a

> complete loss of the stereo-effect occurs when the difference between the angles of convergence required for a model observed stereoscopically and for the visual axes to meet in the plane of the screen reaches a value of 1.6°. This occurs approximately when the parallax between a pair of points in the left and right images is 0.03 of the distance to the screen, i.e., when

$$|P|_{max} = 0.03R.$$

For one screen size I have been using, 1300 mm wide, the maximum recommended parallax (0.03 × 1300 mm) is about 40 mm. I have found Valyus's advice to be fairly accurate. For screen parallaxes at or beyond this value, some, but not all, observers will be unable to fuse the image. Negative parallax values several times the rule given by Valyus are permissible for objects moving rapidly out of the frame or held on screen only briefly.

What causes this is the breakdown of the accommodation/convergence relationship. Specifically, Valyus is telling us about objects being brought too far forward of the plane of the screen. At the plane of the screen or, the stereo window, objects will have zero parallax. Moving them beyond 0.03 times the width of the screen, Valyus asserts, will cause viewers discomfort. If an exaggerated 3-D effect is wanted, objects can be made to appear spectacularly beyond the plane of the screen with values of ½, 1/3 or even lower for $|P|_{max}$, provided the shot holds adequate monocular depth cues. It is the first and most serious mistake of the 3-D novice to attempt exaggerated screen parallaxes, shots in which objects are placed in theater space. Not only will this cause a breakdown in the accommodation/convergence relationship, but it is entirely unnecessary: A shot that has appropriate perspective cues will have a convincing "out of the screen" effect with very low values for $|P|_{max}$.

Valyus arrives at his recommendations, he says, according to strictly geometrical considerations. However, he admits that in the case of positive values for parallax, or when image points will be in screen space,

> constructions made according to the laws of geometrical optics do not give a correct solution to the problem in this case. The physiological laws governing discrimination of planes in depth impose limits on the geometrical constructions defining stereoscopic space. (p. 374)

The interested reader is referred to Valyus's book for more details. We will return to this point repeatedly when discussing transmission systems.

For one thing, useful stereoscopic photography can be carried out with divergence, thus upsetting geometrical arguments, and this will be discussed elsewhere. For another, Duke-Elder has stated, according to Levonian (1954), that people are able to exercise only the middle third of their relative convergence without visual fatigue. Accordingly, the safest practice would be to restrict screen parallaxes to a narrow range on either side of the screen surface boundary layer.

If the middle third of relative convergence can be used without fatigue, given the restrictions governing placement of images in theater space, the safest screen parallaxes to employ would be those lowest possible positive values that would place the image near and at the zero parallax plane. Using a shooting scheme like this, it is possible to represent a broad, even seemingly full range of depth, since stereopsis, as we will see (page 193), is scaled or weighted by extrastereoscopic cues.

The limitations of the relationship between convergence and accommodation may be strongly felt, for many individuals, when one shot is replaced with another. If, for example, we have a medium shot of a person composed so that he is in screen space—that is, behind the plane of the screen—and we cut to a closeup of that person so that he appears in the plane of the screen, the eyes of the viewer must reconverge from the medium shot to closeup.

For some people, and in my experience they are a minority, the required effort of convergence can cause strain, but some care should be taken during photography to set camera convergence properly to help minimize this effect. It may be impossible to anticipate editorial needs fully during photography, in which case the only recourse may well be to make corrections by means of lateral image shifts through optical printing. However, in most respects, editing stereoscopic films is like editing planar films.

DIVERGENCE

In a crossed-lens-axes (CLA) system of stereoscopic photography, corresponding image points beyond the plane of convergence have steadily increasing values. In Figure 3.8 I have identified three zones: In zone 1, fusion may be difficult because of large values for negative screen parallax, which produce images in theater space. The next zone, 2, is divided into two parts, (a) and (b), with screen parallaxes ranging between $-t_e$ and $+t_e$. The negative zone will produce images in theater space, but generally within acceptable values for screen parallax so that fusion can take place. (For large screen projection, homologous image points with negative parallax

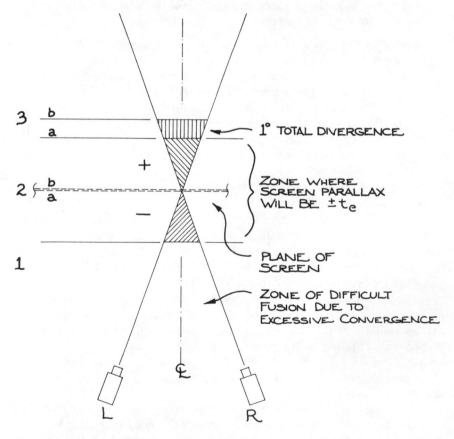

3.8. *Zones of screen parallax.*

values very much greater than t_e are permissible, more or less according to the rule given by Valyus above.) The positive portion of the zone, (b), is the region where nearly all photography should take place, and it lies in screen space. Zone 3, also divided into parts (a) and (b), is the region of divergence; it will continue to produce images in screen space, but image points with values of screen parallax, or p, larger than t_e. Part (a) of zone 3 will yield parallaxes with up to a total of 1° of divergence. Here I am referring to the divergence of both eyes added together, so that the left and right eyes have ½° each, outward rotation, for a total divergence angle of 1°. Part (b) will produce parallaxes with divergence greater than 1°.

All combinations of focal lengths, interaxial, and convergence settings will produce the results graphically displayed in Figure 3.8. Screen parallaxes increase rapidly as we move away from the point of convergence, and with greater values of interaxial and focal length.

If the eyes are looking at a distant scene, their optical axes will be parallel. Divergence, the outward rotation of the eyes, does not occur when looking at the visual world, but it can occur when looking at stereoscopic effigies. If positive screen parallaxes are greater than the value of the observer's interocular, the eyes will need to rotate outward for fusion to take place. In zone 3(a) divergence is acceptable, whereas in zone 3(b) divergence is beyond acceptable limits.

Most people's eyes can accept a small amount of divergence without strain. I learned this by laterally shifting or rotating one projector to produce divergent conditions of any desired degree and by numerous photographic tests. At the screen, with a ruler, I measured screen parallaxes, and by using trigonometry I converted these measured distances into angular measure. The method for calculating divergence is given on page 191.

DISPARITY, HOROPTER, PANUM'S AREA, DIFFERENTIAL PARALLAX

A pair of eyes are looking at an object, an arrow. But what do the eyes really see when part of the arrow is closer to the eyes than other parts of it? The eyes are converged on point B, while lines Bb_l and Bb_r are respectively the optical axes of the left and right eyes. Points a_l, b_l, c_l, a_r, b_r, and c_r lie on the retinas of the eyes, but only points b_l and b_r lie in the portion of the fovea where fusion takes place. As can be seen from the drawing, it is not possible to converge on the arrowhead A, shaft B, or feather C at the same instant. The rays from the various points of the arrow cross at the rear nodal points of the lenses of the eyes, O_l and O_r.

The distance between points a_lb_l and a_rb_r is not the same, and the difference between these distances is called *disparity*. The corresponding quantity for a photographic system is called *parallax*.

The angle of convergence for the eyes is given, by convention, as angle b_lBb_r, sometimes also defined as the quantity parallax. Whether the quantity is called disparity and is given in terms of distance measured on the retinal surfaces, or whether it is specified in terms of angular measure formed by the crossing of the lens axes, it is basically the same, and one quantity can be related to the other trigonometrically.

If the left and right eyes are converged on point B, we know that points in front of and behind B will appear doubled, more or less depending on how far they are from B. This is the zone of single, clear binocular vision, which corresponds with what is known as *Panum's Fusional Area*. Panum's Area is a statistical entity, not an anatomical one. It is elliptically shaped, with the minor axis vertical, and it is largest at the periphery of the retina and smallest at the fovea.

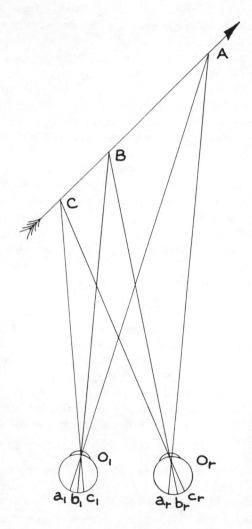

3.9. *Disparity*.

Panum's Area is an important concept for setting the allowable tolerances for the alignment of corresponding image points in stereoscopic projection. Different values are given by authorities depending on the measurement techniques (Ogle, 1972). Typical values might be 20' of arc horizontal and one half or one third of that for the vertical. Assuming that the figures given here are correct, we could state that the vertical separation between homologous points must be kept to within, say, 10' of arc for a viewer. To exceed this value is to invite the eyes to attempt fusion of vertically separated corresponding points, which for projected stereoscopic images is to promote fatigue and strain.

Let us return to the drawing: Points close to B, for example, will have little doubling, since there is not much retinal disparity. However, the single point of convergence B is not the only place in space where image points will be seen as single points. For every position of the eyes there will be a locus of points in space where image points will be seen single; this locus is known as the *singleness horopter*.

The horopter in Figure 3.10 is shown as a portion of a circle, and in this case the nodal points of the eyes and the point of convergence must lie on the circumference of the circle.

All points lying on the horopter will form images on corresponding points of the left and right retinas. They will have zero disparity. Forming a single image from the left and right eye images is called fusion.

The three-dimensional version of our circular horopter is the surface of a sphere, and this is called the Vieth-Mueller horopter.

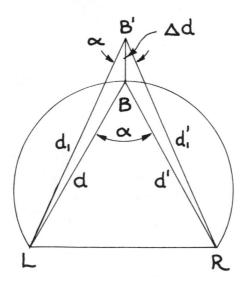

3.10. *Singleness horopter.*

In the diagram, point B^1 lies off the horopter and is at distance Δd from point B. If the eyes (t_e apart) are converged on B, then B^1 will appear to be doubled, as we have explained. Disparity and angular parallax are a measure of the same thing, but let us be more specific. The binocular or stereoscopic parallax of image point B^1 with respect to the point of convergence, B, is defined as the difference between the angles, α and α_1, or $\Delta\alpha$. Stereoscopists also call the quantity *differential parallax*, and perceptual psychologists who specialize in stereopsis call it *relative parallax* or *disparity*. The subject was first developed, I believe, by Helmholtz. He called the equivalent quantity "depth-intervals."

We will now relate $\Delta\alpha$ and Δd by a functional relationship. Let us take the simple case of essentially symmetrical convergence, in which the image points lie almost equidistant from the left and right eyes, L and R. The asymmetrical case is more complex and need not concern us yet. It is obvious from geometrical considerations that $\Delta\alpha$ and Δd are proportional to each other, but the problem is exactly how.

We can assume that t_e, the interocular, is small compared to the distance of the image points in question B and B^1, so we can express angular measure in terms of radians. Thus

$$\alpha = \frac{t_e}{d^1} \quad \text{and} \quad \alpha_1 = \frac{t_e}{d_1^1}$$

$$\Delta\alpha = \alpha - \alpha_1 = \frac{t_e}{d^1} - \frac{1}{d_1^1}$$

$$= \frac{t_e d_1^1}{d^1 d_1^1} - \frac{d^1 t_e}{d^1 d_1^1}$$

$$= \frac{t_e(d_1^1 - d^1)}{d^1 d_1^1}$$

But $d_1^1 - d^1 = \Delta d$, and we can take $d^1 d_1^1 = d^2$, where d is the average distance, since we are dealing with the symmetrical case.

Hence

$$\Delta\alpha = \frac{t_e \, \Delta d}{d^2}$$

Differential parallax is inversely proportional to the square of the average distance between the image points and directly proportional to the distance between the two points. The constant of proportionality for a given observer is t_e, the interocular distance.

We can also write this relationship

$$\Delta d = \frac{\Delta\alpha d^2}{t_e}$$

Δd may be thought of as the perceptual threshold of relief, or the minimum depth for which stereopsis can be thought to function.

It is clear that stereoscopic depth perception does indeed fall off as distance increases, and this relationship gives us a theoretical basis for quantifying exactly how rapidly this occurs. Since there is an inverse square relationship at work, stereopsis must fall off very rapidly.

STEREOSCOPIC ACUITY

Is it possible to evaluate, along theoretical lines, the threshold of stereoscopic acuity for observing distant objects? How meaningful would this quantity be? And could we then specify the limits of stereopsis or of a stereophotographic system?

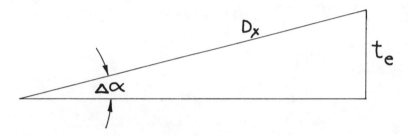

3.11. Limiting distance for stereoscopic acuity.

It should be possible to establish some limiting distance for stereoscopic acuity given two facts: the stereo base of the system, which is about 65 mm for the average human eyes, and the resolution or visual acuity of that system. Using these and simple trigonometry, we should be able to arrive at a calculation. From the drawing, we specify $\Delta\alpha$ to be acuity in terms of angular measure, D_x to be our threshold distance, and t_e to be the interocular. Then

$$D_x = \frac{t_e}{\tan\Delta\alpha}$$

Judge (1950, p. 44) takes the quantity of visual acuity to be synonymous with the resolving power of the eye, similar to photographic resolution. He tells us that "the human eye, in the case of the average person, is unable to distinguish between two points, or vertical lines, when the distance between them subtends an angle at the eyes of about one minute of arc." According to Valyus (1962, p. 42), "this quantity differs from the angle defined as the resolving power of one eye, and depends greatly on the extent to which the subject possesses stereoscopic vision." Valyus further states that $\Delta\alpha$, or stereoscopic acuity, varies in relation to the intensity of background illumination, observation time, and the brightness of the object observed. The graph of the statistical distribution of stereoscopic acuity, reproduced here as Figure 3.12, is based on Soviet measurements of 106 people. About 30% of this group had a stereoscopic acuity of a little more than 6'' of arc. For calculations, Valyus also states that acuity is usually taken to be 30'', and he goes on to calculate the maximum threshold distance for 5'', 10'', and 30''.

For 10'',

$$D_x = \frac{65}{\tan 10''}$$

$$= 1341 \text{ m}$$

Arguing along strictly geometric lines, we see that, given the empirically determined $\Delta\alpha$, in terms of disparity or stereoscopic perception, an object further away than 1341 m cannot be perceived as deeper. Observers with eyes further apart than normal or with greater acuity can have an extended radius of stereoscopic vision.

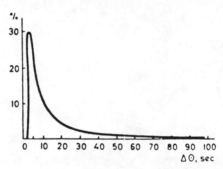

3.12. *Graph of statistical distribution of stereoscopic acuity.* (Valyus, 1962)

We must also understand that the quantity $\Delta\alpha$ varies with the factors Valyus enumerates. For example, it may well be that prolonged observations of a distant target could yield a greatly increased radius of stereoscopic perception. Moreover, the calculation assumes a fixed observer, and human beings do not remain fixed for very long. Motion parallax probably plays a very important part in depth perception of distant objects, and it may not be entirely separable from stereopsis. After a time, a depth effigy of the distant scene may be synthesized by the mind from the cues of stereopsis and strongly related motion parallax. Even slight side-to-side movements of the head are significant.

Let us extend this line of argument to the stereoscopic camera, where we should be able to use the same relationship for determining the maximum threshold distance, or radius of stereoscopic acuity, for a camera, using the concept of photographic resolution, similar to that employed by Judge for his calculations with regard to the eye.

We will take the example of a super 8 system, which was the medium of experimentation in this study, but we might apply this calculation to any photographic system, taking into account resolution of camera film, camera and projector, screen surface and sheet polarizers employed for image selection. We can assume a resolving power of 40 lines per millimeter for a super 8 system viewing original camera film. If a test chart ruled with vertical black lines, alternating with equal spaces of white, were filmed and projected with the system, such resolution is achieved when forty lines remain separately discernible in a space one millimeter across on the film. If we attempt to photograph more lines per millimeter, they would appear to be blurred together.

Since the super 8 frame is 5.5 mm wide, there are a total of 220 resolvable vertical line elements. A super 8 15mm lens has a horizontal angle of view of 22°. Thus the resolution in terms of angular measure for this focal length, or $\Delta\alpha$, is 22° per 220 lines, or 0.1°.

$$D_{rc} = \frac{65}{\tan 0.1°}$$

$$= 37.2 \text{ m}$$

The subscript $_c$ refers to the camera.

The assumed stereo base is 65 mm. For longer bases, the stereoscopic photographic threshold would be larger, and increasingly so for high-resolution photographic systems. Such a calculation says nothing about how an observer would interface with the system, but different values for background illumination, length of observation, and brightness of image points would alter the acuity.

Wider lenses, or those with numerically shorter focal lengths, would necessarily have lower values for $\Delta\alpha$. Since shorter focal lengths reduce the stereoscopic photographic threshold, and longer focal lengths add to it, the photographic stereoscopic threshold is proportional to focal length.

In the event that larger-format motion picture systems are employed, the threshold will be increased by a factor of about 2 for 16mm, or 4 for full-frame 35mm formats. Thus the thresholds for photographic systems will remain appreciably below that of the normal, unaided pair of eyes.

Stereopsis operates effectively only for relatively short distances. There is universal agreement on this point, and any observer can confirm it. The factor that chiefly limits stereopsis is the interocular separation.

Stereopsis, in developmental terms, is closely linked with the sense of touch. As our eye-hand coordination develops in childhood, the close-in sense of stereopsis, and other visual depth cues, become linked with the tactile sense. Quite obviously we cannot touch objects great distances from our bodies, and this may help to establish the close-in nature of this visual cue.

Observers of stereoscopic films are quick to point out that backgrounds look flat. Similar views in the visual world also lack stereoscopic depth, but the stereocinema, which suddenly and effectively calls attention to the sense, makes the observer more keenly aware of this.

I hasten to point out that the calculations carried out above, while in fact reinforcing the assertion that stereopsis operates at relatively close distances, should be taken with the proverbial grain of salt. Although these geometrical arguments do follow familiar observations, they themselves prove nothing. The literature is full of various estimates of the limits of stereoscopic acuity, perhaps to some extent depending on their authors' own limits of acuity.

ORTHOSCOPY

Judge (1950, p. 423) and others give as a necessary condition for orthoscopy the relationship

$$V = Mf_c$$

where V is the distance of the viewer from the screen, M is the frame magnification; and f_c is the focal length employed in photography.

The orthoscopic condition may be defined as that particular combination of shooting and projection variables that produce a stereoscopic effigy appearing exactly like the real object or scene at the time of photography. This is a geometric constraint based on object magnification.

If the subject imaged subtends the same angle in space, or covers the same portion of the retina during projection as it would for the observer at the scene, then we have one basic condition for achieving orthoscopy. The relationship stating that viewing distance during projection is proportional to the product of linear magnification and camera focal length can be taken as a definition of what is meant by viewing an image in proper perspective, and Kingslake (1951) and others generally accept this point of view not only for projection but for viewing prints.

Indeed, only if the relationship $V = Mf_c$ is fulfilled will the relative size of foreground and background objects be maintained in true perspective. That is, their relative sizes according to the rules established by the painters of the fifteenth century, as translated into the standard for rectilinear perspective in modern lenses, will be maintained when the viewing distance is given by the camera focal length scaled up by linear magnification.

For orthoplanar representations, this is the only geometrical-perspective condition that must be fulfilled. But for stereoscopic projection, there are several others as well (see page 225).

However valid the reasoning may be in support of the $V = Mf_c$ relationship, photographers and cinematographers are concerned with producing the most pleasing image, not one that necessarily conforms to the logic of the geometry of perspective. Photography is a pragmatic undertaking, like any craft or art, and practical considerations and good results outweigh theoretically *correct* solutions.

The case for strict adherence to orthoscopic conditions is not a strong one in my view. For the usual projection situation, it can never be achieved, since the viewer would be between the projection beam and the screen itself. If we used rear-screen projection, there still could be only one seat in the screening room for which orthoscopy could be fulfilled.

I have observed that wide departures from this condition for planar and stereoscopic work are allowable and in many situations desirable, and marked departure from focal lengths predicted by the condition $V = Mf_c$ is suggested elsewhere in this book.

A useful alternative to the expression $V = Mf_c$ may be written as

$$V = \frac{Qf_c}{f_p}$$

since it can be shown that Q/f_p is equivalent to M, or frame magnification, where Q is the distance from projector to screen and f_p is the projector focal length that must be employed to fill a given screen at that distance. If the camera focal length used is 10 mm, and M is about 250 (a 1.3-m-wide screen for super 8), then the distance V, where the orthoscopic condition may be fulfilled, is $V = 250 (10 \text{ mm}) = 2.5$ m.

If we are going to place the projector at $Q = 5$ m, and want to know the focal length of the projection lens, then by substituting into $V = Qf_c/f_p$, after first solving for f_p, we can calculate

$$f_p = \frac{Qf_c}{V}$$

$$f_p = \frac{5,000 \text{ mm} (10 \text{ mm})}{2500 \text{ mm}}$$

$$f_p = 20 \text{ mm}$$

As it turns out, just about every super 8 projector with a zoom lens includes a 20-mm range. By simple calculations such as this, it is possible to decide on placement of projector with respect to screen and the arrangement of seating in the screening room.

One should bear in mind that people usually choose seats in a movie screening room starting at about the center, and then from there on back. Only as seats become difficult to find, after the center and rear of the house fill up, will people sit closer to the screen. The seats closest to the screen are the most difficult seats in the house for stereoscopic projection. Vergence angles for the eyes are greatly increased.

VIEWING DISTANCE AND PERCEIVED DEPTH

Stereopsis is a highly individual phenomenon, and various observers will perceive the same effigy in various ways. Nevertheless, one of the first things most people notice about stereoscopic projection is that the farther they are from the screen, the greater the apparent depth of the image. The concept of orthoscopy says that the theoretically ideal place from which to view the image can be given by $V = Mf_c$. An image viewed closer than V will have reduced depth, and one farther will have increased depth. Observation bears this out, but it is also possible to demonstrate geometrically that this is the case.

The observed increased depth, as one moves away from the screen, can be explained in terms of perspective considerations. A subject filmed with a lens of short focal length should be viewed from a distance that is correspondingly closer than one shot with a longer lens, as given by $V = Mf_c$. For example, a shot taken with a wide-angle lens does not have noticeably exaggerated perspective when viewed from relatively close, but it does when viewed from farther than V predicted by Mf_c. This effect is used by planar photographers who wish to control the perspective effect of their photography.

Similarly, for stereoscopic photography or projection, viewing an image from a distance greater than the recommended V will produce a heightened perspective effect. As we will learn on page 161 stereopsis is scaled by perspective. Thus photography with stressed perspective will also have an exaggerated three-dimensional effect. A similar argument can be advanced for the reduction in depth by moving closer to the screen than that predicted by Mf_c.

When the stereoscopic image is viewed closer than the recommended Mf_c, increased palpability or tangibility is often experienced. The image in some sense seems more tactilely satisfying or, if you like, more real, when viewed closer; and conversely, the image appears more magical or more artificial to many people from farther away. Not all observers report this effect, but many do.

The relationship of the viewer to the image points of the stereoscopic effigy is shown in Figure 3.13. Here V is the distance of the spectator from the screen, t_e is the interocular distance, homologous image points l and r have screen parallax p, Y is the distance from the image points on the screen to where they appear in theater space—assuming that the eyes behave like a rangefinder—and Z is the distance the observer perceives point l_1.

It can be shown, using our nomenclature, geometrically that Z is proportional to V (Spottiswoode and Spottiswoode, 1953, p. 25). Since Z is directly proportional to V, when the spectator doubles his or her distance from the screen (fig. 3.13), the spectator's distance to the image point l will likewise be doubled. In other words, an object that appears halfway between the screen and the observer will appear halfway between the screen and the observer no matter what distance the observer is from the screen. This explains the phenomenon of increased depth, or elongation of the effigy, with increased distance from the screen. Moreover, this will be true for all image points that constitute the effigy. Helmholtz (1925, p. 355), using a different approach, arrives at the same conclusion.

Whether an observer's vision follows this expectation is a nice question. Human eyes do not locate objects in space along the lines of a camera or military rangefinder. Perceptual psychologists have established that there is no correlation between the muscular effort of vergence and distance. Thus, the basic assumption of the argument is suspect.

I have conducted some experiments to gain insight into this question. Stereoscopic images have been projected onto a rear-screen surface that conserves polarization. The screen was 86 centimeters across, and viewers, wearing the usual spectacles and standing, observed the screen from several meters away. A rear projection setup was chosen to avoid shadows that would have been cast had conventional front projection been employed.

First, people were asked to estimate how far in front of the screen an object appeared to be. Several images projected with negative parallax were used—a clump of berries and goldfish. People's estimates of the distance from the surface of the screen to the effigy varied considerably.

The observers were next asked to hold a finger in space adjacent to the effigy. Persons were free to move in the projection room. Everyone placed his or her finger in accurate juxtaposition with respect to the theater space effigy.

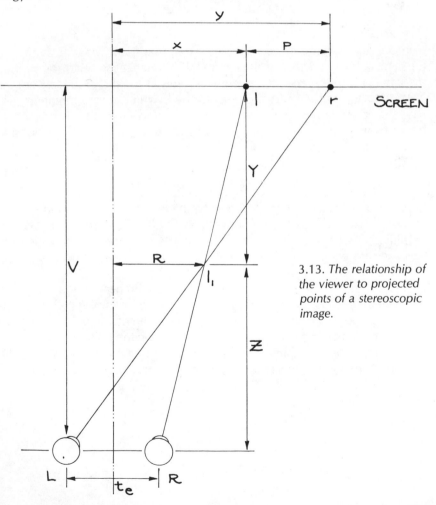

3.13. The relationship of the viewer to projected points of a stereoscopic image.

Estimates of distance not involving the finger as a pointer may have varied because the objects were projected out of scale. A clump of berries only 60mm across was projected 600mm across, and fish only 30mm long were projected 500 mm long. But motion picture images are frequently projected this way. Only rarely do effigies have unit object magnification.

Once an observer placed the finger on or adjacent to the object, his or her estimates of distance became more accurate. Now the observer simply had to estimate the distance from his or her finger to the surface of the screen, a relatively simple, everyday problem.

THE DEPTH-RANGE EQUATION: SIMPLE CASE

Rule (1941) gives the following relationship, which we will call the *depth-range equation* or *screen parallax equation*:

$$P = \frac{Mf_c t_c}{D_0 - D_m} \text{ or } P = \frac{Mf_c t_c}{D_0} - \frac{Mf_c t_c}{D_m}$$

Here P is the maximum screen parallax, M is the frame magnification, f_c is the camera focal length, t_c is the interaxial distance, D_0 is the distance from the camera to the plane of convergence, and D_m is the distance from the camera to the farthest object photographed, which correspondingly will have the greatest screen parallax. When D_m is very large, the term $Mf_c t_c/D_m$ becomes very small and can be taken to be zero, so that the relationship simplifies to the form

$$P = Mf_c t_c/D_0$$

Since we will return to this relationship many times in the course of this study, some effort will be made to derive the equation so that an intelligent nonspecialist can follow the argument. We will follow, more or less, the simplified proof first offered by Rule (April 1941) for the case in which the lens axes are parallel (as shown in the drawing). This is the usual arrangement for still stereoscopy.

This is the simple case of parallel lens axes with near and far points on the median line, chosen because of the complexity of the geometry of converging lens axes. The drawing uses our usual nomenclature. The distances W_1 and W_2 on the film plane are the distances from the point where the lens axes intersect the film plane to the image points formed by points X and O. The proof involves only similar triangles and simple algebraic manipulations:

From similar triangles,

$$W_1 = \frac{f_c t_c}{2D_0}$$

$$W_2 = \frac{f_c t_c}{2D_m}$$

In order to find the distance between the image points produced by X and O, we subtract and simplify:

$$2(W_1 - W_2) = f_c t_c \left(\frac{1}{D_o} - \frac{1}{D_m} \right)$$

The maximum film parallax of image point X is twice the distance $W_1 - W_2$, since the parallax is measured by comparing image points on the left and right film planes.

$$P_f = f_c t_c \left(\frac{1}{D_o} - \frac{1}{D_m} \right)$$

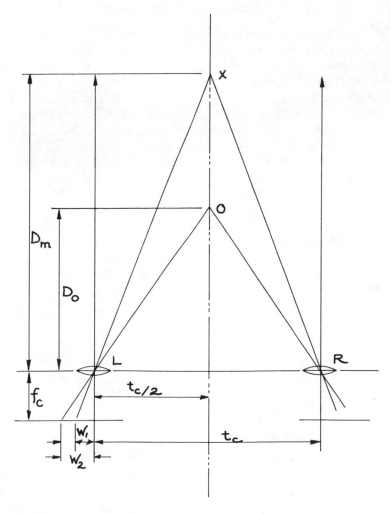

3.14. *Depth-range diagram, simple case.*

This relationship can be used for calculating the maximum parallax on the film, which generally is not terribly useful for filmmakers, although this would be of considerable interest to technicians doing optical printing. (The relationship can also be used to obtain approximate values for retinal disparity.) We are most concerned with screen parallaxes. The film parallax multiplied by the frame magnification will give us the desired quantity for screen parallax, P_s:

$$P_s = Mf_c t_c \left(\frac{1}{D_o} - \frac{1}{D_m} \right)$$

THE DEPTH-RANGE EQUATION: GENERAL CASE

The foregoing derivation of symmetrical convergence on a foreground point, with the maximum background point behind it, also on the median line drawn perpendicular to and bisecting the interaxial, has been attributed to Rule; but he is anticipated (as is everyone else in the field) by Helmholtz's *Treatise on Physiological Optics,* Volume III (1925). The interested reader will find the derivation in a slightly different context beginning on page 330 in a section called "Laws of Stereoscopic Projection."

We will now follow Spottiswoode and Spottiswoode (1953), who stopped short of deriving the relationship for the general case, for symmetrical convergence, but with the background point off the median line. We will add the last few steps to complete the form we desire. In Figure 3.15, X is the distant point and O is the near point intersected by the lens axes. The perpendicular distances from the lens plane for X and O are D_m and D_o. Lengths l and r are distances along the film plane measured from the point where the lens axes cross to the images of X and O, f_c is camera focal length, t_c is the interaxial, θ is the angle of convergence, and other angles and distances are as marked.

$$r = f_c \tan (\beta - \Theta)$$

$$l = f_c \tan (\gamma + \Theta)$$

and

$$\tan \gamma = \frac{a}{D_m}, \tan \beta = \frac{b}{D_m}$$

Substituting and expanding:

$$r = f_c \cdot \frac{b - p \tan \Theta}{D_m + b \tan \Theta}$$

and

$$l = f_c \cdot \frac{a + p \tan \Theta}{D_m - a \tan \Theta}$$

If $a \tan \Theta$ or $b \tan \Theta \ll p$ (l-r), the expression may be disregarded from the equations above. Spottiswoode and Spottiswoode tell us that even for large practical values of Θ, the assumption holds good. By simplifying and combining, we have

$$l - r = p = 2f_c \tan \Theta - \frac{t_c t_c}{D_m}$$

Let's note that

$$\tan \Theta = \frac{\frac{1}{2}t_c}{D_o}$$

And by substitution and simplification,

$$p = f_c t_c \left(\frac{1}{D_o} - \frac{1}{D_m}\right), \text{ etc.}$$

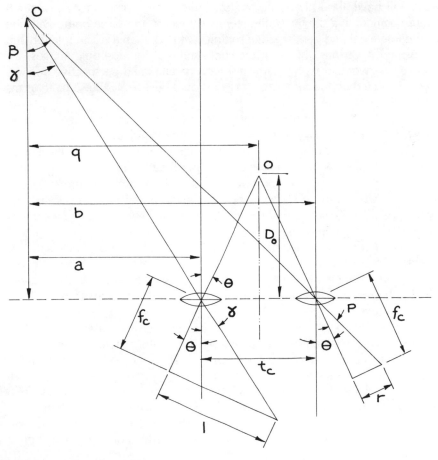

3.15. Depth-range diagram, general case.

Spottiswoode and Spottiswoode also give the equivalent case for lateral shifting of lenses, and their book is recommended to those interested in a rigorous mathematical treatment entirely in Euclidean terms. Some of the relationships they give would be helpful to equipment designers and optical printing specialists.

SCREEN PARALLAX INVARIANCE

This is a good place to explain a very important point about screen parallax as related to frame magnification, comparing photography and projection of various formats.

If we compare two formats, say super 8 and 16mm, we note that the 16mm format is approximately twice the width of the super 8 format and that the angle of view of 16mm lenses will be equal to the angle of view of super 8 lenses when they have approximately double the numerical value. In other words, if we are filming with a super 8 12mm lens, a 16mm 24mm lens will have about the same angle of view. If we first placed a super 8 stereo camera and then a 16mm stereo camera at the same point, with the same interaxial and convergence setting, without changing the relationship between the various objects in the shot, and took stereoscopic images, we would discover that with regard to screen parallax and perspective, the images projected on the same size screen would be exactly the same in terms of stereopsis.

We can see that this must be so from the basic depth-range equation $P = Mf_ct_c(1/D_o - 1/D_m)$, since M for the 16mm projection must be about half M for super 8 projection on the same size screen, while f_c for the 16mm camera must be about twice f_c for the super 8 camera.

M and f_c are inversely proportional as we go from one format to the other, and they vary in such a way that, given equal camera parameters, screen parallax for lenses with the same angle of view projected on screens of the same size will be equal.

I can find no statement of this in the literature, but it obviously is fundamentally correct, and a key to the understanding of technical stereoscopic filmmaking. The invariant nature of photography with various formats, given that shots are set up the same and projected on the same size screen, has not been pointed out.

On an intuitive level, I sense that this must be the case, since a two-dimensional projection of a perspective space onto a plane of a given size will result in an image of a given size. Two such projections, with a fixed distance for the base line between the centers of projection (or lenses), will result in fixed parallax relationships. Whether or not the transmission system includes a large format for recording the picture information, or whether the system uses a small format, or uses none at all and actually projects the twin image à la camera obscura, the parallax relationships of effigy points must remain the same.

chapter 4

Transmission Systems: Classical Developments

In this chapter and the next we will review the work of the pioneers who advocated various transmission systems for producing pleasing stereoscopic motion picture images. Inevitably, as may be the case for today's filmmakers, many of these workers had to design the apparatus they used.

Raymond and Nigel Spottiswoode (1953) appear to have coined the term *stereoscopic transmission,* by which they meant ". . . the transfer of a scene in the solid spacial world to a distant place where it is recreated in its original three dimensions . . . . Thus the transfer of a scene in space by a storage medium such as film, and its recreation elsewhere in space, as in a cinema, may be called stereoscopic transmission." To this definition I would add that animation or various kinds of computer simulations not originating in the solid, spatial world would certainly come under the heading of stereoscopic transmission, and the term ought also to include live television, which may not involve any sort of storage medium.

The technical aspects of photographic stereoscopy, since its inception, have been a subject of controversy. The principal innovators, Wheatstone and Brewster, had widely differing points of view. Psychologists such as Helmholtz soon became interested in stereopsis and stereoscopy, and Helmholtz's remarks on the subject were given in his *Optik,* Volume III, published in Germany in 1866.

The discussions of these early workers are necessarily concerned with still stereoscopy, but with the growing importance of motion pictures correspondingly greater interest was shown in transmission theory as applied to projected moving images. There was a peak in the literature in the early 1950s, corresponding to the theatrical motion picture industry's period of greatest interest in the stereoscopic form.

Norling, an early motion picture stereographer, had some interesting remarks to make in 1939 and subsequently, but the first systematic approach to the problem of photographic stereoscopy and projection is in the work of Rule, who clearly stated the depth-range relationship (page 133). Rule's basic formulation was incorporated in an elegant and, for the filmmaker, difficult mathematical form in the early 1950s by the Spottiswoode brothers and Smith. As far as I have been able to determine, they were the only people to have used their system for actual cinematography.

Kitrosser (1953) of the Polaroid Corporation described the Polaroid Interocular Calculator, a circular slide rule relating camera variables and image size; Spottiswoode et al. created a similar circular rule, which they called a Stereomeasure. Both formulations are based substantially on the work of Rule. The Natural Vision system, perfected by Milton and Julian Gunzburg, was used to photograph nine Hollywood features beginning in the latter part of 1952. The system of photography advocated by Julian Gunzburg had some interesting aspects that are worth discussing.

Yet another circular rule was offered in 1953 by Hill, of the Motion Picture Research Council, a Hollywood-based organization funded by the film industry. Hill's system is based on the work of Luneberg, a mathematician who believed that perceptual space could be described by non-Euclidean geometry. The systems of Rule, of Spottiswoode et al., and of the Polaroid Corporation are based on the assumption that psychological space can be described in terms of Euclidean geometry.

Levonian in 1954 and 1955, using the system of coordinates employed by Luneberg but assuming that perceptual space can be considered to be Euclidean, developed a system of his own for a master's thesis. It is, to say the least, a precocious work.

In 1954, MacAdam, a Kodak researcher, while investigating tolerances for slide mounting, noticed that stereoscopic photography is strongly dependent on the extra-stereoscopic depth cues of geometrical perspective.

Twenty years later, Ousjannikova and Slabova (1975) published a description of the Soviet Stereo 70 system. This article became available to me late in 1977, at which time I commissioned a translation. The Soviet system is based on a great deal of effort and careful observation, the result of many years' continual engagement in the art. Their general recommendations are similar to my own independently derived system.

The following pages will summarize these contributions briefly, drastically condensing many lengthy arguments, to offer a coherent synopsis of the foundations of this obscure branch of intellectual activity. The interested reader should consult the original sources for a complete account.

The mathematical notation of the original papers has been retained, partly because readers will have a less difficult time if they should choose to review any of the articles. Whenever possible, the original drawings have been reproduced in order to retain the character of the work more faithfully; for this reason it is also helpful to employ the author's notation. I have not felt entirely comfortable about this, since it would be better to use a uniform nomenclature, but I have provided Table I, correlating the variables of the various transmission systems, as an aid.

This account of transmission systems has been divided into two portions, one reviewing classical and the other modern ideas. The most important distinction between the two, aside from the obvious arbitrary chronological division, is that classical workers have advised avoiding divergence, whereas modern workers have accepted its necessity.

	Helmholtz	Norling	Rule	Spottiswoode	Hill	Soviet	Lipton
Parallax	$e_1 - e_{11}$ (retinal disparity)		X	Z		P	P
Interaxial		I	T	t_c	b	B	t_c
Interocular	2a	e	e	t	e	B_3	t_e
Distance from camera to plane of convergence	ρ_1 (Distance from eyes)	d	d_0	$\dfrac{1}{D_1}$	p	L_p	D_0
Distance from camera to far plane	ρ_{11} (Distance from eyes)	D	d_{max}	$\dfrac{1}{D_0}$		L	D_m
Camera focal length	b	f	f	f_c	f	F	f_c
Frame magnification		M	M	M	M	K	M
Frame width		W	w	w	w_p	a_k	w
Screen width		s	s	W	W_s	A	s
Distance of spectator from screen		D_v	V	V	v	L_0	V
Distance of spectator from fused image point				I		D	
Nearness factor				N			
Nearness ratio					ρ		
Object magnification					m	m	m
Divergence		0°	0°	0°	1°	1°	1°

4.1. Correlating various mathematical nomenclatures used throughout this book.

This, then, is a review of the thoughts of the people who laid the foundations for the stereoscopic cinema. Because of their experimentation and passion for the medium, today's filmmakers are in a better position to take up the call and make stereoscopic movies.

WHEATSTONE AND BREWSTER

Wheatstone and Brewster engaged in a continuing controversy about stereoscopy. It is probably true that the heart of the controversy really lies in the different styles of the men, at least as far as their personalities are manifested in print. Wheatstone appears to have been patient, careful, and dignified. Brewster strikes me as having been hasty, emotional, with great ego involvement in the priorities of discovery. Wheatstone took five years, from 1833 to 1838, before publishing the invention of the mirror stereoscope and his discovery of stereopsis. It is probable that he anticipated Brewster's 1844 announcement of the invention of the lenticular stereoscope. Brewster passionately denounced Wheatstone's claim to priority, maintaining that both the stereoscope and stereopsis were well known many years before.

The controversy extended to technical differences in setting camera convergence angles and so bears directly on this discussion. Wheatstone's first photographic recommendations, published in 1852 in the *Philosophical Transactions* of the Royal Society of London, advises setting camera convergence angles for a single camera, placed in two positions to produce a stereopair:

> We will suppose that the binocular pictures are required to be seen in the stereoscope at a distance of 8 inches before the eyes, in which case the convergence of the optic axes is about 18°. To obtain the proper projections for this distance, the camera must be placed, with its lens accurately directed towards the object, successively in two points of the circumference of a circle of which the object is at the center, and the points at which the camera is so placed must have the angular distance of 18° from each other, exactly that of the optic axes in the stereoscope. (p. 7)

Citing experimental evidence to support his view, Wheatstone seems to be advising that the convergence angle of photography be set according to the convergence angle for the eyes when looking through a stereoscope. Perhaps he assumed that the subject is best understood in terms of similar triangles, in which the geometry of viewing is to be repeated in photography.

As I have indicated, Brewster (1856) mounted a bitter attack against Wheatstone, denying him credit for inventing the stereoscope (Brewster is given priority in the invention of the lenticular stereoscope) or discovering stereopsis. Comparing the lower values of angles of convergence derived based on the interaxial and subject distance, rather than interocular and stereopair distance, Brewster pounced on Wheatstone's mistake: "As such a difference is a scandal to science, we must endeavor to place the subject in its true light . . ." (p. 149). Wheatstone's observations based on work done with large lenses, Brewster charged, are unfit for stereoscopic work.

To be fair to Wheatstone, it may be that, whatever method he used, suitable mounting of the stereopairs by means of lateral shifts of either image with the flexible mirror stereoscopic would have compensated for any errors in photography.

Brewster quotes Alfred Smee, the originator of what is usually known as the "target method" for setting convergence:

> A spot may be placed on the ground-glass on which the point of sight should be made exactly to fall. The camera may then be moved 2½ inches, and adjusted till the point of sight falls again upon the same spot on the ground-glass when, if the camera has been moved in a true horizontal plane the effect of the double picture will be perfect. (p. 153)

Smee was obviously using a single camera moved through the necessary interaxial distance for successive exposures. Setting small angles for convergence is terribly difficult, but the method Smee hit upon, aligning the axes by making a spot on the finder screen coincide with the subject to be placed in the plane of convergence, is exceedingly accurate, very simple, and preferred to this day.

Stereoscopic photography is a practical subject. It should be easy to observe results and to learn from experience. It is strange, to say the least, that Wheatstone could have come up with his peculiar method. It ought to take very little experience with stereoscopic photography to demonstrate the weakness of this approach. How is it possible that so many workers over the years have recommended procedures that cannot produce good results? The explanation may lie in the highly idiosyncratic nature of stereoscopic perception.

THE STEREOSCOPE AND MOTION PICTURE IMAGES COMPARED

If we consider the transmission system with which Brewster and Wheatstone were dealing, we find that there are differences between photography for the stereoscope and for the motion picture screen. The transmission of a stereoscopic effigy begins with the subject in space and ends with the perception of the eye-brain of the beholder. To accomplish all of the stages in transmission, there must be the camera and its film, and in the case of presentation with a stereoscope, film processing and positioning the pair in the viewer.

When a stereograph is viewed in a stereoscope, the two photos—usually transparencies—are viewed through two lenses. The stereopair is held at a more or less fixed distance from the lenses, and it is rear illuminated, say with a built-in source of illumination, or the stereoscope uses ambient light through frosted or translucent plastic. The purpose of the lenses is to help the eyes focus on the photographs a few inches from the spectator. Since the left image is viewed by the left eye and the right by the right eye, image selection presents no difficulty. In motion picture presentation, however, the polarized images are superimposed on each other and selection takes place immediately in front of the eyes of the spectator by means of sheet polarizers.

For both the stereoscope and motion pictures, the image ought to be placed so that most of it plays at or behind the screen surround. Homologous image points in exact superimposition will appear to be in the plane of the screen. Superimposed homologous points and the image points that make up the boundary of the surround have zero parallax and will appear to be in and to define the plane of the screen. In the case of a projected stereography, image points with zero parallax—perfectly superimposed—appear to be in the plane of the screen, which is the plane of the stereowindow. For stereopairs in a stereoscope, image points must have a somewhat different relationship to appear at the stereowindow: They must have the same distance from the edges of the left and right borders. In other words they must be some distance X from the left border for the left image and the corresponding point for the right image must also be distance X from its left border.

The stereoscope uses a substantially different method for establishing the stereowindow, created by the two rectangular boundaries or borders that surround the left- and right-image pairs. For motion picture work, the screen

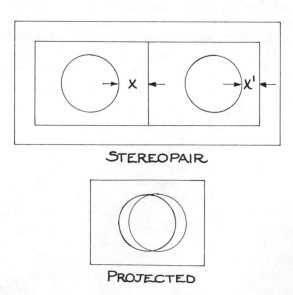

STEREOPAIR

PROJECTED

4.2. *Mounted stereopair and projected stereo image.* Stereowindow is defined by aperture of mount or by screen surround. Depth of a homologous point in relationship to stereopair aperture is given by distance from points to that aperture.

surround itself, a single boundary, creates the stereowindow through which the image is viewed. But transparencies for the stereoscope are mounted adjacent to each other, and the window is created by the two borders surrounding each image.

The stereo worker can adjust the pair of images by laterally shifting one or both, or with mount borders of the appropriate width. Depending on how the mount openings are cut, they can have various degrees of "forwardness," creating a spatial boundary that best suits the parallax content of the slide and setting the compositional elements behind the effective window.

In terms of the geometry of the transmission system, this is an important difference between viewing stereo effigies through the stereoscope and viewing them on a motion picture screen.

On the other hand, one obvious difference turns out to be of no importance. The fact that lenses are used to help the eyes focus on the stereopair does not reduce the difficulties imposed by the breakdown of the accommodation/convergence relationship. Stereoscope lenses will help the eyes focus on the plane of the transparency, but the discrepancy—between the convergence produced by image parallax and focusing (accommodation) to the plane of the slide—remains, since the lenses help the eyes focus for one distance and one distance only. Thus, looking at a stereogram through a stereoscope in terms of A/c breakdown is similar to looking at stereo movies projected on a screen.

In terms of the actual visual perception, the most important factors remain the perspective of the image and the retinal disparities produced by the stereopair parallaxes. Viewing a stereoscopic image through a stereoscope and seeing a motion picture on a screen ought to be similar experiences. For the stereoscope to fulfill the orthoscopic condition, the relationship $V = Mf_c$ becomes $V = (1)f_c$, since frame magnification must be 1. Then, since V is obviously equal to f_c, the lenses used in the stereoscope must have the same focal length as the lenses used in the camera (assuming the spectator needs no refractive correction).

One advantage the stereoscope has over projection is that it can "seat" the viewer at the proper distance, whereas people in a theater are free to select seats that are either too close or too far, based on perspective considerations. But frankly, I cannot convince myself that fatigue or eyestrain are necessarily caused by violations of the $V = Mf_c$ condition. My experience leads me to believe that wide departures from it can still produce acceptable images without strain, or in fact, with little noticeable distortion.

Some stereoscopes allow the lenses to be focused to match the idiosyncrasies of human vision; but just as important, the lateral shift of the lens pair not only adjusts the instrument's interaxial to match the viewer's interocular but also allows some manual control by the viewer to aid fusion in the case of a stereograph with a very large depth range, or for slides mounted to various standards. These alterations of the interaxial of the viewing device are not available to projected moving picture images.

Less expensive stereoscopes, such as the View-Master models, use lenses of longer focal length, producing less magnified images with lower values for the resulting retinal disparities corresponding to the lower parallax of homologous points. In movie terms, this puts the observer at the back of the house, the most forgiving position for viewing. Moreover, the exaggerated depth effect is pleasing to many viewers.

These considerations made me ask myself why stereoscopic images could not be projected on a motion picture screen as successfully as when viewed through a stereoscope. In principle, I could see no reason why this ought not to be achievable, but in practice, nearly all theatrical screenings I had witnessed as an adult involved a great deal of visual discomfort.

HELMHOLTZ

Hermann Ludwig Ferdinand von Helmholtz has made contributions in physics, physiology, and psychology, but we are concerned here with his efforts toward the transmission of stereoscopic images, given in the last volume of the *Handbuch der physiologischen Optik*, which first appeared in 1866. Helmholtz is credited with the invention of the telestereoscope, a mirror device similar to Wheatstone's original stereoscope. It extends the interocular distance, thereby exaggerating depth effects, and is the basis for one kind of military rangefinder. Helmholtz also made a basic improvement to Brewster's lenticular stereoscope by adding a variable interocular control to help match the subject's eyes to the vagaries of mounted stereographs. It is not generally recognized that Helmholtz derived the basic depth range equation, anticipating Rule, who has received the credit.

Let us look at the drawing reproduced from the *Optik* (Figure 4.3), showing the relationship between the eyes of an observer viewing an image through a stereoscope and the resulting spatial image. The eyes are at points P and Q; AB represents the stereoscopic drawing, CD is "the line of intersection of the median plane with the visual plane," and the point S is some point in space to be reproduced stereoscopically.

Let $2a$ represent the interocular distance, b the distance from the eyes to the plane of the stereopair, and ρ "the distance between the object and a plane through the centers of the two eyes perpendicular to the visual plane."

Helmholtz defines a quantity he calls the stereoscopic difference, which we call stereoscopic parallax, and he shows that

$$e_1 - e_{11} = 2ab(1/\rho_1 - 1/\rho_{11})$$

an expression which is equivalent to the depth-range relationship.

Helmholtz sought to establish theoretical limits for the acuity of binocular vision and to compare this with the acuity of monocular vision. His conclusion that the limit of binocular accuracy is equal to the limit of monocular acuity is no longer accepted. Some people have stereoscopic threshold angles measured in a few seconds of arc. This is more than ten times their minimum angle of resolution acuity.

He also made a number of interesting observations on the binocular nature of luster, reflection, and refraction, by explaining that, to use my own terminology, the asymmetrical nature of such reflections from surfaces, or refractions through materials, produces the glitter or shimmer that only stereoscopic photography can capture.

Von Kries, in an appendix to the 1910 German edition, further theorizes about stereoscopic photography by defining P/B as the telescopic power, where P is the distance of plate from the camera lens and B is the distance at which the image is viewed. This corresponds with our V/f_e, or actually is the reciprocal of that ratio, which is image magnification, M.

In a confusing section, Von Kries throws about the terms *homoeomorphous*, which seems to be interchangeable with *orthomorphous* and *tautomorphous*, or *orthoscopic*; but he also introduces nice distinctions: *orthoplastic*, for a stereoscopic image that has the same proportion as the original, *hyperplastic*, for an image with depth values too large, and *hypoplastic*, for depth values too small. Von Kries's enlightened point of view maintained that successful stereoscopic photography will produce an image similar to the original but not necessarily congruent with it. This disagrees with the viewpoints of a number of workers who were concerned with achieving orthostereoscopic views.

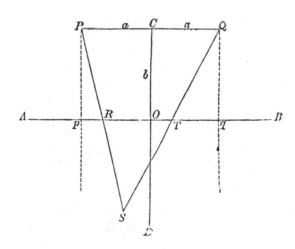

4.3. *Stereoscopic difference of Helmholtz.* Eyes *P* and *Q* observe homologous points *R* and *T* in a stereopair. See text. (Helmholtz, 1910)

NORLING

One of the best-known practitioners of stereoscopic cinematography was John Norling. Together with J. F. Leventhal, he produced in 1935 at the Loucks and Norling Studios anaglyphic short subjects distributed by MGM under the title *Audioscopiks*. These were commercially successful in the American and Western European markets.

In 1939, Norling produced a stop-motion, animated, black-and-white stereoscopic film, depicting the assembly of a Plymouth automobile. Projection used polarized light for image selection. The following year, a color version of the film was presented, and both films were shown at the Chrysler exhibit at the New York World's Fair to more than 5 million people.

Although the terms *zero center line* or *crossed-lens-axes system* were not then used, Norling seems to be one of the first to recognize the advantages of this approach, which he used in the Chrysler exhibit. A dual 35mm system was employed with interlocked Selsyn motors for cameras and a similar electrical interlock for the projectors. The theater was equipped with an aluminum lacquered screen 17 ft wide.

The stereo camera, made up of two Bell & Howell machines, had a fixed interaxial of about 3½ in. Despite the fact that Norling favored lateral lens shifts for setting convergence, the cameras were angled inward or outward, as the occasion required. Although there must be some geometric or keystone distortion inherent in a pair of projectors 5 ft apart with a throw of 90 ft., the total convergence angle for the projectors was only a little over 3°, and this should produce very little geometric distortion.

For the Golden Gate International Exposition in San Francisco in 1940, Norling used a different system for a film commissioned by the Pennsylvania Railroad. This involved mechanical rather than electrical camera synchronization and parallel projection rather than the crossed-lens-axes system. Norling probably switched to mechanical interlock because of the complexity of his Selsyn system, and it may be that mechanical interlock of the cameras placed restraints on the rotation of left and right units to achieve convergence. If my inferences are correct, a parallel-lens-axes projection system might be a better choice. The relative merits of crossed-lens and parallax-axes systems will be discussed in the content of the work of Rule.

In the early 1950s Norling showed a dual-system 35mm camera, which even today is an advanced instrument. Two rolls of film, immediately adjacent to each other, ran side by side through the machine. A periscope-type lens system set the continuously variable interaxial distances of from 1½ to 4 in., and a rack-over binocular finder allowed the cinematographer to anticipate the stereo effects.

Between 1939 and 1953, Norling published a number of articles containing basically the same material. A genuine enthusiast about stereoscopic filmmaking, Norling needed to publicize his own efforts, but he also felt the need to guard certain "trade secrets" from competitors. This accounts for the lack of specific recommendations in his material relating to the important variables of camera-to-subject distance, interaxial, and focal length.

THE RELATIONSHIP $Wed/sf = I$

The closest Norling (1953) comes to any sort of explicit advice is the following relationship (Norling's notation), which is found in other sources as well:

$$I = \frac{Wed}{sf}$$

where

I = interaxial distance
W = frame width
e = interocular distance
d = camera-to-subject distance
s = screen width
f = camera focal length

From the definition of linear magnification, the ratio of s to W, we have

$$\frac{W}{s} = \frac{1}{M}$$

which may be substituted into the above to obtain

$$I = \frac{ed}{Mf}$$

What about the relationship is predictive? How can it be used by a working filmmaker? Let us suppose the following (units in inches): W (the width of the super 8 frame) is 0.21, and s (the width of the Eastman Ektalite model 3) is 40; then M is 190. Assuming an interocular of 2.5, with a 0.50 (13mm) lens, and a subject distance of 60, we get $I = 1.58$. My experiments show that this is not a bad choice for the interaxial. However, if we use a focal length of half the previous value and take $f = 0.25$ (6mm), we obtain $I = 3.12$, which, experiments show, is bad advice. The relationship as stated has I inversely proportional to f, which gives poor results in many practical cases, since shorter focal lengths may also require values for the interaxial that are less than the average interocular.

I have actually led the reader into a trap, since the equation is not meant to be applied to the crossed-lens-axes system. But I do not feel bad about this, since I was misled by Norling's presentation, and I believe that many others have also gone astray here. The relationship was meant to be used only for the case of parallel projection, which we will explore more fully on page 135. In this context, it is used to control the position of photographed objects with respect to the stereowindow. The position of photographed objects changes with magnification, and on larger screens they come forward of the window. By reducing the interaxial, one can control the stereoscopic juxtaposition of window and effigy.

Norling did present some more meaningful concepts in a 1952 article in the *PSA Journal,* where he defines the parallax index in an attempt to relate screen parallax to angular measure, a far more accurate method for determining acceptable limits for audience tolerance of homologous image points than simply giving the distance between those points:

$$P = \frac{D_v}{I_n}$$

where D_v is the viewing distance and I_n is the interocular.

The *P* value is given in relationship to a version of the depth-range equation derived from the diagram for the simplified case of asymmetrical convergence, with one lens axis perpendicular to the stereo base:

$$I = \frac{W}{PF} \times \frac{Dd}{D - d}$$

where *I* is called the *parallactic difference.*

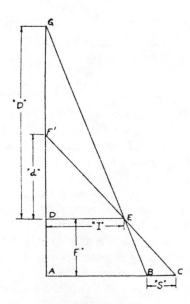

4.4. *Derivation of Parallax Index, P. D and d* are the distances to the far and near plane of objects *G* and *F*, respectively. Lenses of focal length *F"* are located at *D* and *E*, separated by interaxial *I*. *W*, given in the equation in text, is the format width. *S* is the distance between image points *B* and *C*, which correspond to *F'* and *G*. (Norling, 1953. Reprinted with permission from the *SMPTE Journal,* Volume 60, March 1953. Copyright Society of Motion Picture and Television Engineers, Inc.)

HYPERSTEREOGRAPHY

Concerning the orthoscopic condition, or at least a version of it, Norling stated that it will exist when "the projected views shall subtend the same angles for the eyes as for the camera lenses used in taking the picture" (1939, p. 619). But he understood the impossibility of achieving this condition, since it would reduce the audience to one person in the single geometrically preferred position. He knew that the image will change shape when viewed from different parts of the house, and that the distortions can be disturbing when viewed off axis.

One of the most important aspects of the stereoscopic cinema, he stated, has little to do with depth, but rather with luster and textures, which are better reproduced binocularly. Norling also noted the necessity of careful alignment of the camera lens axes in the horizontal plane to avoid vertically displaced homologous image points, and the need for the careful matching of focal lengths of camera optics.

The following example was given by Norling (1939, p. 621) to illustrate his conception of the effect of hyperstereoscopy (photography with an enlarged interaxial):

> Thus if we were to make a stereogram of the Empire State Building, which would require a field of approximately 2000 feet in width, taking the picture from a distance of 5000 feet, and using a lens separation of 2500 inches, 1000 times that of the normal, the building would appear to be 5 feet away and to be 1/1000 as big. Theoretically, one should experience, in viewing such a stereogram, what one would experience in viewing a model of the building constructed on a scale of 1000 to 1. . . .
>
> The capacity to see objects in absolutely true *relative* scale is probably lacking in most individuals. Thus, even though we know that, theoretically, the observer should see the Empire State Building at 1/1000 of its real size, he would probably still think of it as big and his probable reaction would be that he would think he were seeing it without a shrinkage in size unless some reference object, such as a yardstick, were artificially introduced into the scene.

Expressing the argument as it usually is given, Norling pointed out that hyperstereoscopic views tend to reduce distant subjects to modellike proportions. Yet extended interaxials are the only way that stereoscopic depth can be brought to shots of distant subjects. In this case, the usual interaxial of 2 or 3 in. will produce as much stereoscopic depth as a painted backdrop. Some people, when shown such images, complain about this lack of depth. One trick frequently employed is to add a foreground object, such as a tree, placed in or near the plane of convergence so that the background can be set off stereoscopically.

The effigy produced by the extended interaxial is often compared to that which would be perceived by a giant; in our example, his eyes would be 1000 times farther apart than ours. Thus, it seems all the more reasonable that hyperstereoscopic effects produce modellike results.

Another opinion, somewhat at odds with Norling's, is given by Kodak researcher MacAdam (1954, p. 285), whose work is presented later. He said:

> If the cameras are separated much more than the normal interocular distance, the binocular disparities can be experienced for objects much further from the original scene than is normal for human vision. The natural and quite involuntary interpretation of such an experience is that the distances in the image are no greater than those for which stereopsis normally occurs. On the basis of this very effective clue, all distances in the scene are underestimated. Consequently, all objects in the scene are perceived proportionately closer than the original objects. Their shapes, however, are distorted and close objects appear smaller than identical objects at a distance.

In a footnote (p. 285), he added: "The assertion is sometimes encountered, that use of a camera separation greater than normal interocular separation causes perception of a miniature model of the scene, reduced in all dimensions but otherwise undistorted."

He gave (p. 285) a numerical example to illustrate his point and concludes with:

> The enlargement of distant objects (or relative dwarfing of close objects) also distorts the shapes of objects that occupy much depth in the scene. Such enlargement of distant objects and distortions of all objects are inevitable consequences of use of camera separations greater than the normal interocular distance.

We are in a transitional period; people have had little experience looking at stereoscopic effigies. When there is a conflict between the cue of stereopsis and other depth cues, as there is in hyperstereoscopic reproduction, it is difficult to know how the mind will evaluate the scene and which cue will take precedence. It is very likely that hyperstereoscopic views can, in time, become part of a new grammar of the stereoscopic film, pleasing for people to experience, an accepted convention of stereoscopic filmmaking. Of course, in such a case, proper handling of the shot, the choice of interaxial, focal length, and compositional elements will determine the esthetic outcome.

To continue with Norling's work: He understood the great importance of the converging stereo camera to filmmaking, and that the "normal" or fixed parallel-lens-axes still cameras used to this day did not provide adequate control of juxtaposition of the photographed object with respect to the stereowindow. (In projection, the window is the border surrounding the image.) In reference to rotation of cameras and lateral lens shifts—two methods for adjusting convergence—he clearly prefers the latter, emphasizing the need for the elimination of keystone or geometric distortion resulting from rotation or angling of cameras.

The crossed-lens-axes system was employed by Norling for the 1939 World's Fair and by Spottiswoode et al. for the Festival of Britain in 1950, thus becoming the system that set the standard for theatrical presentation in the early 1950s. In the parallel-lens-axes system, the lenses of the camera and projector are parallel, and no convergence or toeing of the lenses is employed. The camera lenses in the crossed-lens-axes system are converged on the subject that is to be placed in the plane of the screen, and the projection lenses are adjusted so that their lens axes cross at the center of the plane of the screen.

For viewing stereograms through a stereoscope, the parallel system passes muster, more or less. In many better-quality stereoscopes with lenses of shorter focal length, the borders of the image are indistinct, since they are perceived only peripherally; hence the less pressing need for accurate placement of the effigy with respect to the stereowindow.

The advantages of the crossed-lens-axes system for the projection of moving stereoscopic images must have become clear to Norling, perhaps when first working with anaglyphs. Stereopairs are viewed side by side in a stereoscope, probably obscuring the underlying geometry of the situation to a certain extent. But images overlaid on each other, the anaglyph's green and red images, clearly illustrate that objects with zero screen parallax are perceived in the plane of the screen, while the rest of the effigy is perceived in terms of positive or negative screen parallaxes.

Norling employed many of the general principles of a good stereoscopic transmission system, in terms of both engineering parameters and recommendations for photography. He helped disseminate information about an art form that had, then and now, few practitioners. Not the least of his accomplishments was the design of a camera that, in most ways, still serves as a model for a first-rate stereoscopic instrument.

RULE

John T. Rule was a professor of mathematics at MIT, who between 1938 and 1941 published articles on stereoscopic drawing, a geometrical analysis of stereoscopic image distortions, a treatment of the geometry of projection of stereoscopic images, and stereoscopic still photography. His approach was rigorously based on Euclidean geometry, yet he understood that stereoscopy is a practical art and that departures from theory were acceptable if better results could be achieved.

His work, the most formally developed and coherently organized writing to appear on the subject up to that time, greatly influenced the mathematical analysis of transmission theory published in the early 1950s by Spottiswoode et al., by Hill, and by Levonian.

Although Rule's work was based on the use of the geometrical principles of convergence as a psychological range-finding device, or what the perceptual psychologist would call the theory of projection, he understood that there were limits to this notion.

> . . . it is assumed that the stereoscopic image of any point lies at the intersection of the two projected lines from the eyes through the images of the

> point on the stereograph . . . Though this is an acceptable assumption it should be pointed out that it is not entirely true and that therefore it does not lead to perfect results. It can be quickly proved to be untrue by cutting the two halves of the stereograph apart and varying the separation between them. It will be found that this separation may be considerably altered without any detectable effect on the image either in shape, size, or location. On convergence principles, the image should grow larger and recede as the halves are separated. (1938, p. 314)

This is a repeatable experiment (first carried out by Wheatstone) that readers engaged in stereoscopic projection may try, by laterally shifting one of their projected images with respect to the other. As long as excessive negative or positive screen parallaxes are not produced, situations that would prevent comfortable fusion, the stereoscopic image will maintain its shape and size.

In an article coauthored with Vannevar Bush in 1939, Rule stated definitely "that the absolute convergence of a single point never determines its apparent depth in a stereoscopic image. Its relative convergence with other points is used by the brain to locate it with regard to those points after the general position of the image is fixed." This comes as no surprise, since Dove and other psychologists have shown that convergence cannot be considered a depth cue. Although convergence enables the eyes to fuse retinal images, disparity itself is the important depth factor.

In terms of a geometrically derived theory of transmission, convergence and film parallax can be made to be mathematically interchangeable. But the situation is more complex than an analysis of parallax alone will provide, since additional extra-stereoscopic cues play a tremendously important role in the mind's evaluation of depth. One can see mathematically based transmission theories as brave attempts to specify, in functional terms, quantities that probably defy numeration. Nevertheless, a geometrical analysis of the problem may produce useful results, if only by allowing us to observe how actual events depart from prediction.

Rule and Bush defined "an orthoscopic view [as one] . . . in which the resultant image is of exactly the same size and shape and has the same location with respect to the observer's eyes as the original scene."

There are powerful psychological factors against an observer ever seeing such an orthoscopic view. In the screening room, the effigy is seen hanging in space surrounded by a black rectangle (the so-called stereo window). Sitting, you are watching events that you often observe only when moving or standing. You know you are still sitting in a theater, and a host of factors follow from this: There is tactile deprivation, for one thing. You can never touch the effigy. You can watch an attacking African lion and still wonder if you remembered to turn off the car lights. The person in the next row might have an annoying nervous cough. You might be aware that the floor underfoot is sticky from spilled soft drinks.

Specialists in stereoscopy, those who have taken the trouble to write down their thoughts, are extremely concerned with the concept of ortho-stereoscopy. Yet people who write about the technical aspect of convention-al photography or filmmaking are not as concerned with the companion concept of presenting the spectator with an orthoview in terms of perspec-tive. One of the conditions of orthoscopy, namely the relationship $V = Mf_e$, is also the orthoperspective relationship.

Art, especially the visual arts and the cinema in particular, is not iso-morphic with visual experience. There is a great deal in common between the visual world and its photographic counterpart, but the two experiences markedly depart from one another. It may well be that art expresses itself most clearly in these departures, which one is free to call distortions.

No one writing about planar filmmaking suggests that audiences will become uncomfortable when wide-angle or telephoto views are projected. The image is a distortion, but audiences discount this or have become so accustomed to the effect that they readily accept the image as a natural part of the experience of the cinema.

But stereoscopists seem to have become obsessed with this point out of all proportion, if you will forgive the expression, to its merit. Perhaps this is closer to the truth: People have so little experience looking at stereoscopic images that it is possible that they can be annoyed by these departures from orthoscopy. We are at a time when audiences are not familiar with stereo-scopic conventions.

In "The Shape of Stereoscopic Images" (1941b), Rule details a geomet-rical approach for evaluating distortions of stereoscopic images by develop-ing functional relationships between camera and viewing or projection vari-ables. Photographers might find the geometry difficult and the arguments obscure, based on the assumption that perceptual space can be described by Euclidean geometry, but this treatment might be helpful to psychologists who want to test and measure departures from these predictions, in order to learn something about the nature of perceptual space.

Of far greater interest to us is Rule's "The Geometry of Stereoscopic Projection" (1941a), probably the seminal work in the field. Rule comes from a tradition in which parallel lens axes for taking and projection were considered de rigeur. Implied in Rule's approach is that the parallel system is the method employed by the purist.

In the parallel scheme, the lens axes of both camera and projector are always parallel. It is sometimes expedient, in the parallel scheme, to depart from strictly parallel placement of the projection lens axes and to use effec-tive parallel projection by maintaining the distance of homologous infinity points at the average interocular spacing. Such a situation could arise with dual projection when the physical size of the projectors prevents them from being set close together.

In parallel projection, the homologous infinity points are always spaced at the interocular distance. And no matter what size screen is used, or how large the image is magnified, the homologous points for infinitely distant objects will always be so maintained.

The most curious aspect of parallel projection is that the larger the screen employed, the farther the effigy moves in front of the stereowindow, or plane of the screen.

The left-hand portion of Figure 4.5 illustrates the geometry of photography. The photographic plate is shown to be in front of the lens for simplicity. Cube ABCD is being photographed by a stereocamera with lenses whose interaxial distance, e, is equal to the interocular, and f is the focal length of the lens.

The drawing on the right gives the case for parallel projection of the cube's image. Various screen sizes for given magnifications are illustrated. When the magnification is M = 2, then the front edge of the cube is in the plane of the screen. As we go to larger screen sizes, with correspondingly greater values for M, the cube is brought in front of the plane of the screen.

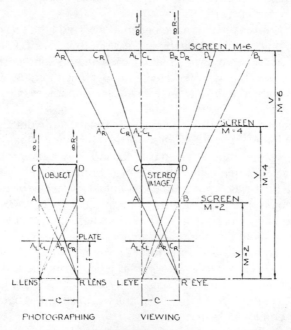

Fig. 1. Parallel projection.

4.5. *Parallel projection.* Object on left, image on right. The photographic plate with image points $A_L C_L$ and $A_R C_R$ is placed in front of the lenses, to simplify the drawing. When the cube ABCD is projected on a screen at a magnification of 2 (M = 2), then the front edge, AB, is seen in the plane on the screen. When M = 6, the edge AB is seen to be one third of the way from the eyes to the screen. As magnification is increased, objects come forward on the screen if parallel projection is maintained. (Rule, *Journal of the Optical Society of America,* Volume 31:325–34, 1941. Reprinted by permission.)

Rule derives this formula, whose purpose is to enable the photographer to place the desired object in the plane of the screen, by suitably reducing the interaxial distance:

$$T = \frac{Wed}{sf}$$

The reader will recall that this relationship was introduced earlier, on page 127 in connection with the work of Norling. The notation here is slightly different. Whereas Norling used I for interaxial and W for frame width, Rule uses T and w, respectively. As shown, we may write this equation in terms of frame of linear magnification in the form

$$T = \frac{ed}{Mf}$$

In other words, for a given screen size or magnification of the image as the projection variable, we can calculate for the camera variables of focal length, format size, and distance from the lens to the near object, an interaxial setting that will place our near subject in the plane of the screen. The image, if too far in front of the plane of the screen, could produce serious eyestrain in cases of large values of screen parallax, because of a breakdown of the accommodation/convergence habitual response, or because the near object is cut off by the surround (see page 220).

This imposes a serious practical photographic difficulty. It requires cameras that can substantially diminish their interaxial distances to create a corresponding reduction of screen parallax, which may not be able to supply an ample stereopsis cue. In other words, markedly reduced interaxials may produce images that look flat.

The relationship $T = wed/sf$ has been erroneously quoted out of Rule's context as a means for predicting the interaxial. But specifically it refers to the parallel scheme, and the value for the interaxial predicted this way only specifies that the near object will be placed in the plane of the screen. It does not guarantee that the object will be correctly represented stereoscopically.

Rule gives his derivation of the basic depth range relationship, which has already been given (page 133), for what he calls nonparallel projection (and what I refer to as the CLA or crossed-lens-axes system). Rule undervalues the CLA system, believing that it causes serious geometric distortions, a view I have discovered is still shared by some contemporary workers.

While the parallel projection system always results in a constant value (nominally the interocular distance) for the separation of distant homologous points, regardless of the size screen employed, the CLA system will present increased separation for homologous distant points as the screen size increases. In fact, for CLA, all screen parallaxes, both positive and negative, will vary in direct proportion to M. Only object points at the plane of the screen will retain their constant value of zero parallax.

While parallel projection will result in an image with constant values for the maximum positive screen parallax for any size screen, the stereowindow—made up by the borders provided by the two frames—recedes, and objects are brought forward out of the plane of the screen as the size of the screen is increased. On the other hand, no matter what size screen is used, CLA projection maintains the important compositional constancy of the stereowindow (the screen surround itself) so that the filmmaker can specify which portion of the shot will be in front of the screen and which behind, or in language I prefer, which portions of the shot will be in theater space and which in screen space.

For the case of CLA photography, a film shot for a screen 10 feet wide that would have maximum positive screen parallaxes equal to the interocular (say, 65 mm) will have, on a 20-ft-wide screen, maximum values for screen parallax of twice the interocular, or 130 mm. This will produce divergence for distant image points.

There are some experts, Rule among them, who feel that divergence, or the turning outward of the eyes, which does not occur naturally in human vision, should not be allowed in stereoscopic projection. There is evidence to support their position, and it is easy to demonstrate that divergence can cause eyestrain. Therefore the parallel projection system, which, when properly executed, will always avoid divergence, has a strong appeal. However, some slight degree of divergence is permissible; others argue—and I agree—that the advantages of the CLA system far outweigh the consequences of increased parallax and divergence for larger screen sizes.

One possible approach with the CLA system is that films can be shot for a maximum screen size so that projection on a smaller size screen would reduce parallax and produce no divergence. And, while the absolute values in terms of screen parallax may sound horrendous, the most meaningful measure is retinal disparity, or the more easily handled and entirely equivalent quantity of angular measure (actually a simple trigonometric function of the value of the screen parallax and distance from the screen). Since people sit farther away from large screens, the effects of large values of parallax are minimized.

Before leaving the work of Professor Rule, I would like to cover two additional points. Rule, in the context of parallel projection, stressed the importance of the relationship $V = Mf_e$ and pointed out that this equation could be used as a guide for predicting optimum seating for fulfilling the orthostereoscopic condition.

Rule also identified (1941a) a cause for what stereoscopists usually call by the pleasantly descriptive term *cardboarding*. This is a frequently observed condition in which "objects appear to lie in planes at different depths, [but] they themselves appear flat."

If a stereograph is taken with an interaxial of, say, 63 mm in Rule's example, or taken so that it is meant to be viewed by an individual with an interocular of 63 mm, someone else with an interocular of 70 mm will see an apparent compression in depth of the effigy. Rule demonstrates this with a drawing (Figure 4.6) that shows how this will take place for squares compressed into trapezoids. It seems intuitively evident that scenes shot with a certain interaxial, when viewed by an individual with a larger interocular, will appear to have reduced depth, and naturally enough, the converse ought to be true.

Others have explained the causes of cardboarding in other ways. Spottiswoode et al. (1952) claim that it arises from projected images that have maximum screen parallaxes less than the interocular. I have also observed that the use of lenses of longer focal length, without extended interaxials, produces cardboarding. The explanation for this, probably best given by MacAdam (1954), is that stereopsis is scaled to extra-stereoscopic, or monocular, depth cues in general and to perspective specifically. Long lenses, as will be familiar to many photographers, tend to compress perspective and "flatten out" a scene. Hence the resulting cardboarding.

Daniel Greenhouse, a visual psychophysicist and stereoscopist, has told me that flat lighting and the inability to incorporate motion parallax in stills contributes to the cardboarding effect.

The example of the mismatched interocular and interaxial given as a cause of cardboarding is one further reason to be suspicious of the philosophical basis of the doctrine of orthoscopy. In actual practice, the condition

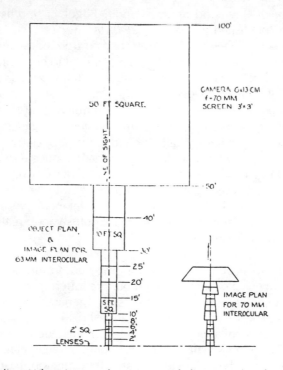

4.6. *Cardboarding.* When interocular (70mm) of observer exceeds interaxial (63mm) of the stereograph. (Rule, *Journal of the Optical Society of America*, Volume 31:325–Volume 34, 1941. Reprinted by permission.)

can be fulfilled only for those few people with an interocular separation that exactly matches the interaxial separation used in photography. For everyone else, there can never be an orthoscopic view. Orthoscopy is even more difficult to achieve than has been indicated. From the consideration of perspective alone, as we have discussed, an orthoview is out of the question for all but one theoretically perfect seat in the house. We can also intuit that the camera interaxial must be equal to the interocular of the viewer, and as mentioned, the values for maximum positive screen parallax must be equal to the viewer's interocular. These last two conditions limit the geometrically correct view or orthoview, to a handful of people in any given audience. Chosen from this handful, one lucky person must be selected to sit in the seat determined by $V = Mf_c$.

A successful system of stereoscopic photography, while mindful of the orthoscopic conditions, should not slavishly adhere to these constraints, for they will create impossible limitations. It is better to do pleasing photography than theoretically perfect photography, especially when the axiomatic basis of the theory is suspect.

SPOTTISWOODE ET AL.

The work of Raymond Spottiswoode, Nigel L. Spottiswoode, and Charles Smith, published in the *Journal of the Society of Motion Picture Engineers* (1952) and then in a book by the Spottiswoodes alone, *The Theory of Stereoscopic Transmission* (1953), was meant to be the foundation for all subsequent work in the field. If the authors' intentions had been fulfilled, the theory would have provided basic information for designers of stereoscopic apparatus, for technicians in the film industry, and for filmmakers.

Here is a fully developed mathematical system using elegant and powerful techniques—even if essentially limited to the applied mathematics of a sophomore science major (as in fact is the mathematics in most scientific papers)—accompanied by a highly articulate and persuasive text. Raymond Spottiswoode was a noted authority on motion picture technology when he became the director of the Festival of Britain's Telekinema. As a result of this involvement with the stereoscopic cinema, Spottiswoode realized that the form was in a tentative state.

His goal, shared by his colleagues and coauthors, was to enunciate the underlying principles of stereoscopic transmission, to turn a puzzling subject—undeveloped and with spotty literature offering contradictory advice—into a coherent system based on a single general equation that yielded physical variables and functional relationships in very much the same way that Maxwell's equations codified electromagnetic theory. From their general equation, approximately eighty further functional relationships were developed. This rich theory of stereoscopic transmission, based on simple geometrical postulates, might be able to explain a number of curious observations as well as offer practical advice. What more could one ask?

Because the system of Spottiswoode et al. is developed more fully and expressed at greater length than any of the others, more abridgment of their exposition was necessary. As usual, I will present my own comments as well. I may not have clearly separated them from the summary, so I suggest that the interested reader return to the original sources.

The basic assumption of the system is that the eyes function like range-finders and gauge depth by triangulating or converging on objects in space. Psychologists call this a projection theory of stereopsis, and as has been mentioned, it was first proposed by Kepler. Closely tied in with this assumption is the use of Euclidean geometric postulates as the axiomatic basis of the mathematical system. In essence, a straight line in a Euclidean space is one in which s, the shortest distance between two points, in a coordinate system where x, y, and z are distances measured along the three mutually perpendicular axes, can be described by the relationship (attributed to Pythagoras)

$$s^2 = x^2 + y^2 + z^2.$$

It is difficult to persuade most people, since it flies in the face of common sense, that the Euclidean description of space is a purely arbitrary but useful construct. However, Euclidean geometry does not describe events on a cosmic scale. This is one of the modern additions to our understanding of the universe, proposed by Einstein in his theory of special relativity. More about this in the context of Hill's use of Luneberg's work.

The two implicit assumptions of the Spottiswoode transmission theory are that convergence of the eyes is a depth cue and that local space, or perceptual space, may be described in terms of a Euclidean metric. Both assumptions are demonstrably false and have been shown to be false in repeated experiments by psychologists specializing in depth perception. At the time of the writing of the Spottiswoode et al. theory, this was well known, and Spottiswoode et al. acknowledge it. Nevertheless, they insist that their concept is basically correct, and in view of the fact that a true description of the nature or geometry of perceptual space was wanting (and is still wanting), they would plunge ahead and do the best they could, hoping that their work would be sufficiently flexible to stand future modification.

On purely teleological grounds, one must seriously question a theory built on fundamentally incorrect postulates. Of course, the test of theory is utility; if the system is useful and predicts the physical situation accurately, then fundamental principles be damned.

The pregnant nature of the stereoscopic cinema offers us an unusual opportunity to study the interrelationship between technology and esthetics. Art forms are based on technology, in terms not only of mastery of craft and materials, but in the relationship of that mastery to perception. Until recent years media had ancient traditions. Painting, music, and theater were invented thousands of years ago, printing only a few hundred years ago, and the cinema was invented only a few years after the birth of my grandfather.

Certain important aspects of the thinking of Spottiswoode et al. did immediately influence the Hollywood theatrical industry (they advocated the CLA system, which they called ZCL, for zero center line), but their theory is only of limited use to the stereoscopic filmmaker. The work of Spottiswoode et al. occupies one of those unique niches in the history of technology, valuable because it is "false doctrine." It is something to push against.

Spottiswoode et al. first derive and define the nearness factor, $V/P = N$, where V is the distance from the spectator to the screen and P is the distance from the spectator to the fused image point I—given at the intersection of rays from the left eye (L) to the left image point l, and from the right eye (R) to the right image point r, as shown in fig. 3.10. (In the drawing Z is used in place of P, and vice versa. In my nomenclature, P is screen parallax, and Z is the distance to the fused image point. In Spottiswoodes' Z is parallax and P the distance to fused points.)

We should note that uncrossed screen parallaxes, Z_s, which produce the sensation of an image in screen space, have by definition a positive value, and crossed screen parallaxes, which produce images in theater space, have a negative value.

In mathematical form, the relationship $V/P = N$ states that the ratio of the spectator's viewing distance from the screen to his or her distance from the fused image point is a constant, no matter what distance the viewer may be sitting from the screen. If an object appears to be halfway out from the screen to the spectator when he or she is 10 ft from the screen, it will also be halfway out when he or she is seated 20 ft from the screen. Another way to put this is that the shape of the image becomes elongated in proportion to distance.

For the case where $P = \infty$ then $N = O$ and Z_s (screen parallax) $= t$ (the interocular). The image then appears at infinity. For the case where $P = V$ then $N = 1$ and $Z_s = 0$, the image is in the plane of the screen. For the case where $P = V/2$ then $N = 2$ and $Z_s = -t$. This corresponds to the image being halfway out from the screen.

Spottiswoode et al. have decided that the best possible stereoscopic presentation is what they call the zero center line (ZCL) system—what I have been calling the crossed-lens-axes (CLA) system—in which projectors are aligned so that identical prints projected by left and right machines will appear in perfect coincidence on the screen. Theirs, the clearest exposition of the virtues of this system, was probably influential in establishing it as the theatrical standard in the early 1950s.

It is interesting to note that although the exposition of the system is based on the assumption that the polarized-light method for image selection will be employed and that spectators will be wearing glasses, there is nothing inherent that would prevent it from being equally applicable to autostereoscopic systems, in which selection takes place at the screen rather than at the eyes of the beholder.

A new unit of distance is established called the rho, defined as

$$\text{distance in } \rho = \frac{6,000}{\text{distance in inches}}$$

A metric rho is also defined, although the actual units used in the exposition are as given above. Reciprocal distances are employed because of the form of the depth-range equation (see page 114) and the arbitrary multiplying factor of 6000 is chosen to give convenient values for rho.

The concept of depth content, or the range in space that the image occupies, is as follows: If there is a difference in nearness factor of 2 between the nearest and furthest parts of the image, for example when $N = 0$ (this describes the far plane) and $N = 2$ (N_2) (an image halfway between the screen and spectator), then we write ΔN_2. It is important to realize that ΔN_2 might also express the depth content of a scene that ranges from N_1 to N_3, where the image would extend from the plane of the screen to 2/3 the way out.

The general equation is derived in this form:

$$P = \frac{Ap}{C - Bp}$$

where the distance P of a fused image point is given in terms of p, the distance from the camera to the original point, and in terms of three factors—A, B, and C. The A factor is Vt, a function of the spectator and his or her distance from the screen (t without a subscript represents the interocular, with the subscript c—for camera—the interaxial, and with the subscript p, the distance between the projection lenses). The B factor is determined by lens convergence, and in its simplest form

$$B = \infty_{z_s} - t$$

where $\infty\, z_s$ represents the screen parallax for an infinity point and t is the interocular. "B is the excess of screen parallax of a point originally at infinity over the separation of the human eyes."

Spottiswoode et al. favor only the condition in which $B = 0$, although in some special cases they will allow B to be negative. In other words, divergence is never allowed. Divergence would come about when the value of $\infty\, z_s$ is greater than t, so that B would be positive. They define the following classes of "B-ness":

1. When $B = O$, the ortho-infinite class, the proportions of the image are linear and the infinity points are correctly represented.
2. When B is positive, the hyper-infinite class, the image is presented in a nonlinear fashion (compressed), and objects short of infinity are represented to be at infinity.
3. When B is negative, the hypo-infinite class, the image is nonlinear; cardboarding results, and objects at infinity are represented closer than infinity.

The C factor of the general equation is made up of variables that determine screen parallax for an object at a given distance from the camera:

$$C = Mf_c t_c$$

Thus C is the product of magnification, focal length of the camera lenses, and interaxial separation. As each increases, so does the screen parallax.

The depth-range equation is then

$$D_N - D_o = \frac{NtK}{C}$$

where D is in the reciprocal unit rhos and K is the rho constant, which for inches is 6000.

The transmission theory provides certain objective tests of image distortion. Two are classified under the heading of stereoscopic magnification: depth magnification, m_d, and width magnification, m_w. A third distortion is called binocular magnification, m_b.

Stereoscopic magnification is defined as the ratio of the stereoscopic image size to the real object size. The two types of stereoscopic distortion are

$$m_d = \frac{Vt}{Mf_c t_c} \left(\frac{B}{Nt} + 1 \right)^2$$

$$m_w = \frac{t}{t_c} \left(\frac{B}{Nt} + 1 \right)$$

The shape ratio μ is defined as

$$\mu = \frac{m_d}{m_w}$$

Binocular magnification is

$$m_b = \frac{Mf_c t_c}{Vt}$$

The British authors claim that stereoscopic magnification and binocular magnification may be perceived as separate entities by trained observers and that some spectators are more sensitive to one than the other.

A circular slide rule device, the Stereomeasure, was built to coordinate the camera variables so that a cinematographer (or stereotechnician, the term used by the authors) might rapidly set up a shot for projection on a given fixed-size screen. The assumption is that the cinematographer would prefer to select the focal length, as is usually the case, and that the other parameters would follow as a result.

The technician need not understand the theory's derivation but could rely on the Stereomeasure and on experience. While the theory might be criticized on the basis of its sheer complexity, which is only hinted at here, the Stereomeasure eliminates complex calculations and the need to select the appropriate relationships.

But there is no getting around the fact that we are dealing with a complex system, which probably cannot be grasped without both mathematical training and filmmaking experience. A good understanding of the psychology of depth perception would not hurt either.

As a formal exposition, the system is hard to fault. It is a thorough job, elegantly executed, even if at times the elegance tends to conceal rather than illuminate. The use of A, B, and C factors, which appear in various relationships, is confusing. Instead of clarifying the physical significance of the system, these factors, it seems to me, obscure what was going on.

In their introduction (1953), the authors explain that they are not engaged in esthetic arguments but rather in questions of a technical nature. This point of view is really difficult to take seriously, since this is an exposition of the techniques of an art form. Yet this attitude may well have permeated their approach and led to substituting rigidity for common sense.

They make a clear exposition of the orthostereoscopic condition and specify it with greater clarity than earlier writers. The condition for orthostereoscopy or geometric congruence occurs when

$$B = O, \qquad t_c = t, \quad \text{and} \quad V = Mf_c$$

In other words, screen parallaxes must be equal to the interocular, the interaxial for photography must be set equal to the interocular, and the size of an object's image as projected on the retina must be the same as it would have been if viewed in "real life."

Whether or not this system is easy to understand has relatively little to do with its basic correctness. There are no guarantees that the universe is explicable—or, if explicable, simple. The system is difficult to understand without a background in the physical sciences or mathematics. Its complexity would not interfere with its utility in the context of equipment design, or in the solving of problems connected with optical printing. But the exposition and difficulty of the concepts make the theory inaccessible to filmmakers.

Another grave problem is the use of reciprocal units. I cannot believe that most people would ever get used to such a system, and the simplification in formalism that results from this choice is offset by unpleasantness in the field. Extreme reductions for interaxial spacing are often called for, which, apart from camera design problems, would in my view lead in many cases to images without satisfying stereoscopic depth. The need for reduced interaxials arises from the exclusion of divergence for infinity or distant points. (There is a similarity here compared with Rule's disallowal of divergence in the parallel projection scheme.)

The authors propose that much of the image might be placed in front of the screen, in theater space. In order to accomplish this, they suggest the addition of a stereowindow printed on the film itself, so that the limitations of the screen surround might be circumvented by providing a window whose boundaries actually have negative parallax. (This suggestion is similar to the practice followed by still stereographers in the mounting of stereographs for projection.) This proposal is a consequence of not allowing divergence for distant points in an effort to extend the depth range of the shot.

The difficulty with this suggestion is that a great range of screen parallaxes, or ΔN, especially those with negative values, would tax the habitual accommodation/convergence response to the very limit. Moreover, printed-on stereowindows will reduce the width of the screen, and this is further aggravated by psychological factors that tend to diminish the size of the image when brought forward, at least according to some accounts (R. Spottiswoode himself, in a change of heart in 1969 in *The Focal Encyclopedia of Film and Television*, p. 775).

It is not at all certain that uniformly good results would be produced from following recommendations prescribed by this system, since not only are its axiomatic bases (that the eyes locate objects in space by convergence) suspect, but also the authors have, for the most part, left out any consideration of the effects of extra-stereoscopic cues. These monocular cues, which are essentially beyond numeration, have so heavy a scaling effect on stereopsis that they cannot be omitted.

It can also be demonstrated that entirely adequate, and even pleasing, depth effects for very distant objects can be supplied with what is called a *B minus* or negative system. It is not necessary, or even desirable, to have screen parallaxes made equal to the value of the interocular for photography of distant vistas, for example. Values for screen parallax of one half or one third of the interocular give better results, since distance in such a case is gauged in terms of monocular cues. Such reduced values for screen parallax help prevent the breakdown of accommodation/convergence and reduce eyestrain.

In summary, the major problem with the Spottiswoode system is that it is very difficult to think in its terms. The formal construction of the theory ultimately precludes its comprehension by people conversant with the technical aspects of filmmaking, and as far as I know no one outside of the Spottiswoode group ever used this transmission system to film a motion picture. Perhaps this quote from the shorter journal version (1952) will make this clear:

> If the director says that he wishes an actor seated at a table to be represented at $N = 0.5$, while another's hand must come out from the screen three-quarters of the way toward him. The concept of the nearness factor is easily grasped, even by studio personnel to whom the rest of the stereo shooting procedure remains something of a mystery; but it affords the connection of ideas most necessary to establish between director and stereotechnician. (p. 253)

Having known a few directors, I believe it is no underestimate of their talent to say that in my wildest dreams I cannot imagine one calling for a table at $N = 0.5$. If this is "the connection of ideas" to bridge the gap between creator and technician, something is terribly wrong.

In the fifteen years following the publication of his transmission system, Raymond Spottiswoode came to realize that this major intellectual effort was not to influence others and provide the basis for a flourishing stereocinema. His tone was pessimistic and discouraged by 1969:

> Even if this were done [technical progress of an improbably high order], it is improbable that the resulting three-dimensional picture would provide a sufficiently increased realism or entertainment value to warrant its extra complexity. 3-D films may play a minor role in the scientific world as they continue to do in that of the still photograph, where they can offer perfect realism for a single viewer with relatively simple equipment. Only the further development of holography will show whether an extra measurable dimension justifies itself commercially in terms of added entertainment value. (p.775)

Nevertheless, the work of Spottiswoode et al. helped to lead to an understanding of a number of key points: the virtues of the crossed-lens-axes system and the full advantage of camera variables in controlling the shape of the stereo image and the depth range of a shot.

POLAROID

The Polaroid Corporation quite obviously had a vested interest in helping photographers achieve good results with stereoscopic photography and projection. Kitrosser (1953) described the Polaroid Interocular Calculator, based, so it seems, on the work of Rule and experimentation done at Polaroid. The Interocular Calculator (which might less confusingly have been named Interaxial Calculator) correlates the width of the projection screen or print with negative width, interaxial distance, focal length, and near and far distances permissible without displaying excessive convergence or divergence. A distinction is made between focal length and lens-film distance, which in most cases are very nearly equal. For what might best be described as extreme closeups, the lens-film distance will exceed the focal length, and that figure ought to be used as the basis for calculations.

The variables of the Polaroid Calculator are arranged on circular scales, and with a little practice a photographer can quickly determine the permissible depth range for a given camera setup, or starting with a depth range requirement set up the desirable camera variables.

The Calculator is a useful device and can help avoid the eyestrain caused by excessive distance between homologous points with negative or positive parallax values. However, it does not take into account extra-stereoscopic cues, such as perspective. In order to increase the depth range of a

shot, it recommends the proportional reduction in interaxial. This will eliminate eyestrain caused by excessive parallax values for distant or very close
homologous image points, but strict adherence to this advice will result in
photographs that lack full three-dimensional depth.

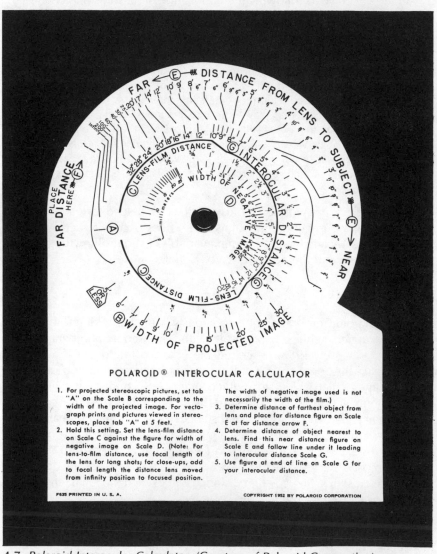

4.7. *Polaroid Interocular Calculator.* (Courtesy of Polaroid Corporation)

chapter 5

Transmission Systems: Modern Developments

NATURAL VISION

The Natural Vision System grew out of Hollywood scriptwriter Milton Gunzburg's attempt to find the proper medium for his story "Sweet Chariot." The script called for shots of automobile engines, and tests in the usual planar process were disappointing.

Julian Gunzburg (1953), an opthalmologist and devoted amateur stereographer, suggested to his brother that the film be shot in 3-D. The Gunzburgs employed the services of cameraman Friend Baker, who designed a rig that would hold two facing Mitchell studio cameras, shooting into a pair of mirrors set at right angles to each other—45-degree angles to the lens axes—an arrangement similar to Dudley's rig for the Festival of Britain. They must have shot tests with their stereocamera in order to demonstrate the system, but "Sweet Chariot" seems to have been abandoned.

The Gunzburgs succeeded in selling their idea to independent producer Arch Obler after having been turned down by major studios, and in December 1952 the film *Bwana Devil* was released in Natural Vision. This started the great Hollywood 3-D craze, and soon major studios were filming in the Natural Vision process itself, or in any one of many similar systems of interlocked cameras.

The hardware, the camera, for such a system is virtually useless without the software, or information needed to do good photography, and Julian Gunzburg served as technical consultant on the set for a number of major studio films.

Gunzburg rejected the notion of controlling the depth range of the subject by varying, usually reducing, the camera interaxial. He also preferred the crossed-lens-axes system and decided on a fixed interaxial of 3.5 in., no matter what focal length was employed. Gunzburg felt that the long focal lengths used for studio work would profit from the increased depth effect to be obtained by an increased interaxial separation. Focal lengths for the Natural Vision camera varied from 35 to 100 mm. (For equivalent 16mm focal lengths, divide by 2; for super 8, by 4.)

Gunzburg argued that by fixing the interaxial he was following nature's practice, which keeps the human interocular fixed. Variations to the interaxial, he reasoned, might produce camera misalignment, leading to "Chinese" parallax, or vertical disparity, which has no depth content and can only produce strain.

Gunzburg advocated the use of variable convergence during the shot. He stands alone in all of the literature with this idea. It is interesting to note that the cinematographers at Universal, with their own rig, used this kind of variable interaxial during shooting. Let me make this clear: The use of convergence to establish the subject in the stereowindow, or the plane of the screen—or to control the depth content of the shot so that compositional elements appear either in screen or in theater space—was accepted. It is this variation of the convergence control during photography that is the most interesting aspect of the Natural Vision System.

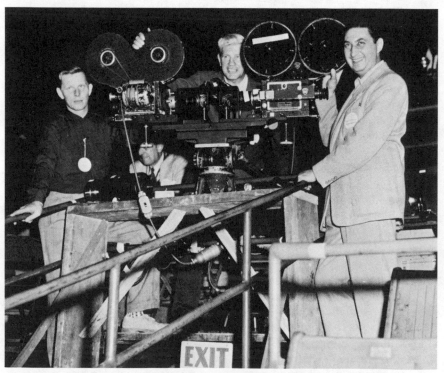

5.1. *Natural Vision camera*. (Gunzberg, "The Story of Natural Vision," *American Cinematographer*, Volume 34:612–6, 1953. Reprinted by permission.)

Suppose the camera dollies in to the foreground subject during a shot. If the camera lens axes are crossed at the subject at the start of the shot, they will be crossed behind the subject at the end of the shot and the subject will be placed in theater space. But by continuously varying the convergence control (like "riding" the focus control) so that the foreground subject remains in the plane of convergence, the subject will remain at the stereowindow, or in the plane of the screen if you prefer, throughout the entire shot during projection. Gunzburg argued again that he was taking his lead from the way in which the human eye functions. After viewing Hollywood films of the period using Gunzburg's variable-convergence method (which he called the variable-parallax method, to distinguish it from Rule's variable-interaxial method), I can say that it can work very well indeed. Old hands at stereography, or those with a conservative streak, might find it to be a violation of established procedure, but it is quite an enjoyable effect to observe. In many instances, if handled with skill, the effect can be concealed. During a pan, for example, we can start with one convergence setting and end up with another. I consider this a genuine contribution to the art.

I used the technique in the feature film, *Rottweiler*, photographed with my organization's system, known as the Future Dimensions process. Filmed in the summer of 1981 in North Carolina, we followed convergence on just about every dolly shot in the picture. The results are completely unobtrusive and helped maintain adequate depth range in many difficult situations. In fact, just about any camera control that can be varied in the appropriate circumstances ought to be varied. This is true for focal length, interaxial, and convergence, and I believe that advanced stereo motion picture cameras will someday allow all these parameters to be controlled by the cinematographer, or perhaps by an on-board computer.

However, I find a fixed interaxial set at 3.5 in. (about 86 mm) to be a grim restriction, probably motivated more by mechanical and optical limitations of the Natural Vision rig than any other factor. Nevertheless, after it had been debugged, the Natural Vision camera produced good results.

For studio photography, I can see how Gunzburg's system could get by with one fixed, and somewhat longish, interaxial. Portraits and medium shots with a 3.5 in. interaxial should appear acceptable, and control of the divergence of background points can be manipulated at will by simply adjusting the distance between performers and background. In documentary work, or when shooting beyond the controlled confines of the studio, a fixed, extended interaxial would be a decided drawback, since the cinematographer cannot usually control the blocking or environment to the same extent as theatrical filmmakers.

Gunzburg also accepted a total divergence of 1° for background homologous points, which is in agreement with the systems proposed by Hill, MacAdam, the Soviets, and the author but in disagreement with the systems of Rule and of Spottiswoode et al.

Since he was an eye physician, Gunzburg asked these interesting questions about stereoscopic vision: What percentage of the people have binocular vision? What percentage will see a stereo picture as a flat picture? What percentage of the people might be expected to be actually disturbed or distressed by the stereo picture? Would stereo do any harm to any viewer?

According to his research, Gunzburg reports that perhaps less than 5 percent of the population will be uncomfortable watching the stereo picture because of a variety of eye defects: "aberrations in the focusing apparatus, abnormalities in fusion functions, imbalance between the eyes in refraction, image size, color balance, and, of course, pathological conditions" (p. 612).

He estimates that "perhaps only 75 percent of the population have so-called normal binocular vision; but the percentage of viewers who would be aware of the stereo effect and benefit from it might bring the total percentage to well over ninety percent" (p. 612).

Gunzburg felt that if many of these correctable eye defects were treated, viewers would then be able to appreciate stereo films. Stereo films can actually alert viewers in need of treatment, and he further believed that stereo films can provide a valuable form of eye-training exercise.

Practically speaking, though, the Natural Vision and other similar double-band systems—because of errors in photography or projection—often produce serious eyestrain for many people with normal vision and, far from being a service to those with defects in vision, turn out to be an irritant to just about everyone.

HILL

The Hollywood motion picture industry spends relatively little on research. Technological improvements have often come from beyond the orbit of the major studios, as was the case for sound, color, and wide- or giant-screen projection.

The Motion Picture Research Council, now defunct, was the major exception to Hollywood's short-sighted indifference to improving motion picture technology. The council, originally part of the Academy of Motion Picture Arts and Sciences, became a separate entity devoted to aiding the Hollywood studios in 1947. It investigated lighting, rear projection and traveling matte procedures, a number of other technical matters, as well as stereoscopic transmission.

The Council's transmission system was the work of Armin J. Hill (1953), and Dr. Hill's circular calculator was offered to the industry to help the cinematographer come to grips with the problems of the new medium.

The mathematical treatment employed by Hill is quite a bit more difficult than anything else encountered in the literature, primarily because Hill's work is based on Luneberg's hypothesis (1947) that perceptual space can be described by a non-Euclidean metric.

Although I am in no position to argue with the mathematical manipulations of Hill's system, implicit in his work are two assumptions that warrant examination. Hill's contribution is based on the variable object magnification, rather than frame magnification, as is the case for other systems, notably the Spottiswoodes'. Object magnification is the ratio of the projected image size to the size of the original object. For example, a man 6 ft tall is photographed and the image is projected on a screen so that it is 12 ft high. The object magnification, or M value, according to Hill, is 2. Object magnification is dependent on frame magnification, since the greater the frame magnification the greater the size of the object's image. (For the exact functional dependence, see page 171) Hill assumes that image distortion is directly related to object magnification, and bases his work on this assumption. "One of the most noticeable effects when stereoscopic pictures are projected on a full-sized theater screen contrasted to their projection on the comparatively small screens used in amateur photography is the distortion in any subject matter which comes forescreen" (p. 468).

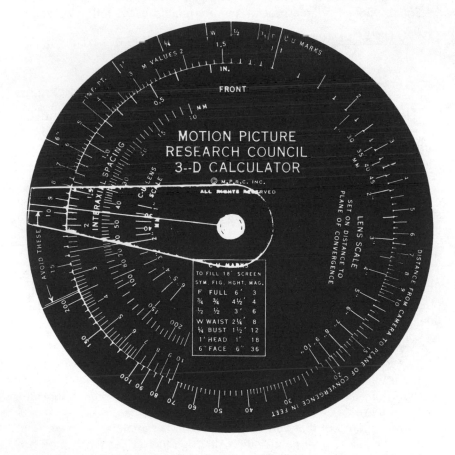

5.2. *Hill's circular calculator.* (Hill, 1953b. Reprinted by permission of *American Cinematographer.*)

Hill is wrong to attribute the distortion to object magnification. He may be confusing distortion with excessive screen parallax caused by large-screen magnification. In any case, I have not observed the effect he describes. The important variable is probably the size of the retinal image. People sit farther away from large screens than from small screens, and an image 1 m wide viewed from 3 m away will cover the same portion of the retina as an image 2 m wide viewed from 6 m away. Object magnification in itself cannot determine the distortion of an image.

Using straightforward Euclidean geometry, Hill derived the equation:

$$\rho = \frac{\rho^1}{\overline{m} + (\overline{m} - 1)\,\rho^1}$$

Here ρ is the distance or nearness ratio, and $\overline{m}$ is the "reduced" magnification given by $m(b/e)$ where m is object magnification and b/e is the ratio of interaxial to interocular distance. Distance (or nearness) ratios are similar to the Spottiswoodes' nearness factor and are related in the following way:

Hill's distance ratio	Spottiswoodes' nearness factor
infinity	0
1	1
−0.5	2
−0.8	5

Next Hill translated these results into a modified bipolar coordinate system, which made it easier for him to transform the results using Luneberg's metric,

$$ds^2 = \operatorname{csch}^2 \gamma \,(\gamma + \mu)\,(\gamma^2 d^2\gamma - d\phi^2 - \cos^2 \phi\, d\Theta^2)$$

As a point of reference for the mystified reader, the metric of Euclidean space is given by the following familiar Pythagorean relationship expressed in the Cartesian form:

$$ds^2 = dx^2 + dy^2 + dz^2$$

Hill then graphically plotted results using his relationships as transformed by the Luneberg metric to study the distortion inherent in photography, given a certain distance from the object compared with image distortion.

He then states the following relationship for interaxial setting:

$$b = e/G\,\rho + a/\rho_y - a$$

Here G is what he calls the "gigantizing" factor, determined empirically and related to object magnification. The circular calculator designed by Hill is based on these theoretical and experimental results.

I must point out that Luneberg's hypothesis remains unproved, more than three decades after publication. Although there does seem to be general agreement that perceptual space and Euclidean space differ, a survey of the literature indicates that the discipline of perceptual psychology, or specifically that portion devoted to the study of stereopsis, has generally passed over Luneberg's work. Whereas Luneberg suggests one particular family of possible metrics, specifically Lobachevskian saddle-shaped space, to describe perceptual space, there is some evidence that another class of metrics may provide a more accurate description.

In particular, Batto (1977) argues that perceptual space is best described not by the Lobachevskian but rather by the Riemannian model. The important point about all of this for stereoscopists is that the basis of Hill's system is suspect.

One approach is to bypass all this hocus-pocus and try to make Hill's calculator work by doing some photography. It was a relatively straightforward job to photostat a reproduction of the calculator and recreate the device by mounting the copies on card stock. A cursor was made out of celluloid, and then the various parts were joined with a brass roundhead fastener. Despite this effort, I could not get useful results from the device, probably because the gigantizing factor G had been calculated for the 35mm format and because the object magnifications for theatrical screen sizes are about seven times greater than those encountered in my work on screens from 1 to 1.7 m wide. It may well be that Hill's calculator did help cinematographers of the 1950s. I simply have not been able to verify this.

THE NON-EUCLIDEAN NATURE OF PERCEPTUAL SPACE

The object of this study is to aid in creating easy-to-view and pleasant-to-observe stereoscopic motion pictures, primarily employing the polarized-light method of image selection. It is not intended to be a text on the psychology of depth perception, and the discussion of this branch of perceptual psychology is limited to that which may help unravel the highly specialized puzzle of transmission theory. Readers seeking a broader understanding of stereopsis are advised to consult Gregory (1973), Charnwood (1964), Kaufman (1974), Ittelson (1960), or the fine bibliography in Rock (1975).

One of the most difficult areas in the study of binocular depth perception has to do with the nature or geometry of perceptual space, and its relationship to media such as painting or the photographed image. Spottiswoode et al., assuming that perceptual space is congruent with Euclidean axioms, arrived at a certain transmission system, while Hill, adopting Luneberg's tenet that perceptual space follows the hyperbolic geometry of Lobachevsky, arrived at an entirely different system. It is necessary to understand, even in simple terms, the basis of these arguments for a fuller understanding of the history of stereoscopic motion picture technology.

Leonardo introduced the concept of perspective in his notebooks, according to Gregory (1973), as an exercise in geometry. Leonardo considered the perspective view of an image to be a projection of the spatial objects onto a plane surface, specifically a sheet of glass, a technique in the form of the camera obscura later used by Dutch painters. Leonardo was interested in considerations that went beyond geometrical perspective, and he added to his discussion of perspective aerial perspective, the blue haze in front of distant objects, and shadow and shade. Although specific rules may be laid down for the geometrical portion of this system, the application of aerial perspective to painting is quite another matter and defies exact quantification.

The rules of perspective are now taken for granted in our culture. First enunciated by painters, then codified by opticians and cameramakers, it is still not at all clear whether perspective is a discovery or an invention of the Renaissance. Do the rules of perspective shed light on innate truths, or do they present an arbitrary but satisfying system for ordering perceptual space?

We know from the history of painting that at other times in other cultures there were other ways of representing the depth of painted objects. Chinese perspective placed objects that were supposed to be farther away higher up in a composition, and retained the constant size. Zulus, who live in round huts in clearings in deep forests, have trouble interpreting photographs or paintings that incorporate the rules of Renaissance perspective.

The images projected on the retina more or less conform to the laws of geometric perspective, but the mind's interpretation of those images goes far beyond this easily codified system. At the core of our understanding of stereopsis lies this problem: How do these two retinal images, one very slightly different from the other, become a single stereoscopic view of the world? How can minute horizontal shifts caused by the slight displacement (65-mm nominal) of the two centers of perspective be turned into a new sensation, stereopsis?

A clue to the puzzle is that these left- and right-retinal images, formed according to the rules of perspective assuming Euclidean space, ultimately produce a new kind of perceptual space that is not Euclidean.

In my survey of the literature, I cannot find a modern authority who would disagree with the statement that visual space is non-Euclidean. To people who are not mathematical specialists nor experts in perceptual psychology, this must seem very peculiar, since the immediate environment as we know it—the rooms and the streets of our world—quite clearly reflects the ordering of space according to Euclidean postulates.

The one readily understandable and pertinent quality of space is the concept of the shortest distance between two points, defined as the *geodesic*. For Euclidean space, the geodesic is the straight line, in terms of familiar Cartesian coordinates:

$$ds^2 = dx^2 + dy^2 + dz^2$$

where s is the distance between the two points. This is the quadratic differential form of the theorem of Pythagoras. (Written this way to match Hill and Luneberg's form for easier comparison.)

The shortest distance between two points on the surface of a sphere, like the earth, is not a straight line but is formed by the intersection of a plane passing through the center of the sphere with the surface of the sphere itself, and is the minor arc of a great circle. The shortest distance between two points on the surface of a sphere of radius 1 is given by the quadratic differential

$$ds^2 = dx^2 + \sin^2 x \cdot dy^2$$

Since the work of Einstein even little children may be heard to talk about the curvature of space, which in relativistic terms tells us that the shape of space is determined by the distribution of bodies, or the mass of those bodies in space.

Although the Euclidean metric, or rule for the everyday space of a manifold of points, is usually given by the Pythagorean relationship, in the context of what we have just discussed it may seem less peculiar to the reader now that this is just one arbitrary way of describing space; it is used because it is convenient to do so. For building houses, laying out city streets, or constructing furniture, the implied manifold is Euclidean and we accept the resulting metric of this space—that the shortest distance between two points is a straight line— and all the other qualities of Euclidean space following from this, for example, that parallel straight lines never meet.

Through day-to-day use, the Euclidean view and the commonsense view have become congruent. Therefore it may seem baffling to state that the shape of visible or perceptual space has been incontrovertibly shown in repeatedly duplicated experiments to be non-Euclidean. These "alley" experiments, conducted by Ames, Hillebrand, and Blumenfeld, are a variation of experiments to determine the shape of the horopter. Aguilinus conceived the horopter, or the location of points in visual space producing retinal images on corresponding points, to be a straight line. Others, notably Vieth and Mueller, have shown that a circle or sphere may better describe the horopter. Later technical modifications to the shape of the horopter, taking into account the location of the nodal point of the eye's lens and the center of the eyeball's rotation, are essentially variations based on the Euclidean manifold.

Today it is believed that corresponding retinal points are not laid out symmetrically. Because of these asymmetries in the shapes of the retinas there will be departures from the simple horopter.

The alley experiments are based on lines drawn at right angles to the horopter. One would expect that subjects asked to order targets in straight lines would order these targets, more or less, along straight lines. This does not occur. Since experiments depart significantly from predictions based on Euclidean assumptions, it is reasonable to assume that perceptual space is best described in terms of non-Euclidean geometry.

Luneberg, working at the Dartmouth Eye Institute, published his "Mathematical Analysis of Binocular Vision" (1947), based on the experiments of

Ames—also at Dartmouth—and others who worked on alley experiments. These showed that the horopter derived from the assumption of a Euclidean manifold, or simple plane geometry, was incorrect. Luneberg sought to uncover the appropriate manifold, or shape of perceptual space, and in doing so he expressed the metric or rule for that space

$$ds^2 = \frac{1}{\sinh^2 \sigma(\gamma + \mu)}(\sigma^2 d\gamma^2 + d\phi^2 + \cos^2 \phi \, d\Theta^2)$$

Unlike the usual constructs employed by perceptual psychologists, this formalization does not explain in terms of a model, like Kepler's projection theory. It simply states that perceptual space can be described by this metric. Presumably the constants in the expression have physical significance.

Whether or not Luneberg successfully achieved his goal is impossible to say, at least based on a reading of subsequent literature. Following his death, an attempt to continue his work by Hardy et al. (1953) produced equivocal results, with the authors remarking that the project had to be abandoned because they were unable to obtain the help of, or even find, a mathematician of Luneberg's originality.

Suppes (1977) calls into question Luneberg's results by claiming, for one thing, that alley experiments performed outside the smaller experimental space of the laboratory produce different results. Suppes states that experiments performed in a large, open space, on lawns for example, do not conform to Luneberg's metric for hyperbolic space. But Suppes, in the best available review of the subject, does not doubt the basic concept that perceptual space is non-Euclidean.

This is an exceedingly difficult subject. In a sense, it seeks to explain in mathematical terms our relationship to the visual world, or to provide an interface between the world of visual sensation and the mind.

Spottiswoode et al., by ignoring this, worked out a system that simply does not correspond to the interface of humans and the stereoscopic recording of the visual field.

Hill jumped the gun and used an unproved theory to justify his work. Even if the model of Luneberg should prove to be correct, and there seem to be few Lunebergeans at work to verify this, Hill's manipulations are still suspect and the experimental basis for his work is doubtful.

It is important to remember that most photographic imaging systems, motion pictures included, use optical systems that have been made to conform to the Euclidean metric of visual space or, in other words, to the perspective projection first and most clearly enunciated by Leonardo in the sixteenth century. The perspective described by Leonardo is based on some innate relationship between the human nervous system and tangible space on the one hand, and on the arbitrary needs of the painter to interpret the visible world in terms of a flat or planar surface, i.e., the visible field. It may seem inconceivable to us that the choice of rectilinear perspective is in fact arbitrary, yet had Leonardo painted on the inner or outer surface of a sphere or a cylinder, different sorts of perspective rules would have been formulated.

For centuries, Western man has learned how to look at the visual space that surrounds him, in part because of his relationship with media. Renaissance painters have taught us how to look at the world. Specifically, they have taught us that the objects of space are ordered according to one particular and arbitrarily chosen system of perspective, not any better or any worse than the systems used by the Chinese or the Zulus.

It should come as no surprise that lens designers have sought to create pleasing images that conform to this cultural bias. Perhaps the truth of this assertion can be indicated by those exceptions to the usual optical modalities, the fisheye lenses that have come into use in recent years and the large-screen motion picture systems that were in vogue in the 1950s and 1960s.

Fisheye lenses, a kind of ultra-wide-angle lens, are designed to conform to projection on the surface of a sphere rather than on a plane. They exhibit what is usually called barrel distortion. If images taken with such optics are projected on the inside surface of a sphere, they will reassume their natural shape.

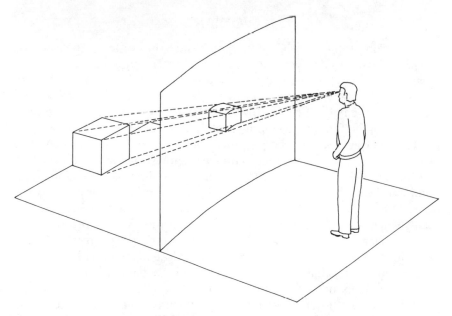

5.3. *A different kind of perspective.* Image of an object projected onto a cylindrical surface. Photographic optics are generally corrected to produce linear perspective, since images will be projected onto the surface of a plane. However, it is also possible to produce lenses that are geometrically corrected for other surfaces, such as a section of a cylinder, if, for example, projection is to take place on a Cinerama-type screen. Such optical systems have been used for 70mm photography and projection under the trade names D-150 and Ultra-Panavision.

The important aspect of all this, for the stereoscopic filmmaker, is that the lenses conform to arbitrarily enforced standards of rectilinear perspective. The spatial images are recorded by a pair of Euclidean image makers. We are then left with the problem of how this Euclidean imaging system interfaces with the eye-brain. It is not as if the imaging system is some sort of a neutral entity; synergistic qualities occur in terms of the interface of this optical-mechanical system with the human nervous system.

Given the present state of knowledge about binocular stereopsis, a theoretical basis for a stereoscopic transmission system does not exist; such a formulation is premature. It may turn out that it is entirely beyond numeration because of the concomitant factors of extra-stereoscopic depth cues. A parallel may be drawn between Leonardo's codification of the rules of perspective made up of a strictly specifiable geometric projection and the unspecifiable variables of aerial perspective—shadow and shade, and so forth—which Leonardo left to painterly discretion.

We will see a different approach to the problem of a transmission theory in the work of MacAdam (1954), Ovsjannikova and Slabova (1975), and myself. Before proceeding to these discussions, it will be instructive for the sake of completeness to review the work of Levonian.

LEVONIAN

Levonian (1954a, 1954b, 1955) published his system, *Stereoscopic Cinematography: Its Analysis with Respect to the Transmission of the Visual Image*, as his Master's thesis at the University of Southern California. The experimental basis was carried out with a pair of interlocked Kodak Cine Special 16mm cameras; the mathematical analysis, in particular the error analysis, and the formal development of the subject are good.

Levonian accepts Luneberg's version of the non-Euclidean nature of visual space, but he claims that "Luneberg shows that when the convergence angle of the eyes is small (as it is in 3-D motion pictures), the visual world can be approximated by the Euclidean manifold." However, as is known to mathematicians specializing in the field, " . . . a metric referring to points which are infinitely close also determines metric relations of points which are far apart" (Luneberg, 1947). In other words, the expression for the geodesic for points in a space which are very close together will also determine the metric for that space. For this reason, Levonian's small-angle assumption may not be correct.

Nevertheless, he employs the modified bipolar coordinates used by Luneberg to derive his system. His system is similar to that of the Spottiswoodes except that he has used angular measure rather than line elements as a basis. He then formulates expressions that are similar to the familiar depth range expression, but in terms of trigonometric functions. Perhaps his most peculiar assertion is that the shape of the stereoscopic image may be controlled by varying the plane (or point) of convergence at the time of photography. The camera angle of convergence suggested by his system at the time of photography is an effort to obtain a pleasing image. But this will not provide the needed correction, since the shape or depth of the stereoscopic image is independent of the convergence angle. This was understood by Wheatstone, Rule, and MacAdam, among others. It has been repeatedly verified experimentally that the shape of the stereoscopic image is independent of the convergence angle used for photography or for viewing.

In my view, Levonian's transmission system will not provide useful recommendations for stereoscopic cinematography; but, as with Spottiswoode, there is much of use here for equipment designers. Levonian's analysis of the registration problems in a stereoscopic projection system, and in blowups to larger formats, is valuable, as is his analysis of geometric distortion. His empirically verifiable conclusion is that asymmetrical camera convergence—say, with one camera set at right angles to the interaxial base line—will produce little more distortion than symmetrical convergence, with equal angles chosen for the camera lens axes. Practically speaking, it is much simpler and quicker to set the angle of a single camera.

The problem of keystoning in a practical stereoscopic projection system has been greatly exaggerated by other workers (especially Dewhurst, 1954). In a well-designed system, misalignment of homologous image points due to keystoning will be very low, especially over the major or central portion of the screen, and shape distortions will also be of little consequence for most subjects.

MacADAM

David L. MacAdam's paper "Stereoscopic Perception of Size, Shape, Distance and Direction" (1954) had a very beneficial effect on my research. MacAdam was a researcher at Kodak, given the job of establishing standards for mounting Stereo Realist format slides. It turns out to be a difficult task to mount these separated left and right stereogram transparencies accurately. In the course of his research, MacAdam became interested in the problems of stereoscopic motion picture projection, and he formulated recommendations for photography based on perspective considerations. Unfortunately, his paper was published after the stereo bubble burst, too late to make a practical contribution.

MacAdam's thesis is that

> serious distortions can be avoided if stereoscopic pictures are shown with nearly correct perspective. That means that each person or object in the projected picture should fill just about the same angle at the eyes of the observers as he did at the camera [$V = Mf_c$ consideration]. There seems to be a liberal tolerance on this requirement, so that the familiar rule that the focal length of the projector should be twice the focal length of the camera is satisfactory in most theaters. However, in the past, this rule has been violated frequently. The resulting false perspective is often noticeable, but not objectionable in flat motion pictures. (p. 272)

He goes on to say that it is not possible to compensate for these perspective distortions by varying the camera interaxial. This is, quite obviously, entirely at odds with the systems proposed by Spottiswoode et al.

MacAdam tells us:

> Objects photographed with telephoto lenses, and exhibited at greater visual angles than they subtended at the camera, appear too thin. This is called the "cardboard" effect and is a direct result of false perspective. Nothing can fully remedy this, except to reduce the magnification or to put the observer farther from the screen, so as to restore the angular subtenses of the original scene with respect to the camera. In most cases, the required distance from the screen exceeds that for which stereopsis is experienced, and the perception then does not differ in effect from conventional single-image projection. (p. 285)

He also comments, "Use of camera separations less than the interocular distance is usually not troublesome. The result is intermediate between binocular and monocular perceptions, so that conflicts [between stereoscopic and monocular cues] are reduced" (p. 281).

And to drive the point home:

> . . . it is no exaggeration to point out that no choice of camera separation can eliminate false perspective, or correct distortions caused by false perspective. On the other hand, if perspective is correct, then considerable variations of camera separations seem to be tolerable. The same cannot be said for considerable deviations from correct perspective, even when the camera separation is equal to the normal distance between the two eyes. (p. 282)

In support of his argument, MacAdam quotes from Lord Charnwood's *Essay on Binocular Vision* (reprinted 1965): "Stereopsis has no scale and is capable of many interpretations, the choice of interpretation being made in response to some outside factor. The most important of these is recollection of past experience, which is generally able to select the scale factor which makes possible a solution compatible with the subject's expectations" (p. 283).

MacAdam's point of view is that stereopsis is scaled to perspective cues, Charnwood's "recollection of past experience."

While the primary emphasis in MacAdam's paper is on stereoscopic motion pictures, he manages to give a fine review of the subject of photographic perspective. In drawings like the one reproduced, as Figure 5.4, he shows the effect of three camera locations and the resulting perspectives of two blocks and a wall. The rearward block is twice the height of the close one. The progression from left to right illustrates the use of telephoto, normal, and wide-angle lenses.

> For an observer just as far in front of the screen as the camera is shown to be in front of the nearest object, the perspective is correct. The observer gets a correct idea of the shapes and relative locations of the objects. If he

recognizes any one of the objects in the scene and knows its size, then he perceives its distance correctly and therefore correctly perceives the distances and sizes of all the rest of the objects.

The drawing on the left shows the perspective, with overlap, obtained with a camera located twice as far away as previously. If the resulting picture is viewed so that the image of the foremost object subtends the same visual angle as previously, but twice as great an angle as it did at the camera, then false perspective results. The observer gets the wrong ideas of the shapes and relative locations of the objects. If he recognizes the front object, he may perceive its front face as being the correct size, at the same distance as he formerly perceived it. But it and all other objects appear too thin, and too close together. At the right, the camera is shown at only one-quarter the original distance. If the resulting picture is viewed so that the front object subtends the same angle as previously, but one-quarter the angle it did, false perspective again results. If the observer recognizes the front object, he may perceive its front face as being the correct size, at the same distance as formerly. But it and all other objects will appear to be elongated in the direction away from him. (p. 273)

Although this is a description of perspective perceived by a viewer observing planar images, it is practically a casebook of stereoscopic distortions that will result from similar camera setups when projected and viewed on a screen.

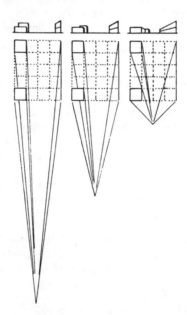

5.4. *Three viewpoints.* "Ground plans of three camera locations and (above) outlines of resulting perspectives of two blocks and a wall. The more distant block is a cube. The closer block is only one-half as high." (MacAdam, 1954. Reprinted with permission from the *SMPTE Journal*, Volume 62:271–93. Copyright 1954, Society of Motion Picture and Television Engineers, Inc.)

Placing this in the context of stereoscopy, MacAdam writes:

> Perceived space is dependent primarily on monocular clues, most frequently the known size of familiar objects which are naturally visualized at such distances that they appear of normal size. Stereoscopic perception then spaces all other objects relative to that distance. This is the only, and quite subsidiary, role of stereopsis in the perception of distance. If the perspective in the picture is incorrect, that is, if the object on which the perception is based was not at a distance from the camera equal to the distance at which it is perceived, then stereopsis emphasizes the false perspective. (p. 285)

MacAdam also discusses what is called movement or motion parallax, which is a monocular depth cue to distance resulting from the continuously varying perspective when you move your head or change your point of view. MacAdam believes that because movement parallax is missing from stereoscopic projection, many individuals who may have difficulty properly perceiving stereoscopic films are actually more sensitive to the movement parallax cue than to stereopsis. When observing a stereoscopic projection, you can confirm this lack of movement parallax by moving your head from side to side. There will be no change in perspective, but rather a sheering or twisting of the projected objects. MacAdam considers this a defect in our stereoscopic system and suggests that a moving camera be frequently employed to create the effect of motion parallax.

MacAdam also believes that the use of zoom lenses will result in false perspective if employed for stereoscopic cinematography.

> The enhancement of depth perception produced by movement of the camera toward the scene cannot be produced by the use of the zoom lens . . . . Pictures taken with zoom lenses may give some sense of approach to the scene. But the sense of depth is merely produced by the enlarged picture, and suffers from the changing distortions as the picture is magnified up to and beyond the size for correct perspective . . . . In stereoscopy, therefore, it is essential to move the camera toward the scene, instead of using zoom lenses, if the sense of approach is desired. Otherwise, the perception will be produced that the scene is being pushed and squashed toward the observer, with the foreground objects and actors shrinking in an unaccountable and perverse manner. (p. 278)

He also discusses the role of convergence in stereoscopic perception; the point he makes is especially important, since many present workers persist in believing that convergence of the eyes is the most important stereoscopic mechanism for locating objects in space.

> If one of a projected stereoscopic pair of pictures is moved sidewards during observation, a powerful perception of approach or recession of the entire scene is momentarily experienced. An excruciating pain may be felt if an excessive divergence is produced. But if the pair is left at a new and not painful separation, the scene will quite soon resume its formerly per-

ceived location and dimensions. During the movement, which of course does not change the visual angles subtended by the images of any objects, each object appears to undergo a rapid change of apparent size, proportional to its apparently changing distance. The size perceived at the end of the movement is so unnatural that the reinterpretation of the whole scene follows, more or less unconsciously and quickly, so as to restore the perception of the normal size, and consequently to re-establish the original perception of the distances. (p. 283)

The lateral shifts of one stereoscopic image with respect to the other are fully equivalent to changes in convergence angle at the time of photography. It is a relatively simple procedure to shift the images as described, and generally speaking, MacAdam's observation is entirely correct. Levonian suggests that corrections in shape distortions can be made by choosing the proper plane of convergence at the time of photography. He is wrong.

MacAdam is substantially correct, I believe, in his assertion that stereopsis is scaled to extra-stereoscopic cues and to perspective cues in particular, and that correct perspective is the way to achieve undistorted stereoscopic images. But pleasing, even if slightly distorted, images can be produced through reductions of the interaxial spacing when used in conjunction with wide-angle optics. Although such compensations may not arrive at a theoretically perfect solution to the problem of stereoscopic distortion, superbly satisfying images can result for this kind of manipulation of camera variables.

MacAdam makes the point that perspective distortions are accepted by viewers when watching planar films. For example, telephoto or long-focal-length photography viewed from any place but in the back of the theater will have substantial perspective distortion, but people have come to accept this flattening of perspective.

MacAdam holds that the addition of stereopsis tends to exaggerate or exacerbate perspective distortions. The pertinent question is whether the distortion is now perceived as objectionable merely because we are unaccustomed to it, given our relative stereoscopic naiveté, or whether we are up against some innate violation of the principles of perception. A strict adherence to MacAdam's concept would place grave limitations on a craft that is already substantially limited with respect to planar filmmaking. The use of telephoto lenses in stereoscopy is indeed difficult, not only because of perspective distortion but to a large extent because increased magnification leads to increased screen parallax which can produce unpleasant divergence.

I do not know whether MacAdam's work involved the use of zoom lenses or whether his suspicions about them come from reasoning alone. Because of his opinions, I was prejudiced against experimenting with zoom optics, despite the fact that these were at my disposal. However, my curiosity finally was aroused, and at the instigation of my research associate, Michael Starks, I undertook my first stereoscopic zoom photography.

MacAdam's description of the stereoscopic zoom is entirely incorrect. I can find no mention in the literature of anyone having made stereoscopic zooms, so there is some likelihood that Starks and I performed the first such zooms in the summer of 1977. This photography and subsequent work has convinced me that, if properly executed, stereoscopic zooms work perfectly well and exhibit none of the expected perspective distortions. Stereoscopic zooms seem to work almost as well as planar zooms, but care must be taken not to produce excessive screen parallaxes through high magnification, say at the end of a zoom-in. Further, the plane of convergence must be set with extreme accuracy to prevent conflicts of stereopsis and interposition with the screen surround. With care, stereo zooms work.

INTERLUDE

Most of the important works in stereoscopic transmission theory were published in the early 1950s, coinciding with the tremendous interest in stereoscopy in the theatrical cinema. In this context, one ought to include Dewhurst's *Introduction to 3-D* (1954) and Ivanov's (not the inventor of the raster screen) *Stereocinematography* (1956). The former has a strong emphasis on prism devices for combining both images on a single band of film. The latter looks to be of great interest, but there is no English translation.

For the next two decades, very little in the field appeared. It is possible to single out Valyus's *Stereoscopy* (1962), which fortunately has been translated from the Russian. It does not concentrate on cinema but includes many sections of interest, although specific advice for the filmmaker is not to be found. An interesting article by Herman, "Principles of Binocular 3-D Displays with Applications to Television" (1971), attempts to show that a television stereopair cannot be successfully displayed using a panoramagram screen.

It is also worth mentioning the April 1974 issue of *American Cinematographer*, although this is primarily interesting as background and "fan" information and makes no specific contribution to transmission theory.

THE SOVIET SYSTEM

The Russian efforts in stereocinematography began in 1940 with the work of director N. Ekk and cameraman N. Renov in their film *Day Off in Moscow*. This was a short subject, presumably projected either anaglyphically or using the polarized light methods for image selection. In 1941, the feature length film *The Concert,* directed by A. Andievskij and shot by D. Surenskij, was projected in the raster screen system invented by S. P. Ivanov.

In an article in Russian entitled "Is 3-D Cinematography?" by Boltjanskij, Komar, and Ovsjannikova (1975), a brief historical outline is given of Soviet stereoscopic cinematographic efforts. It is evident that the Soviets have had an opportunity to develop this medium continuously, with a more-or-less steady production of feature and short films. Cinematographers have sharpened their skills working on many productions over the years. No comparable opportunity has existed in any other society. Surenskij, for example, shot nine stereoscopic films from 1941 through 1970.

NIKFI, the Motion Picture and Photography Scientific Research Institute, an organization operating both to standardize and to advance motion picture technology, has developed the Stereo 70 three-dimensional system, a sensible and intelligent design. This kind of unified research and development effort has no counterpart in the West. My source for this Russian research is an article by Ovsjannikova and Slabova, "Technical and Technological Principles 'Stereo 70' " (1975), which I had translated. These articles did not make their way to American libraries until two years after their Soviet publication had taken place, and I did not have access to English versions until July 1977. After studying the Russian material, I was faced with two conflicting responses. The recommendations for varying camera parameters are very similar to what I had worked out. If I had had earlier access to the article mentioned above, I would have had a far easier, but less interesting, time of attempting to establish these cinematographic variables. The Soviets were the first to publish a workable system for varying camera parameters, and I feel able to confirm this, since I spent two years independently establishing similar recommendations. To be anticipated in this way, the reader may well understand, led to a certain annoyance on the one hand; but on the other, it was pleasing to have arrived at a similar formulation. In terms of formal development, the reader will see that my approach is different.

The optical arrangement of the Soviet system is similar to the one employed by Paillard in a Bolex 16mm system in 1953. Two matched objectives, mounted side by side in a single lens barrel, establish the appropriate interaxial separation for photography through prism systems. Both Leitz and Zeiss offered devices like this prior to the Bolex system for their 35mm still cameras, the Leica and Contax.

By using such an optical arrangement and the 70mm format, the design allows for adjacent placement of two large-size frames, which of course do not suffer from the synchronization problems inherent in two-band systems. Moreover, the use of 70mm film and the existing 70mm cameras allows for the utilization of the existing 70mm infrastructure developed originally for large-screen projection.

The drawings of the Stereo 70 format show stereopairs with projector apertures some 16.7 by 23 mm, with a diagonal of 28 mm. These figures are to within a millimeter or so of the 35mm Edison aspect ratio format. Essentially, then, the Stereo 70 system uses two 35mm Edison aspect ratio frames for stereopairs side by side on the same stock. A suggestion put forth by Chris Condon of Stereovision (*American Cinematographer*, April 1974) is similar but reduces the standard 70mm five-perforation pulldown to three, to produce two smaller but wider aspect ratio (1.85:1) frames and an accompanying saving in film stock. The virtue of the Soviet system, as it stands, is that no modification of the camera or projector intermittent need be undertaken, whereas Condon's suggestion entails changes to the basic mechanism.

(Condon has built both three- and five-perforation machines, and his work may predate the Soviet 70mm efforts.)

One important question is whether or not modern audiences in the West will accept the Edison aspect ratio format, in an era in which theatrical presentations are mostly wide-screen. There is no basic incompatibility between stereo and wide-screen. The choice probably will be based on the arbitrary whims of fad and fashion.

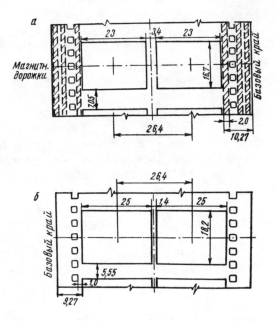

5.5. *Soviet Stereo 70 format.* Top shows projection standards; bottom, camera. Both camera film and prints are on stock 70mm wide. In the West, we use 65mm stock for camera film and use 70mm-wide film for prints only. The Stereo 70 format is identical to the System D-70 offered by Future Dimensions to the Hollywood film industry. (Ovsjannikova and Slabova, 1975)

The Soviets have modified four types of 70mm cameras, including studio reflex, aerial, handheld, and high-speed (slow-motion) models, and a wide variety of optics are available ranging in focal lengths from 28 to 300 mm with available interaxial separations from 26 to 105 mm.

Projection is straightforward: simply placing and correctly adjusting the stereoptic on the 70 mm projector. Projection parameters are described in detail by A. N. Shatskaya in "The Range of Basic Parameters for a Stereo Projector" (1975). For the polarized-light method of image selection, the optics closely resemble the Paillard stereo lens, but a wider interaxial base is needed for the autostereoscopic screen. The same film may be projected using polarized-light image selection, or onto a lenticular screen for 3-D without glasses, but the former appears to be the greatly preferred method.

In the West, 65mm-wide original camera film is release-printed in 70mm, with the additional print width devoted to soundtrack area. The Soviets shoot and print on 70mm-wide stock. There are six magnetic sound tracks used on 70mm print stock, for impressively rich stereophonic sound. Very little 65mm photography is done in the West, since practically all theatrical production is in the 35mm format. For release, producers can choose to blow up their product to the larger format for "road show" presentation.

The Soviets wisely present their Stereo 70 films in relatively small houses of, say, 400 seats, on screens 15 or 20 ft wide. This allows extremely bright projection and relatively low values for screen parallax. This system, or variations of it, is perfectly suited to the many small theaters in the United States cut down from larger houses or built as multiple theater complexes.

The Soviets use the crossed-lens-axes system, and with reference to the drawing shown here, they label the following variables. The top drawing shows the camera optical system without a prism attachment; the bottom one shows the system with a prism attachment. Without the prism, the base B is about 26mm. As pointed out, larger interaxial spacings with various prism attachments are possible. Lateral shifts of the lenses are also possible for setting convergence. The focal length is F, the distance to the plane of convergence is L_p, point O is a midpoint on the plane of convergence, M a point in space in front of the plane, and Q a point behind the plane of

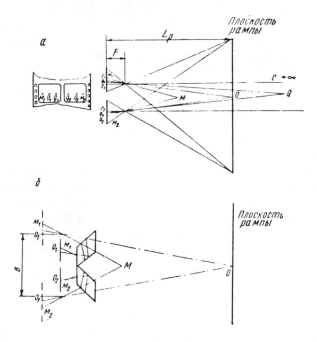

5.6. *The geometry of projection and camera optics of Stereo 70.* Projection (top); photography through prisms (bottom). (Ovsjannikova and Slabova, 1975)

convergence. C is considered to be an infinity point. Lowercase letters signify the points imaged on the plane of the film, so that o_1 and o_2 will coincide if the frames are laid on top of each other, or projected to the crossed-lens-axes standard. Points m_1 and m_2 will then have a film parallax of p_m, points q_1 and q_2 a film parallax of p_q, and infinity points will have a parallax of p_∞.

By definition, parallax values will be negative for the object M, and positive for object points Q and C. Object point O will appear to be in the plane of the screen upon projection, with M in theater space and Q and C in screen space.

The coefficient of projection magnification (or what we have simply called magnification or frame magnification) is given by the expression

$$K = \frac{A_3}{a_\kappa}$$

where A_3, is the width of the screen and a_k the width of the frame. If we define L_3 as the distance from the audience to the screen, B_3 as the interocular of the viewer, p as the screen parallax, and D as the apparent distance from the observer to the spacial image of a point, then—in a relationship I believe was first given by Spottiswoode et al.—we have

$$D = L_3 \; \frac{B_3}{B_3 - P_3}$$

When the object point has zero parallax, or is in the plane of the screen, $D = L_3$. If the image is in theater space, then $D < L_3$, corresponding to a negative parallax. For example, if B_3 is taken to be 65 mm and $P_3 = -65$ mm, given a viewer distance L_3 at 2000 mm, then D, the apparent distance, is 1000 mm, or 1 m, halfway to the viewer, which seems entirely reasonable. If we were to take the case where screen parallax is 65 mm, then we see that D must be equal to ∞, which also seems reasonable. When $D > L_3$, parallax is positive.

It is important to note that the Soviets use the term *seeming* or *apparent* distance for D, and this exercise, based on location of object points when imaged on a stereoscopic screen, does not take into account extra-stereoscopic cues or the fact that convergence itself is not a reliable depth cue.

The maximum value or limit of screen parallax is taken to be a constant called $p_{\infty \, 3}$. In point of fact, this value would depend on the interocular of the observer, but an average value for B_3 is assumed. The limit of parallax on the film, then, is

$$P_{\text{а л л}} = \frac{P_3}{K} = \frac{B}{K}$$

We should be familiar with the form of this expression, since film parallax multiplied by frame magnification gives us screen parallax. If $p_3 > B_3$, we then will have a divergent condition in which the optical axes of the eyes are towed or turned outward. Slight divergence is allowed in the Soviet system, a maximum of 1° total divergence, or ½° for each eye. This practice is condoned by Hill and MacAdam but disavowed by Rule and by Spottiswoode et al. Practically speaking, it becomes all but impossible to do successful stereoscopic cinematography without slight divergence in certain shots.

For a given film parallax, larger values of K will result in increased divergence; so, strictly speaking, films should be shot for one size screen. The lens-raster or autostereoscopic screen used in the Soviet Union, which does not require glasses, is 4 m wide, and the aluminized screen for the polarized light method of image selection is up to 8 m (20 ft) wide. As a compromise, films are shot for a screen 5 m wide.

Ovsjannikova and Slabova emphasize that "stereopsis does not lend itself to strict mathematical evaluation." They briefly discuss the concept of orthostereoscopy, but they point out that the image is generally greater in size than the object photographed. This, of course, will be true to a greater extent for screens used for the projection of theatrical films than for those used for the projection of smaller-format films, such as the super 8 format employed in much of my study.

They then define what they term the scale M, and the perspective θ of a stereoscopic effigy. These characteristics are determined by the ratio of focal length of the camera lens, the distance of the filmed object, the projection magnification, and the distance of the viewer from the screen.

$$M \;=\; \frac{F}{L_p} \quad K = \frac{L_o}{L_p}$$

$L_o = FK$ (in our terms, $V = Mf_c$). This is one of the conditions for orthostereoscopy. The authors have stated the relationship between frame and object magnification, where M is object magnification and K frame magnification.

The derivation of this relationship, it seems, does not appear in the literature, and this is a good place for me to give it. The drawing using Soviet notation shows the related conditions for the object being filmed, and as its effigy would appear upon projection. By definition, we have

$$M \;=\; \frac{H}{h}$$

$$K \;=\; \frac{A_3}{a_k}$$

By similar triangles, we have

$$\frac{h}{A_0} = \frac{H}{A_3}$$

or

$$A_3 \;=\; \frac{H A_0}{h}$$

Then

$$A_3 = MA_0 = Ka_k$$

or

$$M = \frac{a_k}{A_0} K$$

Since

$$\frac{a_k}{A_0} = \frac{F}{L_p}$$

we have

$$M = \frac{F}{L_p} K$$

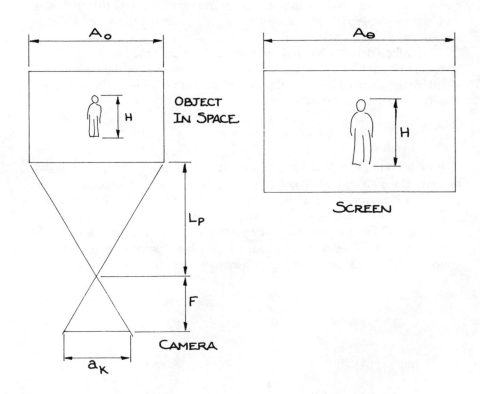

5.7. *The relationship between frame and object magnification.*

Given this relationship, it should be possible to compare the Euclidean portion of Hill's development, done in terms of object magnification, with the development in Spottiswoode, which follows frame magnification. Up to the introduction of the Luneberg metric, the two ought to correspond.

The Soviet authors then give the coefficient of depth transmission θ, or the perspective characteristic, as the ratio of the distance of the viewer from the screen when the orthostereoscopic or correct perspective condition is fulfilled (which they call the *basic* distance) to any given distance for the viewer from the screen:

$$\theta = \frac{L_3}{L_0}$$

When $L_3 < L_0$, θ gives the degree of "compression." When $L_3 > L_0$, θ gives the degree of relaxation.

The authors note that the character of projected space is determined by the selection of focal length and that short focal lengths tend to "stress" or strengthen the depth sense, in which case $\theta \geq 2$, and long focal lengths give a weakened depth sense, where $\theta \approx .3$. For normal perception, $\theta \approx 1$.

Ovsjannikova and Slabova distinguish between two types of stereo filming, which they call filming in proportional ratios and filming with hyperstereoscopy (increased interaxial). In the former case, screen parallaxes at infinity, p_∞, do not exceed the interocular, and the parameters of filming are given, they say, by

$$BF = L_p P_\infty$$

The parallax on the film for a point L_c from the camera is

$$P_{\text{лл}} = \frac{P_\infty (L_c - L_p)}{L_c}$$

The purpose of filming with hyperstereoscopy is to increase the depth sense compared with the relationship given above, and for a change in the depth content, given a constant L_p and F, the interaxial B is increased H times compared with the relationship $BF = L_p P$ and may be written as $B_H = HB$, or $B_H F = Hp_\infty L_p$, and the film parallaxes can be

$$P_{\text{л я}} = \frac{H P_\infty (L_c - L_p)}{L_c}$$

When filming hyperstereoscopically, or when $H > 1$, it is possible to calculate the distance to the far plane that does not produce excessive parallax with

$$L_{\text{д}} = L_p \frac{H}{H - 1}$$

The quantity $L_{\text{д}}$ is also known as the coefficient of hyperstereoscopy.

The tables reproduced here are designed to aid cinematographers to select the camera variables needed to produce the desired effect. The tables use as their reference the object located in the plane of convergence, which is usually a human being. The symbols used are: m, the image magnification, and h_k, the height of the object in the composition; $L_{ол}$ and $L_д$ the limits, in distance from the camera, for the near and far planes; and L_p is the distance to the plane of convergence. Focal length F and interaxial B are also listed, as are comments with regard to the degree of "stereoscopicity": normal, strong, very strong, and weakened.

Additional remarks are made about the nature of stereoscopic cinematography, defining the compositional entities "post-plane" of convergence and "pre-plane" of convergence, which we have called screen and theater space. Recommendations are given about extending objects into theater space, and the authors stress the importance of texture and additional compositional factors that aid stereoscopic cinematography.

The authors discuss a concept, the "support surface," which is actually a measure of stereoscopic resolution, evaluating depth content in terms of

F	B	$L_{бл}$	$L_р$	$L_д$	H	Характер
80	26	1,1	1,4	1,7	5	Очень сильно
»	37	1,2	»	1,6	7,1	» »
300	105	4,95	5,2	5,5	20	» »

F	B	$L_{бл}$	$L_р$	$L_д$	H	Характер
80	26	1,5	1,85	2,5	3,75	Очень сильно
»	37	1,6	»	2,3	5,3	» »
300	105	6,5	6,95	7,5	15	» »

F	B	$L_{бл}$	$L_р$	$L_д$	H	Характер
28	26	1,4	3,2	∞	0,8	нормально
32	26	1,6	3,7	»	0,8	»
40	26	2,0	4,6	»	0,8	»
»	42	2,5	»	26,7	1,2	сильно
»	65	3,0	»	9,9	1,9	очень сильно
50	26	2,5	5,8	∞	0,8	умеренно
»	37	3,0	»	»	1,1	нормально
»	47	3,3	»	21,8	1,4	»
»	52,2	3,5	»	17,4	1,5	сильно
»	65	3,8	»	12,5	1,9	»
80	37	4,8	9,3	∞	1,1	умеренно
»	47	5,3	»	35,8	1,4	»
»	52,2	5,6	»	27,8	1,5	нормально
»	65	6,0	»	19,8	1,9	»
»	75	6,3	»	17,3	2,2	»
»	87	6,6	»	15,5	2,5	сильно
300	105	26,0	34,6	52,0	3,0	умеренно

Рис. 5. Операторские таблицы:
а, б — крупный план; в — средний план

5.8. *Stereo 70 tables.* Recommendations for closeups, head-and-shoulder shots, and medium shot showing entire body. *F, B, L* values and *H* are discussed in text. We can also use these tables to review Soviet optical equipment, which ranges from a focal length of 28 to 300mm, and various possible interaxial settings of from 26mm (no prism set) to 105mm. The last column, **Характер** (character), lists the stereo effect: **умеренно** —weakened; **нормально** —normal; **сильно** —strong; **оуень сильно** —very strong. (Ovsjannikova and Slabova, 1975) discrete planes. A similar concept was introduced by Spottiswoode et al. (1953).

We are also told that more leeway is possible in filming scenery and objects than human beings, since the perspective characteristics and consequent stereoscopic strengthening or weakening of the human face or form is highly noticeable. Comments are made about the modification of calculated results using the relationship $BF = L_pP$ for filming closeups. It is suggested that the interaxial base may be increased by 1.5 to 2 times, and in certain cases up to 3 times, and that similar sorts of more extreme increases for base distance are needed when using $B_HF = HP \propto L_p$ for lenses of long focal length.

Caution is advised when filming pans, which we are told ought to be executed 1.5 to 2 times slower than comparable planar pans. I also found this to be true but attributed my difficulties to lack of precise phasing of my camera shutters. It might seem that no such difficulty would be experienced by the Soviet single-band system. Why, then, must camera motion be slowed down for stereoscopic pans? If the camera shutter does not rotate in a manner to occlude both frames simultaneously, we would then have spurious temporal parallax added especially for rapid camera or subject motion. Perhaps this is the reason for the prescribed caution with regard to pans. Since the left and right frames are side by side in the stereo 70 system, a shutter with vertical sweep would expose both essentially simultaneously, while one with horizontal sweep would cause one frame to be exposed slightly before the other.

It is my feeling that Ovsjannikova and Slabova have succeeded far better than others at formulating a workable stereoscopic system. Their recommendations may be translated directly into terms that are of use to 16mm workers by dividing values for focal lengths in half, and quartered for the super 8 worker. The heart of the matter is not contained in their algebraic relationships for the most part, since these are quite clearly the result of a formalism imposed after the fact on an empirically developed approach. For example, when we are advised to increase the base by various arbitrary factors, the effect is more like witchcraft than science. We are in fact dealing with an art, and the information given in tabular form, bereft of this particular formalism is more to the point. Some of the equations simply lull one into thinking that they will yield useful predictive results for calculating filming parameters. Although film and screen parallaxes may be so calculated to good effect, camera variables may not.

The separation of the subject into hyperstereoscopic and proportional effects seems, to this author, to be peculiar, when coupled with what appears to be the virtual overlooking, in terms of formal development, of hypostereoscopic, or reduced-base, effects, which turn out to be as important in stereoscopic cinematography.

In terms of hardware, there is a very wide selection of interaxial distances, focal lengths, and convergence control. The super 8 system used in this study has a variability of camera parameters that is the equal of the Soviets' with the important exception that it is limited to a minimum interaxial of 66 mm; but hyperstereoscopic effects exceeding the Soviets' are possible with it. The principle of screen parallax invariance (page 118) states that images produced on the same size screens, given equal camera parameters, produce the same screen parallaxes and stereo effects. Therefore, recommendations for one format are good for another.

The only real deficiency in the hardware of the Stereo 70 system is the lack of increased interaxials for the shortest focal lengths available, namely 28mm and 32mm lenses, which are fixed at a base of 26mm. Although many shots may be successfully executed with this reduced base, it does happen that more extended bases are useful for scenery and for human beings several meters from the camera.

Earlier I mentioned Shatskaya's treatment of projection optical variables. This ought to be briefly discussed before taking leave of the Soviet system. Twin lenses, mounted in a single barrel, are employed, and in my view this is the best possible method for a single-band system, since it allows for total control of unwanted binocular asymmetries.

Such dual lenses must have the ability to shift one or both optical centers laterally, so that the axes may be brought into perfect coincidence on the screen. This can be best accomplished while projecting a test film, and although alignment should stay fixed once it is set, periodic checks can be made on the integrity of the crossed-lens-axes condition.

Designers can determine the necessary range of lateral shift, u, of the optics by this simplified relationship:

$$u \simeq \frac{b}{K}$$

Homologous screen points are distance b apart, and K is the frame magnification. Additional relationships are given in the article.

chapter 6

Binocular Symmetries

Early in the course of this investigation, I began to wonder why viewing images through the stereoscope did not produce the same eye-strain people sometimes experience when viewing stereoscopic motion pictures. The important factor, retinal disparity, can be the same in both cases, yet discomfort was often felt looking at movies.

After projecting stereoscopic images daily for more than a year, it occurred to me that there was a symmetrical principle at work in the transmission of these images. In all specifiable ways, with the exception of the asymmetry of horizontal parallax, which provides the stereopsis depth cue, the images should be as alike as possible. My idea was that some symmetrical quality needed by the left- and right-image fields was more easily satisfied with the stereoscope than with motion picture viewing.

The following exposition of the concept of binocular symmetry is important not only for equipment designers but also for filmmakers who use double-band stereo systems, since they must calibrate the two images. Even with access to a single-band precalibrated system, understanding this concept will enable one to trouble-shoot problems and perform adjustments.

There are many possible sources of eyestrain, but frequently the sensation is not felt in the eyes but in some other part of the body. People are completely unfamiliar with the discomfort associated with improperly presented stereoscopic images, since asymmetries of this kind do not occur in daily experience when looking at this visual world. For example, many people, given the proper stimulus, report headaches or nausea or complain that the image is "blurry."

Interestingly, if one or several strain-producing asymmetries are present, generally speaking the unpleasant sensation will be felt in a single part of the body. Strain seems to be cumulative, and repeated exposure to strain-producing factors will produce increased discomfort. To a large extent, the control of strain becomes the control of binocular symmetries.

Once this concept became clearly defined, my primary object was to create images dependably without these binocular asymmetries; in other words, a stereoscopic system controlled to tolerable levels for the enjoyment of strain-free viewing.

Binocular symmetry differs from conventional symmetry—for example, the point symmetry of the mandala—in that two image fields (the left and right images), and not one field, must be considered—and compared. Research indicates that the symmetries of the two fields must be held to within specifiable tolerances or strain will occur. The symmetries are: illumination, aberration (and sharpness), geometry (or linearity), color, image selection, and temporal symmetry and registration.

Improperly executed photography can create strain that is indistinguishable from that produced by the out-of-tolerance system parameters I have just listed. Stereoscopic imaging systems may therefore have elements of strain produced by both poor photography and poor system design. I hypothesize that strain from both areas is additive, and cumulative with time, and symptoms of strain are proportional to the degree of error.

The nonsystematic photographic parameters will be the subject of the following two chapters, which deal with binocular asymmetries. Our concern now is with systematic elements.

When tolerances are supplied, they are the values that I have been able to achieve in my system. If other systems can be made to meet these specifications, it is my assumption that they too will be similarly strain-free. While more work needs to be done, I stand by these figures.

EXPERIMENTAL TECHNIQUES

In the course of a year and a half, about forty subjects in about sixty trials were shown hundreds of shots photographed and projected on a screen 1.3 m wide in my studio with the system described on page 248. The subjects, in groups of from one to eight, viewed the films seated 2.75 to 5 m from the screen. Each subject's interocular measurement was taken, and each was shown Julesz (1971) figure anaglyphs, which are unfakeable tests of stereopsis. They were interviewed at length and were free to volunteer comments.

Upon completion of my 25-minute film, *Uncle Bill and the Dredge Dwellers,* I screened it publicly a number of times toward the end of 1978. A collection of interesting effects, called *Through My Window,* was also shown. The screenings were accompanied by a discussion period, and audience members made many comments. Audience and critical reactions in the press were generally favorable.

It is important to discuss the experimental approach that led to the conclusions given in this and the previous two chapters. After presenting test footage in my studio to my subjects, I began to suspect that shots presented this way were being scrutinized far more critically, in a negative sense, than would be the case if they were part of a completed film. Shots projected out of the context of continuity or filmic structure, as isolated entities, drew more attention and stood out in a way that might actually be counterproductive.

I drew an analogy between this phase of my work and a hypothetical motion picture pioneer who might be engaged in the same sort of research, but with planar apparatus. Audiences, for example, might be flustered by pans. When looking at a pan, what we see rotates in a direction opposite to that of camera motion. This is quite unlike what occurs when we move our eyes or head. Try it, and you will see that the room does not seem to spin around backwards. Yet this is exactly what a motion picture camera will do, lacking the constancy effect of the human nervous system interfaced with the visual world.

Another unpleasant aspect of the pan is that it is seen to be blurry. When moving your eyes, or when panning the eyes and the head, if you prefer, the world does not become a blur. You are, in fact, not conscious of detail, or tend to suppress vision while the eyes are in motion. Only when they come to rest can you pick out detail.

The act of panning a camera and projecting this motion picture film produces an entirely different effect from similar eye movement. Let us suppose that our pioneer planar experimenter showed some pans to an audience. Most people would find the pans unpleasant, and some people would probably complain that they were painful, that they hurt their eyes. There would be, in all likelihood, a minority of viewers who were not disturbed by the effect, and some might even enjoy these blurry moving-backwards shots. But most people would be upset by pans, never having previously seen them (or movies, for that matter).

There are two additional considerations that come to mind: Suppose the pan shots were part of a well-structured film. How would our novice audience react? Suppose our audience had even a few hours of experience looking at motion pictures. How would they then react to the pan?

Just as the pan is not isomorphic with our normal visual experience, many aspects of the stereocinema are similarly nonisomorphic with our perception of the visual world. The breakdown of accommodation/convergence is one such effect, as is the effect of images with negative parallax cut off by the screen surround. Yet another major class of effects might be departures from geometrically predicted orthostereoscopy.

The questions before me were: What is acceptable and what is unacceptable practice? How can I trust the reactions of a rather small population of naive viewers? These people had very little or, in many cases, no experience looking at stereo motion picture effigies. Since it was my work they were viewing, how could I guard against their being influenced by my presence? Their emotional reactions, or possible desire to please, might bias their response. As I have mentioned, in the early days of my work I had no finished film to present, and screening isolated shots out of continuity may have presented additional difficulties. Not the least of my concerns was that some of the viewers might have anomalous stereoscopic perception.

My approach was influenced by my background: I had been trained in the physical sciences, but by inclination I had become an artist. Here, for the first time, I was faced with a challenge that totally engaged both aspects of my mind.

I was faced, or in fact have been faced for the past five years, with the challenge of engineering a good stereoscopic moving image system, and I have found that this engineering problem is totally inseparable from the esthetic problem of making a good stereoscopic film. Other workers, if they are lucky enough to use a well-designed stereoscopic motion picture system (which at the moment usually cannot be obtained off the shelf and must be built to suit the needs of the worker), may tend to lose sight of the inseparable nature of this technology and its accompanying esthetic. It may well be that the perfection of technical details tends to conceal the relationship between scientific and artistic coexpression.

As I shot more and more stereo footage and showed that footage to many subjects, I learned that the perception of the stereoscopic image is highly idiosyncratic and that the same individual will react in different ways at different times to the same effigy. This may well be caused by the relative naiveness of my test population. Generally speaking, people's reactions to the footage became increasingly favorable. But then again, even if they saw the same shot several times, in the intervening months I may have learned enough about improving my projection technique to make significant changes in viewing conditions.

Faced with all of these considerations, I embarked on the following course: I would learn about the idiosyncratic nature of my perception, how it differed from and how it was like that of others, and through intellectual effort and whatever instincts at my disposal I would try to turn myself into an introspective instrument. I would try to learn what was pleasing and what was displeasing to my "normal" or "average" viewer. I would try to learn what it was that caused strain or discomfort; I would also try to see as others saw, so that I might appreciate their perception vis-à-vis the shape or proportion of the effigy.

In fact, I became engaged in learning the same sort of technique that any visual artist tries to master by training his or her esthetic sense. My task was more difficult because my chosen medium was in a tentative state. I had to build my own tools, and I had to learn the engineering principles involved.

I can say that I put a great deal of effort into library research and, with the help of my research associate, Michael Starks, uncovered if not every article, then just about every significant article on stereoscopic cinematography and related topics. I saw no point in repeating the work of others. That is why humanity records its thoughts in printed form, and there was no reason why I should not be a beneficiary of this intellectual tradition.

However, I learned that the needed information did not appear in print. No filmmaker, no engineer, could go to the literature and learn how to do good stereoscopic photography or how to design a good stereoscopic film-making system. The two problems are related. Instruments of a good system will not only conform to a rigorous set of standards to control what I call binocular symmetries, but these instruments will also be designed to incorporate the appropriate creative variables so that successful photography may be conducted. This second aspect relates to the creative control of asymmetries of horizontal parallax, and it is the subject of the last two chapters.

ILLUMINATION SYMMETRY

While previous workers specified that the exposures of the left- and right-image fields, and finally the total illumination projected on the screen, must be equal, practitioners with the notable exception of Norling (1952) do not seem to have understood this: A point-for-point comparison must be made of corresponding image points in these left and right fields, and these corresponding points must have the same intensity when projected.

If stereoscopic exposures are made of a gray card, examination of the left and right images with a measuring device such as a densitometer should register the same density for typical corresponding points: for example, the corners and centers of the left and right images, given by the letters A, B, C, D, and E and A', B', C', D', and E'.

Projection optics must also be free of illumination asymmetry, or discomfort or strain will be produced in the viewer that is cumulative with time and proportional to the extent of the asymmetry. In a good system, the point-for-point difference in intensity of illumination, it is estimated, would be held to within 10%, which can be determined by measuring the screen illumination for each field with a goniophotometer, or in actual practice with the eye of a trained observer. For rapidly evaluating the comparative

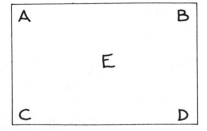 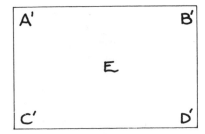

6.1. *Illumination symmetry.*

intensity of projected fields, place red and green filters over the left and right projection lenses. The additive color mixture is yellow, and asymmetries can instantly be isolated as reddish or greenish areas. (Lee primary red and green filters were used.) This technique, which I discovered, is the basis for a disclosure filed with the U.S. Patent office.

Field-dividing devices employing a prism or mirror optic placed over a single objective, known as frame or field dividers (mistakenly called beam splitters), often produce unwanted asymmetry of illumination (vignetting). Since all lenses have illumination intensity and, generally, correction of aberration—in terms of conventional point symmetry, symmetrical about the center of the frame or field—any superimposition of such a split field must produce fields that are unmatched in terms of illumination and aberration. This is why it is preferable to use dual objectives in stereoscopic photographic and projection systems.

COMMENTS

It was the binocular symmetry of illumination that first came to my attention. After that—through experiment, inference, or intuition—I generalized the other necessary symmetrical qualities.

Periodic tuning or tweaking of the camera and projector portions of the system, together with steady improvements in photographic technique, led to increasingly pleasant results, but I noticed that prolonged viewing was still producing discomfort. After investigating many other possibilities, I measured the incident illumination of various portions of the screen for both left- and right-projection beams and tabulated the results. In terms of a point-for-point correspondence of intensity of illumination, there was a serious mismatch.

After an abortive attempt to realign the projection lamp housings, I simply switched the lamps. These lamps have a peanut-size bulb centered in a reflector that is a paraboloid of revolution. The lamps retained their illumination characteristics after being switched. One of the bulbs must have been poorly aligned with respect to its reflector. I replaced it with a new lamp that proved to be a good match for the remaining lamp.

ABERRATION SYMMETRY

The principle of binocular symmetry of aberration (and sharpness) is derived from the fact that aberration and sharpness are symmetrical with respect to a point in the center of the frame. To measure the binocular aberration symmetry and sharpness, one would conventionally measure the extent of the lens aberrations and sharpness of the corresponding positions of left and right fields. In practice, lenses of the same design that are properly assembled should produce good results.

Strictly speaking, classification of binocular asymmetries is arbitrary. For example, illumination asymmetries in a system may result from asymmetrical vignetting, which could be classified as an asymmetry of illumination. But illumination asymmetries may arise from a number of other causes. For example, the symmetry of illumination might also be influenced by unequal development of film, especially in a dual-band system, or by miscalibrated iris diaphragms. In addition, the relationship of various components of the projection optical system (lamps, lens, polarizing filters, screen) can critically influence the symmetry of illumination.

COMMENTS

This classification is a generalization based on the illumination symmetry, and it was intuited on the basis of this work. Aside from the efforts carried out with regard to illumination, I have not done the experiments to substantiate the validity of this proposed symmetry.

GEOMETRICAL SYMMETRY

The binocular symmetry of geometry (or linearity) requires that the image magnification for both fields must be the same, that corresponding left- and right- or homologous points must be aligned horizontally, and that both images must have substantially the same linearity (i.e., a circle in one field must have the same shape as a circle in the other). In the literature, it is usually specified that an acceptable tolerance requires the lenses' focal lengths to be within 0.5% of each other both in photography and in projection.

Geometrical symmetry expresses itself most dramatically in horizontal alignment of corresponding, or homologous, image points. Misalignment of homologous points beyond specified tolerance (placing one image point above the other) can arise from magnification differences in the optics, or from misalignment of the left and right camera lens axes in the horizontal plane, or from errors in frameline settings during projection. Tolerances for alignment of camera lens axes in the horizontal plane are stringent and must be held to less than a 0.2° difference for a good system.

The vertical parallax of homologous points is always undesirable and does not contribute to stereopsis. Its only contribution is to eyestrain, since as the eyes seek to fuse the image pairs, it causes unnatural vertical rotation of one eye with respect to the other.

Since we are concerned with differences in the sizes of objects whose effigies lie in the left- and right-image fields, we can use the following equation, which relates object magnification m and frame magnification M, which was derived (in terms of the Soviet notation, but given here in our notation) on page 171:

$$m = \frac{f_c M}{D}$$

We now have a way to evaluate changes in image size by doing some calculations for a given screen size, assuming seats no closer than some minimum distance. In addition, we must have standards for spurious vertical parallax, which needs to be held to 0.1° or at the very most 0.2°.(See page 103 for a discussion of Panum's Area, the physical basis of this tolerance.)

For a specific set of conditions, we can arrive at a graph like the one shown here. If B is the diagonal of the format, camera lens focal lengths of B must be held to 1%. Focal lengths of $2B$ must be within 0.5% of each other, and those of $4B$ to within 0.1%.

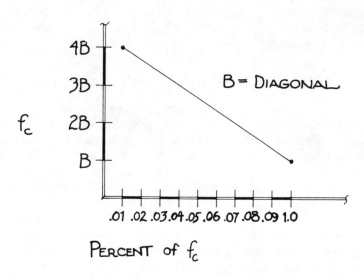

6.2. *Geometrical symmetry.* Vertical axis shows focal length of camera optics in terms of the diagonal of the format, *B*. Horizontal axis shows lens tolerance in terms of percentage of focal length.

As focal length and consequent object magnification increases, greater demands must be placed on matching optics. In the graph given here, the Edison aspect ratio was assumed with seating no closer than twice the screen width. For scope projection, and/or closer minimum seating, stricter tolerances will be necessary.

Similar considerations can be used to arrive at standards for projection optics.

COMMENTS

The need for symmetrical geometry of the left and right fields is obvious and can be substantiated through rather straightforward experimental procedures. If one image is magnified more than the other, homologous points will be altered in all relative directions, except for axial points, which do not shift (but which will change size). While lateral shifts produce spurious parallax that encourages spurious stereoscopic perception, these can be relatively benign. Vertical displacement, on the other hand, is malevolent, since these spurious parallaxes will result in strain.

Some individuals have more tolerance for mismatched image size than others. Images that are quite mismatched may still be fused, but a distinction must be made between fusion and comfortable fusion. Despite the fact that some individuals can fuse images up to one about 15% larger than the other, I doubt that they can do this with comfort for very long.

Zoom projection optics are especially easy to match by using SMPTE registration or similar ruled leader, as will be described in the Appendix.

In addition to lateral shifts of one image with respect to the other, or differing magnifications, one image may be tipped with respect to the other. This effect is extremely unlikely to occur in a single-band system. In double-band systems, cameras and projectors can be tipped, and the effect of this slight rotation, in its own plane, of one image of a stereo pair, is described in a footnote by MacAdam (1954) and in greater detail by Ogle (1950).

REGISTRATION SYMMETRY

Another symmetrical quality, symmetry of registration, may be considered to be a subclass of the geometrical symmetry (or horizontal alignment) of homologous points. It can be understood as the relative time rate of change of the position of these points. This concept may be applied to dual projection, but in single-band systems relative registration for properly oriented images may have identical or perfectly symmetrical registration. It is possible to specify the worst possible relative unsteadiness of two superimposed fields in terms of absolute values for angular measurement. If a specific screen size is given, then specifications can be made in terms of that screen size, taking into consideration the minimum distance of an observer.

For this quantity, and for all the measurable symmetries of the stereoscopic art, the eye of the observer is the last link in the overall optical system. Subjective response is the final arbiter of quality. In an excellent system (properly designed single-band), there would be no relative unsteadiness between left and right fields. But in a good system the worst possible misregistration in angular terms cannot be greater than approximately 0.1°.

Registration can be considered in terms of the vertical and the horizontal. Both components can produce strain, but the vertical is particularly troublesome, as was the case for geometrical symmetry. I have determined experimentally that severe weave, or horizontal unsteadiness, causes a jumping of object position and does indeed lead to fatigue.

COMMENTS

Spottiswoode and Spottiswoode (1953) have defined a quantity called stereoscopic resolving power based on relative movement of images in a double-band system. They claim that as unsteadiness increases, the number of resolvable planes, as spaced from the camera and perpendicular to the plane of the lens axes, similarly decreases. This seems a logical supposition, but in fact I have been unable to observe the effect. Stereoscopic resolution does not decrease despite marked unsteadiness, even if fatigue is a function of this effect.

All double-band systems have observable relative unsteadiness. Simply remove the stereoglasses to observe the phenomenon. The causes could lie in manufacture of the film, exposure in the camera, printing, projection, and film wear. The last cause is insidious, since increases in unsteadiness are quite gradual and may go undetected. With good equipment, though, long life can be expected from an original or a print.

Observing this unsteadiness—usually the vertical component is most noticeable—one should bear in mind that the most visible and worst possible error is being observed.

CHROMATIC SYMMETRY

Color asymmetries arise from processing vagaries or the emulsions themselves for dual-film systems, or from the camera and projector optics, which in the case of camera optics includes any filters used. For projection optics, one must also consider color variations of illumination sources or of the sheet-polarizing filters employed, including those used in viewing devices.

By its nature, this seems to be a relatively benign asymmetrical factor, and some departure in relative color balance is tolerable, although when so easy to correct, unnecessary. Chromatic symmetry in a good system requires the left and right fields to coincide to within 10 or 15 CC filters as supplied by the Eastman Kodak series of color compensating filters.

COMMENTS

I have tried some interesting experiments shooting black-and-white in one camera and color in the other. Exposures have to be carefully made so that color and black and white densities correspond. Some subjects shown such footage simply do not notice what is happening and report that the scene looks like the other color footage into which it had been cut for these tests. On the other hand, many people are instantly aware that something is "wrong." Some are rapidly able to identify the nature of the effect, while others remain bewildered. A great many of the test subjects report that the colors appear to be subdued, or desaturated (my term). A great many also report that the colors seem to shimmer or scintillate. This perception corresponds with my own. No one complained about fatigue or discomfort.

The effect might be used to good purpose in a number of situations. To me, it suggests something magical or wonderful and might be used to illustrate a fantasy, for example.

Helmholtz (1925) and others reported on the phenomenon called binocular color mixing, in which one color is presented to one eye and another to the other eye. What usually is reported by most observers corresponds very closely to the rules of subtractive color mixing (blue plus yellow is equal to green). It is interesting that Helmholtz himself could not see binocular color mixing.

In terms of brain function, the mixing of binocular colors must take place after binocular processing takes place. Mixing black-and-white and color footage probably needs to be explained both by binocular color mixing and in terms of retinal rivalry. Binocular color would explain the desaturated nature of the colors, and retinal rivalry would explain the shimmering effect. I use the word "explain" here merely to indicate that the phenomena are classifiable under these headings, but the terminology itself explains nothing.

TEMPORAL SYMMETRY

Temporal symmetry is a parameter that may be applied mainly to dual-band motion picture systems. It is possible to demonstrate experimentally that synchronization between the left and right image, for average subject motion, must be held to within 100° out of the 360° of a single intermittent cycle for projection, and to far lower values for the photography itself. Although the projection apparatus lent itself to incremental adjustment of phase relationship between left and right shutters, the camera control circuitry was not adjustable. There is no reason why a good dual projection system cannot operate with a phase error of only a few degrees.

Single band systems are not immune from temporal asymmetry effects, as mentioned in connection with the Soviet Stereo 70 system on page 166. For example, when using 35mm over-and-under optics (see page 265), on an Arriflex 2c camera, with a vertical sweep shutter, which occludes one frame before the other, rapid action displays spurious temporal effects. On the other hand, when using an Arri 35BL, which has a horizontal sweep shutter, which occludes both frames simultaneously, no temporal asymmetry can be observed.

COMMENTS

A peculiar rippling or gelatinous effect is seen when objects are in motion and there is phase error. Some people will experience strain or will report that the image appears to be blurry. There is no counterpart in the perception of the visual world; images always arrive at the left and right eyes simultaneously. With motion pictures, we have an opportunity to circumvent expectation.

Out-of-phase shutters will also prove troublesome with camera movement, creating additional flickering for pans, making them more disturbing than usual. On the other hand, these out-of-synchronization images can be used to good creative effect. Shots of waves or rippling water become espe-

ASYMMETRY		CAUSE	
	CAMERA	POST PRODUCTION	PROJECTION
ILLUMINATION	Mismatched *T* stops Asymmetrical vignetting Different emulsions*	Processing* Printing light*	Mismatched lenses Unequal illumination source Polarizers of mismatch transmittance
ABERRATION	Frame splitter employed Mismatched optics	Possible introduction in optical printing	Mismatched optics
GEOMETRY	Excessive keystoning because of convergence angle		Poor alignment of projectors
COLOR	Mismatched optics Mismatched filters Mismatched emulsions*	Unequal processing* Printer lights*	Mismatched optics Sheet polarizers
IMAGE SELECTION	High-contrast subject Subject not in plane of convergence		High-contrast subject Subject not in plane of screen Poor-quality polarizers Head tipping Poor-quality screen
TEMPORAL	Shutters out of synchronization or phase	Rolls printed out of synchronization or cut out of synchronization*	Improperly repaired break* Shutters out of phase* Projectors out of synchronization*
REGISTRATION	Poor registration* Single-band system with frames arranged 180 degrees rotation	Printer adjustment*	Projectors unsteady* Film wear*

*Double-band systems only

6.3. *Catalog of asymmetries.*

cially curious and interesting for many observers, although some people are disturbed by the effect.

In one shot of a distant smokestack, I displaced one band three frames with respect to the other. When projected in synchronization, the short interaxial equal to the average interocular provided no stereoscopic relief. When projected out of synchronization as described, smoke emerging from the stack appeared to be floating toward the audience, coming forward in space from an otherwise flat backdrop of factories and railroad yards. The temporal parallax of the movement of the smoke was used to create spatial parallax. If the direction of relative movement of the bands of film were reversed, the smoke might be made to appear to be receding behind the backdrop. This is a curious effect, which most pairs of eyes will resist, because of the conflict of the stereoscopic cue and the cue of interposition.

DESIRABLE ASYMMETRIES

With the notable exception of glitter, sparkle, or luster, the only desirable asymmetries in a stereoscopic system of photography and projection are the asymmetries of horizontal parallax. These are determined at the time of photography by the photographer. The binocular symmetries listed in the chart can all be considered to be systematic parameters, for the most part within the province of the manufacturer of the camera and projection apparatus. (In the case of double-band systems, these parameters fall within the capability of the filmmaker and projectionist.) The desirable asymmetry of horizontal parallax, which provides the depth information of stereopsis and is the single distinguishable feature of stereoscopic projection—compared with conventional planar projection—must be under the creative control of a skilled photographer. This will be the subject of the discussions in the following two chapters.

chapter 7

Binocular Asymmetries: Depth-Range Relationships

For the projection of a stereoscopic image using polarized light and crossed lens axes, the left- and right-image fields are projected on top of each other in virtual superimposition. The most visible differences between the two fields are produced by the relatively slight horizontal displacement of image points resulting from the different points of view, or perspective, of the left and right camera lenses. These displacements, which we call horizontal screen parallax or simply screen parallax, are the stereophotographic counterpart of retinal disparity and are the only desirable asymmetrical elements in the combined images.

In this chapter I will discuss the depth-range relationship and how to predict acceptable limits for screen parallax before proceeding to explain the manipulation of camera variables to produce the most pleasing stereoscopic effigy, within those acceptable parallax limits.

MAXIMUM PARALLAX

In the basic depth-range or screen parallax equation (see page 114),

$$P_m = Mf_c t_c \left(\frac{1}{D_o} - \frac{1}{D_m} \right)$$

P_m is the maximum screen parallax, M is frame magnification, f_c the camera focal length, t_c the interaxial, and D_o and D_m, respectively, the distance from the camera to the plane of convergence and the distance from the camera to the far plane. We define the distance between D_m and D_o to be the *depth range* and call this quantity ΔD. In the crossed-lens-axes system, an object at distance D_o from the camera will have zero screen parallax, or will appear in the plane of the screen. The object at distance D_m will produce an image with the maximum positive parallax in the shot, and the value of this parallax is a major limiting factor in photography.

The challenge in stereoscopic cinematography is to keep screen parallaxes as low as possible in order to offset the breakdown of accommodation/convergence (A/C) and to avoid large parallax values of image points, which may result in excessive divergence. The maximum screen parallax between homologous points of distant objects should be kept equal to or less than t_e, the interocular.

However, it is often difficult to limit the maximum screen parallax to t_e. We have noted that homologous points equal to t_e lead to optical axes of the eyes that will be parallel. If we disallow values of P_m larger than t_e, we restrict the depth range, making photography and subsequent projection of many subjects impossible. Instead we allow a total divergence of 1°, a value accepted in the literature by writers such as MacAdam, Gunzburg, Hill, Levonian, and Ovsjannikova and Slabova.

It is also possible to consult authorities such as Rule, Spottiswoode, and Norling, who believe that divergence should not be allowed. For six years I showed divergent footage to a number of subjects, and I found that, with qualifications, 1° total divergence, (½° for each eye), was acceptable.

One qualification is that subjects entirely or very nearly at photographic infinity (without important foreground compositional elements) should have no divergence, and in fact look just as deep if the value of screen parallax is less than the average interocular. If the composition requires the viewer to observe the background in preference to the foreground, then divergence ought to be avoided. On the other hand, there are cases in which total divergence greater than 1° is permissible. For example, the background can be dark compared with the foreground.

Stereoscopic filmmaking is an art, and it is impossible to impose a perfectly strict guideline like this. What I am relating consists of my photographic experience acquired over a period of six years under a variety of conditions. I have been my own projectionist for hundreds of screenings, many of them public and outside my studio, so that I have had extensive opportunity to observe the effect of this photography on disinterested spectators.

Figure 7.1 helps illustrate the method for calculating divergence. Let d be the total divergent or excess parallax, V the distance from the viewer to the screen, and θ_d the angle of divergence. When viewing homologous points 65 mm apart, the eyes will be parallel. If we add the divergent parallax d to this, we can compute the angle of outward turning or total divergence of the eyes:

$$\tan \Theta_d \cdot V = d$$
$$P_d = d + t_e$$
$$P_d = d + 65 \text{ mm}$$

The value for P_d, while important, is not the sole determinant of stereophotographic limits. It should be noted that the angle of divergence decreases as the viewer recedes from the screen for a given P_d. Maximum screen parallaxes for divergent homologous points can appear to be very large, even several times t_e, but when analyzed from the point of view of angular measure, divergence can still be held to tolerable limits. Generally speaking, large screens are viewed further away than small screens, and the limit is the maximum screen parallax with respect to those seated closest to the screen. There, viewers' eyes will be converged to subtend the largest angles for all homologous points except those spaced at t_e, which remain constant from all seats. Calculations are based on the correct assumption that all seats further back will give lower values for divergence.

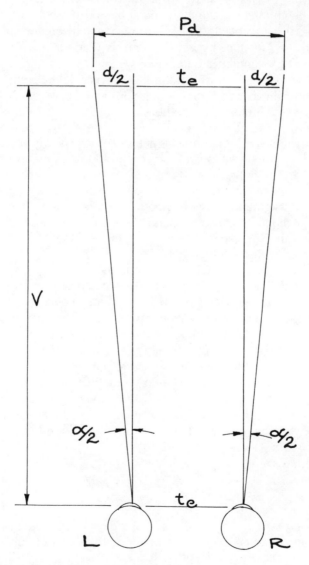

7.1. Calculating divergence.

THE STEREOSCOPIC CONSTANT

The stereoscopic constant K is defined as

$$K = \frac{P_m}{M}$$

When P_m is set at the maximum screen parallax, which will give 1° total divergence, we can write

$$K_d = \frac{P_d}{M}$$

When P_m is set to equal a screen parallax equal to t_e, we have

$$K_e = \frac{P_e}{M}$$

You may wonder why this is not written

$$K_e = \frac{t_e}{M}$$

It can be written this way, but when shooting for a variety of screen sizes, in effect a compromise value for t_e may have to be chosen, since P_m is a function of M. Therefore K_e should have useful or nominal value in order to give a value for P_m close to but not necessarily equal to t_e.

We can now write (by substitution into the basic depth range equation)

$$K_d = f_c t_c \left(\frac{1}{D_o} - \frac{1}{D_m} \right)$$

which can also be written in the more useful form

$$\frac{1}{D_m} = \frac{1}{D_o} - \frac{K_d}{f_c t_c}$$

For the nondivergent, or nominally nondivergent case, we have

$$\frac{1}{D_m} = \frac{1}{D_o} - \frac{K_e}{f_c t_c}$$

HYPERCONVERGENCE DISTANCE

In crossed-lens-axes transmission systems, all photography will have some convergence, including that of objects at photographic or stereoscopic infinity. Workers familiar only with the parallel projection system will find this curious, since parallel lens axes when photographing the image will give the desired results. But if the lens axes of the cameras are held parallel for distant shots, in the CLA system, the result will be zero parallax, since the two images will be essentially identical. In other words, the image of very distant objects will be reproduced incorrectly at the plane of the screen. It is better to have some positive value of screen parallax for such shots so that they will be reproduced in screen space.

But we can find the distance at which to converge the camera lenses in order to achieve screen parallax for distant objects by using depth-range equations. When the distance to the far plane D_m is at stereoscopic infinity, we can set $1/D_m = 0$. Therefore we have the equations

$$\frac{1}{D_o} = \frac{K_d}{f_c t_c} \quad \text{or} \quad D_0 = \frac{f_c t_c}{K_d}$$

in the event that divergence is allowable.

If divergence is not allowable, we can write

$$\frac{1}{D_o} = \frac{K_d}{f_c t_c} \quad \text{or} \quad D_0 = \frac{f_c t_c}{K_e}$$

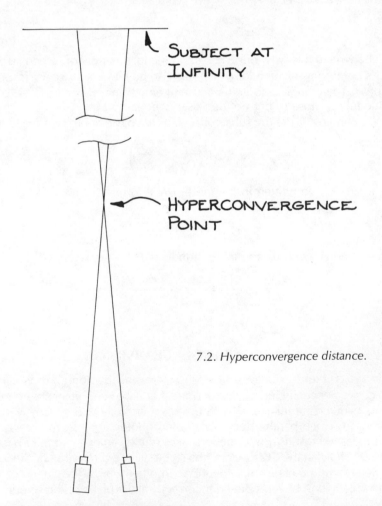

SUBJECT AT INFINITY

HYPERCONVERGENCE POINT

7.2. Hyperconvergence distance.

These relationships define the *hyperconvergence distance* or the distance for which the lens axes must be converged in order to produce acceptable screen parallax for very distant objects. First we have, for D_o, the hyperconvergence distance, or distance to the plane of hyperconvergence, for the case in which a total divergence of 1° is allowed. Second, we have the distance to the plane of hyperconvergence when no divergence is allowed, or when homologous points are approximately t_e apart.

We will use the subscript h to denote the general case of hyperconvergence distance. Thus

$$D_{hd} = \frac{f_c t_c}{K_d}$$

and

$$D_{hd} = \frac{f_c t_c}{K_e}$$

We can now write the generalized depth-range or screen parallax equation:

$$\frac{1}{D_m} = \frac{1}{D_o} - \frac{1}{D_h}$$

This gives us the elegant result of having the reciprocal of the distance to the far plane equal to the reciprocal of the distance to the plane of convergence minus the reciprocal of the distance to the plane of hyperconvergence.

Remembering that we defined depth range $\Delta D = D_m - D_o$, we can write $\Delta D = D_h - D_o$. By substitution into the equation above and simple algebraic manipulation, we obtain

$$D_m \Delta D = D_o D_h$$

Thus the product of the distance to the far plane and depth range is equal to the product of the distance to the near plane and the distance to the plane of hyperconvergence.

We shall see that the concept of hyperconvergence distance leads to additional simplification of the formal development of the subject, and that physical significance of other relationships is similarly clarified. This will be shown when we discuss the concept of the near plane which is halfway between the plane of the screen and the audience.

CALCULATING *K*

Consider now how to compute the stereoconstant K, which is straightforward enough if one is considering a single screen size but becomes more complicated for a range of screens.

As the example let us take the case of dual 70mm projection on large screens of various sizes. The projection aperture of this format is 48.6 × 22mm. Projection is to take place on screens of from 22 × 10 m to 11 × 5

m. I have observed in such theaters that the minimum seating distance from the screen is equal to the height of the screen. Usually 70mm projection is done on large screens, with seats rather close to the screen. One attribute of this kind of filmmaking is that it allows the spectator to observe a screen that subtends a very large angle of view (Szabo, 1976). If the old rule of thumb for seating in a motion picture screening room were followed for the Edison aspect ratio, the distance of the closest seats would be twice the width (or height) of the screen. Given the 1.3:1 aspect ratio, it hardly matters whether one picks width or height as a basis for placement of the nearest seats. In a typical super 8 seating arrangement for a screen 1.3 × 1 m, the closest seats might be placed at, say, 2.5 m.

It may be instructive to do a simple calculation for the screen parallax for a total divergence of 1°. Let us take the largest 70mm screen, which measures 22 × 10 m, and assume that the closest seats are 10 m away. In such a case,

$$\tan \Theta_d \cdot V = d$$
$$(\tan 1°) \cdot 10{,}000 \text{ mm} = d$$
$$0.01746 \cdot 10{,}000 \text{ mm} = d$$
$$174.6 \text{ m} = d$$
$$P_d = d + t_e$$
$$= 174.6 \text{ mm} + 65 \text{ mm}$$
$$= 239.6 \text{ mm}$$

Calculating M for this screen size, we obtain

$$M = \frac{S}{W}$$
$$= \frac{22{,}000 \text{ mm}}{48.6 \text{ mm}}$$
$$= 453.6$$

And finally, K_d:

$$K_d = \frac{P_d}{M}$$
$$= \frac{239.6 \text{ mm}}{453.6}$$
$$= 0.53 \text{ mm}$$

In the same way, we can compute the values in Figure 7.3.

Screen dimensions (meters)	Area (square meters)	M	P_d (millimeters)	K_d (millimeters)	K_e (millimeters) (Pte=65 mm)
22 × 10	220	453	240	0.53	0.14
11 × 5	55	226	152	0.67	0.28

70mm screen parameters, based on minimum viewing distance equal to screen height.

7.3. K values for dual 70mm format.

Looking at the figures tabulated in Figure 7.3, for screens 22 × 10 m and 11 × 5 m, we see a spread in K from 0.53 to 0.67 mm for divergent values, and from 0.14 to 0.28 mm for nondivergent values. When one tries to compute a depth-range table, it turns out that it is far simpler to do photography with large values of K than small values. From the expression for the hyperconvergence distance, $f_c t_c / K$, we see that D_h is inversely proportional to K, so that large values for K place the hyperconvergence plane closer to the camera, making photography easier. Since K is inversely proportional to M, it turns out to be easier to photograph for smaller than for larger screens.

Also bear in mind that seats behind the first row will provide easier viewing conditions, since parallax, in terms of angular measure, decreases, reducing any possible strain produced by A/C breakdown or by excessively divergent homologous points.

The seats in some theaters are closer to the screen than in others, further complicating an already difficult situation. But even seats close to the screen will be acceptable to some patrons, for example, very young people with supple eye muscles. The example I have chosen for illustrating K_e and K_d is the most difficult possible case I have encountered, since it involves projection on very large screens with very close seating.

In looking over the table for K for purposes of calculation, I decided to pick values of K_d equal to 0.57 mm and K_e equal to .18 mm. It is impossible to do perfect photography for a range of screen sizes that runs from 55 to 220 m². Only a compromise is possible. I decided on these K values because they favor the larger screen sizes while still allowing workable values for photography.

COMPUTING D_h

We now have a convenient form of the depth-range equation for computing tables that will aid us in stereoscopic photography. Given a focal length and interaxial setting, knowing the distance from the camera to the plane of convergence, we can look up the allowable distance to the far plane. This distance can be computed to allow 1° total divergence, or no divergence, or anything in between. As you shall see, the working technique has been to compute sets of tables based either on allowing divergence or on essentially no divergence. This makes it possible to select or estimate desirable intermediate values.

These tables include the distance to the plane of hyperconvergence, to allow setting the lens axes for the infinity condition. It is also possible to employ a table of hyperconvergence distances as the basis for computation in the field by nonprogrammable pocket calculator.

At this point, if so desired, we can compute 70mm hyperconvergence tables for the given K values, 0.57 mm for the divergent condition and 0.18 mm for the nominal interocular condition. On very large screens, photography based on K_e will produce homologous points for infinity objects with parallaxes somewhat greater than t_e, whereas on smaller screens, the maximum parallaxes will be less than t_e. The same sort of changes in parallax occur with K_d.

These tables were calculated while I was consulting with United Artists Theaters for their dual 70mm stereoscopic system. Note that the camera used had a range of t_c from 0 to 100 mm, and tables were calculated based on intervals of 10 mm beginning at 15 mm. These 70mm tables are given here as an example of how such tables can be arranged.

As has been mentioned, these tables can be used at the time of photography to compute distance to the far plane D_m from the relationship

$$\frac{1}{D_m} = \frac{1}{D_o} - \frac{1}{D_h}$$

A

Focal length (millimeters)

$K_D = 0.57$ mm

	15	25	35	45	55	65	75	85	95
50	1.316	2.193	3.070	3.947	4.825	5.702	6.579	7.456	8.333
75	1.974	3.289	4.605	5.921	7.237	8.553	9.868	11.184	12.5
100	2.632	4.386	6.140	7.895	9.649	11.406	13.158	14.912	16.667
150	3.947	6.579	9.211	11.842	14.474	17.105	19.737	22.37	25.00

Values in meters

B

Focal length (millimeters)

$K_e = 0.18$ mm

	15	25	35	45	55	65	75	85	95
50	4.167	6.944	9.72	12.5	15.28	18.06	20.83	22.22	26.39
75	6.25	10.417	14.58	18.75	22.92	27.08	31.25	35.42	39.58
100	8.33	13.88	19.44	25.0	30.56	36.11	41.67	47.22	52.78
150	12.5	20.83	29.17	37.50	45.83	54.17	62.5	70.83	79.167

Values in meters

7.4. Hyperconvergence tables. (a) With divergence; (b) Without divergence.

For example, with a 50mm lens, if we are shooting a subject placed in the plane of convergence at 2 m, we can find the distance in the far plane resulting in 1° divergent screen parallaxes, or in nondivergent parallaxes. Let us suppose that t_c is set at 45 mm. For the divergent condition

$$\frac{1}{D_{me}} = \frac{1}{2 \text{ m}} - \frac{1}{3.945 \text{ m}}$$
$$D_{me} = 4.01 \text{ m}$$

For the nondivergent condition, given the same camera parameters

$$\frac{1}{D_{md}} = \frac{1}{2 \text{ m}} - \frac{1}{12.5 \text{ m}}$$
$$D_{md} = 2.4 \text{ m}$$

If we were to pull back the camera just one more meter, so that D_o was equal to 3 m, we would have a great increase in distance to the divergent far plane. For the divergent condition, $D_{md} = 12.5$ m, and for the nondivergent condition, $D_{me} = 3.95$ m.

As D_o approaches D_h, the depth-range increases rapidly. Although useful tables like these can find the needed D_m in a few seconds in conjunction with a simple pocket calculator, a set of tables solving for D_m may be handier. Such tables are presented beginning on page 203 for the various formats.

I have gone to the trouble of doing these numerical examples because a stereoscopic filmmaker may have limited mathematical training but still be faced with the need to produce depth-range tables for specific purposes. The arithmetic is not hard, only tedious; but pocket calculators, particularly programmable models, can vastly simplify the work.

DEPTH-RANGE PARAMETERS

The same kinds of considerations that were applied to large-format work projected on giant screens went into my formulation of depth-range tables for other formats. Instead of the seats beginning at about a distance equal to the height of the screen, as was the case with 70mm, seats are more likely to be placed somewhat further from the screen.

The principle set forth here of the invariance of screen parallax (page 118) holds that all formats projected on the same size screen, given the same camera parameters, will produce images with the same screen parallax and perspective. For this to be true, lenses must have the same angle of view, and the interaxial and distance to the plane of convergence must be set the same.

Given this constancy, depth range for photography with one format will be the same as photography with another. It is important to bear in mind that larger formats tend to be projected on larger screens, but the compensating factor is that people also tend to sit proportionately farther from large screens. Of course, this does not hold true for 70mm panoramic projection. If seating is moved proportionately further away, so that the angle of the large screen subtended at the eye is the same as that of the small screen, given equal photographic parameters, the depth range will be the same for both. This is the case despite the fact that screen parallaxes are greater for the larger magnification, because the most significant factor is actually retinal disparity, which is the same in both cases. One must never forget that the eyes are the final link in the stereoscopic optical system.

THE NEAR-RANGE EQUATIONS

It has been assumed that the volumetric compositional elements selected by the cinematography will lie at or behind the plane of convergence—the plane of the screen during projection—to a far plane of maximum distance. Without even taking into consideration the factors dealing with proper selection of focal length and interaxial setting together with camera to subject distance, the major limitation so far is that homologous points of objects in the far plane tend to move apart rapidly as distance from the camera increases. Once these values exceed some safe limit, strain will be produced, first for audience members in the closest seats, and then, depending on the magnitude of the parallaxes involved, extending backward through the theater rows.

Now let us consider the relationships necessary to predict the effect of objects closer to the camera than the plane of convergence. Let us recall that objects photographed in front of the plane of convergence will by convention be assigned negative values for screen parallax, (crossed parallax) and that these objects will appear in theater space.

In 3-D projection, screen and theater space are bounded by the plane of the screen, and their counterparts in the stereophotographic field are beyond and in front of the plane of convergence; the plane of convergence is the boundary. We will arbitrarily set the limit for theater space parallax at -65 mm. On the basis of parallax considerations alone, objects with -65 mm would appear halfway between all observers and the screen no matter what distance they are from the screen. This implies that the location of objects in space is determined by the eyes functioning in the manner of an optical rangefinder. This is subject to qualification: Extra-stereoscopic cues scale stereopsis. Since this is the case, and on the basis of my observations, it is indeed rare that an object with a parallax value of -65 mm appears to be halfway between the viewer and the screen to every person in an audience.

Most people have no trouble fusing images with a parallax of -65 mm, but those sitting in the closest seats will have a harder time fusing the image than those farther from the screen, since angular measure of parallax is the significant factor. There may be occasions when for shock effect or other reasons the decision is made to place objects even closer to the spectator than -65 mm. However, the filmmaker is advised that extra-stereoscopic cues, such as perspective, can emphasize even low values of negative screen parallax. The use of this alternative is preferable to large negative parallaxes, since stereoscopic photography beyond certain limits can produce unpleasant sensations.

Nevertheless, large values of parallax, quite a bit greater than t_e, can be comfortably fused by many people. According to the rule given by Valyus (page 100), for a thirty foot screen, this works out to almost one foot of negative screen parallax.

Arguments can be made to extend the basic depth-range equation to take into account the near-plane condition. Both Rule (April 1941) and Spottiswoode (1953) have derived this relationship:

$$\frac{1}{D_2} - \frac{1}{D_m} = \frac{2P_e}{Mf_ct_c}$$

It should be noted that the subscript 2 designates the near plane D_2. Recall also the relationship for the hyperconvergence distance:

$$\frac{P_e}{Mf_ct_c} = D_{he}$$

So we can now write

$$\frac{1}{D_2} - \frac{1}{D_m} = \frac{2}{D_{he}}$$

And solving for $1/D_2$ gives us

$$\frac{1}{D_2} = \frac{2}{D_{he}} + \frac{1}{D_m}$$

Thus, by solving for the near-plane distance in terms of the hyperconvergence distance and the far-plane distance, we have expressed what we call the near-range equation. Note the special case when $D_m \rightarrow \infty$:

$$\frac{1}{D_2} = \frac{2}{D_{he}}$$

or

$$\frac{D_{he}}{2} = D_2$$

This result is interesting. To record the stereoinfinity plane, when the stereocamera is set for the hyperconvergence distance, the near plane is halfway between the camera and plane of hyperconvergence.

We can also present the near-range equation in terms of the hyperconvergence distance and the distance to the plane of convergence. The basic depth-range equation

$$\frac{1}{D_m} = \frac{1}{D_o} - \frac{1}{D_{he}}$$

into which the near-range equation is substituted

$$\frac{1}{D_2} - \frac{1}{D_m} = \frac{1}{D_{he}}$$

to produce the desired result:

$$\frac{1}{D_2} = \frac{1}{D_{he}} + \frac{1}{D_o}$$

With regard to this relationship, when $D_o = D_h$, we have

$$\frac{1}{D_2} = \frac{2}{D_{he}}$$

This result has already been given when $D_m \rightarrow \infty$.

Finally, we can solve the near-range equation in terms of the distance to the plane of convergence and the distance to the far plane by similar manipulation to produce

$$\frac{1}{D_2} = \frac{2}{D_o} - \frac{1}{D_m}$$

In this case, when $D_m \rightarrow \infty$, $1/D_m = 0$, but then $D_o = D_{he}$, and we again have

$$\frac{1}{D_2} = \frac{2}{D_{he}}$$

Any one of these relationships properly applied can be used to solve for D_2. Perhaps the most convenient form of the equation is the way it was first given, in terms of D_h and D_m. One suggestion is first to calculate values of D_h (for the nondivergent case) and tabulate these. With this as a basis, compute and tabulate a set of tables solving for D_m, the most important unknown. Given sets of tables for D_h and D_m, we can then, in a straightforward operation, calculate and tabulate values for D_2.

THE TABLES

The basis of the calculations of the depth-range tables for the 70 mm dual format has already been given. This case does not represent a situation likely to be encountered by many filmmakers, but it is interesting because it is the most difficult, in terms of limited depth range. Tables for the super 8, 16 mm, and 35 mm formats may be constructed by similar means. While the K value for the 70 mm format was calculated by assuming that the nearest spectators would be seated a distance from the screen equal to the screen height, the super 8 K values were calculated by assuming that the nearest spectator would be placed at a distance of twice the screen width, and for 16 mm at a distance of twice the screen height. For the 35 mm format, the K values assumed that the closest seats in the house were at a distance equal to the screen height, as is the custom in many theaters.

7.5. SUPER 8 DEPTH-RANGE TABLE

$K_e = 0.2$ mm $K_d = 0.4$ mm   FORMAT Super 8 $F_c = 7$ mm

t_c		1.	1.5	2.	2.5	3.	3.5	4.	4.5	5.	5.5	6.	7.	8.	9.	10.	D_h
								D_o (meters)									
25 mm	D_{me}	∞	∞	∞	∞	∞	∞	∞	∞	∞	∞	∞	∞	∞	∞	∞	0.88
	D_{md}	∞	∞	∞	∞	∞	∞	∞	∞	∞	∞	∞	∞	∞	∞	∞	0.44
	D_2	0.47	0.55	0.61	0.65	0.68	0.70	0.72	0.73	0.74	0.75	0.76	0.78	0.79	0.80	0.80	
45 mm	D_{me}	2.74	31.50	∞	∞	∞	∞	∞	∞	∞	∞	∞	∞	∞	∞	∞	1.58
	D_{md}	∞	∞	∞	∞	∞	∞	∞	∞	∞	∞	∞	∞	∞	∞	∞	0.79
	D_2	0.61	0.77	0.88	0.97	1.03	1.09	1.13	1.17	1.20	1.22	1.25	1.29	1.32	1.34	1.36	
65 mm	D_{me}	1.78	4.40	16.55	∞	∞	∞	∞	∞	∞	∞	∞	∞	∞	∞	∞	2.28
	D_{md}	8.27	∞	∞	∞	∞	∞	∞	∞	∞	∞	∞	∞	∞	∞	∞	1.14
	D_2	0.69	0.90	1.06	1.19	1.29	1.38	1.45	1.51	1.56	1.61	1.65	1.72	1.77	1.82	1.85	
85 mm	D_{me}	1.51	3.03	6.10	15.66	∞	∞	∞	∞	∞	∞	∞	∞	∞	∞	∞	2.98
	D_{md}	3.05	∞	∞	∞	∞	∞	∞	∞	∞	∞	∞	∞	∞	∞	∞	1.49
	D_2	0.75	1.00	1.20	1.36	1.49	1.61	1.71	1.79	1.87	1.93	1.99	2.09	2.17	2.24	2.29	
105 mm	D_{me}	1.37	2.53	4.39	7.82	16.33	73.50	∞	∞	∞	∞	∞	∞	∞	∞	∞	3.68
	D_{md}	2.19	8.17	∞	∞	∞	∞	∞	∞	∞	∞	∞	∞	∞	∞	∞	1.84
	D_2	0.79	1.07	1.30	1.49	1.65	1.79	1.92	2.02	2.12	2.20	2.28	2.41	2.52	2.61	2.69	

7.5. Super 8 depth-range table continued.

K_e = 0.2 mm K_d = 0.4 mm

FORMAT Super 8 F_c = 15 mm

t_c		1.	1.5	2.	2.5	3.	3.5	4.	4.5	5.	5.5	6.	7.	8.	9.	10.	D_h
									D_o (meters)								
25 mm	D_{me}	2.14	7.50	∞	∞	∞	∞	∞	∞	∞	∞	∞	∞	∞	∞	∞	1.88
	D_{md}	∞	∞	∞	∞	∞	∞	∞	∞	∞	∞	∞	∞	∞	∞	∞	0.94
	D_2	0.65	0.83	0.97	1.07	1.15	1.22	1.28	1.32	1.36	1.40	1.43	1.48	1.52	1.55	1.58	
45 mm	D_{me}	1.42	2.70	4.91	9.64	27.00	∞	∞	∞	∞	∞	∞	∞	∞	∞	∞	3.38
	D_{md}	2.45	13.50	∞	∞	∞	∞	∞	∞	∞	∞	∞	∞	∞	∞	∞	1.69
	D_2	0.77	1.04	1.26	1.44	1.59	1.72	1.83	1.93	2.01	2.09	2.16	2.28	2.37	2.45	2.52	
65 mm	D_{me}	1.26	2.17	3.39	5.13	7.80	12.41	22.29	58.50	∞	∞	∞	∞	∞	∞	∞	4.88
	D_{md}	1.70	3.90	11.14	∞	∞	∞	∞	∞	∞	∞	∞	∞	∞	∞	∞	2.44
	D_2	0.83	1.15	1.42	1.65	1.86	2.04	2.20	2.34	2.47	2.58	2.69	2.87	3.03	3.16	3.28	
85 mm	D_{me}	1.19	1.96	2.91	4.11	5.67	7.76	10.74	15.30	23.18	40.07	102.00	∞	∞	∞	∞	6.38
	D_{md}	1.46	2.83	5.37	11.59	51.00	∞	∞	∞	∞	∞	∞	∞	∞	∞	∞	3.19
	D_2	0.86	1.21	1.52	1.80	2.04	2.26	2.46	2.64	2.80	2.95	3.09	3.34	3.55	3.73	3.89	
105 mm	D_{me}	1.15	1.85	2.68	3.66	4.85	6.30	8.13	10.50	13.70	18.24	25.20	63.00	∞	∞	∞	7.88
	D_{md}	1.34	2.42	4.06	6.85	12.60	31.50	∞	∞	∞	∞	∞	∞	∞	∞	∞	3.94
	D_2	0.89	1.26	1.59	1.90	2.17	2.42	2.65	2.86	3.06	3.24	3.41	3.71	3.97	4.20	4.41	

7.5. Super 8 depth-range table continued.

$K_e = 0.2$ mm $K_d = 0.4$ mm   FORMAT Super 8 $F_e = 28$ mm

t_c		1.	1.5	2.	2.5	3.	3.5	4.	4.5	5.	5.5	6.	7.	8.	9.	10.	D_h
25 mm	D_{me}	1.40	2.63	4.67	8.75	21.00	∞	∞	∞	∞	∞	∞	∞	∞	∞	∞	3.50
	D_{md}	2.33	10.50	∞	∞	∞	∞	∞	∞	∞	∞	∞	∞	∞	∞	∞	1.75
	D_2	0.78	1.05	1.27	1.46	1.62	1.75	1.87	1.97	2.06	2.14	2.21	2.33	2.43	2.52	2.59	
45 mm	D_{me}	1.19	1.97	2.93	4.14	5.73	7.87	10.96	15.75	24.23	43.31	126.00	∞	∞	∞	∞	6.30
	D_{md}	1.47	2.86	5.48	12.12	63.00	∞	∞	∞	∞	∞	∞	∞	∞	∞	∞	3.15
	D_2	0.86	1.21	1.52	1.79	2.03	2.25	2.45	2.63	2.79	2.94	3.07	3.32	3.52	3.71	3.87	
65 mm	D_{me}	1.12	1.80	2.56	3.45	4.48	5.69	7.14	8.90	11.10	13.90	17.61	30.33	66.18	819.00	∞	9.10
	D_{md}	1.28	2.24	3.57	5.55	8.81	15.17	33.09	409.50	∞	∞	∞	∞	∞	∞	∞	4.55
	D_2	0.90	1.29	1.64	1.96	2.26	2.53	2.78	3.01	3.23	3.43	3.62	3.96	4.26	4.52	4.76	
85 mm	D_{me}	1.09	1.72	2.40	3.16	4.01	4.96	6.03	7.24	8.62	10.23	12.10	17.00	24.41	36.93	62.63	11.90
	D_{md}	1.20	2.01	3.01	4.31	6.05	8.50	12.21	18.47	31.32	72.72	∞	∞	∞	∞	∞	5.95
	D_2	0.92	1.33	1.71	2.07	2.40	2.70	2.99	3.27	3.52	3.76	3.99	4.41	4.78	5.12	5.43	
105 mm	D_{me}	1.07	1.67	2.31	3.01	3.77	4.59	5.50	6.49	7.58	8.79	10.14	13.36	17.55	23.21	31.28	14.70
	D_{md}	1.16	1.88	2.75	3.79	5.07	6.68	8.78	11.61	15.64	21.85	32.67	147.00	∞	∞	∞	7.35
	D_2	0.94	1.36	1.76	2.14	2.49	2.83	3.14	3.45	3.73	4.00	4.26	4.74	5.18	5.58	5.95	

D_o (meters)

7.6. 16mm DEPTH-RANGE TABLE

$K_e = 0.2$ mm $K_d = 0.47$ mm   FORMAT 16mm $F_c = 12.5$ mm

D_o (meters)

t_c		1.	1.5	2.	2.5	3.	3.5	4.	4.5	5.	5.5	6.	7.	8.	9.	10.	D_h
25 mm	D_{me}	2.78	37.50	∞	∞	∞	∞	∞	∞	∞	∞	∞	∞	∞	∞	∞	1.56
	D_{md}	∞	∞	∞	∞	∞	∞	∞	∞	∞	∞	∞	∞	∞	∞	∞	0.66
	D_2	0.61	0.77	0.88	0.96	1.03	1.08	1.12	1.16	1.19	1.22	1.24	1.28	1.31	1.33	1.35	
45 mm	D_{me}	1.55	3.21	6.92	22.50	∞	∞	∞	∞	∞	∞	∞	∞	∞	∞	∞	2.81
	D_{md}	6.08	∞	∞	∞	∞	∞	∞	∞	∞	∞	∞	∞	∞	∞	∞	1.20
	D_2	0.74	0.98	1.17	1.32	1.45	1.56	1.65	1.73	1.80	1.86	1.91	2.01	2.08	2.14	2.20	
65 mm	D_{me}	1.33	2.38	3.94	6.50	11.47	25.28	260.00	∞	∞	∞	∞	∞	∞	∞	∞	4.06
	D_{md}	2.37	11.34	∞	∞	∞	∞	∞	∞	∞	∞	∞	∞	∞	∞	∞	1.73
	D_2	0.80	1.10	1.34	1.55	1.73	1.88	2.02	2.14	2.24	2.34	2.42	2.57	2.69	2.80	2.89	
85 mm	D_{me}	1.23	2.09	3.21	4.72	6.89	10.26	16.19	29.42	85.00	∞	∞	∞	∞	∞	∞	5.31
	D_{md}	1.79	4.46	17.35	∞	∞	∞	∞	∞	∞	∞	∞	∞	∞	∞	∞	2.26
	D_2	0.84	1.17	1.45	1.70	1.92	2.11	2.28	2.44	2.58	2.70	2.82	3.02	3.19	3.34	3.47	
105 mm	D_{me}	1.18	1.94	2.88	4.04	5.53	7.50	10.24	14.32	21.00	33.97	70.00	∞	∞	∞	∞	6.56
	D_{md}	1.56	3.24	7.05	23.86	∞	∞	∞	∞	∞	∞	∞	∞	∞	∞	∞	2.79
	D_2	0.87	1.22	1.53	1.81	2.06	2.28	2.49	2.67	2.84	2.99	3.13	3.39	3.61	3.80	3.96	

7.6. 16mm depth-range table continued.

$K_e = 0.2$ mm $K_d = 0.47$ mm   FORMAT 16mm $F_c = 25$ mm

D_o (meters)

t_c		1.	1.5	2.	2.5	3.	3.5	4.	4.5	5.	5.5	6.	7.	8.	9.	10.	D_h
25 mm	D_{me}	1.47	2.88	5.56	12.50	75.00	∞	∞	∞	∞	∞	∞	∞	∞	∞	∞	3.13
	D_{md}	4.03	∞	∞	∞	∞	∞	∞	∞	∞	∞	∞	∞	∞	∞	∞	1.33
	D_2	0.76	1.01	1.22	1.39	1.53	1.65	1.75	1.84	1.92	1.99	2.05	2.16	2.25	2.32	2.38	2.38
45 mm	D_{me}	1.22	2.05	3.10	4.50	6.43	9.26	13.85	22.50	45.00	247.50	∞	∞	∞	∞	∞	5.63
	D_{md}	1.72	4.02	12.16	∞	∞	∞	∞	∞	∞	∞	∞	∞	∞	∞	∞	2.39
	D_2	0.85	1.18	1.48	1.73	1.96	2.16	2.34	2.50	2.65	2.78	2.90	3.12	3.30	3.46	3.60	3.60
65 mm	D_{me}	1.14	1.84	2.65	3.61	4.76	6.15	7.88	10.09	13.00	17.02	22.94	50.56	520.00	∞	∞	8.13
	D_{md}	1.41	2.65	4.74	9.03	22.67	∞	∞	∞	∞	∞	∞	∞	∞	∞	∞	3.46
	D_2	0.89	1.27	1.60	1.91	2.19	2.45	2.68	2.90	3.10	3.28	3.45	3.76	4.03	4.27	4.48	4.48
85 mm	D_{me}	1.10	1.75	2.46	3.27	4.18	5.22	6.42	7.81	9.44	11.40	13.78	20.52	32.38	58.85	170.00	10.63
	D_{md}	1.28	2.24	3.59	5.59	8.92	15.49	34.69	956.25	∞	∞	∞	∞	∞	∞	∞	4.52
	D_2	0.91	1.31	1.68	2.02	2.34	2.63	2.91	3.16	3.40	3.62	3.83	4.22	4.56	4.87	5.15	5.15
105 mm	D_{me}	1.00	1.69	2.36	3.09	3.89	4.77	5.75	6.85	8.08	9.47	11.05	15.00	20.49	28.64	42.00	13.13
	D_{md}	1.22	2.05	3.12	4.53	6.48	9.37	14.09	23.16	47.73	360.94	∞	∞	∞	∞	∞	5.59
	D_2	0.93	1.35	1.74	2.10	2.44	2.76	3.07	3.35	3.62	3.88	4.12	4.57	4.97	5.34	5.68	5.68

7.6. 16mm depth-range table continued.

FORMAT　16mm　F_c = 50 mm

K_e = 0.2 mm　　　K_d = 0.47 mm

D_o (meters)

t_c		1.	1.5	2.	2.5	3.	3.5	4.	4.5	5.	5.5	6.	7.	8.	9.	10.	D_h
25 mm	D_{me}	1.19	1.97	2.94	4.17	5.77	7.95	11.11	16.07	25.00	45.83	150.00	∞	∞	∞	∞	6.25
	D_{md}	1.60	3.44	8.06	41.67	∞	∞	∞	∞	∞	∞	∞	∞	∞	∞	∞	2.66
	D_2	0.86	1.21	1.52	1.79	2.03	2.24	2.44	2.62	2.78	2.93	3.06	3.30	3.51	3.69	3.85	
45 mm	D_{me}	1.10	1.73	2.43	3.21	4.09	5.08	6.21	7.50	9.00	10.76	12.86	18.53	27.69	45.00	90.00	11.25
	D_{md}	1.26	2.18	3.44	5.23	8.04	13.02	24.32	75.00	∞	∞	∞	∞	∞	∞	∞	4.79
	D_2	0.92	1.32	1.70	2.05	2.37	2.67	2.95	3.21	3.46	3.69	3.91	4.32	4.68	5.00	5.29	
65 mm	D_{me}	1.07	1.65	2.28	2.95	3.68	4.46	5.31	6.22	7.22	8.31	9.51	12.30	15.76	20.17	26.00	16.25
	D_{md}	1.17	1.92	2.81	3.92	5.30	7.09	9.49	12.89	18.06	26.88	45.35	∞	∞	∞	∞	6.91
	D_2	0.94	1.37	1.78	2.17	2.53	2.88	3.21	3.52	3.82	4.11	4.38	4.89	5.36	5.79	6.19	
85 mm	D_{me}	1.05	1.61	2.21	2.83	3.49	4.19	4.93	5.71	6.54	7.42	8.36	10.44	12.83	15.61	18.89	21.25
	D_{md}	1.12	1.80	2.57	3.46	4.49	5.71	7.17	8.96	11.18	14.04	17.83	30.99	69.39	1912.50	∞	9.04
	D_2	0.96	1.40	1.83	2.24	2.63	3.01	3.37	3.71	4.05	4.37	4.68	5.27	5.81	6.32	6.80	
105 mm	D_{me}	1.04	1.59	2.16	2.76	3.39	4.04	4.72	5.43	6.18	6.96	7.78	9.55	11.51	13.70	16.15	26.25
	D_{md}	1.10	1.73	2.44	3.22	4.10	5.10	6.23	7.54	9.05	10.83	12.96	18.75	28.19	46.32	95.45	11.17
	D_2	0.96	1.42	1.86	2.28	2.69	3.09	3.47	3.84	4.20	4.55	4.88	5.53	6.13	6.70	7.24	

7.7. 35mm DEPTH-RANGE TABLE

FORMAT 35mm F_c = 25 mm

K_e = 0.18 mm K_d = 0.37 mm

D_o (meters)

t_c		1.	1.5	2.	2.5	3.	3.5	4.	4.5	5.	5.5	6.	7.	8.	9.	10.	D_h
25 mm	D_{me}	1.40	2.64	4.72	8.93	22.06	∞	∞	∞	∞	∞	∞	∞	∞	∞	∞	3.47
	D_{md}	2.45	13.39	∞	∞	∞	∞	∞	∞	∞	∞	∞	∞	∞	∞	∞	1.69
	D_2	0.78	1.05	1.27	1.45	1.61	1.74	1.86	1.96	2.05	2.13	2.20	2.32	2.42	2.51	2.58	
45 mm	D_{me}	1.19	1.97	2.94	4.17	5.77	7.95	11.11	16.07	25.00	45.83	150.00	∞	∞	∞	∞	6.25
	D_{md}	1.49	2.96	5.84	14.06	225.00	∞	∞	∞	∞	∞	∞	∞	∞	∞	∞	3.04
	D_2	0.86	1.21	1.52	1.79	2.03	2.24	2.44	2.62	2.78	2.93	3.06	3.30	3.51	3.69	3.85	
65 mm	D_{me}	1.12	1.80	2.57	3.46	4.49	5.72	7.18	8.97	11.21	14.07	17.89	31.16	70.27	2925.30	∞	9.03
	D_{md}	1.29	2.28	3.67	5.80	9.47	17.23	44.83	∞	∞	∞	∞	∞	∞	∞	∞	4.39
	D_2	0.90	1.29	1.64	1.96	2.25	2.52	2.77	3.00	3.22	3.42	3.60	3.94	4.24	4.51	4.74	
85 mm	D_{me}	1.09	1.72	2.41	3.17	4.02	4.97	6.05	7.27	8.67	10.30	12.20	17.20	24.82	37.87	65.38	11.81
	D_{md}	1.21	2.03	3.07	4.43	6.28	8.96	13.18	20.79	38.64	129.86	∞	∞	∞	∞	∞	5.74
	D_2	0.92	1.33	1.71	2.06	2.39	2.70	2.99	3.26	3.51	3.75	3.98	4.39	4.77	5.11	5.41	
105 mm	D_{me}	1.07	1.67	2.32	3.02	3.78	4.61	5.51	6.51	7.61	8.83	10.19	13.46	17.72	23.51	31.82	14.58
	D_{md}	1.16	1.90	2.79	3.86	5.20	6.91	9.17	12.30	16.94	24.47	38.89	525.00	∞	∞	∞	7.09
	D_2	0.94	1.36	1.76	2.13	2.49	2.82	3.14	3.44	3.72	3.99	4.25	4.73	5.17	5.57	5.93	

7.7. 35mm depth-range table continued.

$K_e = 0.18$ mm $K_d = 0.37$ mm

FORMAT 35mm $F_c = 50$ mm

D_o (meters)

t_c		1.	1.5	2.	2.5	3.	3.5	4.	4.5	5.	5.5	6.	7.	8.	9.	10.	D_h
25 mm	D_{me}	1.17	1.91	2.81	3.91	5.28	7.06	9.43	12.78	17.86	26.44	44.12	∞	∞	∞	∞	6.94
	D_{md}	1.42	2.70	4.90	9.62	26.79	∞	∞	∞	∞	∞	∞	∞	∞	∞	∞	3.38
	D_2	0.87	1.23	1.55	1.84	2.09	2.33	2.54	2.73	2.91	3.07	3.22	3.49	3.72	3.92	4.10	
45 mm	D_{me}	1.09	1.70	2.38	3.13	3.95	4.86	5.88	7.03	8.33	9.82	11.54	15.91	22.22	32.14	50.00	12.50
	D_{md}	1.20	1.99	2.98	4.25	5.92	8.25	11.69	17.31	28.12	57.56	450.00	∞	∞	∞	∞	6.08
	D_2	0.93	1.34	1.72	2.08	2.42	2.73	3.03	3.31	3.57	3.82	4.05	4.49	4.88	5.23	5.56	
65 mm	D_{me}	1.06	1.64	2.25	2.90	3.60	4.34	5.14	5.99	6.91	7.91	8.99	11.43	14.36	17.94	22.41	18.06
	D_{md}	1.13	1.81	2.59	3.49	4.56	5.82	7.34	9.23	11.61	14.71	18.93	34.47	89.66	∞	∞	8.78
	D_2	0.95	1.38	1.80	2.20	2.57	2.93	3.27	3.60	3.92	4.22	4.50	5.04	5.54	6.01	6.44	
85 mm	D_{me}	1.04	1.60	2.19	2.80	3.44	4.11	4.82	5.56	6.34	7.17	8.04	9.95	12.10	14.54	17.35	23.61
	D_{md}	1.10	1.73	2.42	3.20	4.06	5.03	6.14	7.40	8.85	10.55	12.56	17.92	26.36	41.58	77.27	11.49
	D_2	0.96	1.41	1.84	2.26	2.66	3.05	3.42	3.78	4.13	4.46	4.78	5.40	5.98	6.52	7.02	
105 mm	D_{me}	1.04	1.58	2.15	2.73	3.34	3.98	4.64	5.32	6.03	6.78	7.55	9.21	11.02	13.02	15.22	29.17
	D_{md}	1.08	1.68	2.33	3.03	3.80	4.65	5.57	6.59	7.72	8.98	10.40	13.82	18.34	24.61	33.87	14.19
	D_2	0.97	1.43	1.87	2.30	2.72	3.13	3.52	3.90	4.27	4.63	4.98	5.65	6.28	6.88	7.45	

7.7. 35mm depth-range table continued.

K_e = 0.18 mm $\qquad K_d$ = 0.37 mm $\qquad\qquad$ FORMAT 35mm F_c = 35 mm

D_o (meters)

t_c		1.	1.5	2.	2.5	3.	3.5	4.	4.5	5.	5.5	6.	7.	8.	9.	10.	D_h
25 mm	D_{me}	1.26	2.17	3.40	5.15	7.84	12.50	22.58	60.58	∞	∞	∞	∞	∞	∞	∞	4.86
	D_{md}	1.73	4.10	12.96	∞	∞	∞	∞	∞	∞	∞	∞	∞	∞	∞	∞	2.36
	D_2	0.83	1.15	1.42	1.65	1.86	2.03	2.19	2.34	2.46	2.58	2.69	2.87	3.02	3.16	3.27	
45 mm	D_{me}	1.13	1.81	2.59	3.50	4.57	5.83	7.37	9.26	11.67	14.81	19.09	35.00	93.33	∞	∞	8.75
	D_{md}	1.31	2.32	3.77	6.06	10.16	19.69	66.32	∞	∞	∞	∞	∞	∞	∞	∞	4.26
	D_2	0.90	1.28	1.63	1.94	2.23	2.50	2.75	2.97	3.18	3.38	3.56	3.89	4.18	4.44	4.67	
65 mm	D_{me}	1.09	1.70	2.38	3.12	3.93	4.84	5.85	6.99	8.27	9.74	11.42	15.69	21.80	31.26	47.89	12.64
	D_{md}	1.19	1.98	2.96	4.21	5.86	8.12	11.45	16.78	26.76	52.14	248.18	∞	∞	∞	∞	6.15
	D_2	0.93	1.34	1.73	2.09	2.42	2.74	3.04	3.32	3.58	3.83	4.07	4.50	4.90	5.26	5.58	
85 mm	D_{me}	1.06	1.65	2.28	2.95	3.67	4.44	5.28	6.18	7.17	8.24	9.42	12.14	15.50	19.76	25.32	16.53
	D_{md}	1.14	1.84	2.66	3.63	4.79	6.20	7.96	10.22	13.22	17.41	23.64	54.09	1586.67	∞	∞	8.04
	D_2	0.94	1.38	1.78	2.17	2.54	2.89	3.22	3.54	3.84	4.13	4.40	4.92	5.39	5.83	6.23	
105 mm	D_{me}	1.05	1.62	2.22	2.85	3.52	4.22	4.97	5.77	6.62	7.53	8.50	10.65	13.15	16.09	19.60	20.42
	D_{md}	1.11	1.77	2.50	3.34	4.30	5.40	6.70	8.23	10.07	12.32	15.15	23.71	41.12	95.87	∞	9.93
	D_2	0.95	1.40	1.82	2.23	2.62	2.99	3.34	3.69	4.02	4.33	4.64	5.21	5.75	6.25	6.71	

7.8. 70mm DEPTH-RANGE TABLE

$K_e = 0.18$ cm $K_d = 0.57$ mm   FORMAT 70mm $F_c = 50$ mm

t_c		D_o (meters)															D_h
		1.	1.5	2.	2.5	3.	3.5	4.	4.5	5.	5.5	6.	7.	8.	9.	10.	
25 mm	D_{me}	1.17	1.92	2.81	3.91	5.28	7.06	9.43	12.78	17.86	26.44	44.12	∞	∞	∞	∞	6.94
	D_{md}	1.84	4.75	22.73	∞	∞	∞	∞	∞	∞	∞	∞	∞	∞	∞	∞	2.19
	D_2	0.87	1.23	1.55	1.84	2.09	2.33	2.54	2.73	2.91	3.07	3.22	3.49	3.72	3.92	4.10	
45 mm	D_{me}	1.09	1.70	2.38	3.13	3.95	4.86	5.88	7.03	8.33	9.82	11.54	15.91	22.22	32.14	50.00	12.50
	D_{md}	1.34	2.42	4.05	6.82	12.50	30.88	∞	∞	∞	∞	∞	∞	∞	∞	∞	3.95
	D_2	0.93	1.34	1.72	2.08	2.42	2.73	3.03	3.31	3.57	3.82	4.05	4.49	4.88	5.23	5.56	
65 mm	D_{me}	1.06	1.64	2.25	2.90	3.60	4.34	5.14	5.99	6.91	7.91	8.99	11.43	14.36	17.94	22.41	18.06
	D_{md}	1.21	2.04	3.08	4.45	6.33	9.06	13.40	21.35	40.63	155.43	∞	∞	∞	∞	∞	5.70
	D_2	0.95	1.38	1.80	2.20	2.57	2.93	3.27	3.60	3.92	4.22	4.50	5.04	5.54	6.01	6.44	
85 mm	D_{me}	1.04	1.60	2.19	2.80	3.44	4.11	4.82	5.56	6.34	7.17	8.04	9.95	12.10	14.54	17.35	23.61
	D_{md}	1.15	1.88	2.73	3.76	5.02	6.60	8.63	11.35	15.18	20.96	30.72	114.42	∞	∞	∞	7.46
	D_2	0.96	1.41	1.84	2.26	2.66	3.05	3.42	3.78	4.13	4.46	4.78	5.40	5.98	6.52	7.02	
105 mm	D_{me}	1.04	1.58	2.15	2.73	3.34	3.98	4.64	5.32	6.03	6.78	7.55	9.21	11.02	13.02	15.22	29.17
	D_{md}	1.12	1.79	2.55	3.43	4.45	5.65	7.07	8.80	10.94	13.65	17.21	29.17	60.87	393.75	∞	29.17
	D_2	0.97	1.43	1.87	2.30	2.72	3.13	3.52	3.90	4.27	4.63	4.98	5.65	6.28	6.88	7.45	

7.8. 70mm depth-range table continued.

FORMAT 70mm F_e = 75 mm

K_e = 0.18 mm K_d = 0.57 mm

D_o (meters)

t_e		1.	1.5	2.	2.5	3.	3.5	4.	4.5	5.	5.5	6.	7.	8.	9.	10.	D_h
25 mm	D_{me}	1.11	1.76	2.48	3.30	4.23	5.30	6.54	7.99	9.72	11.80	14.37	21.84	35.80	71.20	340.91	10.42
	D_{md}	1.44	2.76	5.10	10.42	34.09	∞	∞	∞	∞	∞	∞	∞	∞	∞	∞	3.29
	D_2	0.91	1.31	1.68	2.02	2.33	2.62	2.89	3.14	3.38	3.60	3.81	4.19	4.52	4.83	5.10	
45 mm	D_{me}	1.06	1.63	2.24	2.89	3.58	4.31	5.10	5.94	6.85	7.82	8.87	11.24	14.07	17.49	21.70	18.75
	D_{md}	1.20	2.01	3.02	4.33	6.08	8.56	12.33	18.75	32.14	77.34	∞	∞	∞	∞	∞	5.92
	D_2	0.95	1.39	1.81	2.21	2.59	2.95	3.30	3.63	3.95	4.25	4.55	5.10	5.61	6.08	6.52	
65 mm	D_{me}	1.04	1.59	2.16	2.76	3.38	4.03	4.70	5.41	6.15	6.92	7.73	9.48	11.41	13.55	15.96	27.08
	D_{md}	1.13	1.82	2.61	3.53	4.62	5.92	7.51	9.50	12.04	5.41	20.10	38.56	123.81	∞	∞	8.55
	D_2	0.96	1.42	1.86	2.29	2.70	3.10	3.49	3.86	4.22	4.57	4.91	5.56	6.18	6.76	7.30	
85 mm	D_{me}	1.03	1.57	2.12	2.69	3.28	3.89	4.52	5.16	5.82	6.52	7.24	8.75	10.37	12.11	14.00	35.42
	D_{md}	1.10	1.73	2.44	3.22	4.10	5.09	6.23	7.53	9.04	10.82	12.94	18.71	28.10	46.08	94.44	11.18
	D_2	0.97	1.44	1.89	2.34	2.77	3.19	3.59	3.99	4.38	4.76	5.13	5.84	6.53	7.18	7.80	
105 mm	D_{me}	1.02	1.55	2.10	2.65	3.22	3.81	4.40	5.02	5.65	6.30	6.97	8.35	9.81	11.36	13.01	43.75
	D_{md}	1.08	1.68	2.34	3.05	3.83	4.69	5.63	6.67	7.84	9.14	10.61	14.19	19.00	25.82	36.21	13.82
	D_2	0.98	1.45	1.91	2.36	2.81	3.24	3.66	4.08	4.49	4.89	5.28	6.03	6.76	7.46	8.14	

7.8. 70mm depth-range table continued.

$K_e = 0.18$ mm $K_d = 0.57$ mm

FORMAT 70mm $F_c = 100$ mm

t_c		1.	1.5	2.	2.5	3.	3.5	4.	4.5	5.	5.5	6.	7.	8.	9.	10.	D_h
							D_o (meters)										
25 mm	D_{me}	1.08	1.68	2.34	3.06	3.84	4.70	5.64	6.69	7.86	9.17	10.65	14.27	19.16	26.10	36.76	13.89
	D_{md}	1.30	2.28	3.68	5.81	9.49	17.33	45.45	∞	∞	∞	∞	∞	∞	∞	∞	4.39
	D_2	0.93	1.35	1.75	2.12	2.47	2.80	3.11	3.40	3.68	3.94	4.19	4.65	5.08	5.46	5.81	
45 mm	D_{me}	1.04	1.60	2.18	2.78	3.41	4.08	4.77	5.50	6.27	7.07	7.92	9.76	11.83	14.15	16.79	25.00
	D_{md}	1.15	1.85	2.68	3.66	4.84	6.29	8.11	10.47	13.64	18.13	25.00	61.76	∞	∞	∞	7.89
	D_2	0.96	1.42	1.85	2.27	2.68	3.07	3.45	3.81	4.17	4.51	4.84	5.47	6.06	6.62	7.14	
65 mm	D_{me}	1.03	1.57	2.12	2.69	3.28	3.88	4.50	5.15	5.81	6.50	7.21	8.71	10.31	12.03	13.89	36.11
	D_{md}	1.10	1.73	2.43	3.20	4.07	5.05	6.16	7.43	8.90	10.62	12.66	18.13	26.80	42.70	81.25	11.40
	D_2	0.97	1.44	1.90	2.34	2.77	3.19	3.60	4.00	4.39	4.77	5.15	5.86	6.55	7.20	7.83	
85 mm	D_{me}	1.02	1.55	2.09	2.64	3.21	3.78	4.37	4.98	5.60	6.23	6.88	8.23	9.65	11.15	12.72	47.22
	D_{md}	1.07	1.67	2.31	3.00	3.76	4.57	5.47	6.44	7.52	8.71	10.04	13.19	17.26	22.70	30.36	14.91
	D_2	0.98	1.45	1.92	2.37	2.82	3.26	3.69	4.11	4.52	4.93	5.32	6.10	6.84	7.56	8.25	
105 mm	D_{me}	1.02	1.54	2.07	2.61	3.16	3.73	4.30	4.88	5.47	6.08	6.70	7.97	9.29	10.66	12.10	58.33
	D_{md}	1.06	1.63	2.24	2.89	3.58	4.32	5.11	5.95	6.86	7.84	8.90	11.29	14.14	17.60	21.88	18.42
	D_2	0.98	1.46	1.93	2.40	2.85	3.30	3.74	4.18	4.61	5.03	5.44	6.25	7.04	7.80	8.54	

The 70 mm format uses a 2.2:1 aspect ratio, the super 8 and 16 mm formats a 1.3:1 aspect ratio, and the 35 mm format is given a 2.3:1 or scope aspect ratio. Only the 35 mm format is assumed to be a single-band system, using the over-and-under or twin Techniscope format, but as long as the format sizes maintain standard dimensions, it makes no difference whether they are dual- or single-band. Of the given formats, the greatest variability in screen shape exists for the 35 mm frame. The super 8 and 16 mm formats are almost presented at 1.3:1, and 70 mm at 2.2:1. On the other hand, 35 mm is projected in ratios from 1.3:1 to 2.3:1, with intermediate values of 1.85:1 and 2:1 frequently used. I selected the over-and-under 35 mm system, with its approximately 2.3:1 ratio, because it is a likely candidate for commercial acceptance.

The most important focal lengths for shooting stereo movies will probably fluctuate between values somewhat less than the diagonal of the format to about three times the diagonal, and the tables have entries based on these considerations.

Various factors play a role in the selection of which values to tabulate. It would have been nice to offer additional values for focal lengths, or others for interaxials, which are given here from 25 to 105 mm in steps of 20 mm. Tables with additional K values based on other assumptions about seating and relative screen size could have been offered. To provide all the tables that might be interesting would have taken many more pages. I have tried to give the most useful information in a relatively small number of tables.

Filmmakers who need great precision or who know they are going to be shooting for a specific screen size would do well to calculate their own tables or to use a programmable calculator to produce depth-range limits in the field.

The K values derived were based on a range of frame magnifications of from about 200 to 400. This, it is felt, is typical of motion picture systems. To shoot a stereoscopic film for the largest value of M for a given range of screens would ensure control of divergence and avoidance of a breakdown of the accommodation/convergence ratio for screen points with negative parallax for all screen sizes. However, this might lead to needless restrictions in photography for small screen sizes, and some compromise value of K was chosen favoring the largest screens. Usually 10% was added to the largest K in an attempt to increase depth range. Given a constant value for P_{me} of 65 mm, equal values of M for all formats will have the same value for K_e, and for this reason K_e is usually in the range of 0.2 mm.

The relatively limited depth range for 70mm photography is attributable not to the large screen size but to the custom of having seats very close to the large screen. If the closest seats were twice the screen width away, with suitable adjustment for aspect ratio differences and given equal camera parameters, then depth range for 70mm photography would be the same as that for the super 8 format, for example.

OBJECT MAGNIFICATION AND DEPTH RANGE

Given the basic form of the depth-range equation,

$$P_m = Mf_ct_c\left(\frac{1}{D_o} - \frac{1}{D_m}\right)$$

we can write

$$P_m = \frac{Mf_ct_cD_m}{D_oD_m} - \frac{Mf_ct_cD_o}{D_oD_m}$$

and

$$P_m = \frac{Mf_ct_c}{D_oD_m\,(D_m - D_o)}$$

When discussing the Soviet transmission system, we derived the relationship between object and frame magnification, which is given here in our notation:

$$m = \frac{f_cM}{D_o}$$

By substitution, we have

$$P_m = mt_c\,\frac{D_m - D_o}{D_m}$$

We will call the expression $(D_m - D_o)/D_m$ the *reduced depth range* and write it as $\overline{\Delta D}$. Then we have

$$\frac{P_m}{mt_c} = \overline{\Delta D}$$

Therefore

$$\overline{\Delta D}\quad \alpha\, \frac{1}{m}$$

Thus the depth range, $D_m - D_o$ or ΔD, is inversely proportional to object magnification. The larger the image of the object the less the depth range; the smaller the image, the greater $\overline{\Delta D}$.

Depth range varies with object magnification. Now we will investigate how depth range changes if distance to the plane of convergence and then object magnification remain constant.

If D_o remains constant but f_c varies, then m changes. This must be true because

$$m = \frac{fcM}{D_o}$$

Given the condition that D_o remains constant, in terms of the depth-range relationship,

$$D_m = \left(\frac{1}{D_o} - \frac{K_e}{f_ct_c}\right)^{-1}$$

If D_o is constant (as is t_c) but f_c increases, then D_m decreases. If D_o is constant (as is t_c) but f_c decreases, then D_m increases. To put it another way, given a constant distance to the plane of convergence, increasing the focal length decreases the depth range and vice versa.

If m remains constant, D_o must vary in direct proportion to f_c, as shown by the object-frame magnification equation above. By multiplying both D_o and f_o by any number N, we will keep m constant. Thus

$$D_{mn} = \frac{1}{ND_o - K_e/Nf_ct_c}$$

. or

$$D_{mn} = \frac{N}{1/D_o - K_e/f_ct_c}$$

For the case of hyperconvergence distance given by

$$D_h = \frac{f_ct_c}{K_e}$$

when multiplying f_c by N,

$$D_{hn} = \frac{Nf_ct_c}{K_e}$$

So we can state that increasing f_c and D_o N times also increases D_m and D_h N times. The reader can confirm this by comparing entries in the depth-range tables. For example, given the super 8 format, as we quadruple the value of both f_c and D_o, giving constant image magnification for the object in the plane of convergence, we find that the value of D_{me} is also quadrupled. For $f_c = 7$ mm, and the entry under $D_o = 1.5$ m (for $t_c = 65$ mm), we find $D_{me} = 4.40$ m. For the corresponding entry under $f_c = 28$ mm, $D_o = 6$ m ($t_c = 65$ mm), we find $D_{me} = 17.61$ m.

The same arguments can be advanced concerning D_2, which also varies in proportion to changes in D_0 and f_c, while m remains constant.

We can summarize these observations. Depth range (ΔD, or $D_m - D_o$) is the difference in distance between the far and near planes. It is inversely proportional to m, or object magnification. The larger the projected image of the object photographed in the plane of convergence, the less depth range we will have, other photographic variables remaining constant.

If D_o remains constant and we vary the shot by changing f_c (assuming a constant t_c), object magnification m will decrease proportionately as f_c decreases and vice versa. As the focal length of the shot decreases, object magnification will decrease but depth range will increase, and vice versa.

If we increase the distance to the object in the plane of convergence proportionately with an increase in focal length, object magnification will remain constant, and the distance to the far plane will proportionately increase (assuming a constant t_c).

In other words, given constant image magnification m for the object at the plane of convergence distance D_o, as D_o increases in proportion to f_c, then depth range $D_o - D_m$, or distance to the far plane D_m, increases proportionately (or decreases as D_o and f_c increase).

One implication of this is that one cannot get something for nothing. If one moves back from the object to take the shot in order to increase ΔD, maintaining a constant f_c, then m will decrease. One will get more ΔD, but the composition of the shot may not be acceptable, since the primary object of interest has diminished in size.

If one moves away from the primary object at D_o and increases f_c proportionately to maintain m, ΔD will increase, but because of perspective considerations, the relative juxtaposition of foreground and background will have been altered, perhaps again spoiling the composition. And it may not even be physically possible to move the camera farther away from the subject.

Increasing ΔD this way may be of most use in the studio, where longer distances to the primary object, an actor usually, can be conveniently ar-

constant m, constant t_c		
D_o	1.5 m	3.0 m	6.0 m
f_c	12.5 mm	25 mm	50 mm
t_c	65 mm	65 mm	65 mm
D_{me}	2.38 m	4.76 m	9.51 m
D_{md}	11.34 m	22.67 m	45.35 m
D_2	1.10 m	2.19 m	4.38 m

7.9. *Constant m, constant t_c.*

constant m, t_c varied to account for perspective		
D_o	1.5 m	3.0 m	6.0 m
f_c	12.5 m	25 mm	50 mm
t_c	45 mm	65 mm	85 mm
D_{me}	3.21 m	4.76 m	8.36 m
D_{md}	∞	22.67 m	17.83 m
D_2	0.98 m	2.19 m	4.68 m

7. 10. *Constant m, t_c varied to account for perspective.*

ranged. In the field, or for documentary work, this may be out of the question, since it is usually impossible to remove existing walls, and so forth, in order to compose a shot.

So far no mention has been made of varying t_c in terms of compensation for perspective scaling factors. If you wish to move back from the subject and accept reduced m, shorter focal lengths can possibly call for reduced interaxial distances, further increasing the depth range. However, in many cases, one may not wish to reduce t_c, since increased distance from the subject, shorter focal length notwithstanding, will reduce the stereoscopic effect.

On the other hand, when moving back from the subject in the studio to increase depth range, some increase in t_c is in order, to compensate for relaxed or flattened perspective created by increased distance. This increase in t_c would tend to decrease depth range, but most of the time this is not enough to offset gains produced by shooting from a greater distance.

In the accompanying tables the reader will be able to observe the effects of these factors. I have taken the case of a medium shot of a person, from three distances, with proportional increases in f_c to maintain a constant m. The first table, in which the 16mm format is assumed, gives depth-range data for a constant t_c. The second makes moderate changes in t_c in response to perspective changes.

DEPTH OF FIELD AND DEPTH RANGE

It may seem obvious to some readers that there are certain similarities between the concepts of depth of field and depth range. Depth of field applies to planar as well as stereoscopic photography and is used to establish limits for acceptable focus in front of and behind the plane in space on which the lens is focused. Thus we can draw a comparison between near and far limits of focus and D_2 and D_m, while the distance to the plane on which the lens is focused is comparable to D_0. In addition, I have defined the hyperconvergence distance, D_h, and by so naming it have drawn an immediate comparison between it and hyperfocal distance.

The calculation of depth of field tables is based on an arbitrary constant, called the circle of confusion, which is related to resolution. Sometimes it is taken to be

$$\frac{fc}{1000}$$

At other times, other values may be chosen to increase or reduce the depth of field to correspond to the distance of the viewer from the image, or enlargement of the image. Once again there is a compelling similarity, this time between the circle of confusion and the stereoconstant K, which is selected for divergent and nondivergent maximum screen parallaxes.

Having drawn all of these comparisons, I would like to state that depth of field and depth range are entirely distinct physical entities and have no relationship to each other.

It may be obvious, but it should be said: The lenses of a stereocamera may be focused for one distance and converged on another.

If the limits of depth of field are exceeded, the image will simply appear to be out of focus. Exceeding the limits of depth of field does not result in pain or discomfort. If the depth range criteria are exceeded, homologous image points go beyond allowable standards for fusion, and eyestrain does result.

Depth of field effectively applies to vision with one eye, even if the image is being seen with two. Depth range applies to both eyes working as a team while viewing a stereoscopic effigy. There is no doubt of it. It is the nomenclature that is confusing. For the term "depth range," I believe we can blame Messrs. Spottiswoode. For "hyperconvergence distance," I am to blame.

Although I have taken the trouble to stress that the two quantities are different, as a teaching aid it may be helpful to compare the two. In the sense that limits of object distances close to and far from the camera are given, there is a similarity that might help some people understand the concept.

ACCOMMODATION/CONVERGENCE

Although most people do not experience strain as a result of moderate departures from the habitual accommodation/convergence relationship, there are some who may experience certain difficulties, especially during initial exposure to stereoscopic projection. The eyes are focused on, or accommodate for, the plane of the screen, but are converged in accordance with the value and sign of screen parallaxes. Only when screen parallaxes are zero will accommodation and convergence follow their normal pattern.

In order to minimize any strain resulting from this factor, especially for short audience-to-screen distances, stereoscopic filmmakers should be careful to take certain practical steps. Whenever possible, the object of primary interest ought to be photographed at the plane of convergence, so that it will have essentially a zero parallax and appear in the plane of the screen. Although this advice cannot always be followed, it will prevent the breakdown of accommodation/convergence and also eliminate ghosting resulting from imperfections in the selection technique.

Further, to be compatible with the creation of a decent stereoscopic effect, image points should have the lowest possible screen parallax. A good rule of thumb for quality stereoscopic cinematography is that when viewed without glasses it will appear less doubled or blurry than photography having very large parallaxes. Well-shot and well-projected stereo images tend to resemble planar projected images closely, since values for parallax are low. Such images will not appear to have reduced depth, if the photography is properly executed. It might be too much to expect this approach to be usable for all shots in a film. Nevertheless, in order to produce the most pleasing photography for the greatest number of people, it is good advice to keep in mind.

chapter 8

Binocular Asymmetries: Photographic Variables

In this and the previous two chapters, I discuss my version of a stereoscopic transmission system. In Chapter 6, the necessary symmetrical qualities of the left- and right-image fields were described. In Chapter 7, I wrote about the only acceptable departure from these symmetrical conditions, namely, horizontal screen parallax. I then provided the reader with accurate means for quantifying screen parallax as a function of photographic and projection parameters.

Now it is time to learn how to vary the creative photographic controls in order to produce the most pleasing stereoscopic effigies. If improperly photographed, stereoscopic images may appear distorted to many viewers. Typically the image may appear to be either elongated or compressed. The interrelationship between the stereopsis depth cue, given by screen parallax, and extra-stereoscopic depth cues, principally perspective, is discussed. Guidelines are provided for the cinematographer wishing to control the appearance of the projected image based on its appearance in the visual world and camera controls. The relationships between the important camera variables—focal length, interaxial setting convergence, and distance from the camera to the primary subject are described.

PERSPECTIVE CONSIDERATIONS

The depth-range tables are calculated for those sitting in the closest row to the screen, who will experience the greatest vergence effort when fusing left and right fields. These people will experience the greatest divergence when fusing distant homologous points for shots in which controlled amounts of positive parallax exceeding t_e are allowed, as well as the greatest effort of convergence for effigies with large values of negative parallax. We can specify exactly near and far planes as limits for placement of objects in the photographic field, given a stereoconstant K, camera variables of f_c and t_c, and distance D_o. These limits, ultimately, are based on the resulting screen parallax and the vergence produced by these parallaxes.

We can now establish a second criterion of stereophotography to determine the choice of camera variables in a somewhat less exact sense. This standard is based on perspective considerations; the specifiable parameters are a matter of artistic judgment and are not exactly determinable.

We know that for a given set of f_c, t_c, and D_o, assuming a specified K, we can determine near and far limits for placement of objects in the shot. But how are f_c, t_c, and D_o determined? We know that the near and far limits of object placement in the shot are a function of the nearest viewers' distance from a specific screen. The focal length, interaxial, and distance variables to the plane of convergence are chosen for the most part in terms of perspective considerations, and these are a function of the distance of the average viewer from the screen. Our nearest viewer, who determines depth range, is not the viewer seated at the average distance from the screen. In motion picture screening rooms and theaters, only after the center seats and seats behind the center section are filled will audience members take seats close to the screen. There are exceptions, of course, those who prefer to be overwhelmed by the totality of the motion picture experience and choose the closest seats.

Out of kindness to these people, we have computed the depth-range tables. But it is for the vast majority of people, more or less centrally seated, that camera variables are selected to present the most pleasant images that show the least distortion.

According to the relationship $V = Mf_c$ there will be only one theoretically perfect seat for any given focal length and screen size. But relatively undistorted images occur for viewers placed a liberal distance fore and aft of V, and I find it more helpful to think of shooting for a group than for one privileged individual at V.

The attempt is to aim for the most pleasing photography for our centrally located audience members in terms of perspective considerations and then allow everything else to take care of itself. This is more or less the approach used when photographing planar films, and it is all that any cinematographer can hope to achieve. We must realize that the motion picture experience is far from being isomorphic with the *visual world,* in the sense meant by Gibson (1950). Rather, the challenge is how creatively we use the departures. Departures from orthoperspective will be seen more strongly in stereo than in planar films because stereopsis is scaled by extra-stereoscopic cues, in particular the perspective cue, and perspective distortions are heightened when viewed stereoscopically. The question is whether this perceived exaggeration is a current problem because the viewing population is inexperienced or even unskilled at viewing stereo effigies. Can it be that after acclimation or education to the qualities of the stereo cinema, audiences will adjust themselves to its nonortho- or nonisomorphic nature?

In small theaters or screening rooms such as those for super 8, changing from the ortho seat to one in front or behind it will substantially alter the shape of the stereo effigy. By contrast, in a large theater, even several rows from the ortho seat will not greatly change the shape of the effigy, since the distance represents a proportionately small change in the total distance from the screen.

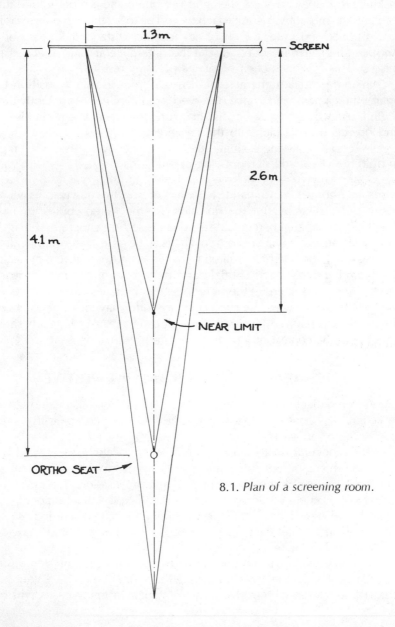

8.1. *Plan of a screening room.*

Those behind the ortho distance V will see an exaggerated depth effect, and those closer than V will see a diminished depth effect. Although it may seem contradictory, those closer than V often report that the image appears more real or tangible, even if less stereoscopic depth is manifested. People viewing the image from a distance greater than V often see a more model-like, less "real" image, but one with increased stereoscopic depth.

It can happen that there will be subjects of interest at more than one distance from the camera. If the action in one plane is more important than another, the most obvious approach would be to set the camera variables for that distance and to let the effigy at the other distance take care of itself. Another alternative might be to split the difference and arrive at a compromise t_c. This approach often produces pleasing results.

In some cases, a character will move from a distant position to one nearer the camera, and I have observed no difficulties. Apparently the eye-brain is used to scaling stereopsis according to perspective in relative terms, and objects moving closer to the camera will always appear to have increased parallax and increasingly stressed perspective. This is what happens in both the visual and stereophotographic fields.

After many years of looking at people and other objects, we have become accustomed to associating a certain perspective cue with its accompanying stereopsis cue. But the question for the stereoscopic filmmaker is whether this habitual perceptual response is so firmly ingrained that departures will cause annoying distortion. If this is the case, stereoscopic filmmaking is going to be a terribly limited form. However, I believe that just as the eye-brain interprets the visual field and makes out of it the visual world, so too the mind will interpret the stereophotographic field as a new version of the visual world. While the stereoscopic world may lack congruence with the usual perception of the visual world, it can have an esthetically satisfying integrity in the context of a motion picture presentation.

CAMERA PARAMETERS AND PERSPECTIVE

Given projection on a screen of a certain size, parallax values are determined by D_o, f_c, and t_c. But how does one select the most pleasing combination of these variables?

The binocular depth sense of stereopsis is scaled or weighted by perspective. This is the guiding principle: If perspective is stressed, then the stereopsis cue should be diminished as a compensation. The magnitude of the stereopsis cue, in the form of screen parallax, is a function of D_o, f_c, and t_c, for a screen of given size. The most important component in this context, the one that produces the essential stereoscopic information, is provided by the interaxial distance, t_c.

If perspective or other monocular cues are stressed, then stereopsis may be relaxed. The perspective of the image is a function of the distance of the object photographed from the camera, which in many cases will be the distance to the plane of convergence, and by f_c, the focal length employed. Objects closer to the camera have stressed perspective, and objects farther away have diminished perspective. Generally speaking, lenses of long focal length tend to flatten or reduce perspective, while short focal lengths tend to stress perspective.

Since these factors scale stereopsis, photography of close objects with lenses of short focal length or wide-angle lenses often requires reduced interaxial distance settings, less than the interocular t_e, 65 mm. Photography with longer lenses, or with lenses frequently described as telephoto, often produces compression or dimunition of perspective when filming distant objects, and this kind of photography may call for interaxial settings greater than t_e.

TOTI-ORTHOSTEREOSCOPY

I would like to introduce a new orthoscopic or orthostereoscopic (the two terms may be used interchangeably) concept that will help in thinking about camera parameters as well as serve to review some useful concepts.

Various suggestions to ensure that the stereoscopic effigy is isomorphic with the object photographed have been put forth by others. From my point of view, these discussions have very little to do with practical stereophotography. Nevertheless, they can provide some sort of a guideline for varying camera controls to produce a pleasing image. The most complete concept of orthoscopy, put forth by Spottiswoode et al. (1953), consists of meeting three conditions: $t_c = t_e$, $f_c = M/V$, and $P_m = t_e$.

I propose one additional test, that object magnification m be equal to 1. When unit magnification occurs, we have what I call the *toti-orthoscopic condition*.

The relationship between object magnification m and frame magnification M is

$$m = \frac{Mf_c}{D_o} = \frac{V}{D_o}$$

This gives us the reasonable result that object magnification (for an object in the plane of convergence) is equal to the ratio of the orthoscopically determined distance from the screen to the distance between the camera and the plane of convergence.

According to the Spottiswoode criteria, m does not have to be equal to 1, and orthoscopy can be maintained for effigies of any object magnification providing that $V = Mf_c$. To achieve toti-orthostereoscopy, by my definition, m must be equal to 1; therefore

$$D_o = Mf_c = V$$

In other words, the toti-orthoscopic condition is fulfilled when the distance to the object is the same as the distance to its image, given additionally that $t_c = t_e$, $P_m = t_e$, and $V = Mf_c$.

It is always possible to fulfill the condition $P_m = t_e$. By setting $D_o = D_{he}$, we can state the hyperconvergence relationship:

$$D_{he} = \frac{f_c t_c}{K_e}$$

Since $t_c = t_e$ and $K_e = t_e/M$, we have

$$D_{he} = Mf_c$$

Object magnification will be 1 and maximum parallax will be equal to the interocular if the object is placed in the plane of hyperconvergence and made to satisfy three conditions specified by Spottiswoode.

It may well be that the toti-orthoscopic condition is the only one in which the interaxial should be set equal to the interocular. For all other conditions, specifically those in which the object is closer to or farther from the camera than specified by the toti-orthoscopic condition, we should expect departures from $t_c = t_e$. This does not mean that successful photography cannot be carried out at $t_c = t_e$, even if object magnification is greater or less than 1, as it is for most motion picture projection. MacAdam (1954) pointed out that once correct perspective is achieved, there may be considerable variation in the interaxial setting.

Whatever its practical merit (which is limited), the toti-orthoscopic condition comes closer to creating an isomorphic reproduction of the visual field within the stereophotographic field than other kinds of orthoscopy. It is as if we were looking through a rectangular aperture cut into a black material of endless extent. This aperture at the time of photography is the same size and shape as the screen on which the film will be projected. But only the spectator at the $V = Mf_c$ distance, which is equal to the distance from the camera to the object, will be able to enjoy the full, although dubious, benefits of toti-orthoscopy.

THE SHAPE OF THE STEREO FIELD

It is far more important to have a feeling for what is happening perceptually in a transmission system as stereophotographic parameters are varied than to rely on mathematical relationships or to have to consult charts. The following model may help the filmmaker get a feeling for what is happening. Think of the stereo field as if it were defined by the frustrum of a four-sided pyramid (that is, a pyramid with its top cut off parallel to its base plane). These two parallel planes correspond to near and far planes, or the plane of convergence and the far plane. The sides of the pyramid are defined by the focal length of the lenses and the shape of the camera aperture.

When perspective is stressed, we can think of this pyramid defining the stereo field as elongated, and all the effigies of objects in the field as similarly elongated, so that they will continue filling the same *proportion* of the volume of the stereo field. These effigies will be stretched both before and behind, along with all the intervening field (empty space) that does not contain effigies.

This elongation will occur when either one or both of two perspective conditions are fulfilled: The distance of the viewer from the screen is greater than the ortho distance, and the distance from the camera to the object is less than the toti-orthoscopic distance. The former condition refers to the projection parameters and the latter to the photographic ones. Given a constant interaxial, as the perspective characteristic of the shot is stressed in the ways described above, the volume of space and the objects in it will be stretched. As the perspective characteristic is reduced or relaxed, the pyramid will pass from elongated through these phases: First it will be similar to that defined by ortho conditions, and then it will become squat or compressed in shape.

The Soviets define the perspective characteristic ол, and we give this ratio in our notation as

$$\pi_S = \frac{S}{V}$$

$S < V$	$D < D_t$	PERSPECTIVE COMPRESSED	
$S = V$	$D = D_t$	NORMAL	
$S > V$	$D > D_t$	RELAXED	
	$t_c < t_e$	STEREOPSIS COMPRESSED	
	$t_c \leq t_e$	NORMAL	
	$t_c > t_e$	RELAXED	

8.2. *Shape of the stereo field.*

The Greek capital letter π (pi) stands for the perspective characteristic, S for any distance from the screen, and V the orthodistance. The subscript S is used to distinguish this condition from the next perspective condition, which involves the concept of toti-orthoscopic distance, given by $V = D_{he} = D_o$, which we may specify as D_t. We write

$$\pi_D = \frac{D}{D_t}$$

π_S is a characteristic of the projected field, and π_D of the field of photographic space.

The shape or stereoscopic characteristic ψ (psi) of the stereo field is also changed by the interaxial distance used in photography. As t_c increases, the field will be elongated, and as t_c is reduced, the shape of the field and the effigies in it will be compressed. If all the other parameters are ortho, then as t_c exceeds t_e the effigies will be stretched or elongated (as stereopsis is increased), and as t_c is reduced below t_e the effigies will be flattened. When $t_c = t_e$ (when ortho conditions are fulfilled), the visual field and the photographed field are congruent. When t_c approaches 0, we arrive at the single-lens or monocular condition in which the field has collapsed into a plane. Fig. 8.2 summarizes these ideas. We can write

$$\psi = \frac{t_c}{t_e}$$

Although we have given functional relationships for the stereoscopic and perspective characteristics of the photographed field, it may be impossible to use these relationships with any degree of precision. It is safe to say that the effects of varying these parameters are additive (or subtractive), and that when the perspective characteristics are relaxed, the proper choice of interaxial, say, a reduced value, can result in an effigy that appears to be pleasing to most observers. Or we might take the example of a shot with a perspective characteristic that is compressed. In this case, increasing the stereopsis cue by increasing the interaxial setting will help to produce a pyramidal field in which the two opposing cues add up to a pleasant image.

In a sense, we are abandoning the principle of orthoscopy, although the concept remains useful as a point of comparison. The pyramidal shape of the stereoscopic photographic field is determined by two psychological cues, perspective and stereopsis; manipulation of camera parameters can change the shape of this pyramidal field. The cues of stereopsis and perspective can be made to work together to produce pleasing images, and one can think of one cue stretching while the other compresses the field to produce a more or less acceptable image.

For the sake of simplicity, I have omitted discussion of other monocular cues, such as the very important cue of motion parallax. The filmmaker should be aware that these also play a part in determining the shape of the stereo field.

COMPARISON WITH THE ORTHO CONDITION

One possible approach for cinematography is to determine the ortho focal length, obtained by solving $f_c = V/M$ for a particular theater or screening room, or to arrive at a compromise value for f_{cv} (the average ortho focal length) if a number of theaters or screening rooms are involved. Photography is then based on this decision. Once the average ortho focal length is determined, we call all lenses with focal lengths less than f_{cv} wide lenses and all those with focal lengths greater than f_{cv} long lenses.

I have provided a sketch of a typical screening installation. Figure 8.1 illustrates my studio setup, where the ortho focal length for the middle seat is 15 mm. As recommended when calculating the depth-range tables, I established a near limit for seating at twice the screen width. The distance from the stereo projector to the screen is about four times the screen width. Up to ten persons can be comfortably seated in my small space. If we were to scale up the space by a factor of 2, then the ortho seat would be at about 8 m rather than 4, and the screen would be 2.6 m wide, but the ortho focal length for photography would remain at 15 mm.

Shots taken with f_{cv} from a distance of several meters can be successfully executed at an interaxial of about 65 mm. If perspective is more or less correct, the filmmaker will find that a rather wide variation in t_c, depending on the subject being photographed, is possible. The viewer's response to familiar objects may somewhat restrict the range of possible values for t_c. The most important subjects to be considered are human beings, and people must be more carefully photographed than anything else. But even for the photography of people, it may be possible to vary t_c by 25% if we are filming a straight-on portrait, or even more for a profile shot.

According to my way of thinking, objects at or near the toti-orthoscopic distance (which, for example, in the case of the super 8 setup given here would be about 4 meters) can be filmed at t_c. As the object approaches closer than $V = D_{he}$, t_c may be reduced, but there is a very wide range of acceptable distances more or less than V that can be photographed at $t_c = t_e$. In fact, the range of variation is probably more than ± 50% of V.

For the moment, we will not consider extreme closeups but only closeups of the head, which, for the ortho focal length and the Edison aspect ratio, are filmed approximately 1.5 to 1.7 m from the camera. In this case, pleasing results may be obtained by reducing the value of t_c. One can select values from t_e to less than half t_e, depending on the proportions of the face filmed and the intention of the filmmaker.

I have avoided giving more than general guidelines for photography and offering precise recommendations that might be tabulated in the form of a chart, as the Soviets have chosen to do. The filmmaker is much better off understanding the basis for selection and control of the stereo effigy in terms of perspective considerations. Moreover, wide departures from any such selection are often permissible because of creative intent, or because such variations may be hard to detect. Depth-range considerations may also play a part in the selection of t_c, and to some extent this value may have to be compromised on that account. However, many workers will find it useful to have a rough guide to setting t_c and I have provided one here.

I can only emphasize that pleasing results can be achieved despite the fact that compromise is involved in every step of the process, from the selection of f_{cv} for various screening rooms to the selection of interaxials based on viewing from distance V, which only one person can occupy.

	Wide	"Normal"	Telephoto
Extreme close-up	$\dfrac{t_e}{N}$	$\dfrac{t_e}{N}$	$\dfrac{t_e}{N}$
Head shot	$\dfrac{t_e}{2}$	t_e	$1.3t_e$
Head and shoulders	t_e	t_e	$1.8t_e$
Top half of body	t_e	t_e	$2t_e$
Full Figure	$1.2t_e$	$1.5t_e$	$2t_e$
Distant	Nt_e	Nt_e	Nt_e

8.3. *Interaxial settings in terms of the interocular,* t_e. The wide lens is assumed to be approximately 0.8 times the diagonal, the normal lens 1.2 times the diagonal, and the telephoto about 2 times the diagonal of the format. This table is meant as a rough guide.

USING LENSES OF SHORT FOCAL LENGTH

We will call lenses of less than the ortho focal length lenses of short focal length, or briefly, short lenses. When f_{cv} is equal to approximately twice the diagonal of the format, lenses with focal length values between f_{cv} and half f_{cv} will be short lenses. Lenses shorter than half f_{cv}, or the diagonal of such a format, we will call very wide-angle lenses.

The diagonal of the super 8 frame is about 7mm, and I consider $f_{cv} = 15$ mm to be the ortho focal length. Focal lengths from less than 15mm are short lenses, and those under 7mm are very short lenses.

For a given object magnification, as focal length and distance to the subject decrease, a shorter interaxial will produce pleasing results. Say we are filming a person's head and shoulders (what is usually called a medium shot) from about 1.7 to 2 m with the 15mm focal length, with an interaxial of somewhat less than t_e. An interaxial of approximately 50 mm can be employed for pleasing results. If we were to use a short lens of $f_c = 7$mm, the super 8 camera should be half the distance from the subject for the same object magnification. The appropriate interaxial would then be about $t_e/2$.

The use of reduced interaxials has the enormous advantage of extending the depth range, which simplifies photography—especially important when filming documentaries where unrehearsed shooting makes it difficult to control blocking or the relationship between foreground and background. Very short or wide-angle lenses, or those with focal lengths of less than half f_{cv}, are useful in this context, since much of the time short focal lengths and short interaxials go together, as we have seen above. Screen parallax is directly proportional to both. Low values for t_c and f_c lead to low values for P_m and increased depth range, making photography on the run simpler to do.

Experiments with focal lengths equal to approximately one half or one third the diagonal of the format (when f_{cv} is equal to the diagonal of the frame) showed that for many shots with the subject about 2 m from the camera, interaxials as low as 12.5 mm produce entirely satisfactory stereoscopic depth effects. These lenses have strongly exaggerated perspective effects, so one would expect low values for t_c to suffice. As a rough rule of thumb for lenses of short focal length, the value for t_c is proportional to f_c with subjects filmed so that they maintain a constant object magnification.

USING LENSES OF LONG FOCAL LENGTH

In my stereoscopic work, I have come to think of my $f_{cv}/2$ focal length as my primary optic. For most of my work in the super 8 format, this corresponds to a value equal to the diagonal of the format, or about 7mm. This is actually the shortest focal length available on the Nizo cameras used in this study, and it provided me with the angle of view I needed for cramped spaces and relatively close subjects. I prefer to be close to people I am filming, since this stresses the intimate relationship between me and my subjects. The short focal length also offers a great deal of depth range, which is important when filming subjects likely to move any distance from the camera in unpredictable ways.

For my work in the 35mm over-and-under format, I continued this practice and got very pleasing results. For example, most of the photography in the film *Rottweiler* was done with a 20mm lens with a 60mm interaxial. The diagonal of the format is 23mm.

I have found that shorter lenses are more useful for stereoscopic cinematography than longer lenses, but this is based on the peculiarities of my experience, and I know there will be filmmakers with other needs and other points of view. However, it can be difficult to use lenses of long or very long focal length, especially for photographing people, because of the reduction of depth range. The difficulties are compounded by the need to increase the interaxial distances to compensate for the compressed perspective lenses of long focal length display when filming distant subjects.

I define lenses of focal lengths greater than f_{cv} to $2f_{cv}$ to be long lenses, and those with values greater than $2f_{cv}$ to be very long lenses.

Medium shots or closeups of people are often taken with lenses of long focal lengths, about $1.5f_{cv}$. Many photographers feel that the slight flattening of perspective, compared to what is obtained with the ortho focal length, is more pleasing. The result will be a greater camera-to-subject distance, which gives more working room, especially convenient when recording sound.

There is much to be said for the use of moderately long lenses in theatrical filmmaking on sets and sound stages. Although the slight increase in interaxial necessary to expand the stereo field reduces depth range, this is offset by the increased depth range that results from moving the camera further away from the subject. This seems to have been the approach used by the Gunzbergs in their Natural Vision system.

In addition to controlling the appearance of the stereo effigy through perspective, we also have the ability to control the shape of the image by variations in t_c. Flattering portraits can be produced using more marked departures from the traditional $1.5f_{cv}$ by manipulating t_c.

Photographing people's faces head-on or three-quarters with focal lengths between f_{cv} and $2f_{cv}$, depending on the characteristics of the face, with t_c values of from 60 to 90 mm, will produce good results, as long as factors such as lighting and the cinematographer's intention are kept in mind. Children and adults with small features can be filmed at $t_c \cong t_e$. For people with more prominent features, the t_e value can be reduced. There is probably more variability in the choice of t_c for profiles than for head-on shots.

Filming faces from great distances with very long lenses is difficult. Using the "normal" interaxial of $t_c = t_e$ will result in flattened or cardboardlike effigies. Although MacAdam (1954) points out that in theory correction of departures from ortho perspective is not possible through interaxial compensation, in practice pleasing results are produced by extending t_c. The resulting image's shape is flattened by the perspective cue and expanded by the stereopsis cue. Different viewers will respond to such an effigy in different ways. In time, people may learn to resolve this conflict of depth cues and judge the effigy with artistic license.

Aside from conflicting cues, we have the problem of limited depth range for distant subjects when using very long lenses with increased values for t_c. If the subject is very close to the background, there is no problem. If the subject is filmed against a featureless background of continuous tonality, such as a blue sky, there will be no homologous background points to fuse when viewing and no accompanying danger of excessive divergence.

CLOSEUPS

The term *closeup* as used here does not refer to full head shots but rather to the kind of photography that is often called macro work. Objects that need to be scrutinized very closely, with the unaided eye or with a magnifying glass, are the area of concern. There are a number of good books and articles on the subject (for example, *Close-Up Photography and Photomacrography*, publication N-12 from Eastman Kodak Company), and I will assume that the reader is versed in the subject.

Before discussing the topic from the point of view of stereoscopic effects, a few words can be said about the means for achieving these closeups. Some lenses focus close to the subject and have long enough focal lengths for adequate coverage. Some zoom lenses feature a macro range that allows for very close focusing. And any lens may have its close-focusing capability extended by using a closeup lens, sometimes called a diopter attachment. For stereo work, it is very important that the diopter power of these lenses be very closely matched, and their optical and geometric centers must coincide to avoid recentration of the images, with consequent spurious parallax.

For cameras with interchangeable lenses, extension tubes or a bellows close-focusing attachment may be placed between the camera body and the lens. The mechanical integrity of this extension unit is very important, since recentration of the image pairs will result from poor alignment.

We can classify our subjects, for the purposes of stereoscopy, into two camps: those with limited depth range and those with greater depth range. Consulting the depth-range tables will reveal that the combination of close-working distances and lenses of long focal length, usually associated with closeup work, leads to very limited depth range.

Objects with limited depth range include coins, bas-reliefs, textured surfaces, and the surfaces of oil paintings or textiles. Generally speaking, one will not have to consult a table when filming objects of such limited depth range if they entirely fill the photographic field and are placed in the plane of convergence.

But even the tables, as set forth here, may not cover all of the possibilities that attract the filmmaker. Therefore it may be necessary to calculate these values as described in the previous chapter.

I think that it is very important to realize that relying on an ortho view or a theoretically correct view of such objects is of very little help. Projected effigies are magnified to many times life size and viewed in a way in which they are never seen in the visual world. What we are concerned with here is producing the most pleasing effigy and exploring the potentials of such a close view. If we wish to exaggerate the effect of a bas-relief or textile structure for didactic or esthetic purposes, comparatively larger interaxial separations can be used. Inanimate objects can be filmed by a single camera moved through the desired t_c.

A good approach when filming new objects is to bracket interaxials and learn by direct experience what produces the most pleasing effect on the screen. One working technique I have used is to do one left take, totaling the running time of the combined right views, and then, by moving the camera in appropriate increments, film the various right views. To be more specific, one can try the following interaxial separations: 10, 20, 30, 40, and 50mm. Suppose each shot will last 20 seconds. First, film the left view for all five interaxial separations, a total of 100 seconds. Then move the camera to the appropriate right views, setting the values for t_c and properly converging the camera for each shot. When projected, the single left view and the series of right views will provide the necessary series of bracketed interaxials. Note that I have assumed asymmetrical convergence with the left camera lens axis perpendicular to the base line. For each new t_c position, the right camera must be properly converged using Smee's method.

Subjects with greater depth range, such as flowers, insects, and models of various kinds, may cover the entire photographic field or only part of it. Since this class of subjects is likely to include animate objects, such as small animals or insects, and since natural movement through wind, etc., may occur, a single repositioned camera technique may be useless.

The interesting question of how such an object can be represented stereoscopically may be considered in very much the same way as the photography of objects with limited depth range. Who is to say what are the proper proportions of a flower only a few millimeters or centimeters across, once it is projected on a screen and measured in meters? An empirical approach is the best, and the particular combination of interaxial and focal length that works can serve as the basis for future work.

The literature usually cautions against using interaxials equal to the interocular because it is assumed that this will exaggerate stereoscopic effects and that the limited depth range will make it difficult to record a background plane only a short distance from our object. Sometimes this difficulty can be overcome by using a textureless card of any desired color set at some convenient distance from the object. If a solid-colored background is not desirable, reduced interaxials can be tried. If drastically reduced, these may give a very limited stereoscopic effect. For example, solving the depth-range equations for a subject 1 m from the camera, using a 40mm super 8 lens with a 15 mm interaxial, gives for maximum distance to the far plane, $D_{me} =$ 3 m and $D_{md} = 1.5$ m.

Another alternative to the low depth range found in such circumstances is relatively elaborate but is worth mentioning because some filmmakers have access to such techniques. Traveling mattes to superimpose a background with a desired foreground could be tried in difficult cases. In addition, rear or front projected backgrounds may be found to be useful.

I have used values equal to t_e for closeups of flowers and plants with a 56mm lens in the super 8 format with very good results. My camera has a minimum $t_c \simeq t_e$, and my photography was done at an interaxial of 66 mm.

However, the literature advises using reduced values for t_c on account of stereoscopic distortion.

Animated puppets or clay animation seem to be ideal subjects to be filmed stereoscopically. The interesting subject of cell animation has been discussed by McLaren (1951) and by the Walter Lantz organization in patent #2,776,594. I suspect that for models that are supposed to substitute for full-sized objects, one could reduce the interaxial in geometric proportion equal to the scale of the model. A rule of thumb might be to choose an interaxial approximately equal to the interocular of models of people that might be included in the shot. This has not been an area of interest to me, so filmmakers will have to conduct their own tests in order to establish proper camera parameters.

HYPERSTEREOSCOPY

So far we have discussed the usual kinds of photography of objects from a few meters to tens of meters from the camera. We have seen that, in general, interaxial settings of from about one third to twice the interocular can be employed successfully. Now let us consider objects very far from the camera.

Given the usual interaxial settings, there would be essentially little parallax information upon projection. Very distant objects photographed with low values for t_c (approximately equal to t_e) will appear as if they have been photographed with a planar camera (which, depending upon your purpose, may be perfectly fine). If we want to impart stereopsis cues to the shot, we will have to use an extended base. The results will be interpreted by different observers in various ways, since large values for parallax are associated with close objects and not distant ones.

It is my assumption that in time audiences will be less troubled by hyperstereoscopic effects and will accept them as a part of the language of the stereocinema. As a matter of fact, it does not seem to be the audience that is troubled by hyperstereoscopy, but rather the experts and writers. For most people, hyperstereoscopic shots are fun to look at.

A number of rules of thumb can be found in the literature for predicting useful values for t_c. Judge (1950) gives two "proofs" to illustrate the soundness of the following:

$$t_c = \frac{D}{50}$$

As an empirical rule this is not bad, for "normal" focal lengths, but there are other experts who allege that better results will be obtained by using $D/25$, for example. Elsewhere in the literature other relationships have also been given. I prefer to use the concept of hyperconvergence distance to supply the interaxial value that will give a full range from 0 to t_e for parallax values. We go about this in the following straightforward way. Recall the relationship for hyperconvergence distance for the nondivergent case:

$$D_{he} = \frac{f_c t_c}{K_e}$$

Solving for t_c yields

$$t_c = \frac{D_{he} K_e}{f_c}$$

Now I will give an example of how to go about using this equation. As I sit at my typewriter, I am looking out the window at San Francisco Bay and the little island just south of the Richmond-San Rafael Bridge, called Red Rock. South of Red Rock, I can see Mount Tamalpais and its peak, and just to the north I can see San Quentin Prison. It is not a very inviting place, but recently it has had a nice paint job. Red Rock I estimate to be about 3 km from the top of my hill. I am using the super 8 format, with a value for K_e of 0.2. First I will consider taking a shot with a relatively long lens, 40mm, and then with the wider 10mm focal length. Solving the equation for the first case, we get a value for t_c of 15 m, and for the second case 60 m. The former is equivalent to Judge's relationship with a constant of 200 instead of 50, and the latter actually works out to 50.

By placing Red Rock at the plane of convergence, or more properly the plane of hyperconvergence, I have assured the largest possible depth range, assuming that the far plane is at stereophotographic infinity. Larger-than-recommended t_c values would produce divergence for background homologous points, and I can find no reason for doing so in this case.

The filmmaker may wish, on the other hand, to reduce the interaxial somewhat, perhaps to values half those indicated by the hyperconvergence relationship. It is really a matter of taste, and when filming distant subjects there will probably be an opportunity to bracket t_c for several values, perhaps t_c, $t_c/2$, $t_c/3$, and so on. Although I have assumed that the object is to be placed in the plane of convergence, there is no reason why it cannot be placed farther back into screen space if this seems to be esthetically valid.

With electronically controlled dual cameras, hyperstereoscopic motion picture photography is relatively easy. All one needs is a long enough cable between the cameras and a crystal control box. Then to align the cameras on the distant target, use a spirit level and sight through the viewfinders themselves, using Smee's method. If there is no motion in the distant object, and if exposures can be accomplished in less time than it takes for the lighting conditions to change, a single camera may be used to do hyperstereoscopy.

COMPOSITION

Usually, whatever composition works for planar photography will also work for stereoscopic photography. There is also a class of compositions that will work stereoscopically and not in the planar mode. Subjects that depend almost entirely on the cue of interposition to provide their depth effect, such as bushes, which are a totally incomprehensible mass of shapes when viewed planarly, spring into life when viewed stereoscopically. The experienced planar photographer has learned to avoid compositions like this. One must learn to see in new ways the visual world to learn something new about the stereoscopic field.

One major exception to this is filming distant vistas. People are disappointed that 3-D distant scenes appear to be flat, when the rest of the frame is rich with stereoscopic depth. But people are not aware that this is also what happens in the visual world. Given an average t_e of 65mm, distant vistas must have little or no retinal disparity (see page 107 for a discussion of the limits of stereoscopic acuity).

Stereographers have added foreground subjects simply to set off the background in depth, or used the techniques of hyperstereoscopy to enhance distant views.

These vistas do not need maximum screen parallax equal to the interocular for the fullest possible depth effect. Low values of P_m, on the order of one half or one quarter of t_e, can give perfectly adequate results while lessening A/C breakdown.

There are a number of compositional tricks that produce more pleasing stereoscopic images and heighten the depth effect. Motion parallax, produced by the dollying (not panning) camera, can greatly heighten the depth effect, and similarly for the photography of sculpture, heightened depth appreciation occurs when the work of art is rotated. Wide-angle lenses, because they exaggerate perspective, can stress the stereoscopic field and produce increased depth effects.

Generally speaking, the kind of lighting that works for a planar film will also work for a stereo film, but some cinematographers may wish to augment the effect dramatically.

Many texts claim that great depth of field in stereophotography is mandatory. They warn that out-of-focus backgrounds have a terribly disruptive effect. In my experience, whatever works for planar photography in this area will also work stereoscopically.

For stereoscopic zooms, once thought to be impossible, the filmmaker must have properly calibrated zoom lenses, with minimal recentration during zooming, whose zoom rate has been synchronized. As we approach either end of the zoom, the shortest and longest focal lengths, care must be taken to avoid unpleasant effects. When zooming to the long focal length, excessive screen parallaxes for background points should be avoided. In a zoom-in, this may preclude a large depth range for the final composition. As the lens zooms wider, avoid including objects in front of the plane of convergence, especially if they enter the composition from the vertical portions of the surround. This encourages conflict between interposition and stereopsis, and leads to the difficulties involving the paradoxical stereoscopic window effect, as we shall see in the next section, "The Image in Theater Space."

The stereo zoom must be carefully planned: The cinematographer must analyze the extreme focal length positions of the shot and satisfy the needs of depth-range and stereoscopic compositional parameters. It is hard to imagine that zooms will ever become as commonplace as they are in planar films. However, many technical difficulties might be overcome if the inter-axial and convergence controls were interlocked and synchronized with the zoom control.

Coordinating zoom lenses and controlling recentration of optics is the subject of a disclosure I have written and filed with the U.S. patent offices.

There is one further important point of departure between stereo and planar composition, concerning images with negative screen parallax. This subject will be considered next.

THE IMAGE IN THEATER SPACE

Images placed in theater space must not be cut off by the screen surround, especially by its vertical edges. Effigies with negative screen parallax values cut off by the vertical surround edges will produce a conflict of the stereoscopic depth cue and the monocular cue of interposition. Stereopsis will tell us that the image must be in front of the screen, but interposition will indicate that the object must be behind the surround window.

Unless there is some very special purpose for them, such conflicts are to be avoided, since they produce eyestrain and confusion in the great majority of viewers. Often people will report that such objects appear to be blurry. This effect becomes progressively worse as more of the subject is eclipsed by the surround or as the value of screen parallax increases. One observation frequently made by spectators is that the object that is in theater space but cut off by the surround tends to be "pulled back" to the screen surface.

Objects in theater space cut off by the horizontal edges of the surround are more easily tolerated. It is true that the interposition cue is still in conflict with the stereoscopic cue, but one source of conflict is eliminated. When looking out a window, say at the left edge of the window, one sees more of the view with the right eye than the left. We have become used to this effect, and any departure from it leads to a direct conflict with out visual experience. In the case of the stereoscopic effigy in theater space, but cut off by the left edge of the surround, we actually see more of the object not with the right eye but with the left eye. This is what I call the *paradoxical stereowindow* effect, and it exacerbates an already difficult situation produced by the conflict of interposition and stereopsis.

For the case of theater space effigies cut off by the horizontal portion of the surround, the paradoxical stereowindow effect is removed, and certain shots may be tolerable if properly executed. For example, it would not do to allow the top of a person's head to be cut off by the top surround edge, whereas a torso may be shown cut off by the horizontal lower edge. A chandelier can be shown to be hanging from the top of the surround; but vertical bars, such as those used for animal cages or jail cells, look peculiar when cut off by both top and bottom of the surround. Experience would be a strong help in establishing personal guidelines for this kind of photography.

One method for bringing effigies of objects into theater space is simply to avoid the surround. A typical example is that of a man placed more or less in the plane of the screen, say a medium shot from the waist up. He points toward the camera, and his hand moves out into theater space without touching the surround.

Practically speaking it is often very difficult to avoid the paradoxical window effect. If images of objects with even large values of negative parallax move into and out of the frame rapidly, they may not produce any disagreeable effect. If images of objects, such as people, are intersected by the vertical surround, they are more easily tolerated if they are dark in color, or cast in shadow.

PRACTICAL PROBLEMS

Herein are a number of specific photographic situations that are worth considering. Most of these situations can probably be handled in a number of different ways. The specific nature of this and the following examples will help the reader begin to think about the unique problems of stereoscopic cinematography. The solutions I offer are only a limited selection of possibilities. The reader may have better approaches than these set forth here. This section is offered to help you practice using the tables by considering problems. No craft can be mastered without practice!

EXAMPLE 1

Suppose we are using the 35mm format and want to take a closeup of a face with the background at a very great distance.

Assuming that our ortho lens for the scope format is $f_{cv} = 35$mm, we probably want to use, say, a 50mm lens. With this lens we would get a closeup at about 1.5 m, even though exact framing of the shot in the field could change this distance. We will use a somewhat reduced t_c, 45mm, which will give a more or less natural effect with the somewhat stressed perspective of the face. Consulting the depth-range table, we find that D_{me} (far plane without divergence) is only 1.7 m and that D_{md} (far plane with divergence) is 1.99 m for $t_c = 45$mm. Clearly, we cannot take this shot unless the background is a textureless surface, such as a blue sky, or unless the background were very dark, very much out of focus, or very overexposed.

One alternative is to frame the face so closely that little or no background shows. Divergent image points in excess of our 1° limit might be acceptable if a very small part of the stereo field is made up of such points. We can see that D_h (the hyperconvergence distance) for nondivergent and divergent points is 12.5 m and 6.08 m respectively, so there is no hope of getting the closeup by moving the camera away from the subject.

We have assumed that our subject is at the plane of convergence, D_o. What if we were to converge behind the subject, placing it at the near plane, D_2, halfway out to the audience? Let us look up a value for D_2 that comes closest to 1.5 m. The table lists 1.52 m in the column for t_c = 45 mm, D_o = 2 m. Still, the D_{md} plane is only 5.84 m.

Another possibility is to move the camera back and simply accept a medium shot, but even this will be hard to achieve with the far plane at infinity. (It can be achieved by using the 25mm-focal-length lens.) The problem of the closeup and very distant far plane is very much easier to handle in the smaller formats, where audiences are seated further from the Edison aspect ratio screen.

If we simply reduced t_c, we would get a flattening of the subject's face, but what if we reduced both f_c and t_c? If we keep 1.5 m for D_o and select a 25mm lens, the subject now occupies half the area. We would no longer have a closeup, but 35mm is often projected on screens 10 m wide, and that is still a lot of head for the audience to look at. To correct for the expansion of the stereo field that would result from perspective considerations, we ought to choose a reduced value for t_c, and 25mm would be a good choice. This would give us a D_{md} of 13.39 m, but if we were to set D_o at 1.69 m, the hyperconvergent divergent distance, or D_{hd}, I think we would have an acceptable solution.

Other alternatives occur to me: For theatrical filmmaking, a painted background or a rear or front projected background is not out of the question; neither is a traveling matte background. Obviously, though, these may not be preferred solutions.

The reader may have begun to realize why I have tabulated values for both D_{me} and D_{md}. If one can avoid divergence in background points, all to the good. But if the shot cannot be achieved any other way, some divergence can be accepted. By having values for both D_{me} and D_{md} in the tables, it is possible to estimate intermediate divergence values that, depending on composition and background, are tolerable.

I suggest that the reader investigate the use of lenses of longer focal lengths with slightly increased interaxial settings. You may be surprised to discover that the case given here, a closeup calling for a great deal of depth range, may be more easily solved by pulling the camera back and using a longer lens while maintaining object magnification.

Another strong possibility is to play the face out into theater space. Converging just a foot or two behind the head will greatly reduce background divergence.

EXAMPLE 2

Consider the following situation: We are filming a closeup of a man holding something in his hand, turned three-quarters to a 16mm camera. The man is 2 m from the camera, the object 1.5 m. The shot will open on his face, and then we want to pan to the object.

For the subject's head and the object, nicely framed with the 50mm focal length, we can try an interaxial of 65mm. If we place the man's face at D_o, we will get values of D_{me} at 2.28 m and D_{md} at 2.81. This allows little depth range for both nondivergent and divergent far planes, but since the closeup is so tight, very little of the background can be seen—only the extreme upper left and right corners of the shot. We do not have to worry about excessive divergence of homologous background points.

Now let us consider what happens as we pan to the object. Since D_2 is 1.78 m, the object will be placed some 0.28 m past the near plane at the conclusion of the pan.

Although we established a near plane halfway between spectator and screen, it might be acceptable to have even greater negative parallax for a shot on the screen for only a short time. I would feel better about panning to the object if the subject moved it closer to the body so that it would not be 1.78 m from the camera. When panning to and finally framing the object, try to compose so that the image, which will be in theater space, avoids touching the vertical portion of the screen surround.

Another possibility might be to halve our distance to the subject and halve our focal length, for the same object magnification of the subject. Then $D_2 = 1$ m, with $f_c = 25$mm and $t_c = 45$ mm. The table tells us that $D_{me} = 1.22$ m, $D_{md} = 1.72$ m, and $D = 0.85$ m. Although $f_c = 25$ mm is the ortho focal length for this format, 45 mm was selected for the interaxial, since perspective will be stressed in this closeup with the subject close to the camera. Further reduction of t_c might also be fruitful, but moving closer to the subject and reducing the value of f_c, to maintain M, is not the answer, because depth range will be reduced.

There are other ways: Let us return to the original camera setting using the 50mm lens and a 65mm interaxial. Suppose we converged on the object at 1.5 m. Would we then have adequate depth range for the starting closeup of the face? Barely, since D_{md} is 1.92 m. If we wanted to try this approach, we might be better off reducing the distance between the object and the face and also placing the plane of convergence midway between the two. Now the subject's face would be set back a bit into screen space, and the object would come forward of the plane of the screen.

Yet another interesting approach would be to follow convergence, in other words, to change the convergence setting during the shot. This must be performed slowly and unobtrusively. If not, the effect may be disturbing. The camera is set so that the subject's face is in the plane of convergence, and during the pan, an assistant reconverges the camera so that the object comes into the plane of convergence. The pan would make the changes in convergence unobtrusive.

The reader might question the validity of such an approach, since an audience expects the object to be closer than the subject's face. Having essentially zero screen parallax may throw off their estimate of distance. Yet objects we are looking at in the visual world always have zero retinal disparity when we fuse them, and we have no difficulty gauging relative distance.

EXAMPLE 3

Let us suppose we are filming a closeup in the 16mm format at a distance $D_0 = 1.25$m, with $f_c = 25$mm and $t_c = 45$mm. A D_0 of 1.25 m is not listed, but entries of 1 and 1.5 m are. We want to know the values of D_{me}, D_{md}, and D_2 for our camera variables.

We could accept the entries under 1.5 m as if they had a built-in safety factor. This might be an appropriate way to work for values of D_{me} and D_{md}, but it will result in a value for D_2 that is too generous. For this reason, we may use the lower value for D_2 listed in the column for 1 m.

The best possible alternatives could be obtained with a calculator, and we would learn that $D_{me} = 1.61$, $D_{md} = 2.62$, and $D_2 = 1.02$ (all in meters).

The next best alternative is to interpolate values from the table. Average the entries for the 1 and 1.5 m columns and obtain $D_{me} = 1.64$, $D_{md} = 2.87$, and $D_2 = 1.02$ (all in meters). These values are close enough to be useful.

EXAMPLE 4

This is the reason for having values for both D_{me} and D_{md} in the depth-range tables: By selecting far planes at appropriate distances, we can include or avoid divergence from our shot. In effect, we can select values from no divergence to a total of one degree divergence.

Suppose we are working in the 16mm format and taking a medium shot of a man with a large painting in the background. The man is talking about the painting, but he is the object of central concern. Attention can be brought to the man rather than the painting in a variety of ways. For example, the painting can be dark, or out of focus.

The parameters of the shot are $D_0 = 2.5$ m, $f_c = 25$mm, $t_c = 65$mm. The man is placed in the plane of convergence at 2.5 m. The painting is 8 m from the camera. Consulting the table, we learn that $D_{me} = 3.61$ m and $D_{md} = 9.03$. Since the far plane, or distance to the painting, is a little less than D_{md}, we will have a little less than 1° divergence.

When the man is the center of attention, it is acceptable to have the effigy of the painting with almost 1° divergence. But if the painting becomes the center of interest of the shot, it would be better to reduce the divergence further or to eliminate it.

There are several techniques for having both the man and the painting reproduced without divergence. We can reduce the interaxial distance between lenses, reduce the focal length, reduce the distance between the object in the plane of convergence and the far plane, or increase the distance to D_0.

If we were to reduce the interaxial t_c to 45 mm, then $D_{me} = 4.5$ m and $D_{md} = \infty$. I think we would still have acceptable depth reproduction of the

man, and certainly the flat surface of the painting would be adequately reproduced. What we have done is to reduce, but not eliminate, the divergence.

By consulting the table and varying the camera variables, we can probably find some acceptable compromise. For example, if we were to move
the man a little further from the camera, say to 3 m, then for t_c = 45mm we
would have D_{me} = 6.43 m, and the image points of the effigy of the painting
at the far plane would have very little divergence.

If it made sense in terms of composition, we could place the man at D_0
= 3.5 m, retaining our original t_c = 65mm. Then we see that D_{me} = 6.15 m.
If the painting were left at 8 m, we would have little divergence, but if none
were desired, it could be brought closer to the camera.

For example, as we double the value of f_c, we must also double the
distance to D_0 in order to maintain the man's image size or magnification.
Given constant object magnification as we change f_c, the far plane will re-
treat in direct proportion to f_c.

Thus we could increase the distance to the far plane of the shot by
maintaining the size of the effigy of the man in front of the painting. But as
we use longer focal lengths, we will wind up showing less of the painting,
and this may not be a satisfactory solution.

Probably the simplest solution that will give good results is to converge
behind the man, placing him out into theater space with a negative parallax
not greater than t_e. This would eliminate background divergence, and give a
pleasing effect of both the man and the painting.

35MM STEREOGRAPHY

Most of the work this book is based on was performed with interlocking
super 8 cameras and projectors. This good-quality but low-cost medium
allowed me to do many experiments. For the better part of six years, I have
investigated motion picture stereography with this format, but in the last year
I have worked in the 35mm medium, which is suited to the needs of the
theatrical film industry.

My company, Deep & Solid Inc. formed an alliance with Stereovision
International Inc. to service the film industry under the Future Dimensions
trade name. Stereovision provided the hardware, and Deep & Solid the stereophotographic expertise. The camera optics, designed by Chris Condon,
image two scope (2.35:1) aspect ratio images above-and-below each other
on a single piece of 35mm film, as shown in Figs. A-5 and A-6. The lenses,
known as System D-35, fit BNCR mount reflex cameras, converting them
into 35 mm stereoscopic cameras. Lenses with focal lengths from 20mm to
63mm have been constructed with various interaxial separations. The projection optics are of the design shown in Fig. A-10.

The system has good binocular symmetrical characteristics and well-
corrected images. Convergence is accomplished by lateral shifts of rear lens

sections, and may be set by scale or the target method. Following or pulling convergence is easily accomplished by rotating the convergence control knob. Although the optics are of a proprietary nature, and cannot be described in detail, they are in certain respects similar to Bernier's non-reflex Spacevision design shown in Fig. 1.27.

After working on the Future Dimensions demonstration reel, a promotional film for the Oldsmobile Division of General Motors, and the feature film *Rottweiler,* I have come to modify the recommendations given in this chapter.

I believe that of the many schemes for placement of stereopairs of images on a single piece of Edison format film, as described on page 260, the over-and-under system is the most practical, has the most advantages, and will probably become the industry standard. The format makes efficient use of the existing frame area, optics can be designed to produce well-corrected images, and the resultant images have a pleasing aspect ratio.

The changes from the recommendations set down heretofore are relatively minor. The major departure is based on the need to extend the depth range in certain shots, especially those involving closeups and medium shots, and to make subjects appear to be closer to people in the audience.

Elsewhere I have advised not to have images of objects with negative parallax playing out into the audience if these images touch the screen surround. I have also stated that images with essentially zero parallax will appear at the plane of the screen. My observations of large screen 35mm projection in the scope aspect ratio have caused me to modify my position.

My first observation was that images with zero parallax appeared to be behind the screen surround, rather than at the plane of the screen. I began to converge behind, rather than at the subject. For example, rather than converging on a person's eyes, I converged a foot or more behind the eyes. This produced, in many instances, images with low negative values of screen parallax. These images now appeared to be, more or less, in the plane of the screen.

I also came to modify my opinion about what constitutes low values of screen parallax. Although minus 65mm may be a large value of parallax for small screen photography, for large screen photography and projection it is rather moderate. I came to use the depth-range tables $^1D_2$ entry as a near limit. This allowed me to converge behind the subject, in many cases greatly extending the depth-range to distant points, thereby avoiding excessive divergent values.

There is no perceptual difficulty with regard to viewing images, typically of people, cut off by the horizontal portion of the surround. For low values of parallax, say under minus 65mm, the vertical edges aren't terribly troublesome when they come in contact with image if care is exercised. Placing the object in a shadow, or dressing an actor in clothes of dark colors, will help blend the image into the vertical edge of the surround. The gaffer can help by flagging light so the object will be darker.

Divergent homologous points can prove to be troublesome when shooting closeups that have a distant background. One thing to bear in mind is that the depth-range tables are very strict, having been calculated for people sitting very close to the screen. In certain circumstances, the advice of the tables can be overruled. This is especially true for backgrounds that are a stop or two less (half or a quarter less light) than the foreground.

Such a situation often occurs with indoor photography. A dark background can tolerate more divergence than a light one. Thus the stereographer can take advantage of exposure differences to enhance his or her ability to extend depth range, making it more comfortable to view photography. Foreground objects occluded by the vertical surround edge, or backgrounds with excessive divergence for homologous points, can be helped by reducing the amount of light falling on these objects.

Closeups, especially those outdoors with distant backgrounds, can prove to be troublesome. If one were to converge on the subject, tremendous parallax values for background points will usually occur. Two techniques can be used. The camera can be pulled back a foot or two, and the convergence can be set a foot or two behind the subject.

In the example given above, for the image of the person with negative parallax, the person will not appear to be in theater space as one might expect. Such an image will usually appear to be at the plane of the screen. It is very important to remember that stereopsis is scaled to perspective, and that for strong theater space effects, more than large values of screen parallax is required. Only objects thrust forward or emerging from the screen with strong foreshortening or other perspective cues will appear to be far out into the audience.

Although it is the major job of the stereographer to make sure that images are pleasant, there is a great deal of pressure to place images as far out as possible into the audience. An unmodulated frenzy of negative screen parallax will prove to be counterproductive, making the few shots that would profit from theater space parallax seem far less effective. Shots that attempt to place objects out into the audience, as dramatically as possible, need to be treated as special effects, and extra time and care are necessary in order to bring them off.

As a rough rule of thumb, strong effects are possible with objects as close as a third to half way to the film plane from the place of convergence. This applies to the great majority of shots in which actors are placed from ten to three feet from the camera, and are called upon to thrust rifles, bloody limbs, arrows, or themselves, into the theater. It must also be understood that lenses with focal lengths from about 20 to 32mm are being used with interaxial separations within 30% of the interocular distance.

Such shots, as I have pointed out, need to be treated as if they are special effects, and it may be necessary to bracket the convergence setting in order to achieve the best effect. Moreover, the editor can select the best of the shots with various convergence settings.

In passing I should point out that a great many shots will profit from following convergence. This is especially true for camera moves toward or away from the subject, wherein the subject is held at approximately the plane of convergence. Such shots are esthetically pleasing, and help to provide needed depth range.

There should be virtually no slowdown of setup time using a modern single band stereoscopic system with an experienced stereographer at the helm. With the exception of certain shots to be treated as special effects, bracketing of convergence is not necessary, and the production can usually proceed at the usual pace. The stereographer must stay in continual contact with the camera crew, and follow the intention of the director as closely as possible. The stereographer is a facilitator, and social skills are, in the long run, as important as the art of stereography. Although it is usually assumed that the stereoscopic cinema must be sold to the public, I submit that public acceptance is guaranteed once a quality system is offered. The technical crews must enjoy working in 3-D. If they don't, the art is doomed.

The major problem of quality control extends from production to exhibition. The stereographer given a proper system with which to work, can guarantee a visually pleasing three-dimensional motion picture. Obtaining the cooperation of the superb technicians working in the film industry makes the task a relatively straightforward one. The major obstacle to quality is the exhibitor. There are approximately twenty thousand theaters in the United States, and it is in their projection booths that the battle for the establishment of the three-dimensional cinema will be won or lost.

Afterword

I have set out to explain how the system of stereoscopic filmmaking, using polarized light for image selection, may be improved so that it could become a viable means of creative expression. I realize that the need for spectacles that must be worn by audience members is an inherent limitation. Nevertheless, I have sought to show that these devices in and of themselves are not the stumbling block, but rather that there are certain symmetrical principles that need to be carefully considered in any system that transmits stereoscopic images.

In addition, if the system of photography I have developed, which in essence limits depth range and considers the relationship between perspective and stereopsis, is used by an experienced practitioner, then pleasingly undistorted images will be produced. This technology can be successfully applied to a wide range of subjects.

But technical limitations are only part of the problem. There are also psychological barriers, which are of equal importance for the future acceptance of the art.

At present, the stereoscopic cinema (outside the U.S.S.R.) is in wretched condition. Stereoscopic films are produced only occasionally, and most of those that are made degrade the form. Many consider the stereoscopic cinema to have a bad reputation. The 3-D cinema is a has-been. Unlike sound, color, and wide screen—refinements that were successively perfected and added—the binocular cinema has not achieved a lasting place in motion picture technology. Critics may say that it was given a chance, in the 1950s, and that it failed, whether for technical reasons or on esthetic grounds. Yet critics of the medium, those completely hostile to it, do it less of a disservice than some of its friends.

Many stereoscopic workers have reached a point where their eye muscles have become very supple, or they have lost the last vestige of objectivity. The films or photographs projected by these enthusiasts are unwatchable by ordinary human beings.

The critics from without will probably greet the arrival of this book with indifference. Their point of view, and it is entirely correct, is that the proof is in the pudding. If good stereoscopic films can be made, they want to see them. Present workers, entrenched in their arcane techniques—the devoted few who have kept the flame lit these dark years—may regard this book as the work of an upstart. They are correct in this, but where I have departed from accepted practice, I did so because the existing traditions do not bring the desired result.

Appendices

APPENDIX 1: THE EXPERIMENTAL SYSTEM

My experimental work began with the observation that much of the apparatus to make stereoscopic films and to study stereoscopic motion picture transmission already existed in the form of easily adaptable super 8 double-system image-sound synchronization equipment. Super 8 cameras, because of their small size, have the added advantage of allowing placement close enough together to obtain reasonably low values for interaxial separation without requiring added-on mirror optics.

The cameras I employed were a pair of Nizo 561 super 8 machines, mounted first on a wooden, then steel, and then aluminum base, maintaining an average interaxial distance of 66 mm. Finally, I mounted the cameras on a special rack-and-pinion base made for me by Edmund Scientific Co. (Figure A.1). The rangefinder circles served as alignment devices for the target method, or Smee's method, of setting convergence (see page 123). An exceedingly accurate technique was evolved to align the lens axes to the horizontal plane, and precision shimming with set screws was used between the cameras and the base. Two quartz-crystal control units manufactured by Super8 Sound of Cambridge, Mass., were modified to run the cameras not only in synchronization, but also with their shutters in phase. Documentation for the conversion was supplied by Jon Rosenfeld, Director of Research at Super8 Sound, and the actual work was carried out by Bob White of Inner Space Systems. To my knowledge, this is the first application of electronic control for a dual stereoscopic motion picture camera.

Stereopairs of motionless subjects were made using a Beaulieu 4008 camera (which accepts "C" mount lenses) mounted on a rack-and-pinion base, so that a variety of focal lengths and interaxial settings were achieved that would not have been obtainable with the Nizo cameras.

Super8 Sound mechanically interlocked dual projectors were employed first with a pair of Eumig 807's and then with the much brighter 824

248

A.1. *Experimental 3-D camera.*

models. I modified the dual projector interlock so that it would function as a stereoscopic apparatus. Tests showed that synchronization was achieved and that the shutter phase could be maintained to within 10° out of the 360° of the intermittent cycle.

Projection was carried out on an Ektalite screen 1.3 m wide joined from stock Kodak units by TIW of Rochester. The high gain of this aluminum-surfaced screen makes up for the light lost by the sheet polarizers and also conserves polarization. Projector sheet polarizers were usually Polaroid HN35 filters, and glasses employing these filters or glasses manufactured by Marks Polarized were used. (More modern screens made by Schudel of San Diego and Biener of Long Island are easier to clean and have a sturdier surface.)

I do not think it would be useful to discuss in detail how to build or use this particular system. In the first place, this dual system is discussed in simplified terms in *Lipton on Filmmaking* (1979). In the second place, there are many possible choices of camera and projector, in the super 8 and other motion picture formats. However, a few remarks about designing and properly calibrating such a system would serve some purpose, since there is very little stereoscopic motion picture equipment available and many film-makers will have to turn to this approach. This will be discussed next, in Appendix 2.

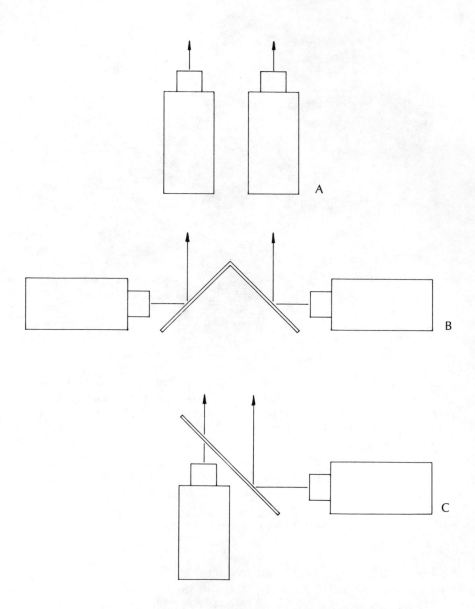

A.2. *Dual camera designs.* (a) Side-by-side (similar to camera in Fig. A.1), (b) lens axes aligned, shooting into 45° mirrors (Natural Vision camera), (c) camera lens axes at right angles shooting into semisilvered mirror (Ramsdell design).

APPENDIX 2: CALIBRATING A DUAL SYSTEM

Because of their small size, super 8 cameras may be mounted fairly close together. Thus I chose to use what is probably the simplest design for a dual-rig camera. Both machines were mounted on a base facing forward. But there are other possible schemes, which have their own advantages and disadvantages. First, let us determine the minimum interaxial of any camera combination. Simply measure the width of one camera and add a few millimeters for working room, or to allow for camera rotation for convergence. That is the approximate minimum interaxial distance if the cameras are to be aligned on a simple base, both facing forward.

However, many larger cameras cannot be conveniently mounted for close interaxial spacing, or the user may desire to reduce the interaxial distance further, since very low values, say one half or one third of t_e, can be very helpful for wide-angle or closeup photography or for increasing the depth range of a shot. Therefore other schemes have been tried, and some of them are shown in the drawings. Some involve the use of total or semireflecting mirrors, and these introduce certain photographic complications. Exposure compensation and color correction may be necessary in order for the two images to match, since light reflected from the mirror will lose about 12% of its intensity, and some spectral portion of the light may be absorbed depending on the characteristics of the metallic reflecting surface.

There can also be the following limitation when shooting into a mirror: Wide-angle lenses may be impossible to use, since they tend to see themselves, or portions of their mounts, reflected in the mirror. In addition, there may be difficulties with properly aligning mirrors, and some provision needs to be made for convergence control.

Inherent in any dual rig are two areas of concern: film and shutter synchronization and optical calibration. So far I have discussed optics, and such calibration is in fact the more difficult of the two. The art of synchronizing cameras by electronic means is well known, and there are relatively straightforward and inexpensive means for ensuring both synchronization of running speed and an in-phase condition of shutters. There are a number of specialists who can help with this, either by adapting off-the-shelf components or by designing original control systems. Let us continue to focus our attention on the more vexing of the two areas and give some general recommendations about optical alignment.

In the course of this study, it occurred to me that there were three useful methods for optically calibrating a dual rig stereoscopic camera: (1) with photographic tests, (2) by sighting through the camera lens and aperture with an optical instrument, and (3) by turning the camera into a projector. I used the first two methods, but it occurs to me that the third approach would be the simplest and quickest, and possibly the most accurate. However, projecting through the camera lens does involve more initial effort than methods 1 and 2.

For method 1, charts or targets are photographed and are projected with calibrated projectors. (I will discuss the method of calibrating projectors shortly.) In this way, by superimposing the left and right images, comparisons may be made of focal length and focusing accuracy, and so on.

For method 2, I was able to sight directly through the aperture of my rear-loading Nizo cameras, using a magnifying glass. The geometry of many cameras will preclude such a direct line-of-sight approach, in which case it may be necessary to use a mirror or to opt for one of the other approaches.

A circular target was observed this way, and left and right images were compared.

For method 3, properly collimated light would have to be introduced into the camera's optical path, in effect turning it into a projector. The source of illumination can be relatively low in intensity, simplifying cooling problems, since highly reflective screen material may be used, and a relatively small image may be projected. A graticule will have to be introduced in front of the film aperture. A frame of the SMPTE registration leader for the appropriate format would serve, or special graticules can be obtained from Century Precision Optics in North Hollywood.

By projecting both images, one on top of the other, instant comparison can be made of focal length, horizontal axes alignment, and focus. Recentration of optics due to shifts in focal length, if zoom lenses are used, can also be observed. For both this and method 1, red and green filters may be used over the lenses so that additive color differences may be used to make it easier to observe results.

The following important optical properties can be evaluated using the enumerated techniques: horizontal alignment of left- and right-lens axes, focus, recentration of axes due to focus, matching focal lengths, recentration of optics for lenses of different focal lengths, or for different focal lengths for prime lenses, and aperture calibration (using a spot meter).

Setting up a dual-camera rig to perform adequately is a relatively tedious task. All the photography I have seen taken with such rigs has exhibited, to some extent, some miscalibration in one or more of these areas. Because the equipment can get out of alignment very easily, calibration procedures which can be used in the field ought to be developed. The only possible salvation of the resulting errors may be costly and image-deteriorating optical printing.

With the notable exception of aperture calibration, all of these matched quantities become all the more serious when employing lenses of long rather than short focal length, since image magnification is greater in these cases. Lack of proper calibration of horizontal placement of lens axes will result in images that may be shifted upward or downward with respect to each other, resulting in spurious vertical parallax. Switching to another set of optics may consequently result in a corresponding relative repositioning of the images, which can be corrected either by optical printing or by the diligent efforts of a maniacally dedicated projectionist.

When focusing, certain lens mounts, more than others, can cause re-centration of optics and the relative or comparative recentration of pairs of optics and produce severe spurious parallax. It is possible to go on catalog-ing such pitfalls and recommending remedies, perhaps even until the result-ing advice exceeded the length of this book. Quite obviously there is a lot to be said for single-band cameras that have been factory precalibrated

APPENDIX 3: SETTING CONVERGENCE

Before I had learned of the target or Smee's method for setting conver-gence, I attempted to set these angles by scale. Costly precision devices for setting small angles are available to the optical industry, but it was my desire to avoid both their expense and their bulk. I found a useful tool, a variable carpenter's angle, the Squangle (Mayes Brothers Tool Manufacturing Co., Johnson City, Tennessee). The Squangle was not meant for setting the small angles needed, from about 0.2° to 4° with an accuracy of about 0.1°. I found that I could set the approximate angle of the optical axes of the lenses by using the Squangle against the bottom edge of the camera and the base. The method was not terribly accurate, and I soon abandoned it.

I did learn one trick, though, for using this technique to greater advan-tage. I fixed one camera's axis at right angles to the base line between the two cameras, and by setting an angle that was about twice as large for one camera only, I was able to increase my accuracy. Later, when I employed the exceedingly accurate target method, I still left one of the cameras fixed at right angles to the base line and rotated only the other. I found that this speeded up the process of setting convergence and led to no noticeable increase in distortion produced by this asymmetrical convergence setting. But this had been predicted by Levonian's analysis (1953).

APPENDIX 4: PROJECTION

The dual stereoprojector must be calibrated for both synchronization and optics. First I will address, in general terms, the problem of synchroniz-ing the two projectors.

There are two approaches, using electrical or electronic means and me-chanical systems. Electronic or electrical synchronization of projectors is a well-established art. Various techniques exist. In many 16mm post-produc-tion centers, projectors are synchronized to each other or to magnetic film recorders electrically by using synchronous motors. This works better if both motors are driven by a common distributor or the same source of AC. An-other, more recent method is to "slave" one projector to another. Such a system does not require projectors with AC synchronous motors. A synchro-nizing pulse generated by one projector is observed by a second projector, and this machine slaves itself to the master machine. The most common theatrical method is to use selsyns, tooth-belted to each projector motor. Separately energized, the selsyns keep the 1725 RPM motors in precise step.

A.3. *Interlocked 3-D projector.*

For my work I used a simple mechanical interlock. Its important advantage, compared with electrical or electronic means, is that it is easy to stop and run in reverse without losing synchronization. It is also very easy to set and maintain shutter phase.

Projectors with inching knobs are natural candidates for interlock conversion. The inching knobs are replaced with suitable timing gears, and an appropriate timing belt is run between the two. It is especially convenient to have some simple means for declutching the belt and gears, since this facilitates threading the projectors and finding start marks.

In the arrangement shown in the photograph, I ran the timing belt around an idler wheel, which could be moved laterally to tension the belt properly. In this way, I could compensate for movements of one projector that were necessary for achieving the crossed-lens-axes mode.

By looking directly into the projection lens, I was able to establish the proper phase relationship between the shutters. This is especially easy to do with the Eumig projectors used, since a low voltage is supplied to the lamps' elements in the standby mode. It is possible to set the shutter blades so that they are in phase, at least for this setup, to within about 10° out of the 360° of the intermittent cycle. Once set, with the timing belt properly tensioned, the phase relationship will never be lost.

Proper belt tensioning is a matter of experience. If the belt is too loose, it will slip. It it is too tight, the projectors will vibrate and the image will become unsteady.

In the rig I used, one projector was located above the other, to make it convenient to reach the controls of both. Geometrical symmetry may be less favorable for this case than for machines placed side by side. Projection tests using a SMPTE leader (Figure A.4) revealed that the asymmetries did not result in troublesome distortion.

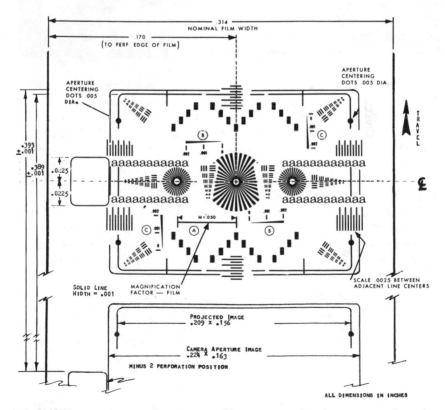

A.4. *SMPTE super 8mm registration test film.* (Reprinted with permission from the *SMPTE Journal.* Copyright Society of Motion Picture and Television Engineers, Inc.)

The projectors must be aligned to the CLA mode. In such a case, two prints made from the same master will project in perfect superimposition. The task of calibrating the optics of the projectors is relatively simple, using the appropriate registration leader provided by the SMPTE. If zoom lenses are used, the size of the fields can be exactly adjusted to coincide. Once this has been accomplished, the fields can be perfectly superimposed by laterally shifting or rotating one of the projectors. Then the projectors are locked down, and the timing belt is tensioned.

APPENDIX 5: CUTTING AND OPTICAL PRINTING

Physical manipulation of the single-band stereoscopic footage exactly corresponds with the handling of planar footage of the same format. All the components of the editing bench can be used to full advantage. The only qualification is that the viewer itself, while retaining its usefulness, will not allow the editor to view the dual images stereoscopically.

It is possible to design and build a stereoviewer, or a simple adaptation to existing designs might be accomplished by placing a stereoscope hood over the viewer's screen. The larger rear-screen devices used for horizontal editing tables might be adapted so that they could be used to superimpose left and right views, which have been filtered by sheet polarizers. A rear-screen material that conserves polarization must be used, and the editor would have to wear stereoglasses.

The cutting of double-band stereoscopic footage is more complex but allows for certain easily achieved effects that would be possible only with optical printing for single-band stereo. Once again, the existing editing equipment may be used. A synchronizer is a necessity, and a four-gang or sprocket unit may serve best if you will be cutting two channels of sound along with your two channels of picture.

Cutting double-band, in terms of actual physical manipulation of film, closely resembles cutting double-system picture and sound, since there is a one-to-one correspondence between left- and right-image bands. There is also a great similarity between A and B rolling and cutting stereo footage. Therefore, filmmakers with good editorial experience will have no trouble adapting to double-band. The same techniques are used, and the same care is necessary.

It can be said that good editing starts in the camera. Start marks, at the head or tail or every shot and on synchronized sound recordings, ought to be provided. This greatly facilitates synchronizing up film with film and sound. If the start marks, in the form of the traditional clapper board or another form, are left off, the editor will have to look for clues in the footage to help find synchronization. I have used a trial-and-error method of screening my footage to establish synchronization with projectors. Since I shoot in documentary style, often without a crew, I have had to leave off start marks. I have been aided in my technique because the Eumig 824 projectors I have used have accurate frame counters. In this way I have been able to log left and right rolls and note positional information on a synchronization cue sheet. Then it is a straightforward task to find the corresponding frames with the synchronizer's frame counter.

Usually left and right bands are cut stacked; that is, there is exact correspondence between where the left and right shots start and stop. However, an interesting effect is possible when left and right cuts are staggered at the end of a shot, that is, if several frames are overlapped. If only one frame is staggered, it is very hard to see or feel any difference between this and a straight or stacked cut. If two or three frames are overlapped or staggered, then one obtains a kind of soft cut, which can be rather pleasing for certain connections between related shots. I used these soft cuts in *Uncle Bill and the Dredge Dwellers* in a sequence of similar shots showing repeated attempts to start a small gasoline motor with a pull-cord.

In this film there is also a sequence in which left and right bands contain totally dissimilar material. At that point there is no stereoscopic effect. Instead we have a form of the binocular cinema which resembles the double-exposure of the planar cinema. However, these binocular effects are more *alive* than planar double-exposures. In fact, the viewer can play with the image, selecting either one by winking the left or right eye.

On some rare occasions out-of-synchronization footage is also very effective. I have used it for waves breaking on a shore. If only a frame out of synchronization, the effect is quite interesting and beautiful. The result is a kind of gelatinous rippling. I have used it to heighten the stereoscopic effect of low-hanging clouds. By shifting one band with respect to the other, temporal parallax becomes a useful substitute for positional parallax by giving, in effect, a broader stereo base producing hyperstereoscopic effects.

It is also possible to interchange left and right bands to achieve pseudoscopic effects. In such a case the left eye will view the right image, and so on.

Pseudoscopy produces a conflict between the stereoscopic cue and all the monocular depth cues. For many shots, the effect is quite upsetting. For example, a closeup of a person's head against a background viewed pseudoscopically would move the background to the foreground and *scoop out* the person's head so that it resembled a mold of the head. Many people when viewing such a shot will be disturbed, but many people will not see that there is anything different about the image. Apparently, for the latter group, pseudoscopic images are so totally foreign and beyond experience that the mind somehow refuses to accept its input and restores the image to familiar form.

The final crutch of the stereoscopic filmmaker and editor may well be the optical printer. It can restore to usefulness footage that was produced with a misaligned camera. Spurious vertical parallax can be cured by an up or down shift of one shot with respect to the other, and it would even be possible to correct for mismatched focal lengths by using a blowup or pullback. Exposure and color correction could also be made.

Even if the equipment has been well tuned and performs flawlessly, and given that the cinematographer made good choices when setting the convergence, editorial judgment may dictate that one shot, because of its relationship to another, must be reconverged.

The cinematographer may have done a closeup and a medium shot this way: The closeup was shot so that the head of the person is in the plane of the screen. The medium shot was done so that the person remains in the plane of the screen. The editor when viewing the shot may decide that, when cutting from one to the other, it looks odd to have both in the plane of the screen. The editor may prefer to place the person into screen space for the medium shot. The optical house or department is then instructed to shift one of the images laterally so that the person's image now appears in screen space.

The editor can specify exactly how much to shift such a shot laterally, or in fact how to make corrections for spurious parallax by actually stepping to the screen, with ruler in hand, and measuring the desired parallax. This divided-by-the-frame magnification gives the optical house the exact dimensions required. Then the direction of shift must be stated, for example, left, right, up, or down (or north, east, south, west).

APPENDIX 6: ANAGLYPHS

My experiments with anaglyphs began in 1953, when I was thirteen years old. I drew stereopair cartoons using red and green pencils and projected these using opaque projectors I built. My recent experiments were performed for the fun of it, and to work with images that are not angle-dependent in the same way as viewing polarized-light displays. Anaglyph glasses retain their selection integrity whatever angle the observer's head assumes with respect to the projected images. With polarized-light-coded stereograms, on the other hand, crosstalk (left image visible to right eye and vice versa) occurs rapidly with even small changes in head angle. So, depending on the subject matter of the image being projected and the photographic technique, anaglyphs may provide more freedom of movement for the observer.

In such a case, the limiting factor for any given stereopair is actually the vertical disparity of homologous points. As it turns out, some additional head-tipping can be allowed with the anaglyph as compared with polarized light, perhaps enough for this to be a significant advantage. However, the anaglyph may be projected not only by additive-light but by subtractive-light methods. An additive-light anaglyph is similar to the polarized-light method, since it involves twin projectors or projection lenses, one with a red and the other with a green filter. In the subtractive method, monochromatic images are printed through colored filters on color stock so that red and green image pairs are superimposed on the same piece of film. The results are entirely equivalent to the additive method but far simpler to project, since any projector can be turned into an anaglyph projector simply by threading up an anaglyph subtractive print.

In my experiments with additive anaglyphs, the source of the stereograms was black-and-white, virtually grainless and very sharp super 8 Plus X reversal film. I tried a wide variety of commercially available filter material over the projection lenses, and I found that the only entirely acceptable pair of filters (for both lenses and spectacles) were Lee primary red and primary green, although corresponding Rosco filters worked almost as well. All other combinations, and I tried scores of them, led to excessive crosstalk or were mismatched in terms of density. Both effects are undesirable because of additional eye fatigue.

The core of the problem can be stated this way: As we reduce crosstalk, we must increase retinal rivalry. Only deeply saturated filters that are essentially complementary can produce minimum ghosting. The choice of these filters, based on the requirements of image selection, leads to retinal rivalry. For many people the resulting flashing or scintillation of color is at least as bad as leakage of the left image through the right filter, and so forth.

We find ourselves in a bind. If we choose less dense filters, or those that are closer together on the color wheel, we can substantially reduce rivalry. But having done this, we discover that spurious images are now objectionable.

As a rough rule of thumb, a good pair of anaglyph filters ought to cause relatively great extinction when laid on top of each other. The same sort of test is applied to sheet polarizers, when an ordinary tungsten lamp, say 40 to 60 W, is viewed through them. Maximum extinction for the case of the polarizers is achieved by rotation of one with respect to the other.

In addition to my additive color anaglyphs, I also tried the subtractive method by having super 8 black-and-white images optically blown up on low-contrast 16mm Ektachrome reversal print stock through colored filters (the work was done by W. A. Palmer Films in San Francisco). The results were very good.

I also experimented with so-called color anaglyphs, using the additive method and printing full-color stereopairs through appropriate filters. From these experiments and from my observations of the commercially available color anaglyph product, I have to conclude that the color anaglyph, so highly touted by inventors, is an entirely hopeless medium. Printing color images through these filters leads to unequal densities and colors and additional eyestrain from retinal rivalry. When colors, say red and green, are sufficiently far apart, a flickering or flashing effect occurs rather than the blending of colors that can come about when similar colors are viewed binocularly. By comparison, a well-made monochromatic anaglyph is a thing of joy.

I should add that anaglyphs lose a great deal of light because of the dense filtration they require. Therefore a very bright light source, and/or a high-gain screen, must be used for best effect, as is the case for polarized-light display.

Children have an easier time with anaglyphs than adults, who more frequently seem to report fatigue and other unpleasant side effects. Nevertheless, the simplicity of presenting subtractive anaglyph prints continues to attract workers, despite the medium's obvious shortcomings. In its simplicity of projection, the anaglyph is very similar to the vectograph. Nevertheless, I feel the technology is a dead end.

APPENDIX 7: SINGLE-BAND FORMATS

Designers of single-band stereoscopic systems face one major question; how to arrange the twin stereo frames within the existing frame. Inventors must somehow arrange the two necessary left and right frames, usually within the area given by the original 1.3:1 Edison aspect ratio. All motion picture formats use this almost square shape, with the exception of the 70mm system, which uses a large frame with a 2.2:1 aspect ratio.

The accompanying drawings illustrate seven major schemes that have been suggested. The reader will discover, after some reflection and doodling, that other variations exist. The basic idea of these designs is to avoid mechanical modification to cameras and projectors in order to retain compatibility with standard hardware. By replacing only the projector or camera optics, or by adding on some sort of optical component to the existing lenses, the full-frame Edison format is converted into a single-band stereo system. In addition, films that have been shot using a dual-band system may be optically printed onto a single band of film.

VERTICAL DIVISION

The first variation, the vertical division, results in a tall and narrow frame and is often accomplished using the same optical attachment for both camera and projector. The design of the attachment most often employed is attributed to Brown and is optically identical to the Wheatstone mirror stereoscope. By a simple combination of mirrors (or prisms), the field of the lens is split in half. A number of such devices have been marketed; their chief merits are low cost and the possibility of adaptation to many pieces of equipment.

This type of device is known in the literature variously as a beam splitter, a frame splitter, or a field splitter or divider. It quite obviously is not a beam splitter, which optically has an entirely different construction and is put to different purposes. (Beam splitters take the place of semisilvered mirrors in optical systems.)

The major difficulty with the frame divider is that it violates the binocular symmetries of aberration and illumination, since the left and right halves of a lens's image must be superimposed on each other.

The vertical orientation of the frame is compositionally suited to few subjects. Moreover, this converter will only operate with lenses of longer

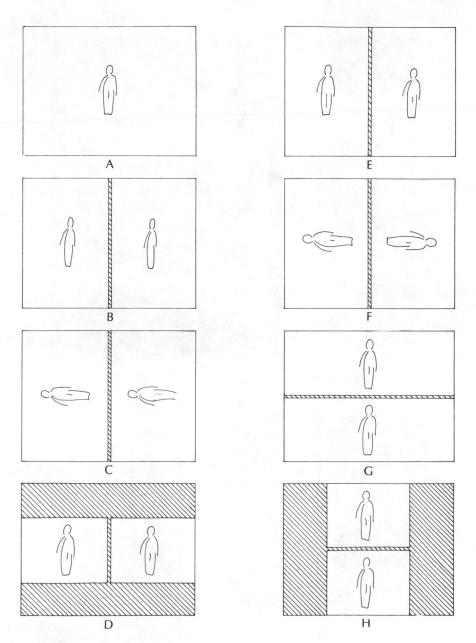

A.5. *Various format designs.* (a) Full Edison format 1.3:1 aspect ratio. (b) Vertical plus anamorphic format (final aspect ratio about 1.3:1). (c) Vertically rotated format, same sense (aspect ratio about 1.85:1). (d) Side-by-side format (1.3:1 aspect ratio shown). (e) Vertical division format (aspect ratio about 1:2). (f) Vertically rotated, opposite sense (aspect ratio about 1.85:1). (g) Over-and-under format (scope, or 2.35:1 aspect ratio). (h) Over-and-under format (aspect ratio about 1:1 as shown).

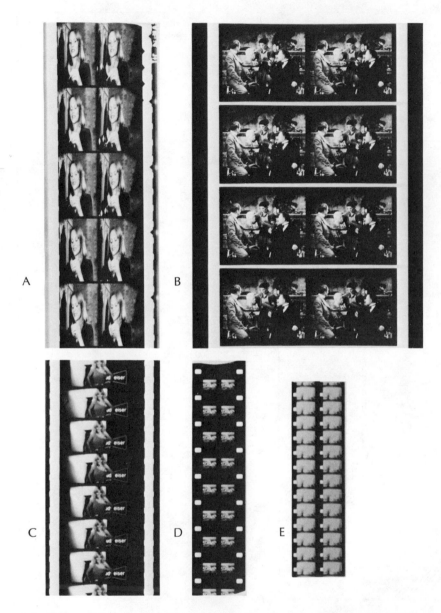

A.6. *Photos of 3-D formats.* (a) 35mm side-by-side squeezed anamorphically. Resulting picture has 1.3:1 aspect ratio. (b) 70mm side-by-side, similar to Soviet Stereo 70 format. Images can be cropped top and bottom to yield wide-screen aspect ratio, or anamorphics can be employed for scope format. (c) Over-and-under on 35mm. The aspect ratio of the projected image varies from 2.34:1 to 1.85:1. (d) 16mm side-by-side format. (e) Super 8 side-by-side format. It is possible to make contact prints from the dual camera system onto this release print stock.

focal lengths. Some variation in convergence and interaxial is possible, but designs of this kind do not usually offer these creative controls.

VERTICAL PLUS ANAMORPHIC FORMATS

The next variation splits the frame vertically but attempts to overcome the unpleasant aspect ratio by using anamorphic components in projection to restore the 1.3:1 aspect ratio. Since the frame is split in half, an anamorphic or "scope" type lens with a ratio of 2:1 is employed to restore the shape of the image for projection.

Stereovision has used this format to release the Warner Brothers' feature *House of Wax,* originally shot in 1953 in the double-band 35mm Natural Vision system. The two images are squeezed optically and printed side by side. Restoration of image geometry takes place in projection. The system has much to recommend it. The full 35mm frame is utilized, which can give good sharpness and, with a high-gain screen and high-intensity source of illumination, good brightness. The projection of *House of Wax* at the Rialto Theater in Berkeley in 1977 is the only example of acceptable stereoscopic projection I have ever seen in a theatrical cinema at a regular screening. A second visit to the theater three days later made quite a different impression. Somehow the projection had gotten so badly out of alignment that the film was greeted with catcalls and hoots by the tortured audience.

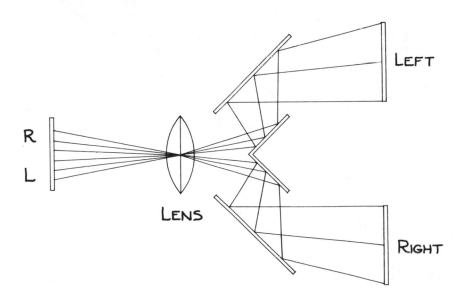

A.7. *Simple frame divider.* A design obviously based on Wheatstone mirror stereoscope, attributed to Brown or Kennedy. It results in an unpleasant (for most subjects) vertical format.

VERTICALLY ROTATED OPPOSITE-SENSE AND SIMILAR-SENSE FORMATS

The vertically rotated dispositions shown here are similar to formats proposed by Norling, and by Dewhurst. One advantage of the vertically rotated opposite- and similar-sense formats is that a pleasant aspect ratio image results, compatible with modern wide-screen projection practices. The full frame is utilized, but taking and projection optical systems tend to be complex. The vertically rotated opposite-sense format maintains the binocular symmetry of illumination, which is violated in the vertically rotated similar-sense format. The intensity of the source of illumination is symmetrical about a point in the center of the full frame, so that the similar-sense rotated image would then have a dimmer left edge of the left frame superimposed over a brighter left edge of the right frame. This could be a major source of eyestrain. (Properly designed graduated neutral-density filters might be used to restore illumination symmetry, but there would be a reduction in total intensity.)

Although the vertically rotated opposite-sense format overcomes this problem, it generates another asymmetry, that of registration, since it will

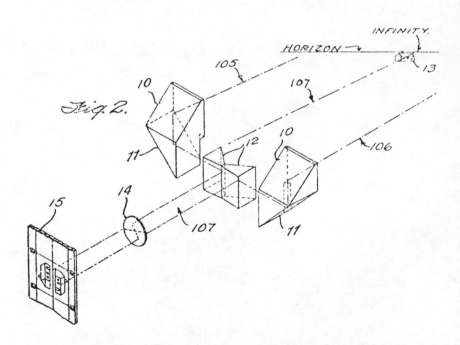

A.8. *Sherbinin frame divider.* Produces vertically rotated opposite-sense tail-to-tail format. Shown here is the camera design. (U.S. Patent No. 2,282,947)

always present the greatest possible relative registration error. Registration error will be identical for both frames, but because of the 180° rotation of one frame with respect to the other the relative unsteadiness is always maximized. This can be a serious flaw that cannot be discounted if we are seeking the most pleasing results. It may be overcome if the registration of camera, printer, and projector are first rate.

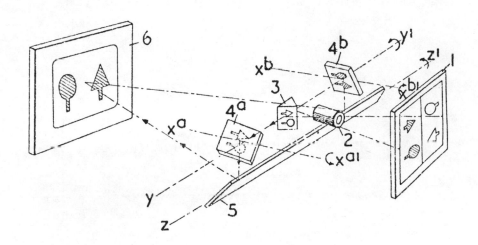

A.9. *Dewhurst frame divider*. It results in vertically rotated opposite-sense head-to-head format. (U.S. Patent No. 2,693,128)

OVER-AND-UNDER (SCOPE) FORMATS

We will next consider the over-and-under format that has been employed for several feature films, such as *The Bubble* and *Andy Warhol's Frankenstein,* both of which were shot in the SpaceVision system invented by Bernier. This over-and-under, or stacked, format results in an aspect ratio of about 2.5:1. While projection optics are relatively straightforward, employing prisms mounted in front of conventional projection lenses, the lens used for photography can be very complex. The problem of maintaining the axes of the taking lenses in the same horizontal plane, while having to displace one image above the other, apparently does not admit of a simple solution. The focal length of the Bernier optic is fixed at 35mm and the interaxial at 65mm. Neither may be varied, but convergence may be altered. The SpaceVision lenses are of very high quality.

A different optic producing the same format is offered by Marks Polarized. It has not been used for making theatrical films, and it loses a stupendous three f stops. Several focal lengths are available with the Marks unit.

Other similar systems are Condon's Stereovision Wide-Screen 3-D, Winton Hock's system, Symmes' D-3, and Findlay's Super 3-D. The Stereovision system uses two lenses mounted in a single barrel for projection, a scheme that could contribute to a reduction of asymmetries. Stereovision offers a set of T/5 lenses of wide, "normal" and long focal lengths that may be used on virtually any modern 35mm reflex camera. The optics are very good and are also offered under the Future Dimensions mark. Symmes' D-3 design, which is similar to Condon's, is also optically well corrected.

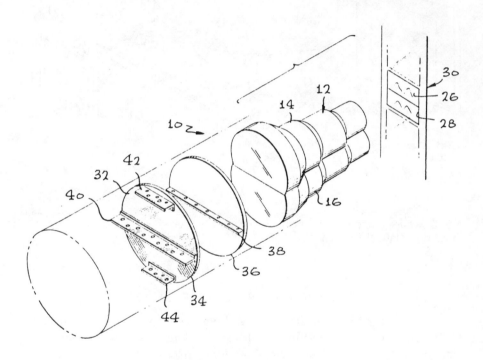

A.10. *Condon's over-and-under projection lens.* This is the only design I know of that can give the necessary symmetrical left and right fields. The design features a UV filter (36) to protect sheet polarizers (32, 34) from heat. Heat sinks (38, 40, 42, 44) also protect filters from heat. (U.S. Patent No. 4,235,503)

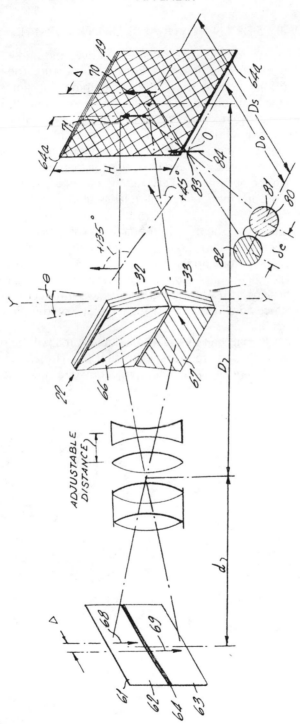

A.11. *Kent's over-and-under projection systems.* Prisms and sheet polarizers are mounted in front of the projection lens. (U.S. Patent No. 4,017,166)

SIDE-BY-SIDE AND OVER-AND-UNDER FORMATS

The following two formats, side-by-side and over-and-under, have this in common: They may both employ the Edison aspect ratio. The over-and-under with the Edison ratio may have little to recommend it, since it is even more wasteful of the available frame than the side-by-side format. However, any aspect ratio up to approximately 2.5:1 could be offered in this format. The side-by-side format, which can also depart from the Edison ratio, is a more promising stereo format. If dual lenses are mounted in a single barrel, all binocular asymmetries may be avoided, since vignetting, aberration, and all lens-related symmetries may be very tightly matched. The images have the same orientation, and there will be no relative unsteadiness between the two frames.

Norling has suggested the use of an anamorphoser, or cylindrical condensing element, between lamp and film, to turn the usual circle of illumination into an ellipse of illumination so that more even and brighter coverage of the side-by-side frames may result. Alternatively, given the present tendency of lamp designs to use an integral reflector, a reflector of suitable design could produce an ellipse of illumination that would more efficiently cover the twin images.

For the 16mm format, half the available image area will be lost in the side-by-side disposition of stereopairs. Although this is inefficient in one sense, in another it is very efficient, since projection of a single-band stereo

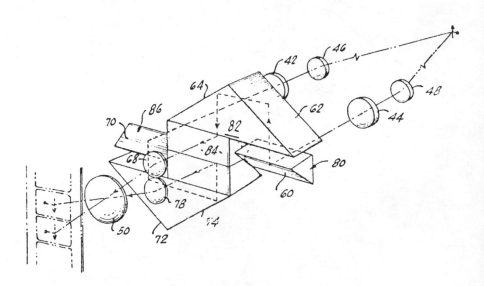

A.12. *Hoch's over-and-under lens.* (U.S. Patent No. 3,825,328)

image is far simpler than dual-band projection. Any standard 16mm projector can be converted to a stereo projector by inserting the dual objectives.

For 35mm the side-by-side has interesting possibilities. Available 16mm optics may be mounted in a single lens barrel for projection, and if desired, the print costs could be reduced by suitable modification of the usual four-perforation pull-down to a two-perforation format.

The Russian Stereo 70mm side-by-side format probably has superb quality. As shown in Figure A.6 on page 262, these two side-by-side Edison-format frames are about the same size as 35mm frames.

APPENDIX 8: SUPPLIERS OF SPECIALIZED EQUIPMENT

POLARIZING SPECTACLES

Supplier	Comments
Marks Polarized Corp. 153-16 Tenth Ave. Whitestone NY 11357	Good-quality, well-aligned sheet polarizers in cardboard frames. I like the frames, although some users do not. They also supply a very comfortable and expensive plastic-framed model. Clip-ons also available for the eyeglass wearer.
Polaroid Corp. 549 Technology Square Cambridge MA 02139	Good-quality, well-aligned sheet polarizers in cardboard frames. I do not like the frames, but some users may. Also very good quality permanent model at relatively low cost.
Stereovision 3421 Burbank Blvd. Burbank CA 91505	Good-quality, inexpensive plastic frames. Good-quality sheet polarizers. Frames designed to be saved and used with fresh filters. More expensive models available.
3-D Video Corp. 10999 Riverside Dr. N. Hollywood CA 91602	Good-quality cardboard frames. 3-D video seems to be able to supply very large quantities for theatrical needs.

Cardboard-framed spectacles are designed to be throwaways, but with care their filters can be cleaned and they can be reused. In small numbers, costs are about $0.40 to $0.50, but half that in quantities. The Stereovision plastic product costs about $0.50. The deluxe Marks and Stereovision glasses cost about $8.00 a pair. The Polaroid deluxe models are half this price and a much nicer design.

PROJECTION SCREENS

Supplier	Comments
Biener Systems 47-20 37th St. Long Island City NY 11101	High-gain TV projection screens, similar to Ektalite but rugged surface. Well-designed.
M. Hodges Instruments 6416 Variel Ave. Woodland Hills CA 91364	Several grades of Liteguarde available. Similar aluminum surface to Ektalite, uses adhesive backing for application to various surfaces.
Hurley Screen Corp. P.O. Box 217 Forest Hill MD 21050	Silverglo material, sound perforated to be mounted on frame.
Schudel Inc. 6873 Consolidated Way San Diego CA 92121	Very high-gain TV projection screens with 52-in. or 67-in. diagonal measurement. Similar to Ektalite but rugged surface. Unfortunate screen curvature produces uneven illumination.
Stewart Filmscreen Corp. 1161 W. Sepulveda Blvd. Torrance CA 90502	Silver 400 material to be stretched on frame. Mounting systems available. Filmscreen 200 rear-screen material works well.
Technicote Corp. 63 Seabring St. Brooklyn NY 11231	Supplies most of the theatrical 3-D screens in United States and Canada. Although they are aluminum-surfaced, the industry calls these "silver" screens.
J. C. Siva 1520 N.E. 131 St. Miami FL 33161	Uses Hodges material for high-gain TV screens.

Note about rear screen material. I have been told that 8-mil callendered plastic, which is used for shower curtains and other applications, works fairly well as a rear screen with adequate conservation of polarization. It is available from plastic supply houses, in great widths and lengths. Be sure to test a sample before ordering.

APPENDIX 9: MATHEMATICAL NOTATION

The following symbols have been used in the exposition of my transmission system. The summaries of earlier developments given in Chapters 4 and 5 have used the nomenclature of the original work.

Symbol	Definition
d	divergent parallax, in excess of t_e
D	distance from camera lens to object
f	focal length
H	height
K	stereoscopic constant
m	object magnification
M	frame magnification
P	parallax, usually screen parallax, even without subscript
Q	distance from projector to screen
t_c	interaxial distance
t_e	interocular distance
V	distance from observer to screen
W	width
θ	convergence angle
π_o	space characteristic
π_s	perspective characteristic

Subscript	Definition
c	camera
d	divergent
e	eyes
f	frame
h	hyperconvergent
i	image
m	maximum
o	object
p	projector
s	screen
t	toti
2	near plane

APPENDIX 10: MISCELLANEOUS INVENTIONS

Over the years, perhaps five thousand patents in the general area of stereoscopy have been issued, and a correspondingly smaller number in the specialized area of motion picture stereoscopy. The two are not entirely separable in many instances. In the course of my investigation, I have collected about 600 patents issued by the United States and British Patent Offices. Selection was based on references to them or their authors in the literature (including other patents) or by searching through the abstracts in *Patent Digest*, a weekly publication of the United States Patent Office. Prior to the turn of the century, before the *Digest*, lists of patents were published.

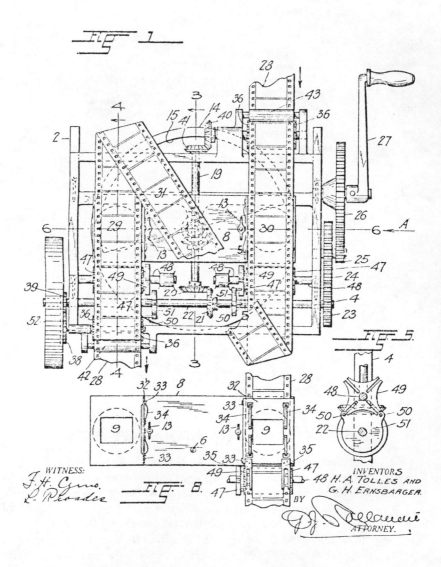

H. A. TOLLES AND G. H. ERNSBARGER.
METHOD AND APPARATUS FOR PRODUCING MOTION PICTURES.
APPLICATION FILED AUG. 30, 1916.

1,308,207.

Patented July 1, 1919.
3 SHEETS—SHEET 1.

A.13. *Tolles and Ernsbarger 3-D camera design of 1919. An exceedingly complex film path that seems to have no advantages.*

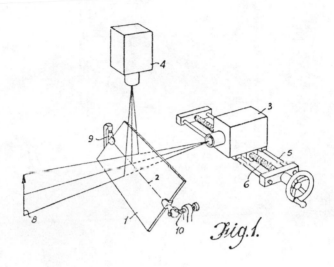

Dec. 15, 1959   N. L. SPOTTISWOODE ET AL   2,916,962

OPTICAL SYSTEMS FOR STEREOSCOPIC CAMERAS

Filed May 24, 1954

Fig.1.

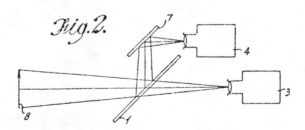

Fig.2.

Inventor
Nigel L. Spottiswoode
Raymond J. Spottiswoode
By

Attorney

A.14. *Spottiswoode's dual camera design.* The only design in this group that is practical.

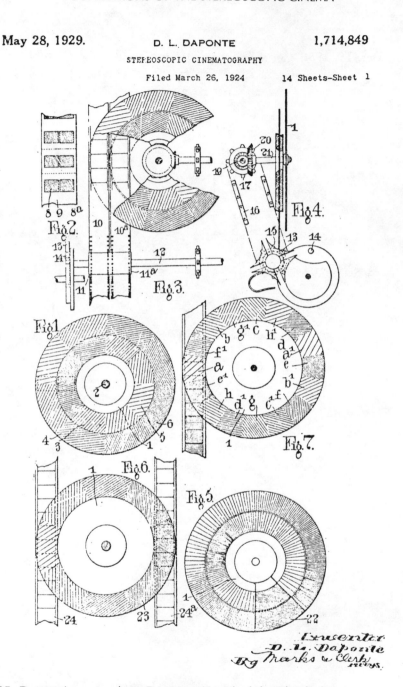

May 28, 1929.

D. L. DAPONTE

1,714,849

STEREOSCOPIC CINEMATOGRAPHY

Filed March 26, 1924

14 Sheets—Sheet 1

A.15. *Daponte's monocular 3-D contraption.* The left and right frames are somehow blended or interleaved together in some magic way to create a stereoscopic effect. If it worked, one ought to be able to view 3-D with one eye shut. This is typical of a number of weird ideas from the inventors. Perhaps I should keep my mind open while my eye is shut.

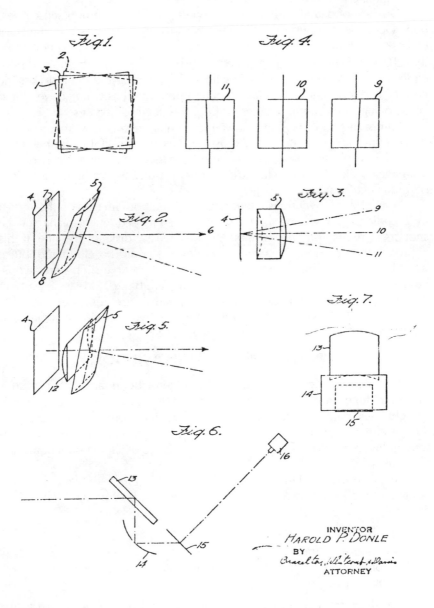

June 22, 1937.   H. P. DONLE   2,084,795
              SYSTEM AND METHOD FOR SECURING THIRD DIMENSIONAL
                      EFFECTS WITH A SINGLE IMAGE
                        Filed Dec. 16, 1933   2 Sheets—Sheet 1

INVENTOR
HAROLD P. DONLE
BY
ATTORNEY

A.16. *Donle's wiggling image.* Can a cylindrical lens placed over a picture be rocked in some way to produce a 3-D effect? If you glue feathers to a turtle, can it flap its shell and fly?

For convenience, I used the following arbitrary categories: cameras, TV systems, polarization, monocular stereoscopy, synthetic stereoscopy, projection, autostereoscopic-still, autostereoscopic-movie, volumetric displays, stereoscopes, and miscellaneous. A few dozen of the most important or interesting patents are listed in the Bibliography.

One test of patentability, I had assumed, was the common-sense question: Does the invention work? Does the invention do what the inventor claims? A significant number of the patents I have examined do not. More than 10% of those in my own collection are based, on psycho-optical principles that, if correct, would have gained the inventor the highest possible honors, and most certainly if the invention performed as claimed we would be enjoying stereoscopic movies without the need for glasses.

Entries in two of my categories, monocular stereoscopy and synthetic stereoscopy, are subject to the most serious doubts. If the former class worked, it would be possible for a one-eyed person to observe a stereoscopic image, while the latter class tries unsuccessfully to synthesize a stereoscopic effect from planar images.

A number of inventions attempt to combine both images on the screen by blending or dissolving them together in some sequence, using special shutters in projection with variable neutral-density disks or the like. If this approach worked, individual selection devices could be elminated, but it would also be true that a one-eyed person could observe such stereoscopic images. Monocular and synthetic stereoscopy are based, at least in part, on the false premises that motion and spatial parallax are equivalent and that the persistence of vision can be used to help the eye-brain integrate left and right views into a true stereoscopic effigy.

APPENDIX 11: THE STEREOWINDOW

The stereowindow is defined as the edge or boundary that surrounds the three-dimensional image. It is usually made up of a border of black straight lines, parallel to the horizontal and vertical, forming a rectangle. In the system advocated in this book, CLA, the screen surround and the stereowindow correspond. The screen surround is the black material bordering the screen.

Berssenbrugge (1948) discusses the subject of the stereowindow in the context of the stereoscope. He defines four methods of image framing that are of interest:

1. The sharp frame at infinity.
2. The foreground frame.
3. The foreground frame requiring accommodation of the eye.
4. The blurred frame.

The sharp frame at infinity could be achieved by having the projector apertures aligned so that they form a window with a parallax of 65 mm for the vertical portion of the surround. The parallel-projection scheme advocated by Rule and others would automatically fulfill this condition. However, parallel projection is often carried out using the screen surround to mask off portions of the frame. This results in an effective foreground frame, or stereowindow, corresponding to the screen surround.

Method 1, as given here, will result in all objects playing in space in front of the window. I find this a disturbing effect. It certainly invites greater conflict of the stereopsis cue and interposition at the vertical portions of the surround. It ought to be noted that the only stereoscopic cues for window placement are given by the vertical portions of the surround.

Method 2, the foreground frame, has been described throughout this book. In the CLA system, which is almost universally adopted by theatrical filmmakers, camera lenses converge on the object to be placed at the stereowindow. Upon projection, the object will appear to be in the same plane as the surround.

Method 3, foreground frame requiring accommodation, is frequently used by still stereoscopists projection slides. By masking portions of the vertical frame, they can add parallax to the stereowindow and move it forward of the surface of the screen. In this way, they can place the window where they please with respect to the image.

Spottiswoode et al. suggest using a window printed on the motion picture print to increase the depth range of the shot and to bring the images out closer to the audience. They also mention that they have perfected a means for imparting parallax information to the horizontal portion of the window. They do not describe the method.

The blurred-frame technique, method 4, might be employed to soften the abrupt transition from screening room environment to stereo effigy. It could be accomplished by a variety of means, either by using masks in front of the projector lens or by optical printing.

In the 1950s, experiments were carried out using gray surrounds that would have some projector light spilled on them to soften the transition from screen image to theater darkness. Although this technique was used to a limited extent in some houses, it obviously has passed into oblivion.

Some people viewing stereo films prefer a relatively high level of ambient room light. They find it less tiring to view the images this way. Perhaps the gray surround and the blurred frame need further experimentation.

I personally like looking at stereo projection in fairly dark rooms with the window corresponding to the surround, or what has been called in this section the foreground frame method. It may well be that this is all a matter of taste. Whatever people get used to, they like. I am reminded of several screenings of the United Artists' dual 70mm system I saw on a 50-ft-wide screen. Many of the images were composed so that the background had zero parallax. All other objects had negative parallax. For example, a shot of the pyramids with a camel in the foreground played with the pyramid at the plane of the screen and the camel in the row in front of me. I disliked it and found it uncomfortable to view, but other viewers did not seem to mind.

APPENDIX 12: THREE-DIMENSIONAL TELEVISION

Motion picture and television systems are strongly related. Both dissect the image of the moving subject into a series of pictures, which when suitably played back, give the illusion of motion. These moving image systems, one storing the images chemically, the other transmitting or storing electronically, are subject to the same stereoscopic transmission theory that has been discussed in these pages.

The construct of symmetrical left- and right-image fields holds for both. For television imaging, because of the smaller screen sizes generally encountered, geometric and angular tolerances may be relaxed. But we should approach this conservatively, since some people may prefer to sit very close to their television sets, projection or large-screen television is becoming increasingly popular, and program material prepared for television may also be displayed as motion pictures.

With regard to the desirable asymmetry of screen parallax and the photographic parameters used to control depth range and the shape of the stereoscopic image, my experiments have led me to believe that photography for the motion picture medium will work well for television. Projection onto the small screen results in pleasing images even if the original photography was intended for the large movie screen and our demonstration films have been successfully transferred to videotape for viewing with a television system designed by my organization.

As of this writing, stereoscopic motion picture systems are in only occasional use and stereoscopic television is used even less frequently. It is at present confined to special industrial, medical, and military purposes. For example, the handling of isotopes with robot arms is facilitated for the operator by viewing the procedure three-dimensionally. But these uses involve highly specialized solutions that may not solve the general problem.

I will define the solution to the general problem as a three-dimensional television system that can be successfully used by nonspecialist consumers in place of, or in addition to, the present planar system. Such a system would have a high degree of compatibility with the present television infrastructure. For example, videodiscs and tape cassettes presently available could be encoded stereoscopically, disc players and tape machines would need no modification, cable and broadcast transmission could be carried out essentially as at present, new stereoscopic television sets could receive planar transmissions, and present planar televisions could receive stereoscopic transmissions two-dimensionally.

Moreover, planar television quality would be preserved; that is, sharpness would remain adequate, color good, and there would be no other degradation of image quality. Ideally, individual selection devices would not be needed, but if they are, the glasses ought to be inexpensive, lightweight and comfortable, and of course they must use neutral lenses. Anaglyphs are unacceptable.

The major aspects of these systems fall into three areas: cameras or telecines, encoding the signal for transmission or recording, and display.

The same sorts of solutions to the camera problem that have been applied by motion picture workers have also been used by television workers. These include dual cameras with or without various mirror or prism arrangements, frame dividers for single-camera systems, and rotating mirrors used in conjunction with single cameras for eclipse or sequential systems. Since we have discussed the first two categories, we need only consider the third at this time. A typical example from the published art is given in the drawing shown here, from Beste's 1966 patent. We see that the prism, 42, sends light from the right and left lenses to a single television camera. Shutters at 36 and 34 alternately occlude the left and right images in synchronization with the interlace. (We will return to the concept of interlace shortly.)

Now let us turn to the area of signal encoding. Various schemes have been proposed for transmitting or recording a pair of images given an unaltered bandwidth. If one is able to opt for doubling the bandwidth to contain two channels, the problem is in many ways simplified. Such a strategy might be acceptable for cable transmission, but it probably would not be acceptable for broadcasting through the air and would also lead to great difficulties with regard to recording and playback apparatus.

One of the first ideas to appeal to inventors was to apply the system of television interlace or alternate odd and even field scanning for stereoscopic encoding. For planar television, in this country 30 complete pictures are transmitted each second. In Europe the number is 25. But each of these whole images is broken up into two parts. A system of interlacing two fields for each picture is used to eliminate flicker. Thus 60 fields are used here and 50 abroad. One pair of odd and even fields, which sweeps out the television picture like intermeshed fingers of the left and right hand, makes up a complete picture.

Inventors such as Goldsmith (1951 for RCA) have tried to take advantage of the interlace system in order, for example, to place the right picture on the odd field and the left picture on the even field.

Goldsmith, in the patent drawings shown here, further proposes to rotate the raster through 90° to provide a vertical pattern that can be positioned behind a parallax stereogram barrier for viewing without glasses. This is not a practical idea, since the viewing zones are limited and head movement is strongly restricted.

Dockhorn in his 1957 patent borrows a page from Hammond's 1924 patent with a mechanically occluding or eclipsing shutter. Kratomi (1973) and Roese (1975) take the idea a step further by synchronizing the fields with electro-optical shuttering devices worn in spectacles. These would be less cumbersome than mechanical occluders.

Goldsmith (1972) and Tesler (1973) do away with alternate interlaced encoding of the stereoscopic signal and use ideas similar to those employed for color television encoding. Essentially, a difference signal is created by subtracting the left from the right image, and this is encoded in an unused portion of the carrier wave. Decoding takes place at the receiver. Thus, a single image, either the left or the right, is transmitted with stereoscopic information as a difference signal carrier (in Goldsmith's version). Planar sets ignore the difference signal, but stereoscopic sets use it to reconstruct the missing image.

Such a scheme would overcome one difficulty of alternate interlace. For alternate interlace, the usual planar receiver will pick up both left and right images and more or less superimpose these as a blurry image. This is what happens when you look at stereoscopic motion picture projection without the glasses. Systems using a difference signal would produce a sharp image on the planar receiver.

Of course, I am assuming that the difference signal can be made to give good results. It certainly is an attractive idea, since it might overcome another of the alternate interlace faults, namely, severe flicker. For alternate interlace we are reducing, the total number of images to each eye from 60 to 30 (or from 50 to 25 in Europe). Therefore there will be flicker, since 30 or 25 pictures per second is considerably below the critical fusion frequency (about 45 images per second).

I will pause for a moment to make some parenthetical remarks. The reader may have noticed that I have discussed both methods for encoding the signal and display. The two areas are separable, but it is expedient to have made some mention of display systems to clarify the intention of the encoding system. We will concentrate on display shortly.

I feel I must also remark that the inventions cited here are taken from the literature not necessarily because they are inspired or perfected manifestations, but rather because they are typical or easily illustrate certain important points. I can only make an educated guess about how well most of these inventions perform because the systems discussed here are, for the most part, from the patent literature. Inventors are not required to submit working models, and in most cases it is my suspicion that these devices have never been built and if built, would not perform well.

I must also emphasize that this is a very complex subject, worthy of its own book. However, in the interests of brevity, I have omitted many comments about the systems discussed here and have, in fact, omitted mention of some systems that may possibly lead to a fully realized manifestation of three-dimensional television.

So far we have discussed electronic means for encoding stereoscopic information. There are also optical means that may be employed, using frame dividers, similar to those used for motion picture work. Butterfield has shown devices of this kind for industrial and medical applications. Images are placed side by side on a cathode-ray tube (CRT) and viewed through a hood, or stereoscope. Results are adequate for the purpose of handling dangerous materials from a distance, or for imaging through a binocular microscope.

May 17, 1966   H. E. BESTE   **3,251,933**

THREE-DIMENSIONAL TELEVISION SYSTEM

Filed Oct. 31, 1962   2 Sheets—Sheet 1

Fig. 1

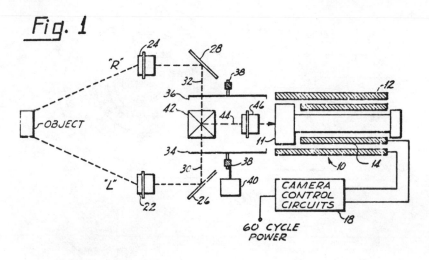

Fig. 2

Fig. 3

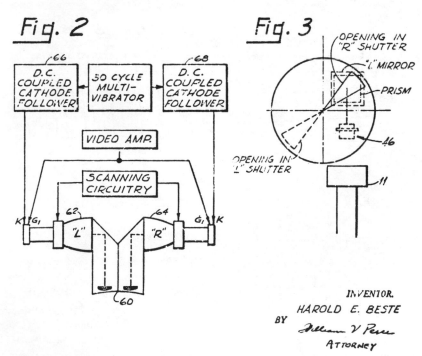

INVENTOR.
HAROLD E. BESTE
BY
        William V Pervic
        ATTORNEY

A.17. *Beste's alternate-field system.*

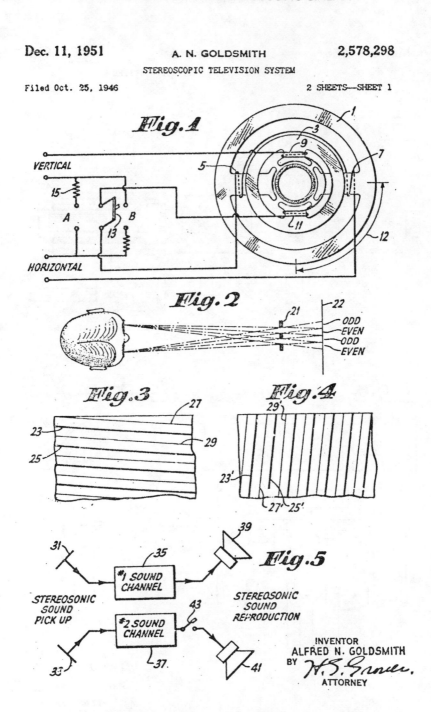

Dec. 11, 1951   A. N. GOLDSMITH   2,578,298
              STEREOSCOPIC TELEVISION SYSTEM
Filed Oct. 25, 1946   2 SHEETS—SHEET 1

Fig.1

VERTICAL

15

A   B

13

HORIZONTAL

Fig.2

21   22
ODD
EVEN
ODD
EVEN

Fig.3   *Fig.4*
27   29'
23
29
25
23'
27' 25'

Fig.5
39
31   35
#1 SOUND
CHANNEL
STEREOSONIC   STEREOSONIC
SOUND   SOUND
PICK UP   REPRODUCTION
43
#2 SOUND
CHANNEL
33   37   41

INVENTOR
ALFRED N. GOLDSMITH
BY
ATTORNEY

A.18. *Goldsmith's alternate-field system.* He would rotate the raster through 90°
and view through a parallax grid barrier.

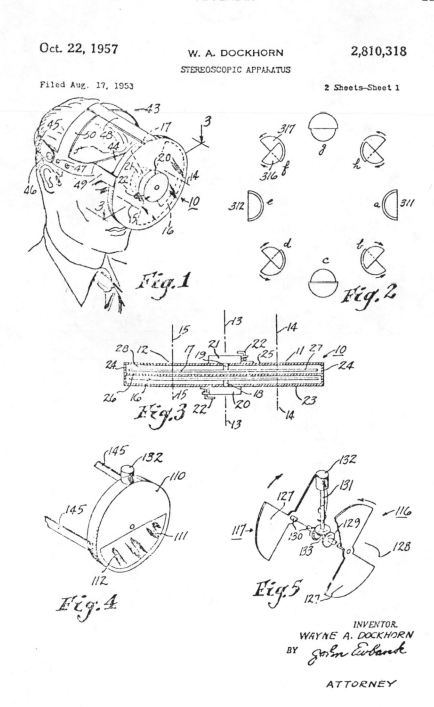

Oct. 22, 1957

W. A. DOCKHORN

STEREOSCOPIC APPARATUS

2,810,318

Filed Aug. 17, 1953

2 Sheets—Sheet 1

Fig.1

Fig.2

Fig.3

Fig.4

Fig.5

INVENTOR.
WAYNE A. DOCKHORN
BY
John Ewbank

ATTORNEY

A.19. *Dockhorn's occluding viewer.*

PATENTED SEP 2 1975   3,903,358

SHEET 1 OF 2

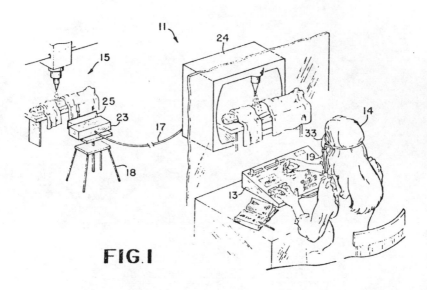

FIG.I

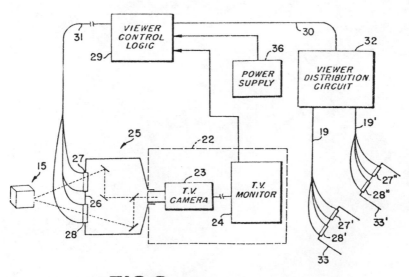

FIG.2

A.20. *Roese's alternate-field system using electro-optical shutters.*

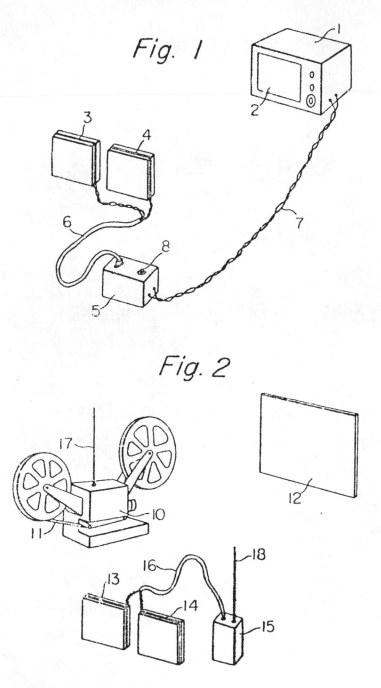

Fig. 1

Fig. 2

A.21. *Kratomi's electro-optical image-selection device.* It is shown here applied to both television and movies.

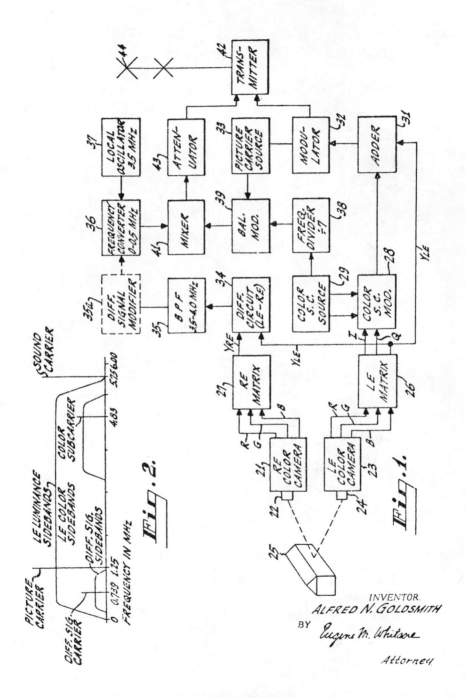

A.22. *Block electronic diagram of Goldsmith's compatible system.*

Butterfield and others have applied the frame-divider concept to display using polarized light for image selection by using a projection television receiver. Projection televisions usually use aluminum-surface screens, which conserve polarization. An optical device is added to the projection lenses to produce properly superimposed and polarized images.

In the foregoing, I have discussed several means for displaying the encoded stereoscopic pairs of images. Mentloned were autostereoscopic displays using raster screens, occlusion using mechanical and electro-optical shuttering devices, viewing the CRT through a stereoscope, and projection television using polarized light for image selection.

A.23. *Stereoscopic television inventor James Butterfield.* Shown here at the viewing hood of his industrial system.

In addition to autostereoscopic displays using raster barriers, inventors have described lenticular screens. These would hardly improve the situation for observing interdigitized stereopairs, since viewing zones would be extremely limited in number and extent. The basic difficulty with autostereoscopic television displays is the same as that for motion picture displays. A large number of images from separate perspective viewpoints are needed in order to provide broad viewing zones. Only broad zones can provide freedom of seating placement and of head movement. A practical system might need a score or more of channels to achieve these ends. This poses grave problems for transmission and storage of autostereoscopic information.

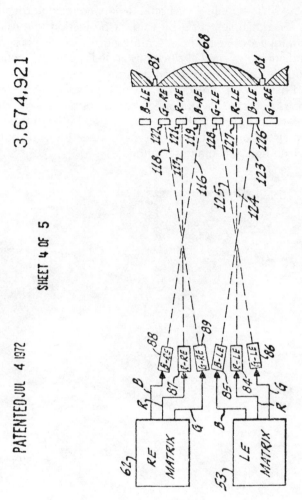

PATENTED JUL 4 1972

SHEET 4 OF 5

3,674,921

INVENTOR.
ALFRED N. GOLDSMITH
BY
Eugene M. Whitacre
Attorney

A.24. *Interdigitized parallax stereogram television system.* Design for a CRT placing phosphors behind lenticules. From Goldsmith's 1972 U.S. Patent No. 3,674,921)

Maurice Tripp, of the Skia Corporation, seems to have demonstrated in the early 1970s an autostereoscopic system of very advanced design which overcomes most of the significant problems of prior art. Tripp's disclosure, U.S. Pat. No. 3,932,699, is more interesting for what it leaves out than what it includes. My associate, Starks, and I visited Tripp in his laboratory and saw examples of his work in the form of large photographic transparencies. The television system had been taken apart but we were able to examine components. A large diameter lens is used for photography, in conjunction with a lenticular screen covering the face of the light sensitive tube of the television camera. Viewing is carried out on a CRT with a fiber optic faceplate, one side of which has the usual phosphor coating. The other side of the fiber optic screen is a lenticular grid.

Turning to display devices working in conjunction with stereopairs, we find two possibilities: sequential occlusion and polarization. The two are not distinctly separable, since polarized images may be presented in sequence.

The heart of the problem is that CRT rear-screen projected television images are produced with electrons, and electrons cannot be treated like light to carry polarization information. Therefore polarization must occur at the surface of the screen after the excitation of phosphors.

In many ways, it would be preferable to use polarizing spectacles instead of electro-optical shuttering spectacles. They would be less expensive, and since they are passive devices, they do not need to receive synchronization information from the receiver. Electro-optical shuttering glasses are active devices that need to be in touch with the scanning rate of the interlace by means of cables or some wireless scheme. Shuttering selection devices, unlike polarizing spectacles, allow for quite a bit of head tipping, and it is my observation that this can make viewing more comfortable.

Huffman (1958) uses an idea by Land originally applied to the display of still stereopairs. He places two CRTs at right angles and views the image through a semisilvered mirror. The CRTs are covered with sheet polarizers, and the viewer wears the appropriate glasses. This is an idea with defects we need not enumerate.

We have discussed the possibilities of projection television, and a recent patent by Tan (1978) combines aspects of both rear-projected and front-projected systems. The idea attracted some attention in the press, probably because the patent is the property of Philips, the electronics giant. A CRT has its image transmitted through a sheet polarizer, and a projection television is used to throw a second image onto the surface of the CRT. The projection optics contain a second sheet polarizer. It seems an ingenious but cumbersome manifestation.

Vanderhooft (1957) and Geer (1965) have attacked the problem in a different way. They steer the left and right images to thin parallel sections of the surface of the CRT. As may be seen in the drawings, both inventors like the idea of using lenticular sheets juxtaposed in front of the screen surface for autostereoscopic viewing. We have discussed the problems of presenting

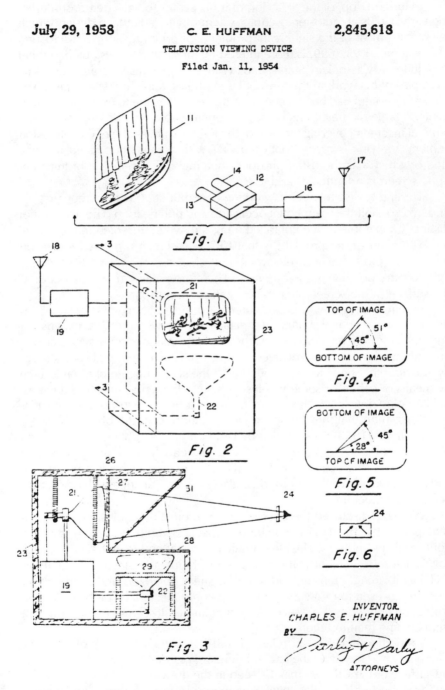

July 29, 1958   C. E. HUFFMAN   2,845,618

TELEVISION VIEWING DEVICE

Filed Jan. 11, 1954

Fig. 1

Fig. 2

Fig. 3

TOP OF IMAGE
51°
45°
BOTTOM OF IMAGE

Fig. 4

BOTTOM OF IMAGE
45°
28°
TOP OF IMAGE

Fig. 5

Fig. 6

INVENTOR.
CHARLES E. HUFFMAN
BY
ATTORNEYS

A.25. *Huffman's 3-D television system.* CRTs coverd with sheet polarizers facing at right angles to each other.

interdigitized stereopairs autostereoscopically. In addition, Vanderhooft and Geer would have to deal with the thickness of the faceplate of the CRT and resulting misalignment of image strips and lenticules. Of course this would also be a consideration if strips of sheet polarizers were applied to the face of the tube. It might be better to place the polarizer strips inside the CRT. A thin glass plate with phosphors on one side and polarizers on the other would do the trick.

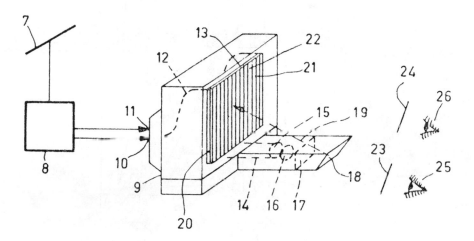

A.26. *Tan's front- and rear-screen 3-D television display.*

The ordinary CRT cannot be used to steer the electron beam accurately to an exact spot on the phosphor surface of the tube. If it could, the job of inventing color television would have been vastly simplified. Special beam index tubes have been suggested that would use a sensor and feedback system to ensure that the electron beam accurately scans the phosphor surface. This kind of a design might be applied to a polarized display, but the lack of progress in its application to color television makes me suspect that it would be a formidable task.

Bonne of Honeywell (1974) takes a different position. He plans to change the angle of polarization at the surface of the screen by using PLZT ceramics positioned after the polarizer. In this way, passive glasses might be used, with left and right images presented in sequence. The PLZT ceramic, probably made up of a mosaic of the material, would function in synchronization with the interlace. Honeywell actually built such a device, and other large PLZT displays have been built for classified military purposes.

Next, I will discuss volumetric display possibilities. We will take a look at three typical suggestions. Ketchpel (Hughes Aircraft, 1964) shows a special CRT with a spinning, disc-shaped phosphor screen. Persistence of vision

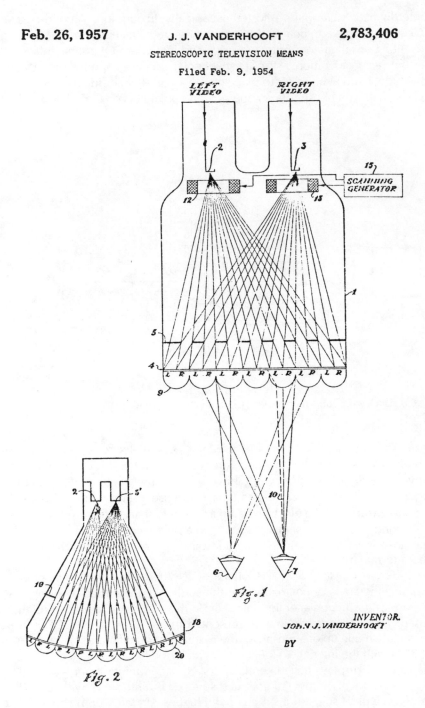

A.27. *Vanderhooft's interdigitized parallax stereogram tube.*

May 18, 1965   C. W. GEER   3,184,630
                THREE-DIMENSIONAL DISPLAY APPARATUS

Filed July 12, 1960   2 Sheets-Sheet 1

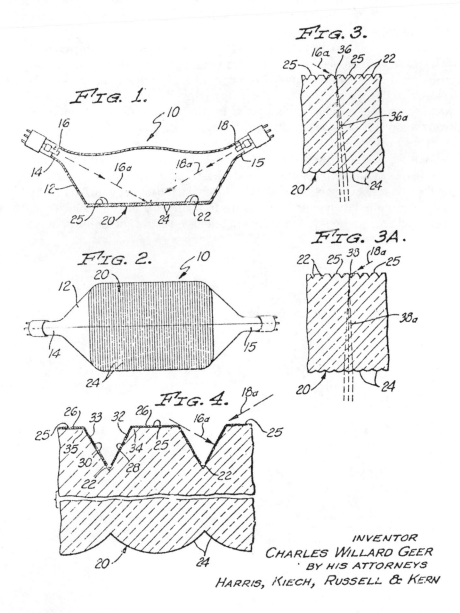

A.28. Geer's interdigitized parallax stereogram tube.

would help create the stereoscopic effigy. A little thought shows that such a contraption will produce transparent images, which one can see through. This is fine for the display of some kinds of graphics or radar, but not for general depictions of the visual world. A similar comment can be made about Rowe's 1977 patent using a cloud of phosphorescent particles floating in a twin-gun CRT. The particles glow where the beams collide. By properly steering the electron beams, a three-dimensional Cartesian coordinate tracing of the image can be created.

We now come to the idea of Munz (1971), who suggests using a plurality of spaced screens as shown in the drawing. This concept, whatever other problems it may contain, has in common with all volumetric systems the following: The spatial extent of the effigy depends on the actual physical thickness of the volume encompassed by the device. Objects cannot be brought forward of the near-screen surface, and they can extend backward in space a distance that, at best, can be measured in centimeters.

For the past seven years, in efforts predating my motion picture work, I have investigated the possibility of a stereoscopic television system encoding the odd and even fields with left-and-right stereoscopic image pairs. My associates and I designed several systems for achieving this end. One of our main goals was to preserve the existing television infrastructure so that our

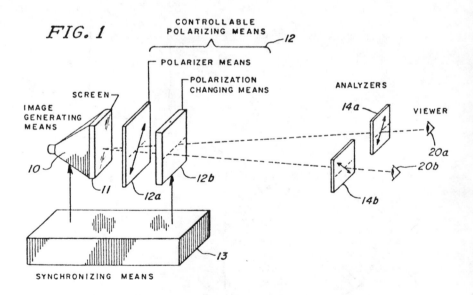

A.29. Bonne's alternate-field display.

July 7, 1964   R. D. KETCHPEL   3,140,415

THREE-DIMENSIONAL DISPLAY CATHODE RAY TUBE

Filed June 16, 1960   4 Sheets-Sheet 1

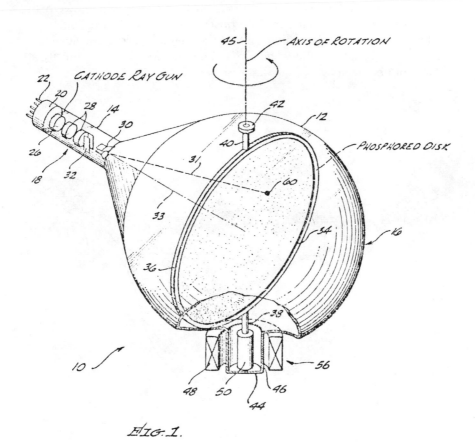

FIG. 1.

INVENTOR.
RICHARD D. KETCHPEL,
BY
ATTORNEY.

A.30. *Keptchel's spinning phosphor screen volumetric display.*

system would be a compatible one. We wanted our invention to be viewable with either passive (polarization) or active (electro-optical occlusion) selection devices, and we desired to preserve the existing bandwidth. On November 20, 1981, at 1:40 P.M., my co-inventor Jim Stewart plugged in the final component, and we observed flickerless high-quality, three-dimensional television images that achieved our design goals. The system was designed with the assistance of my associate Michael Starks. Initially we plan to market the system for industrial purposes, and the readers of this book may find it interesting to learn that it affords a splendid video assist viewfinder for cinematography so that images may be previewed stereoscopically at the time of photography.

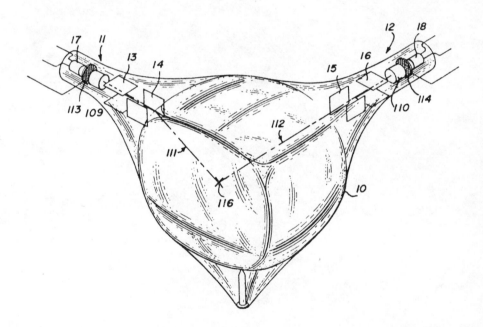

A.31. *Rowe's phosphorescent cloud display.*

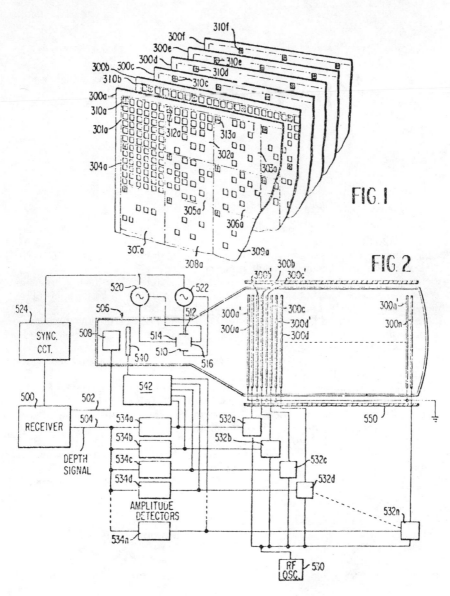

FIG. 1

FIG. 2

INVENTOR

A.32. *Munz's multiple-screen display.*

Bibliography

Abramson, Niles H. 1977. Three-dimensional information. *SPIE* Vol. 120, Three-dimensional imaging.

Adair, Paul E., ed. 1972. *Everything you wanted to know about 3-D but were ashamed to ask!* Dallas: privately published.

Adams, Oscar S. 1955. Stereogram decentration and stereo-base as factors influencing the apparent size of stereoscopic pictures. *Am. J. Psychology* 68:54–68.

Aigner, Hal. 1970. The coming 3-D movie revolution. *Take One* 2:6–8.

Anderton, John. Method by which Pictures Projected upon Screens by Magic Lanterns are Seen in Relief. 542,321. Ap. Jul. 5, 1893; Pat. Jul. 9, 1895 (Jul. 7, 1891 in England).

Anonymous. 1977. Microsurgery for strokes and visual disorders. *Science News* 115(5):69 (Feb. 3, 1977).

Baker, Friend F. (assignor to Baker & Worth, Inc.). Stereoscopic Attachment for Use with Cameras. 2,627,201. Ap. Aug. 23, 1949; Pat. Feb. 3, 1953.

Banning, Thomas A., Jr. Stereoscopic Television Including Means to Select Either Three-Dimensional or Two-Dimensional Reception. 3,358,079. Ap. Aug. 2, 1963; Pat. Dec. 12, 1967.

Bartley, S. Howard. 1969. *Principles of perception.* New York: Harper & Row.

Bassett, Raymond C. (assignor to International Telephone and Telegraph Corp.). Three Dimensional Display System, 3,335,217. Ap. Sept. 14, 1964; Pat. Aug. 8, 1967.

Battro, Antonio M. 1977. *Visual Riemannian space versus cognitive Euclidean space.* Dordrecht, Holland: D. Reidel Publishing Co.

Bautze, Jeff. Simulated Stereoscopic Television Projection System. 4,151,549. Ap. Dec. 19, 1977; Pat. Apr. 24, 1979.

Beachell, C. E. 1953. A 35mm stereo cine camera. *J. SMPTE* 61:634–41.

Benton, Stephen A. 1975. Holographic displays—a review. *Optical Engineering* 14(5):402–7.

Bernier, R. V. 1951. Three-dimensional motion picture applications. *J. SMPTE* 56:599–612.

———. (assignor to Tru-D Co.). Three Dimensional Cinematography. 3,531,191. Ap. Oct. 21, 1966; Pat. Sept. 29, 1970.

———. (assignor to Synthetic Vision Corp.). System and Apparatus for Projecting Three Dimensional Motion Pictures. 2,729,138. Ap. Jul. 17, 1951; Pat. Jan. 3, 1956.

———. Three-Dimensional Adapter for Motion-Picture Projectors. 2,478,891. Ap. Nov. 4, 1947; Pat. Aug. 16, 1949.

Beverly, K. I. and Regan, D. 1974. Visual sensitivity to disparity pulses: Evidence for directional selectivity. *Vision Res.* 14:357–61.

Biroc, Joseph. 1952. Hollywood launches 3-D film production. *American Cinematographer* 33:336–37, 350–52.

———. 1974. Hollywood launches 3-D production. *American Cinematographer* 55(4):452, 486–89.

Bishop, P. O.; and Henry, G. H. 1971. Spatial vision. *Annual Review of Psychology* 22:119–61.

Bjelkhagen, Hans I. 1977. Experiences with large-scale reflection and transmission holography. *SPIE* Vol. 120, Three-dimensional imaging.

Black, Stephen R. 1977. Digital processing of 3-D data to generate interactive real-time dynamic pictures. *SPIE* Vol. 120, Three-dimensional imaging.

Blakemore, Colin. 1970. Binocular depth perception and the optic chiasm. *Vision Res.* 10:43–47.

Boltjanskij, A. G.; Komar, V. G.; and Ovsjannikova, N. A. 1975. 3-D cinematography. *Tekhnika Kino i Televidenia* No. 3:10–13.

Boltjanskij, A.G.; Ovsjannikova, N.A.; and Khanukaev, D. R. 1978. 3-D films projection according to the system "Stereo 70." (In Russian.) *Tekhnika Kino i Televidenia* No. 4:1–11.

Bonnet, Maurice (assignor to La Reliephographie). Relief Photograph Having Reflecting Back. 2,500,511. Ap. Dec. 7, 1945; Pat. Mar. 14, 1950.

Boring, Edwin G. 1929. *A history of experimental psychology.* New York: Appleton-Century-Crofts, Inc.

Bowen, A.; Moir, J.; and Turner, H. 1951. Projection in Britain's "Telekinema." *International Projectionist* 11–13.

Boyle, John W. 1953. Filming the Marciano-Walcott bout in 3-D. *American Cinematographer* 34:318–19, 350–52.

Brewster, David, Sir. 1856. *The stereoscope: Its history, theory, and construction.* Reprinted 1971. New York: Morgan and Morgan.

Brooks, Gene M. 1953. Filming a 3-D feature in the Korean battle zone. *American Cinematographer* 34:426–27, 449–50.

Brown, Theodore. 1906. La projection stéréoscopique directe. *Photo-Revue* 43–44, 83–85, 171–73, 196–97, 212–13.

Burckhardt, C. B. 1968. Optimum parameters and resolution limitation of integral photography. *J. Optical Soc. Amer.* 58 (1):71–76.

Burrows, A. A.; and Hamilton, V. E. 1974. Stereopsis using a large aspheric field lens. *Applied Optics* 13(4):739–40.

Burtt, George. 1953. 3-dimension optical effects. *American Cinematographer* 34:96–142.

Butterfield, James F. 1970. Three dimensional television. Paper presented to the SPIE 15th Annual Technical Symposium, Anaheim, Ca., Sept.

———. 1972a. Stereoscopic television. Paper presented to OSA Meeting on "Design and Visual Interface of Binocular Systems," Annapolis, Md., May 24.

———. 1975. A teaching stereo-video microscope. *SPIE* 66:212–14.

———. 1977. Very high resolution stereoscopic television. *SPIE* Vol. 120, Three dimensional imaging.

Cameron, James R. 1953. *Third dimension movies and expanded screen.* Coral Gables, Fla: Cameron Publishing Co.

———. 1969. *Theatrical projectionists' guide.* Coral Gables, Fla.: Cameron Publishing Co.

Chandler, J. S.; and De Palma, J. J. 1968. High-brightness projection screens with high ambient light rejection. *J. SMPTE* 77:1012–24.

Charnwood, Lord. 1965. *An essay on binocular vision.* New York: Hafner Publishing Co.

Cheng, Richard Tien-Ren. 1971. *Coefficient generator and cursor for the Stereomatrix 3-D Display System.* Urbana, Ill.: University of Illinois Press.
Cherkasova, D. N. 1971. Short-range stereophotogrammetric photography. *Soviet J. Optical Technology* 38(5):306–13.
Chubb, L. W.; Grey, D. L.; Blout, E. R.; and Land, E. H. 1954. Properties of polarizers for filters and viewers for 3-D motion pictures. *J. SMPTE* 62:120–24.
Clark, Charles G. 1953. Practical filming techniques for three-dimensional and widescreen motion pictures. *American Cinematographer* 34:107, 129, 138.
Cogan, Alexander I. 1977. The other role of vergence eye movements. *SPIE* Vol. 120, Three-dimensional imaging.
Cohen, Nathan. 1953. Single-film, single projector 3-D. *American Cinematographer* 34:319.
Cohn, T. E.; and Lasley, D. J. 1976. Binocular vision: Two possible central interactions between signals from two eyes. *Science* 192:561–63.
Collender, Robert B. Three Dimensional Unaided Viewing Method and Apparatus. 3,178,720. Ap. Jun. 2, 1961; Pat. Apr. 13, 1965.
———. Three Dimensional Unaided Viewing Apparatus. 3,324,760. Ap. Dec. 30, 1964; Pat. Jun. 13, 1967.
———. 1967. The Stereoptiplexer: Competition for the hologram. *Information Display* 5(Nov./Dec.):27–31.
———. 1968a. True stereoscopic movie system without glasses. Part 1. *Information Display* 5(July/Aug.):25–38.
———. 1968b. True stereoscopic movie system without glasses. Part 2. *Information Display* 5(Sept./Oct.):24–30.
———. 1972. Standard theatre stereoptics without glasses. *Information Display* 9(July/Aug.):18–25, 9(Sept./Oct.):12–17.
Condon, Chris. 1974. The stereovision 3-D system. *American Cinematographer* 55(4):414.
Cornwell-Clyne, Adrian. 1954. *Kinematography and new screen techniques.* London: Hutchinson's Scientific and Technical Publications.
Cowan, E. W. 1966. Stereoscopic viewer for measuring positions and angles in three dimensions. *Review of Scientific Instruments* 37(8):1004–6.
Dalzell, J. Moir. 1953. *Practical stereoscopic photography.* London: Technical Press.
De Biterro, D. J. 1969a. A front-lighted 3-D holographic movie. *Applied Optics* 9(2):498–99.
———. 1969b. Holographic panoramic stereograms synthesized from white light recordings. *Applied Optics* 8(8):1740–41.
Denisyuk, Yu. N. 1973. Holograph motion pictures. *Sov. Phys. Tech. Phys.* 18(12):1549–51.
Denisyuk, Yu. N.; Ramishvili, N. M.; and Chavchanidze, V. V. 1970. Production of three-dimensional images of two-dimensional objects without lenses or holography. *Optics and Spectroscopy* 30:603–5.
Dewhurst, Hubert. Photography, Viewing, and Projection of Pictures with Stereoscopic Effect. 2,693,128. Ap. Oct. 21, 1948; Pat. Nov. 2, 1954.
———. 1954. *Introduction to 3-D.* New York: The Macmillan Co.
Dickson, William K.-L. Camera 728,584 Ap. Jan. 13, 1903; Pat. May 19, 1903.
Dudley, Leslie P. 1951a. *Stereoptics: An introduction.* London: MacDonald and Co.
———. 1951b. Stereoscopy in the Telekinema and in the future. *British Kinematography* 18(6):172–81.
———. 1970. A new development in autostereoscopic photoscopy. *J. SMPTE* 79:687–93.
———. Integral Photography. 3,613,539. Ap. July 26, 1968; Pat. Jan. 23, 1968.
Duhauron, Louis Ducos (assignor to Eugene Demole). Stereoscopic Print. 544,666. Ap. Sept. 19, 1894; Pat. Aug. 20, 1895 (Sept. 15, 1891 in France).

DuMont, Allen B. (assignor to Allen B. DuMont Laboratories). Dual Image Viewing Apparatus. 2,832, 821. Ap. Jan. 11, 1954; Pat. Apr. 29, 1958.
Dunn, Linwood G; and Weed, Don W. 1974. The third dimension in Dynavision. *American Cinematographer* 55(4):450–51.
Edelson, Edward. The bizarre new world of holography. *Popular Science* 214(3):87– 91, 168.
Editors, *American Cinematographer*. 1953a. Is 3-D dead. . . ? *American Cinematographer* 34:585–86, 608 11.
———. 1953b. One camera, one film for 3-D. *American Cinematographer* 34:269.
———. 1953c. Producers Service's 3-D camera. *American Cinematographer* 34:116, 130–31.
———. 1953d. Some basic principles of 3-D cinematography. *American Cinematographer* 34:266.
———. 1953e. 3-D television. *American Cinematographer* 34:320, 340.
———. Columbia Studio's 3-D camera. *American Cinematographer* :215, 234–36.
———. 1974a. The Spacevision 3-D System. *American Cinematographer* 55(4):432–33, 448–49, 472–74.
———. 1974b. The Stereovision 3-D System. *American Cinematographer* 55(4):414.
Editors, *Cs. cas. fys.* 1973. Od kinematograficke holografie k holograficke kinematografii. *Cs. cas. fys.* A 23:217–19.
Editors, *Motion Picture Projectionist*. 1932. No let-up on third dimension pictures. *Motion Picture Projectionist* 5:14.
Eisenstein, S. M. 1949. About stereoscopic cinema. Penguin Film Review No. 8. London:Penguin.
Enright, James T. 1970. Stereopsis, visual latency, and three-dimensional moving pictures. *Amer. Sci.* 58:536–45.
Fairall, H. K. (assignor to Multicolor Ltd.). Binocular Nonstop-Motion-Picture Camera. 1,784,515. Ap. Nov. 21, 1925; Pat. Dec. 9, 1930.
Ferragallo, Roger. 1974. On stereoscopic painting. *Leonardo* 7:97–104.
Forbes, John. 1953. Elgeet stereo attachments fit most 16mm cameras and projectors. *American Cinematographer* 34:384, 394–95.
Foster, Frederick. 1953. A stereo camera for two-strip 16mm 3-D photography. *American Cinematographer* 34:428–29, 450–52.
Fowell, Frank. 1931. Are stereoscopic "movies" possible? *Motion Picture Projectionist* 4:11–12.
Gabor, Dennis. System of Photography and Projection in Relief. 2,351,032. Ap. Aug. 3, 1940; Pat. Jun. 13, 1944.
———. System of Projecting Pictures in Stereoscopic Relief. 2,351,033. Ap. Aug. 3, 1940; Pat. Jun. 13, 1944.
———. Optical System Composed of Lenticules. 2,351,034. Ap. Aug. 3, 1940; Pat. Jun. 13, 1944.
Gannaway, Robertson R. (assignor to Belmont Radio Corp.) Three-Dimensional Display. 2,578,970. Ap. May 21, 1949. Pat. Dec. 18, 1951.
Garity, William E. (assignor to Walter Lantz Productions, Inc.). Method of and Means for Producing Stereoscopic Animated Cartoons. 2,776,594. Ap. Aug. 18, 1953; Pat. Jan. 8, 1957.
Garnov, V. V.; Dobovick, A. S.; and Sitsinskaya, N. M. 1968. Speed photography with stereoscopic grid cameras. *Soviet J. Opt. Tech.* 35:9–13.
Gavin, Arthur. 1953a. Shooting 3-D films. *American Cinematographer* 34:109, 110, 134–39.
———. 1953b. 3-D Film Festival open to both amateurs and "pros." *American Cinematographer* 34:330, 341–42.
———. 1953c. 2-D, 3-D, wide screen, or all three . . . . *American Cinematographer*

34:210–15, 235–36.

Geer, Charles Willard. Three-Dimensional Display Apparatus. 3,184,630. Ap. Jul. 12, 1960; Pat. May 18, 1965.

George, Nicholas; and McCrickerd, J. T. 1969. *Holography and stereoscopy.* Springfield, Va.: Clearinghouse for Federal Scientific and Technical Information.

Gernsheim, Helmut; and Gernsheim, Alison. 1956. L. J. M. Daguerre, the world's first photographer. New York: World Publishing Co.

Gibson, James J. 1950. The perception of the visual world. Boston: Houghton Mifflin Co.

Gillott, H. F. 1955. *The effect on binocular vision of variations in the relative sizes and levels of illumination of the ocular images.* London: British Optical Association.

Glaser, I. 1977. Imaging properties of holographic stereograms. *SPIE* Vol. 120, Three-dimensional imaging.

Goldovskii, E. M. 1958. *Problems of panoramic and wide-screen cinematography.* (In Russian) Moscow.

Goldsmith, Alfred N. (assignor to Radio Corp. of America). Television Apparatus. 2,384,260. Ap. Sept. 21, 1944; Pat. Sept. 4, 1945.

———. Three-Dimensional Television System. 3,674,921. Ap. Nov. 12, 1969; Pat. July 4, 1972.

———. (assignor to Radio Corp of America). Television Apparatus. 2,384,260. Ap. Sept. 21, 1944; Pat. Sept. 4, 1945.

———. Stereoscopic Television System. 2,578,298. Ap. Oct. 25, 1946; Pat. Dec. 11. 1951.

———. Three-Dimensional Television System. 3,674,921. Ap. Nov. 12, 1969; Pat. Jul. 4, 1972.

———. Stereoscopic and Stereosonic Television System. 2,566,700. Ap. Oct. 30, 1946; Pat. Sept. 4, 1951.

Goodman, J. W. 1968. *Introduction to Fourier optics.* New York:McGraw-Hill. pp. 198–272.

Gorbarenko, V. A. 1975. Microstereoprojectors. *Sov. J. Opt. Technol.* 43(4):229–32.

Gregory, R. L. 1966. *Eye and brain: The psychology of seeing.* New York: World University Library.

———. 1977. Seeing in depth. *SPIE* Vol. 120, Three-dimensional imaging.

Gruber, Wilhelm B. Stereoscopic Viewing Device. 2,189,285. Ap. Jan. 29, 1939; Pat. Feb. 6, 1940.

Gulick, W. Lawrence; and Lawson, Robert B. 1976. *Human stereopsis: A psychophysical analysis.* New York: Oxford University Press.

Gunzberg, Julian. 1953. The story of Natural Vision. *American Cinematographer* 34:534–35, 554–56, 612–16.

Hamlyn, D. W. 1957. *The psychology of perception: A philosophical examination of gestalt theory and derivative theories of perception.* London: Routledge and Kegan Paul.

Harding, Lloyd E. 1931. Stereoscopic motion pictures. *Motion Picture Projectionist* 4:14–16.

Hardy, LeGrand et al. 1953. *The Geometry of Binocular Space Perception.* Columbia University Library, New York.

Hawkins, Richard C. 1952. *An initial investigation of the problems of editing the dramatic stereoscopic film.* University of California, Los Angeles: M.A. thesis.

Helmholtz, H. von. 1925. Helmholtz's Treatise on Physiological Optics. Vol. III 3rd Ed. Optical Society of America. Menasha, Wisconsin. 281-709.

Herman, Stephen. 1971. Principles of binocular 3-D displays with applications to television. *J. SMPTE* 80:539–44.

Hett, John H. 1951. A high-speed stereoscopic Schlieren system. *J. SMPTE* 56:214–18.

Higuchi, H.; and Hamasaki, J. 1978. Real-time transmission of 3-D images formed by parallax panoramagrams. *Applied Optics* 17:3895–3902.

Hill, Armin J. 1953a. A mathematical and experimental foundation for stereoscopic photography. *J. SMPTE* 61:461–86.

————. 1953b. The Motion Picture Research Council 3-D calculator. *American Cinematographer* 34:373.

Hiser, Ernest F. 1952. Drawing in three dimensions for animation and stereoscopic processes. *J. SMPTE* 59:287–92.

Hoch, Winton C. Optical System for a Stereoscopic Motion Picture Camera. 3,825,328. Ap. Sept. 10, 1973; Pat. Jul. 23, 1974.

————. Stereoscopic Motion Picture Film. 3,339,998. Ap. Nov. 23, 1966; Pat. Sept. 5, 1967.

Howard, Bernard. 1953. 3-D in industrial film production. *American Cinematographer* 34:374–75, 400–1.

Huffman, Charles E. (assignor to Allen B. DuMont Laboratories, Inc.). Television Viewing Device 2,845,618. Ap. Jan. 11, 1954; Pat. Jul. 29, 1958.

Institute of Stereoscopic Research. 1974. Calculations for stereo cinematography. *American Cinematographer* 55(4):424–25.

Ittelson, William H. 1950. *Visual space perception.* New York: Springer Publishing Co.

Ivanov, Boris T. 1956. *Stereocinematography.* (In Russian.) Moscow.

Ives, Herbert E. (assignor to Bell Telephone Laboratories, Inc.). Stereoscopic Motion Picture. 2,012,995. Ap. Feb. 9, 1929; Pat. Sept. 3, 1935.

————. 1931. Optical properties of a Lippmann lenticulated sheet. *J. Optical Soc. Amer.* 21:171–76.

————. 1932. Projecting motion pictures in relief. *Motion Picture Projectionist* 5:10–14, 20–22.

Iwane, Waro (assignor to the President of Hokkaido University). Three-Dimensional Television System 4,062,045. Ap. Feb. 24, 1976; Pat. Dec. 6, 1977.

Jacobson, A. D.; Evtuhov, U.; and Neeland, J. K. 1968. Motion picture holography. *Applied Physics Letters* 14(4):120–22.

Jeater, Don. 1978. Dimensions of the third kind. *Film Making* 16 (Oct.):35–37.

————. 1978. The third dimension. *Film Making* 16(Nov.):20–21.

Jennings, W. Wheeler; and Vanet, Pierre. 1952. New direct-vision stereo-projection screen. *J. SMPTE* 59:23–27.

Jeong, Tung H. 1967. Cylindrical holography and some proposed applications. *J. Optical Soc. Amer.* 57:1396–98.

————. 1978. Holography now in the USSR. *Optical Spectra* Apr. 1978:40–42.

Jones, R. Clark; and Shurcliff, William A. 1954. Equipment to measure and control synchronization errors in 3-D projection. *J. SMPTE* 62:134–41.

Jones, Robert C. (assignor to Polaroid Corp.). Synchronous Stereoscopic Motion Picture Projection System. 2,843,005. Ap. Mar. 22, 1957; Pat. Jul. 15, 1958.

Jones, Robert C.; and Shurcliff, William A. (assignors to Polaroid Corp.). Synchronization Tester for Related Motion Picture Frames. 2,854,883. Ap. May 27, 1953; Pat. Oct. 7, 1958.

Judge, Arthur J. 1950. *Stereoscopic photography: Its application to science, industry and education.* London: Chapman and Hall.

Julesz, Bela. 1971. *Foundations of Cyclopean perception.* Chicago: University of Chicago Press.

————. 1977. Recent results with dynamic random-dot stereograms. *SPIE* Vol. 120, Three-dimensional imaging.

Kakichashvili, Sh. D.; Koaleva, A. I.; and Rukhadze, V. A. 1967. Circular holography of three-dimensional objects. *Optics and Spectroscopy* 24:333.

Kanolt, Clarence W. Stereoscopic Picture. 2,140,702. Ap. Aug. 31, 1934; Pat. Dec. 20, 1938.

———. Production of Stereoscopic Motion Pictures. 1,882,646. Ap. Jul. 26, 1929; Pat. Oct. 11, 1932.

Kapany, N. S. 1972. Three-dimensional optar. *SPIE Proceedings* 31:107–12.

Kaplan, Sam H. 1952. Theory of parallax barriers. *J. SMPTE* 59:11–21.

Kaszab, Nicholas T. Screen for Stripe-Composite Stereoscopic Pictures. 2,271,196. Ap. Jul. 19, 1939; Pat. Jan. 27, 1942.

———. Screen for Stereoscopic Pictures. 2,150,225. Ap. Jul. 20, 1937; Pat. Mar. 14, 1939.

Kaufman, Lloyd. 1974. *Sight and mind: An introduction to visual perception.* New York: Oxford University Press.

Kaufman, Lloyd; Bacon, Joshua; and Barroso, Felix. 1972. Stereopsis without image segregation. *Vision Res.* 13:137–147.

Kent, Arthur P.; and Marks, Mortimer (assignors to Marks Polarized Corp.). Apparatus for Converting Motion Picture Projectors for Stereo Display. 3,851,955. Ap. Feb. 5, 1973; Pat. Dec. 3, 1974.

Ketchpel, R. D. 1963. Direct-view three-dimensional display tube. *IEEE Transactions on Electron Devices* 10:324–28.

King, M. C.; and Berry, D. H. 1970. Varifocal mirror technique for video transmission of three-dimensional images. *Applied Optics* 9(9):2035–39.

Kingslake, Rudolf. 1951. *Lenses in photography.* Rochester, N.Y.: Case-Hoyt Corp.

Kingslake, Rudolf, ed. 1965. *Applied optics and optical engineering.* Vol. II, Ch. 2. New York: Academic Press.

Kitrosser, S. 1953. Polaroid interocular calculator. Photographic Science and Technique Section B of *PSA Journal* 19B(2):74–76.

Komar, V. G. 1977. Progress on the holographic movie process in the USSR. *SPIE* Vol. 120, Three-dimensional imaging.

Krause, E. E. 1954. *Three dimensional projection.* New York: Greenberg.

Krulikoski, S. J., Jr.; Kowalski, D. C.; and Whitehead, F. R. 1971. Coherent optical parallel processing. *SPIE* 9:104–10.

Kurtz, H. F. 1937. Orthostereoscopy. *J. Optical Soc. Amer.* 27(10):323–39.

Kurtz, R. L.; and Perry, L. M. 1972. Holographic motion picture camera allows front surface detail to be recorded in real time using a continuous wave laser. *Applied Optics* 12(4):888–91.

La Brecque, M. 1972. Photographic memory. *Leonardo* 5:347–49.

Land, Edwin H. (assignor to Sheet Polarizer Co.) Field Divider. 2,106,752. Ap. Dec. 3, 1934; Pat. Feb. 1, 1938.

———. Polarizing Optical System. 2,099,694. Ap. Mar. 6, 1934; Pat. Nov. 23, 1937.

Land, E. H. 1953. Stereoscopic motion pictures: A special report to the Directors of Polaroid Corporation. Cambridge, Mass.: Polaroid Corp.

———. 1977. Six eyes of man. *SPIE* Vol. 120, Three-dimensional imaging.

———. 1978. Our "polar-partnership" with the world around us. *Harvard Mag.* Jan.–Feb.

Lateltin, H. 1931. Requirements for stereoscopic pictures. *Motion Picture Projectionist* 4:42.

Laube, Grover; and Halprin, Sol. (assignors to Twentieth Century-Fox Film Corp.). Means for Making Stereoscopic Pictures. 2,838,975. Ap. Mar. 19, 1954; Pat. Jun. 17, 1958.

Layer, H. A. 1971. Exploring stereo images: A changing awareness of space in the fine arts. *Leonardo,* 4:233–38.

————. 1972. Figurative photo-sculpture with 3-D pointillism. *Leonardo* 5:55–58.
————. 1974. Stereo kinematics: The merging of time and space in the camera. *American Cinematographer* 55(4):438–41.
Lecuyer, R. 1945. *Histoire de la photographie.* Paris: Baschet et Cie.
Leith, E. N. 1976. White-light holograms. *Sci. American* 235:20:80–95.
Leith, E. N.; Brumm, D. G.; and Hsiao, S. S. H. 1972. Holographic cinematography. *Applied Optics* 11(9):2016–23.
Levelt, W. J. M. 1968. Psychological studies on binocular rivalry. Paris: Mouton & Co.
Levonian, E. 1954a. Stereography and the physiology of vision. *J. SMPTE* 62:199–207.
————. 1954b. Stereoscopic cinematography: *Its analysis with respect to the transmission of the visual image.* M.A. thesis, University of Southern California.
————. 1955. Stereography and the transmission of images. *J. SMPTE* 64:77–85.
Liebes, S., Jr. 1977. Mars Viking 1975 Lander interactive computerized video stereophotogrammetry. *SPIE* Vol. 120, Three-dimensional imaging.
Lightman, H. A., ed. 1974. Special issue: 3-D motion pictures—past, present and future. *American Cinematographer* 55(4):367–494.
————. 1953. Terror in 3-dimension. *American Cinematographer* 34:218–19, 242–43, 245.
Limbacher, J. L. 1968. *Four aspects of the film.* New York: Brussel and Brussel.
Linksz, A., M. D. 1964. *An essay on color vision and clinical color-vision tests.* New York: Grune and Stratton.
Linschoten, J. 1956. *Strukturanalyse der binokularen Tiefenwahrnehmung.* Djakarta: J. B. Wolters.
Linssen, E. F. 1952. *Stereo-photography in practice.* London: Fountain Press.
Lipton, L. 1977. How to make your own 3-D movies. Part 1. *Super 8 Filmmaker* 5(7):30–33.
————. 1977. Getting behind the 3-D camera. Part 2. *Super 8 Filmmaker* 5(8):30–32.
————. 1978. Shooting your own 3-D movies. Part 3. *Super 8 Filmmaker* 6(1):45–47.
————. 1978. The cinema in depth—from Hollywood to super-8 3-D. *American Cinematographer* 59(5).
————. 1979. *Lipton on Filmmaking.* New York: Simon & Schuster.
————. 1982. "Filming *Rottweiler* in 3-D". *American Cinematographer* (in press).
Luneburg, Rudolph K. 1947. *Mathematical Analysis of Binocular Vision.* New Jersey: Princeton University Press.
MacAdam, D. L. 1954. Stereoscopic perceptions of size, shape, distance, and direction. *J. SMPTE* 62:271–93.
McCrickerd, J. T. 1972. Comparison of stereograms: Pinhole, fly's eye, and holographic types. *J. Optical Soc. Amer.* 62(1):64–70.
MacDonald, R. I. 1977. Three-dimensional television by texture parallax. *Applied Optics.* 17:168–170. Jan. 15, 1978.
McLaren, Norman. 1951. Stereographic animation—The synthesis of stereoscopic depth from flat drawings and art work. *J. SMPTE* 57:513–21.
Mahler, Joseph (assignor to Polaroid Corp.). Means for Forming Images. 2,346,774. Ap. Mar. 27, 1947; Pat. Apr. 18, 1944.
Mark, Howard. 1977. Three-dimensional viewing of tomographic data—the Tomax System. *SPIE* Vol. 120, Three-dimensional imaging.
Marks, Alvin M. Three Dimensional Display System. 2,777,011. Ap. Mar. 5, 1951; Pat. Jan. 8, 1957.
Marks, Alvin M.; and Marks, Mortimer. 3-Dimensional Camera. 3,990,087. Ap. Oct. 21, 1974; Pat. Nov. 2, 1976.

Marks, Alvin M.; and Marks, Mortimer, M. Moving Screen Projection System. 3,248,165. Ap. Feb. 24, 1964; Pat. Apr. 16, 1966.
Marks, Alvin M.; and Marks, Mortimer, M. (assignors to Mortimer Marks). Method for Producing Apparent Three Dimensional Images. 2,952,182. Ap. Aug. 18, 1954; Pat. Sept. 13, 1960.
Martin, L. C.; and Wilkins, T. R. 1937. An examination of the principles of ortho-stereoscopic photomicrography and some applications. *Journal of the Optical Society of America.* Oct., 1937:340–349.
Martin, M. 1975. Three-dimensional projection apparatus. *IBM Technical Disclosure Bulletin* 18(2):384.
Mayhew, J. E. W.; and Frisby, J. P. 1976. Rivalrous texture stereograms. *Nature* 264:53–56.
Mekas, Jonas. 1970. *Movie journal: The rise of the new American Cinema 1959–71.* New York: Collier Books.
Millet, Eugene (assignor to Paillard, S.A.). Optical Device for a Stereoscopic Camera with a Horizontal Movement of the Film. 2,767,629. Ap. Apr. 13, 1954; Pat. Oct. 23, 1956.
Millet, Eugene. 1952. Some geometrical conditions for depth effect in motion pictures. *J. SMPTE* 59:517–23.
Montebello, Roger L. de. 1977a. The synthalyzer for three-dimensional synthesis, and analysis by optical dissection. *SPIE* Vol. 120, Three-dimensional imaging.
———. 1977b. Wide-angle integral photography. *SPIE* Vol. 120, Three-dimensional imaging.
Morgan, Michael. 1975. Stereoillusion based on visual persistence. *Nature* 256:639–40.
Moses, Robert A., M.D. 1975. *Adler's Physiology of the Eye:* Clinical Application. 6th ed. St. Louis: C. V. Mosby.
Murroughs, T. R. 1953. Depth perception with special reference to motion pictures. *J. SMPTE* 60:656–70.
Nakayama, Ken. 1977. Geometric and physiological aspects of depth perception. *SPIE* Vol. 120, Three-dimensional imaging.
Noaillon, Edmond H. V. Art of Making Cinematographic Projections. 1,772,782. Ap. Dec. 18, 1928; Pat. Aug. 12, 1930.
———. Art of Making Stereoscopic Projection of Pictures. 2,198,678; Ap. Jun. 25, 1937; Pat. Apr. 30, 1940.
Noll, A. Michael. 1965. Computer-generated three-dimensional movies. *Computers and Automation* 14:20–23.
Norling, John A. 1939. Three-dimensional motion pictures. *J. SMPTE* Dec: 1939: 612–634.
———. 1951a. The stereoscopic art. *PSA Journal* 17:703–8, 738–42; 18:19–25, 122–25.
———. 1951b. Stereoscopic motion pictures. *International Projectionist* Aug. 1951:12–28.
———. 1952a. Stereoscopic motion pictures. *American Cinematographer* 33:66, 78–80, 110, 130–32.
———. 1952b. Stereoscopic motion pictures. *International Projectionist* Feb. 1972:9–11.
———. 1953. The stereoscopic art—A reprint. *J. SMPTE* 60:268–307.
———. Stereoscopic Camera. 2,753,774. Ap. Feb. 12, 1953; Pat. Jul. 10, 1956.
Oboler, Arch. 1974. Movies are better than ever—In the next decade! *American Cinematographer* 55(4):453.
Ogle, Kenneth N. 1950. *Researches in binocular vision.* Philadelphia: W. B. Saunders and Co.

————. 1967. Some aspects of stereoscopic depth perception. *J. Optical Soc. America* 57:1073–81.

Ogle, Kenneth N.; and Wakefield, Janice M. 1966. Stereoscopic depth and binocular rivalry. *Vision Res.* 7:89–98.

Okoshi, Takanori. 1976. *Three dimensional imaging techniques.* New York: Academic Press.

————. 1977. Projection-type holographic displays. *SPIF* Vol. 120, Three-dimensional imaging.

Okoshi, Takanori; and Hotate, K. Projection-type white-light reconstruction of 3-D images from a strip-shaped hologram. *Applied Optics* 14(12):3078–81.

Onosko, T. 1974. '53: The new era—A brief history of the three-dimensional film. *The Velvet Light Trap* (11):12–16.

Ovsjannikova, N. A.; and Slabova, A. E. 1975. Technical and technological principals "Stereo 70." (In Russian.) *Teknika Kino i Televidenia* 16–26.

Palmer, D. A. 1961. Binocular eye movements and stereoscopic depth discrimination. *Optica Acta* 9:11–12.

Pirnat, Charles Raymond. 1972. *Observer position detector for the Stereo-matrix 3-D Display System.* Urbana, Ill.: University of Illinois.

Polyak, Stephen, M. D. 1957. *The vertebrate visual system.* Chicago: University of Chicago Press.

Pratley, Gerald. 1952. The latest 3-dimensional films prove that the movies still have an ace up their sleeve. *Films in Review* 170–174.

Purves, Frederick, ed. 1960. *The focal encyclopedia of photography.* New York: Macmillan Co.

Quigley, Martin, Jr., ed. 1953. *New screen techniques.* New York: Quigley Publishing Co.

Raloff, Janet. 1978. Dancing holograms. *Science News* 113(9):141.

Ramsaye, Terry. 1964. *A Million and One Nights.* New York: Simon and Schuster.

Ramsdell, Floyd A. (assignor to Worcester Film Corp.). Apparatus for Making Stereo-Pictures. 2,413,996. Ap. Feb. 5, 1944; Pat. Jan. 7, 1947.

Rawson, Eric G. 1968. 3-D computer-generated movies using a varifocal mirror. *Applied Optics* 7(8):1505–11.

————. 1969 Vibrating varifocal mirrors for 3-D imaging. *IEEE Spectrum* 6:37–43.

Reijnders, Franciscus Henricus. Apparatus for Taking Stereoscopic Pictures without Abnormal Stereoscopic Effects. 2,595,409. Ap. Feb. 10, 1947 (Jul. 5, 1941 in Netherlands); Pat. May 6, 1952.

Richards, Whitman. 1970. Anomalous stereoscopic depth perception. *J. Optical Soc. Amer.* 61(3):410–14.

————. Stereopsis and Stereoblindness. *Exp. Brain Res.* 10:380–88 (1970).

Rock, Irvin. 1975. *An introduction to perception.* New York: Macmillan Publishing Co.

Roe, Alvin D. 1953. Simplified single-film system for 3-D exhibition. *American Cinematographer* 34:485–509.

Roese, John A. Liquid Crystal Stereoscopic Television System. 3,821,466. Ap. May 25, 1973; Pat. Jun. 28, 1974.

————. PLZT Stereoscopic Television System 3,903,358. Ap. May 22, 1974; Pat. Sept. 2, 1975.

Ronchi, Vasco. 1957. *Optics, the science of vision.* New York: New York University Press.

Ross, John; and Hogben, J. H. 1973. Short-term memory in stereopsis. *Vision Res.* 14:1195–1201.

Rowan, Arthur. 1953. Stereo-Cine Corporation is newest 3-D filming organization. *American Cinematographer* 34:60, 78–81.

Rowe, William Guy. Three-Dimensional Display Devices. 4,063,233. Ap. Dec. 14, 1975; Pat. Dec. 13, 1977.

Rule, John T. 1938. Stereoscopic drawings. *J. Optical Soc. Amer.* 28:313–22.

———. 1941a. The geometry of stereoscopic projection. *J. Optical Soc. Amer.* 31:325–34.

———. 1941b. The shape of stereoscopic images. *J. Optical Soc. Amer.* 31:124–29.

Rule, John T.; and Bush, Vannevar. 1939. Stereoscopic photography. In *Handbook of Photography,* ed. Henny and Dudley, Whittlesey House.

Ryan, Roderick T. 1977. *A history of motion picture color technology.* New York: Focal Press.

Ryan, William H. (assignor to Polaroid Corp.). Method for Producing Stereoscopic Prints Containing Improved Light-Polarizing Images and the Product of Said Method. 2,811,893. Ap. Apr. 7, 1954; Pat. Nov. 5, 1957.

Sauer, F. C. 1937. A method of making stereoscopic illustrations. *J. Optical Soc. Amer.* 27:350–54.

Sauer, Hans (assignor to Zeiss Ikon Aktiengesellschaft). Means for Projecting Stereoscopic Pictures. 2,241,041. Ap. Feb. 11, 1939; Pat. May 6, 1941.

Sauer, Hans (assignor to Zeiss Ikon Aktiengesellschaft). Stereoscopic Camera 2,267,952. Ap. Feb. 24, 1939; Pat. Dec. 30, 1941.

Saunders, S. B.; and De Palma, J. J. 1969. An abridged goniophotometer for evaluating projection screen and other diffusing materials. *J. SMPTE* 78:628–30.

Savoye, Francois. Equipment for the Projection of Stereoscopic Views and Films. 2,421,393. Ap. Jan. 23, 1942; Pat. Jun. 3, 1947.

———. Stereoscopic Motion-Picture Projection System. 2,441,674. Ap. Jul. 13, 1945; Pat. May 18, 1948.

Sawchuck, A. A. 1978. Artificial stereo? *Applied Optics* 17:3869–73.

Schapero, Max; Cline, David; and Hofstetter, Henry William. 1948. *Dictionary of visual science.* New York: Chilton Book Co.

Schensted, Roy E. Process for Stereoscopic Motion Pictures in Colors. 2,283,466. Ap. Apr. 1940; Pat. May 19, 1942.

Selle, Walter. 1971. "3D" im Bücherspiegel. West Berlin 37:Deutsche Gesellschaft für Stereoskopie.

———. 1973. Der Stereofilm verlangt nach neuen Normen. *Fernseh-und Kino-Technik* (7,8):227–30, 279–80.

Sellers, Coleman (assignor to himself and G. Burnham). Exhibiting Stereoscopic Pictures of Moving Objects. 31,357. Pat. Feb. 5, 1861.

Shamroy, Leon. 1953. Filming the big dimension. *American Cinematographer* 34:216–17, 230–31.

Shatskaya, A. N. 1974. The range of basic parameters for a stereo projector. (In Russian.) *Teknika Kino i Televidenia* 18:43–45.

Sherman, Revel A. 1953. Benefits to vision through stereoscopic films. *J. SMPTE* 61:295–308.

Shurcliff, William A. (assignor to Polaroid Corp.). Synchronization Indicator for Plural Projected Images. 2,827,823. Ap. Oct. 7, 1953; Pat. Mar. 25, 1958.

———. 1954. Screens for 3-D and their effect on polarization. *J. SMPTE* 62:125–33.

Simon, William. 1977. A spinning mirror auto-stereoscopic display. *SPIE* Vol. 120, Three-dimensional imaging.

Smith, Charles W. 1977. The two-eyed film comes back. *Sight and Sound* 46:88–89.

Smith, William M. 1953. Apparent size in stereoscopic movies. *Amer. J. Psychology* 66:488–91.

Soboleva, G. A., ed. 1972. *Topics in Holographic Cinematography.* (In Russian.) Moscow: Nauchno-issledovatelskii Kinofotoinstitut.

Sopori, B. L.; and Chang, William J. C. 1971. 3-D hologram synthesis from 2-D pictures. *Applied Optics* 10(12):2789–90.

Spottiswoode, Raymond. 1952. Progress in three-dimensional films at the Festival of Britain. *J. SMPTE* 58:291–303.

———. 1970. Film and its techniques. Berkeley: University of California Press, pp. 374–79.

Spottiswoode, Nigel Lawrence; and Spottiswoode, John. Stereoscopic Cameras. 2,891,441. Ap. Aug. 10, 1954; Pat. Jun. 23, 1959.

Spottiswoode, Nigel Lawrence; and Spottiswoode, R. J. (assignors to National Research Development Corp.). Optical Systems for Stereoscopic Cameras. 2,916,962. Ap. May 24, 1954; Pat. Dec. 15, 1959.

Spottiswoode, Raymond; and Spottiswoode, Nigel. 1953. *The theory of stereoscopic transmission and its application to the motion picture.* Berkeley: University of California Press.

Spottiswoode, Raymond; Spottiswoode, Nigel L.; and Smith, Charles. 1952. Basic principles of the three-dimensional film. *J. SMPTE* 59:249–85.

———, eds. 1969. *Focal encyclopedia of film and television techniques.* London: Hastings House, pp. 775–82.

Suppes, Patrick, 1977. Is visual space Euclidean? Synthese 35: 397–421.

Sutherland, Ivan E. 1968. A head-mounted three-dimensional display. *AFIPS* 33:757–64.

Symmes, Daniel I. 1974a. 3-D cine systems. *American Cinematographer* 55(4):421, 468–69.

———. 1974b. 3-D: Cinema's slowest revolution. *American Cinematographer* 55(4):406–9, 434, 456–57, 478–85.

Szabo, Will. 1976. Some comments on the design of large-screen motion-picture theaters. *J. SMPTE* 85:159–63.

Tamura, Shinichi; and Tanaka, Konichi. 1978. Multilayer 3-D display adapter. *Applied Optics* 17:3695–96.

Tan, Sing Liong (assignor to U.S. Philips Corp.). Display Device for Three-Dimensional Television. 4,122,484. Ap. Oct. 6, 1976; Pat. Oct. 24, 1978.

Tannura, Philip. 1953. Cine amateurs can make 3-D movies, too. *American Cinematographer* 34:120–23.

Tennant, John A., ed. 1899. Stereoscopic photography. *The Photo-Miniature* 1(5):207–49.

Tesler, Vladimir Efimovich. Compatible Stereoscopic Color Television System. 3,896,487. Ap. Aug. 2, 1973; Pat. Jul. 22, 1975.

Thomson, C. Leslie. 1954. *Build your own stereo equipment.* London: Fountain Press.

Tiltman, R. F. 1928. How "stereoscopic" television is shown. *Radio News* 10:418–19.

Tilton, Homer B. 1977. An autostereoscopic CRT display. *SPIE* Vol. 120, Three-dimensional imaging.

Traub, Alan C. 1967. Stereoscopic display using rapid varifocal mirror oscillations. *Applied Optics* 6(6):1085–87.

Tripp, R. Maurice. *Three-Dimensional Television.* 3,932,699. Ap. Nov. 26, 1973; Pat. Jan. 13, 1976.

Trondeau, Albert W. (assignor to Warner Bros. Pictures, Inc.). Stereoscopic Camera System. 2,868,065. Ap. May 11, 1953; Pat. Jan. 13, 1959.

Tsunoda, Yoshito; and Takeda, Yasatsugu. 1975. Three-dimensional color display by projection-type composite holography. *IEEE Transactions on Electron Devices* Ed-22.

Tyler, Christopher William. 1974. Stereopsis in dynamic visual noise. *Nature* 250:781–82.

———. 1977. Spatial limitations of human stereoscopic vision. *SPIE* Vol. 120, Three-dimensional imaging.

Valyus, N. A. 1962. *Stereoscopy*. London, New York: Focal Press.

Veda, Mitsuhiro; Adachi, Tohru; and Sato, Takuso. 1974. Three-dimensional reconstruction of the structure of an object from projections using a TV system. *Bulletin of the Tokyo Institute of Technology* 125:43–49.

Verber, Carl M. 1977. Present and potential capabilities of three-dimensional displays using sequential excitation of fluorescence. *SPIE* Vol. 120, Three-dimensional imaging.

Verma, Shiv Prakash. 1972. *Perspective transformer for the Stereo-matrix 3-D Display System*. Urbana, Ill.: University of Illinois Press.

Vlahos, Petro. 1965. The three-dimensional display: Its cues and techniques. *Information Display* 2:10–20.

———. 1974. The role of 3-D in motion pictures. *American Cinematographer* 55(4):435, 490–92.

Volkov, Yu. T.; Chernyi, I., and Ahdanov, D. D. 1966. Stereoscopic photographic range-viewfinder. (In Russian.) *Soviet Journal of Optical Technology* 34:544–48.

Vysotskii, M. Z. 1972. *Wide Screen and Stereocinematography*. Moscow: Isdatelstvo "Iskustvo."

Wald, George. 1950. Eye and camera. *Scientific American*. 183:2 :1–12.

Wales, Ken. 1974. The Video West, Inc. Three Dimensional Photographic System. *American Cinematographer* 55(4):410–11, 446, 471.

Waliman, Lawrence H. 1972. *Blast: A stereoscopic television display*. Urbana, Ill.: Department of Computer Science, University of Illinois.

Wanless, Harold R. 1965. *Aerial stereo photographs*. Northbrook, Ill.: Hubbard Press.

Weber, Frank Anton. Camera for Taking Stereoscopic Images Without Abnormal Stereoscopic Effect. 2,792,745. Ap. Jan. 7, 1952; Pat. May 21, 1957.

Weber, F. A. 1952. Stereofilm making with the Veri Vision Camera. *American Cinematographer* 33:204, 220.

Weed, Don; and Oakley, Kenneth H. 1974. Cine-Ortho: 3-D movies for eye training. *American Cinematographer* 55(4):454, 470.

Weinberg, S. A.; Watson, J. S.; Gramiak, R.; and Ramsey, G. H. 1954. Stereo X-ray motion pictures. *J. SMPTE* 62:377–82.

Weiner, Melvin L. 1969. The development of a new three-dimensional photographic process through utilization of a horizontal-depth projection screen method without the use of stereoscopic vision. *Applied Optics* 8(6):1225–28.

Weiner, Melvin L. Proximal Reproduction Process for Three-Dimensional Perception. 3,339,454. Ap. Oct. 19, 1965; Pat. Sept. 5, 1967.

Weldon, Roger J.; and Myers, John T. 1965. Apparent motion in depth induced by continuous variation of the stereo base. *J. Optical Soc. Amer.* 55:896–97.

Westfall, R.; and Knutsen, E. V. 1976. Factors affecting the cleanliness of motion-picture film. *J. SMPTE* 85(11):853–59.

Wheatstone, Charles. 1838. On some remarkable, and hitherto unobserved, phenomena of binocular vision (Part the first). *Philosophical Transactions of the Royal Society of London* 1838:371–94.

———. 1852. On some remarkable, and hitherto unobserved, phenomena of binocular vision (Part the second). *Philosophical Transactions of the Royal Society of London* 142(7):1–17.

Whiteside, Stephen Earl. 1973. *The Stereomatrix 3-D display system*. Urbana, Ill.: University of Illinois Press.

Wildi, Ernst. 1953a. Closeup photography with 16mm single-film stereo systems. *American Cinematographer* 34:598–99, 602, 604–6.

———. 1953b. How to shoot 3-D movies in 16-millimeter. *American Cinematographer* 34:278–82.

————. 1953c. Shooting a 16mm travel film in 3-D. *American Cinematographer* 34:430–31.

Williams, Alan D. 1974a. 3-D motion picture techniques. *American Cinematographer* 55(4):420–25.

————. 1974b. A 3-D primer. *American Cinematographer* 55(4):412–13, 466–67.

Wilman, C. W. *Simplified stereoscopic photography*. London: Percival Marshall & Co.

Yamanchi, Satoshi (assignor to Ricoh Company, Ltd.). Method and Color Television Picture Tube for Reproducing Three-Dimensional Image 4,214,257. Ap. Oct. 4, 1978. Pat. Jul. 22, 1980.

Index